Siachin Conflict to Kargil War

Siachin Conflict
to
Kargil War

Capt. (Retd) Brahmdutt Vats

PRASHANT PUBLISHING HOUSE
DELHI-110094

Published by :
PRASHANT PUBLISHING HOUSE
C-34, 28 Foota Road, Gali-3,
West Karwal Nagar, Delhi-110094
Phone : 011-22963970, Mob. : 9810396373, 8826258746
e-mail.: prashantpublishinghouse@gmail.com

Siachin Conflict to Kargil War

First Published 2019

ISBN : 978-93-88526-18-0

PRINTED IN INDIA
Published by Mr. R.K. Jha M/s Prashant Publishing House and Published at H.S. Offset House Press, Delhi.

Contents

Preface

The Siachen conflict, sometimes referred to as the Siachen War, was a military conflict between India and Pakistan over the disputed Siachen Glacier region in Kashmir. A cease-fire went into effect in 2003. The contended area is nearly 1,000 square miles (2,600 km) of territory. The conflict was started in 1984 by India's successful capture of the Siachen Glacier as part of Operation Meghdoot. India took control of the 70-kilometre-long (43 mi) Siachen Glacier and its tributary glaciers, as well as all the main passes and heights of the Saltoro Ridge immediately west of the glacier, including Sia La, Bilafond La, and Gyong La. Pakistan controls the glacial valleys immediately west of the Saltoro Ridge. According to TIME magazine, India gained more than 1,000 square miles (3,000 km) of territory because of its military operations in Siachen.

The Siachen Glacier is the highest battleground on earth, where India and Pakistan have fought intermittently since 13 April 1984. Both countries maintain permanent military presence in the region at a height of over 6,000 metres (20,000 ft). More than 2000 people have died in this inhospitable terrain, mostly due to weather extremes and the natural hazards of mountain warfare.Siachen is seen as a major military setback by the Pakistani Army. Pakistani generals perceives the Siachen glacier as their land that had been stolen by Indians. When India occupied the Saltoro Ridge in April 1984, Benazir Bhutto publicly taunted the Pakistan Army as "fit only to fight its own citizens". When, in June 1987, the Indian Army captured the 21,153 foot high "Quaid Post" and renamed it to "Bana Top", in honour of Naib Subedar Bana Singh, Bhutto once again publicly taunted the Pakistani generals, telling them to wear bangles if they cannot fight on the Siachen.The military conflict between India and Pakistan in the vicinity of the Siachen glacier is now more than thirty years old.

One of the principal findings of this analysis is that while there is broad consensus that Kargil-like operations are not viable in the current international environment, violence in various forms remains a legitimate—if not the only—

means to achieve Pakistan's political objectives in Kashmir. As will be explicated in greater detail later, Pakistan understands that it paid heavily for its adventurism in Kargil and that the international community will not support the use of overt force to alter the status quo. Stated more precisely, Islamabad has concluded that the use of Pakistani troops in Kargil invited political failure, and consequently its incentive to repeat such an operation is very small at present.

Kargil War also called as the Kargil conflict, was an armed conflict between Indian and Pakistani forces that took place between May and July 1999 in the Kargil district of Kashmir and along the Line of Control. In India, the conflict is also referred to as Operation Vijay which was the name of the Indian operation to clear the Kargil sector. The cause of the war was the infiltration of Pakistani soldiers and Pakistan backed militants into areas on the Indian side of the Line of Control (LoC) to occupy military posts vacated in the winter. India responded by launching a major military and diplomatic offensive to drive out the Pakistani infiltrators. Reportedly, the Pakistan infiltration in the Kargil sector was reported by the local shepherds. The Indian Army launched a number of patrols to the area to estimate the extent of the infiltration. Initially, Pakistan blamed the fighting entirely on independent Kashmiri militants, but documents left behind by casualties and later statements by Pakistan's Prime Minister and Chief of Army Staff revealed involvement of Pakistani paramilitary forces, led by General Ashraf Rashid. The Indian Army, later on supported by the Indian Air Force, recaptured majority of the positions on the Indian side of the LOC within two months of the conflict that were trespass by the infiltrators, according to official count, an estimated 75%–80% of the intruded area and nearly all high ground was back under Indian while 20-25% is still in Pakistan control the reason why India can't claim victory as India was unable to take back the whole area- India's then Chief of Army Staff VP Malik, expressing his views on Operation Vijay.

This is a reference book. All the matter is just compiled and edited in nature, taken from the various sources which are in public domain.

This book will be of interest to students and scholars of political science, international history, and international relations. Diplomats bureaucrats, journalists, and the interested lay reader will find this book engaging.

—Editor

1

Introduction

BATTLEFIELD OF SIACHEN

The dispute over Siachen is the only conflict between two neighbours where inhospitable terrains have claimed more lives than actual combat. The majority of an estimated 2, 700 people, who were killed on both sides of the Saichen glacier, died not because they were fighting each other, but because of the extreme conditions in which they live — avalanches, exposure and altitude sickness caused by thin, oxygen-depleted air.

That is perhaps the reason why it is called the highest-altitude battlefield in the world. Situated in the East Korakoram range, it is the longest glacier in Himalayas at 77 kilometres in length and three kilometres in width. Both India and Pakistan spend billions in order to maintain troops — access to the area from the Pakistani side is much better in terms of road connectivity, than the Indian side. India also has to spend more comparatively because the troops are actually camped on a glacier, which is supported by a fleet of helicopters.

The Karachi Agreement, which India and Pakistan signed in July 1949, is considered to be the genesis of the conflict. This agreement demarcated ceasefire lines between India and Pakistan but stopped at a point NJ 9842. After the war of 1971, the LoC was not delineated beyond this point.

The access provided by Pakistan to climbers and mountaineers from its side to various areas led India to believe that Pakistan had snatched and unilaterally extended the LoC from NJ 9842 to the Karakoram Pass, thus eating into over 10,000 square kilometres of Indian territory.

The famous army mountaineer, Colonel Narendra Kumar, whose pioneering exploration paved way for India to take the glacier in early 1984, accidently discovered Pakistan's "cartographic aggression" displayed on commercial American maps, while out on an expedition with a German expedition team. Colonel Kumar, in whose name an Indian post is named, found that the maps showed a line from NJ 9842 — which was the last point delineated on the LoC between India and Pakistan — drawn straight to the Karakoram Pass, instead of going north, as was internationally accepted.

After convincing his seniors, the colonel was permitted to carry out a counter-expedition in 1978. "As we reached Siachen, Pakistani helicopters were flying over us... and they were firing out coloured smoke," Colonel Kumar said in an interview in 2014. According to him, the rubbish left behind by mountaineers and climbers had convinced them that Pakistan was taking over the area. Pakistanis were also alarmed when they found cigarette packets and food packages on the main Siachen glacier; by then, they were convinced India was also trying to set up a base in the area.

Had Indian intelligence agencies not learned about an interesting shopping trip in London in 1984, Pakistan might have seized control of the entire mountain region. "We found out that Pakistanis were buying lots of specialist mountain clothing in London," Colonel Kumar said in the interview. Later a Pakistani army officer admitted the mistake of buying from the same store as the Indians. New Delhi immediately dispatched troops to Siachen, beating Pakistan by a week. On 13 April, 1984, Indian troops snatched control of the Siachen glacier a week before Pakistan could. The race to deploy troops in extreme circumstances, devoid of any human or animal presence, started that year.

A soldier's nightmare

Stephen P Cohen, a prominent expert on South Asian security — while dismissing the geographical importance of Siachen in a military context — once described the standoff between India and Pakistan in Siachen as "a struggle of two bald men over a comb." It was perhaps the most fitting line, which explains the madness over a region that has only given body bags to both the nations. Army officers and reports published over the years say soldiers suffer weight loss of around 15 kilograms every 90 days. Most of them, because of the prolonged use of oxygen masks, complain of hearing loss, eyesight and memory loss. They breath the purest — albeit scarce — oxygen, sleep in ice-caves, and endure blizzards and storms with thunderous velocity of 150 kilometres per hour that sometimes continue for weeks on end.

Soldiers need special equipment, apparel and gear to survive. Reports of people getting incapacitated due to frostbite are normal. There is not enough oxygen to light fires for even cooking purposes.

On the diplomatic front

In June 2005, when former Prime Minister Manmohan Singh flew to the Siachen base camp to talk to soldiers, he said that, the "time has come to convert this battlefield into a peace mountain. It must become an example of peace wherein nobody feels any threat and there is no scope for conflict." This came in the wake of lobbying groups putting pressure on both the countries to avoid confrontation in the mountains.

India has been insisting that the line needs to be demarcated beyond the point it was left without delineation all along the 110-kilometre-long Actual Ground Position Line (AGPL) before considering demilitarisation, and Pakistan wanted to keep the status quo with troops moving to the pre-1984 position.

The tragedy that struck the Pakistani side in 2012 had triggered peace talks between two nations, but failed to break the ice.

"We are keeping men there because it is now a line of control. And the moment you demilitarise it, you will have another Kargil. Conditions are today far better for the soldiers than they were few years ago." an army officer says.

Interestingly, as the improvement in technology and equipment has made things better for soldiers from both the sides, they have realised that the biggest problem in the area is not the altitude, but disposal of human waste.

The question people in India and Pakistan should ask themselves is why they need to waste precious human lives on what is often called a 'block of snow'. The tragedy that took place on Wednesday could have been avoided, had there been no need to keep troops in such hostile circumstances.

FIGHTING 'GENERAL GLACIER'

There is no doubt that the biggest problem is fighting "General Glacier", not the enemy. MoD data shows that India has lost almost 900 soldiers since 1984 — mostly to natural calamities and illnesses caused by oxygen deprivation and temperatures dipping to -50 degrees Celsius. While the army's average yearly death count has significantly reduced in the last five years due to better equipment and technology and is much better than Pakistan's annual casualty average, almost all Indian casualties in recent years accrue to the weather or health conditions. The casualty figures also do not reflect the hidden cost of Siachen — many soldiers come back with life-long problems of memory loss, blood clots in vital organs and other life-threatening issues. There is, for example, the case of Lt Col Rajesh Mehta, documented by the journalist Nitin Gokhale. The officer suffered such serious blood clotting in his limbs that three of them had to be amputated.

Army troops in Siachen are rotated every three months but to be deployed in a place where simply being around can be life-threatening is a Herculean task indeed.

Demilitarization?

Talk on demilitarization in the past has fallen through because of Pakistan's refusal to validate actual ground positions on the glacier. At a disadvantage in Siachen, Pakistan has long been a votary of demilitarization but the fear is that a withdrawal without guarantees could simply allow Pakistan to walk into vacated posts. It is often forgotten that the Kargil War was justified by General Musharraf as a means of cutting Indian troops in Siachen and as a response to what Pakistan sees as Indian aggression there.

After the Pakistani Army suffered heavy losses in the Gayari sector in 2012, its then chief General Kiyani again called for vacating Siachen. Yet, at a time when Siachen is a symbol of muscular nationalism and emotive territorialism, it is difficult to reach even for low-lying fruits in the India-Pakistan face-off. Meanwhile, soldiers continue to die.

The other side of the story

The Gayari tragedy in 2012 led to an emotive public debate in Pakistan's media on the human costs of the Siachen standoff. Then army chief General Ashfaq Pervez Kiyani called for the demilitarization of Siachen, a position that Pakistan, at a military disadvantage in the glacier, has long supported. In 2015, a play called 'Siachen' by Anwar Maqsood debuted before packed audiences. Its script was approved by Pakistan's Inter-Services Public Relations (ISPR).

Pakistan's high commissioner to India Abdul Basit also repeated the call for a mutual withdrawal of troops on February 11, 2016. India's response, enunciated by Lt General DS Hooda, GOC-in-C, Northern Command is clear: "If we have to talk about the withdrawal (of troops from Siachen), first the actual positions on the ground, where we are today and where our posts are, need to be authenticated."

INDO-PAKISTANI WAR OF 1965

The Indo-Pakistani War of 1965 was a culmination of skirmishes that took place between April 1965 and September 1965 betweenPakistan and India.

This conflict became known as the Second Kashmir War and was fought by India and Pakistan over the disputed region of Kashmir, the first having been fought in 1947. The war began following Pakistan's Operation Gibraltar, which was designed to infiltrate forces into Jammu and Kashmir to precipitate an insurgency against rule by India. The five-week war caused thousands of casualties on both sides. It ended in a United Nations (UN) mandated ceasefire and the subsequent issuance of the Tashkent Declaration.

Much of the war was fought by the countries' land forces in Kashmir and along the International Border between India and Pakistan. This war saw the largest amassing of troops in Kashmir since the Partition of British India in 1947, a number that was overshadowed only during the 2001–2002 military standoff between India and Pakistan. Most of the battles were fought by opposing infantry and armouredunits, with substantial backing from air forces, and naval operations. Many details of this war, like those of other Indo-Pakistani Wars, remain unclear.

Pre-war Escalation

Since Partition of British India in 1947, Pakistan and India remained in contention over several issues. Although the Kashmir conflict was the predominant issue dividing the nations, other border disputes existed, most notably over the Rann of Kutch, a barren region in the Indian state of Gujarat. The issue first arose in 1956 which ended with India regaining control over the disputed area. Pakistani patrols began patrolling in territory controlled by India in January 1965, which was followed by attacks by both countries on each other's posts on 8 April 1965.

Initially involving border police from both nations, the disputed area soon witnessed intermittent skirmishes between the countries' armed forces. In June 1965, British Prime Minister Harold Wilson successfully persuaded both countries to end hostilities and set up a tribunal to resolve the dispute. The verdict, which came later in 1968, saw Pakistan awarded 350 square miles (900 km^2) of the Rann of Kutch, as against its original claim of 3,500 square miles (9,100 km^2).

After its success in the Rann of Kutch, Pakistan, under the leadership of General Ayub Khan, believed the Indian Army would be unable to defend itself against a quick military campaign in the disputed territory of Kashmir as the Indian military had suffered a loss to China in 1962. Pakistan believed that the population of Kashmir was generally discontented with Indian rule and that a resistance movement could be ignited by a few infiltrating saboteurs. Pakistan attempted to ignite the resistance movement by means of a covert infiltration, codenamed Operation Gibraltar. The Pakistani infiltrators were soon discovered, however, their presence reported by local Kashmiris, and the operation ended in a complete failure.

The War

On 5 August 1965 between 26,000 and 33,000 Pakistani soldiers crossed the Line of Control dressed as Kashmiri locals headed for various areas within

Kashmir. Indian forces, tipped off by the local populace, crossed the cease fire line on 15 August.

Initially, the Indian Army met with considerable success, capturing three important mountain positions after a prolonged artillery barrage. By the end of August, however, both sides had relative progress; Pakistan had made progress in areas such as Tithwal, Uri and Poonch and India had captured the Haji Pir Pass, 8 km into Pakistan-Administered Kashmir.

On 1 September 1965, Pakistan launched a counterattack, called Operation Grand Slam, with the objective to capture the vital town of Akhnoor in Jammu, which would sever communications and cut off supply routes to Indian troops. Ayub Khan calculated that "Hindu morale would not stand more than a couple of hard blows at the right time and place" although by this time Operation Gibraltar had failed and India had captured the Haji Pir Pass. Attacking with an overwhelming ratio of troops and technically superior tanks, Pakistan made gains against Indian forces, who were caught unprepared and suffered heavy losses. India responded by calling in its air force to blunt the Pakistani attack. The next day, Pakistan retaliated, its air forceattacked Indian forces and air bases in both Kashmir and Punjab. India's decision to open up the theater of attack into Pakistani Punjab forced the Pakistani army to relocate troops engaged in the operation to defend Punjab. Operation Grand Slam therefore failed, as the Pakistan Army was unable to capture Akhnoor; it became one of the turning points in the war when India decided to relieve pressure on its troops in Kashmir by attacking Pakistan further south.

India crossed the International Border on the Western front on 6 September, marking an official beginning of the war. On 6 September, the 15th Infantry Division of the Indian Army, under World War II veteran Major General Prasad, battled a massive counterattack by Pakistan near the west bank of the Ichogil Canal (BRB Canal), which was a *de facto* border of India and Pakistan. The General's entourage itself was ambushed and he was forced to flee his vehicle. A second, this time successful, attempt to cross the Ichhogil Canal was made over the bridge in the village of Barki, just east of Lahore. These developments brought the Indian Army within the range of Lahore International Airport. As a result, the United States requested a temporary ceasefire to allow it to evacuate its citizens in Lahore. However, the Pakistani counterattack took Khem Karan from Indian forces which tried to divert the attention of Pakistanis from Khem Karan by an attack on Bedian and the adjacent villages.

The thrust against Lahore consisted of the 1st Infantry Division supported by the three tank regiments of the 2nd Independent Armoured Brigade; they quickly advanced across the border, reaching the Ichhogil (BRB) Canal by 6 September. The Pakistani Army held the bridges over the canal or blew up those it could not hold, effectively stalling any further advance by the Indians on Lahore. One unit of the Indian Jat Regiment, 3 Jat, had also crossed the Ichogil canal and captured the town of Batapore (Jallo Mur to Pakistan) on the west side of the canal.

The same day, a counter offensive consisting of an armoured division and infantry division supported by Pakistan Air Force Sabres forced the Indian 15th Division to withdraw to its starting point. Although 3 Jat suffered minimal casualties, the bulk of the damage being taken by ammunition and stores vehicles, the higher commanders had no information of 3 Jat's capture of Batapore and misleading information led to the command to withdraw from Batapore and Dograi to Ghosal-Dial. This move brought extreme disappointment to Lt-Col Desmond Hayde, CO of 3 Jat. Dograi was eventually recaptured by 3 Jat on 21 September, for the second time but after a much harder battle due to Pakistani reinforcements.

On 8 September 1965, a company of 5 Maratha Light Infantry was sent to reinforce a Rajasthan Armed Constabulary (RAC) post at Munabao – a strategic hamlet about 250 kilometres from Jodhpur. Their brief was simple. To hold the post and to keep Pakistan's infantry battalions from overrunning the post at bay. But at Maratha Hill (in Munabao) – as the post has now been christened – the Indian company could barely manage to thwart the intense attack for 24 hours. A company of 3 Guards with 954 heavy mortar battery ordered to reinforce the RAC post at Munabao could never reach. The Pakistani Air Force had strafed the entire area, and also hit a railway train coming from Barmer with reinforcements near Gadra road railway station. On 10 September, Munabao fell into Pakistani hands, and efforts to capture the strategic point did not succeed.

On the days following 9 September, both nations' premiere formations were routed in unequal battles. India's 1st Armoured Division, labeled the "pride of the Indian Army", launched an offensive towards Sialkot. The Division divided itself into two prongs, was forced back by the Pakistani 6th Armoured Division at Chawinda and was forced to withdraw after suffering heavy losses of nearly 100 tanks. The Pakistanis followed up their success by launchingOperation Windup, which forced the Indians back farther. Similarly, Pakistan's pride, the 1st Armoured Division, pushed an offensive towards Khem Karan, with the intent to capture Amritsar (a major city in Punjab, India) and the bridge on River Beas to Jalandhar.

The Pakistani 1st Armoured Division never made it past Khem Karan, however, and by the end of 10 September lay disintegrated by the defences of the Indian 4th Mountain Division at what is now known as the Battle of *Asal Uttar* (lit. meaning – "Real Answer", or more appropriate English equivalent – "Fitting Response"). The area became known as 'Patton Nagar' (Patton Town), because of the large number of US-made Pakistani Patton tanks. Approximately 97 Pakistani tanks were destroyed or abandoned, with only 32 Indian tanks destroyed or damaged. The Pakistani 1st Armoured Division less 5th Armoured Brigade was next sent to Sialkot sector behind Pakistani 6th Armoured Division where it didn't see action as 6th Armoured Division was already in process of routing Indian 1st Armoured Division which was superior to it in strength.

The war was heading for a stalemate, with both nations holding territory of the other. The Indian army suffered 3,000 battlefield deaths, while Pakistan suffered 3,800. The Indian army was in possession of 710 miles^2 (1,800 km^2) of Pakistani territory and the Pakistan army held 210 mile^2 (550 km^2) of Indian territory. The territory occupied by India was mainly in the fertile Sialkot, Lahore and Kashmir sectors, while Pakistani land gains were primarily south in deserts opposite to Sindh and in Chumb sector near Kashmir in north.

THE 1965 INDO-PAK WAR THROUGH THE EYES OF SAINIK SAMACHAR

"Pak troops on the run." "Fleeing raiders exterminated." "Pakistani soldiers utterly demoralised." The headlines in *Sainik Samachar* left nothing to the imagination. As India waged a furious battle on its western front, the official publication of the defence ministry worked hard to ensure that morale stayed high and India's image remained one of glory.

A fascinating narrative of the war unfolds in the yellowing pages of the 1965 editions of *Sainik Samachar*, a journal of the Indian armed forces that was born in 1909 and is today published in 13 languages every fortnight.

While the war was on, *Sainik Samachar* was brought out every week. Words like "loyal", "united", "glorious" and "brave" leaped out of its pages as the publication scripted a narrative that exalted the achievements of India at war. It captured every significant speech of (then) President Sarvepalli Radhakrishnan, Prime Minister Lal Bahadur Shastri, Defence Minister Yashwantrao Balwantrao Chavan, and Information & Broadcasting Minister Indira Gandhi.

Niceties were discarded and it openly called Pakistan the cunning aggressor. Every little report that even remotely hinted that a certain assault might have found India on the backfoot was aggressively countered. And every tiny slip by Pakistan was celebrated.

It drew attention to how the nation stood as one in this testing time, with film stars like Balraj Sahni, Sunil Dutt and Mala Sinha going all out to keep the soldiers pepped up.

It tapped into news agency and newspaper reports, reprinting dispatches from the front, splashing on its pages pictures of captured infiltrators, tanks and ammunition, and published letters and documents to show that the infiltration was orchestrated not by civilians but by the Pakistan government under Operation Gibraltar.

It was the first draft of the history of the 1965 war. Carefully bound old editions of *Sainik Samachar* are kept in high-security North Block. Old issues of the magazine, dated and bound in the same shade of red, line the shelves of a grey steel and glass cupboard.

Rummaging through the shelf, the heart skips a beat on realising that while the January-June editions are available, the critical July-December collection is missing — it was during this period, from August 5 to September 22, that the war was fought.

A helpful employee finally finds the collection tucked away in one corner. Some of the pages have come loose and there are notings on others. The cover pages of some war editions have "record copy" scribbled on them. "These are treasures," says Hasibur Rahman, the magazine's editor-in-chief. "We don't allow these copies to go out of this office."

In its edition of May 9, *Sainik Samachar* carried the first report of hostilities between the two neighbours. It was called "Pak Aggression on Kutch-Sind Border: Jawan Shows His Mettle".

Staking claim to large parts of the Rann of Kutch, Pakistani forces intruded in massive strength in April 1965. "The police pickets this time had something much more formidable on their hands than smugglers, innocent stragglers or unwary patrolmen," *Sainik Samachar*said. Pakistan's plan was to take India by surprise and get it to concede the disputed 3,500 square miles of the region. The forces came with Patton tanks and 106 mm recoilless guns.

Drawing from a report by a special correspondent of *The Hindu*, the journal soon proclaimed: "The Pakistani gamble in Kutch has failed." It quoted this dispatch of the correspondent from the Rann of Kutch: "A visit to the operational area dispels from one's mind any wrong notion or apprehension that Pakistan has taken complete possession of any area of particular length or breadth." Lauding the armed police force manning the pickets, the report said: "The heroic defence of the Central Reserve Police, inflicting heavy casualties on them in the very first attack was a bad blow to Pakistan." That event, which took place on the night of April 9 when CRPF's

Sardar Post in Kutch came under heavy shelling, is today celebrated as Valour Day by the paramilitary force.

There were, however, reports that India suffered an initial setback and fell back in the Biar Bet and Point 84 sectors of Kutch. *Sainik Samachar* countered this vehemently in an article titled "Jawan foils Pakistan's plans". "At the border, the Rann of Kutch is overlooked by a rim-like formation 100 feet to 150 feet high. Attacking forces at the height are in an immeasurable superior position," it said.

"Pakistan," it added, "whipped up worldwide political propaganda that the Indian army had been disgraced in battle. This is not true... With the odds so heavy against them, the forces could only employ attrition tactics... This has been accomplished and the enemy has suffered heavy casualties." Speaking about the aggression in Kutch, Defence Minister Chavan informed Lok Sabha on April 26 that the morale of "our people and the forces is high and they are determined to resist any affront to our sovereignty and territorial integrity at any cost".

To buttress the point, *Sainik Samachar* carried a small agency report on the same page as Chavan's Lok Sabha statement. "Servicemen throughout the country have made requests to Army Headquarters here that they be posted along the Kutch-Sind border... There is said to be unprecedented enthusiasm to go to the 'front' to 'roll back' the Pakistani aggressors."

This spirit was reiterated in an interview done by the Press Trust of India with the commanding officer of a battalion stationed in Kutch — of course, he wasn't named. "We swatted them like flies, nearly 150 of them were down, killed or wounded," he said.

The Pakistanis, added the report, were taken aback by Indian firepower and threw in more tanks, six of which went up in flames. Another report talked about "a brave lieutenant colonel and his equally courageous second-lieutenant son" who fought shoulder-to-shoulder in Kutch.

And then there were reports, almost hilarious, of inaccurate shelling by Pakistan artillery: "Pakistani shells, more often than not, pounded the sand of the Rann of Kutch and incidentally helped to dig up the earth which our Jawans subsequently used for bunkers."

In Kutch, British Prime Minister Harold Wilson finally succeeded in persuading the warring countries to end hostilities and resolve the dispute. Pakistan would eventually get 910 square km of the Rann of Kutch against its claim of 9,100 square km.

Soon, the attention shifted to Kashmir. On reading *Sainik Samachar*, it becomes clear that Pakistan's strategy changed little between 1947, when it first fought India, 1965 and 1999 when the last war happened in the Kargil-Drass sector. On each occasion, India claimed that the attackers were Pakistani soldiers masquerading as tribesmen on a mission to "liberate" Kashmir.

In its August 29 issue, the journal reproduced the fiery speech delivered by Prime Minister Shastri from the ramparts of the Red Fort on this very day, five decades ago. "Pakistan has invaded Kashmir," thundered the diminutive, mild-mannered Shastri. "I use the word 'invasion' deliberately. It is absurd to say that civilian raiders have infiltrated into Kashmir from Pakistan-occupied Kashmir."

A few pages down came proof of this "invasion" in the form of a picture of two captured Pakistani officers — Captain Mohammad Sajjad and Captain Ghulum Hussain — blindfolded, handcuffed and held by a soldier in fatigues.

In an account that bears a striking similarity to the way in which the Kargil conflict of 1999 started, *Sainik Samachar* reported: "Early this month (August), Pakistan unleashed a new campaign of sabotage and terror in Jammu & Kashmir. It took the form of armed infiltration, fanning across the cease-fire line (now called the Line of Control) into areas in India for saboteur operations. The first crossing was reported to have occurred on the evening of August 5 in the Mendhar sector of Jammu."

Between 26,000 and 33,000 Pakistani soldiers had crossed the LoC dressed as Kashmiri locals. The Indian troops, it wrote, recovered badges that indicated the ranks of the raiders who had in their possession arms that were available only to regular troops. "The infiltrators had come with large sums of money," it reported. "One of the captured officers had with him Rs 4,700 in Indian currency."

If that wasn't enough, a set of "'top secret' instructions issued by Major-General Akhtar Hussain Malik of the Pakistan army to Brigadier (Amir Abdullah Khan) Niazi for infiltration operations in Kashmir" was reproduced by *Sainik Samachar*. The document gave information on funds, method of operation, ration and ammunition. "You will be self-sufficient to operate for at least two weeks," stated the note.

In another reproduced report, the magazine said that in its "campaign to let loose terror in Kashmir, the Pakistan authorities, the captured documents reveal, also took recourse to enlisting criminals," among them history-sheeters and those accused of abduction. The claim was backed with copies of letters by senior officers of the Pakistan army to senior police officers in Sialkot and to the city magistrate of Lyallpur.

Sainik Samachar noted that Pakistan's confidence came from two factors: one, faced with a military onslaught, India, which had then suffered heavy losses in its 1962 war with China, would not be able to defend Kashmir; and two, it would be possible to trigger a resistance movement in the people of Kashmir who were dissatisfied with Indian rule.

As the war peaked, the journal went all out to debunk these theories. "The people of Kashmir have not only given no quarter to the Pakistani raiders but have throughout helped the Indian army in smashing them and preventing them from their nefarious acts," it declared in bold with a photo feature of the "large quantities of arms and ammunition" left behind by "fleeing Pakistanis".

The writing was melodramatic, with the Indian soldier shown as the invincible hero and the Pakistani infiltrator as the meek, bumbling, demoralised villain. Inevitably, as the two countries were at war, jingoism crept into the narrative.

An army observer who was an eyewitness to a "regular western movie style battle about 30 miles west of Srinagar" narrated how a group of over 20 Pakistani raiders who were trying to flee across to their side of the cease-fire line were engaged and exterminated by our security forces. "The raiders were demoralised," he wrote. And among the material captured from them were some women's clothes that "the raiders had obviously been using to disguise themselves."

Several pages were devoted to how poorly the Pakistani soldiers were treated by their government. One report spoke of how surprised the Pakistani soldiers, captured in Kashmir, were on finding that "stories of Indian Army atrocities on the civil population, on which they had been systematically fed, were a tissue of lies."

These soldiers then said that going back to Pakistan-occupied Kashmir was out of the question because they knew they would be shot by the Pakistan authorities for having failed in their mission. The treachery of the "masters" of the captured soldiers was played out in detail. Here's an account:

"What will you make of three weeping sobbing Pakistani soldiers, each having 13 years army service to his credit but each more demoralised than the other? A large party of Pressmen met these Pakistani soldiers recently and almost all were moved to pity. The soldiers talked in tears of their children, their young wives left behind and their aged children uncared for by anyone. But they also talked of other things, and more bitterly the treachery of their masters and the disgusting game of deceit and fraud played on them by their officers. The three Naiks said they had been told that they were being taken for 'army exercises', and it was only after they had crossed the cease-fire line and received Indian currency notes that they had some idea of their mission."

Ever country that has been in war has its own war history, its own version of the conflict. India and Pakistan are no exception. By the end of August, Pakistan did make some progress in the Tithwal, Uri and Poonch sectors of Kashmir, and Indian troops captured the crucial Haji Pir Pass pushing their forces 8 km into Pakistan-occupied Kashmir.

Sainik Samachar also reported extensively from the Khem Karan sector in Punjab, which came to be called the "graveyard of tanks". It was at Khem Karan that Abdul Hamid of The Grenadiers engaged and destroyed several Patton tanks, fighting till his dying breath — a feat for which he was awarded the Param Vir Chakra posthumously. Hamid found repeated mention in *Sainik Samachar* for several months.

To lend authenticity to the reports of victory, the journal carried reports from other publications. One such report, "Story of the great tank battle in Kasur", by journalist Inder Malhotra reproduced from *The Statesman*, said: "It was about 24 hours after the decisive victory in the Kasur sector on September 11 that we visited the area. It was in this battle that our men smashed a massive enemy attack, captured 15 Patton tanks, destroyed many more and sent the famous First Armoured Division of Pakistan reeling back in defeat and disarray."

The high point for the Indian troops in this war was the capture of Burki, a village less than 10 km southeast of Lahore. "Burki village falls to our troops," said one headline. It was captured on the night of September 10.

The article that accompanied pictures of India's conquest of Burki recounted: "The road to Burki is littered with burnt and charred shells of Pakistani military vehicles.... The village is deserted except for one blind 80-year-old Nabi Baksh... Indian jawans looked after him and fed him and he is full of praise for them. 'They are my true sons now,' he said."

The war of 1965 also saw some old friendships waning and new relations being forged. *Sainik Samachar* took note of this, sparing no opportunity to point out Pakistan's growing and disturbing proximity to China after its old ally, the United States, refused to come to its aid and issued a statement declaring its neutrality.

A report by the United News of India, carried in bold, spoke of Pakistan President Ayub Khan's secret deal with the Chinese premier, Chou En-lai. "President Khan has promised her (China) to allow the use of East Bengal (current day Bangladesh) as a base for war against India," reported the agency.

In a broadcast to the country on September 19, published in the journal, Defence Minister Chavan made this point: "Pakistan, particularly encouraged by her Chinese ally, may try a desperate effort to attack us in the position we have gained and these attacks will have to be beaten back in the same way as the previous attacks that were made by Pakistan."

War is a time when a nation comes together. India did too. And *Sainik Samachar* captured every act that showed solidarity with the soldiers. Here are some examples: Defence Minister Chavan received 7,000 telegrams and letters from industrial concerns, business houses and social and cultural organisations. Among them were letters from college students who wanted to go to the front.

A religious centre in Varanasi offered to educate students of martyred jawans free of cost. A student body gave Rs 1,001 to the National Defence Fund. Maharaja Tej Singh of Alwar donated rifles and pistols to the state government. And Delhi Milk Scheme, or DMS, gave ghee worth Rs 1,000 for jawans in hospitals.

Marketing also took on a war vocabulary as is evident from the advertisements in the pages of *Sainik Samachar*. JK Synthetics, which marketed synthetic yarn under the Jaykaylon brand, advertised that paratroopers could come "sailing down to unexplored ground without fear" because they had safe parachutes with best nylon chords.

India and Pakistan were not isolated in the war of 1965. And China wasn't the only external player. The world was watching closely. Foreign journalists flew in to report on the conflict.

In one interview to *All India Radio*, George de Carvalho, the Pulitzer-winning war correspondent of *Life*, said American military aid to Pakistan "was intended to contain communism and was used against India and was a violation of Pakistan's undertaking to the United States... Obviously one is very upset to see American weapons used against a great and peaceful nation and one only hopes that this warfare will come to an end as soon as possible."

It finally did following diplomatic intervention by the Soviet Union and the United States. On September 22, Prime Minister Shastri announced in the Lok Sabha "that orders were being issued to field commanders for a complete ceasefire at 3.30 am on Thursday, September 23, following Pakistan's acceptance of the terms of the United Security Council." That said, Shastri added that India had to be watchful and vigilant.

Peace returned. The two countries went back to their original positions. The boundaries remained unchanged. Some days later, on October 3, addressing a mammoth gathering at Gurudwara Bangla Sahib, Shastri offered these words of sanity: "It is obvious that in the present world, a war cannot continue for long. There is always intense international diplomatic activity. There was a time when a war could be fought to the finish and an issue could be decided by victory or defeat. Now the world is drawn much closer."

A GLACIAL FIGHT

It is 33 years since humanity established a permanent presence on the snow-clad Siachen glacier and converted the 'land of roses' into the world's highest battlefield. On April 13, 1984, India launched Operation Meghdoot to capture the 76.4 km-long glacier on the Saltoro ridge, narrowly thwarting Pakistan's own attempts in the process. A platoon of 4 Kumaon led by then Captain Sanjay Kulkarni planted the Indian flag at Bilafond La. The operation continues till date, making it the longest continuing one of its kind in the world. But the guns on the glacier have fallen silent following the 2003 ceasefire along the Line of Control (LoC) and the Actual Ground Position Line (AGPL) across the Siachen. The LoC has flared up intermittently, but ceasefire along the AGPL has held since.

Siachen is a legacy of Partition. While the LoC was delineated and accepted by India and Pakistan up to point NJ9842, the glacier was left unmarked. India claims the area based on the Jammu and Kashmir Instrument of Accession (1947) and the Karachi Agreement of 1949, which define the ceasefire line beyond NJ9842 as "running Northwards to the glaciers".

DEMILITARISING SIACHEN

Siachen is often referred to as a low-hanging fruit, an issue to be sorted out by both sides before addressing the Kashmir question. However, it may not be that simple for historical, operational and practical reasons.

Pakistan's calls in the recent past for demilitarising Siachen stem from a position of desperation to save the lives of its soldiers from the extreme conditions there, while at the same time continuing cross-border terrorism along the LoC.

India has shown willingness for demilitarisation conditional on first authenticating the 110-km AGPL, which is the current position on the glacier. But Pakistan refuses, which means that once India vacates the posts, Pakistan may try to occupy them. India currently has the advantage of height as it commands higher ground, and any demilitarisation without proper delineation and acceptance of the current positions would be disastrous. Retaking once-occupied peaks is near impossible. Pakistan made several unsuccessful attempts at retaking the posts till 2003. In July 1998, the then Defence Minister George Fernandes said, "India needs to hold on to Siachen both for strategic reasons and wider security in the region."

The biggest enemy on the glacier has always been the weather. The Indian Army, which holds the highest posts at heights of 21,000 ft, has learnt to adapt and now has a well-oiled system in place. However, the series of recent untimely avalanches on the glacier and the resultant spikes in casualties show that the challenge of changing weather patterns is new.

As status quo continues amidst attempts at demilitarisation, the pressing concern is tackling the changing weather patterns. Some studies have been initiated to access the rate of glacier melt, and the Army is re-assessing the vulnerable posts in an attempt to shift some of them. These need to be accelerated and technology infused to save the soldier.

THE BEGINNING OF THE CONFLICT (1947-49)

In 1947, when British India was partitioned into India and Pakistan, Hari Singh, the autocratic and unpopular Maharaja of Kashmir and Jammu, a predominantly Muslim state, resisted the pressure to join either Pakistan or India hoping to get independence or autonomy from both countries. To buy time and to accomplish this goal, he signed a standstill agreement with Pakistan on August 16, and tried to sign a similar agreement with India. However, following the declaration of independence, communal rioting erupted in Punjab between the Hindus, Sikhs and Muslims when the state was being divided between India and Pakistan. In September, the rioting spilled into Kashmir against the Muslims. The Muslims in the Western part of Kashmir rebelled against the Maharaja and established their own independent (Azad) Kashmir government. Seeing this as an opportunity to force the rump state to accede Pakistan, on October 22, 1947, the got to fifteen miles from the state's capital city, Srinagar. Alarmed by this invasion, Hari Singh sought India's military assistance, but India refused to help unless the Maharajah signed the instrument of accession, a standard procedure under which other princely states had acceded to India or Pakistan. India agreed to the accession after receiving the consent of Sheikh Abdullah, the secular and popular leader of the National Conference (NC) in the state.

Singh signed the accord on October 27 and on the same day Indian armed forces entered Kashmir to repel the raiders. The local Muslims, mostly members of the NC provided the logistical support for the Indian troops. This intervention by India infuriated Pakistani Governor-General Mohammed Ali Jinnah. On the evening of October 27, he ordered Lt. General Sir Douglas Gracey, chief of the Pakistan army, to dispatch Pakistan regular troops into Kashmir, but Field Marshall Auchinleck, the Supreme Commander of the transition period persuaded him to withdraw his orders. In November, Jinnah approved the transfer of military supplies to the raiders and in early 1948 sent Pakistan regular troops to join their effort as "volunteers" and did not admit to Pakistan's direct involvement until much later in July 1948. On January 1, 1948, India's Prime Minister Jawaharlal Nehru following the advice of British Governor General Lord Mountbatten and contrary to the wishes of his Deputy Prime Minister Sarder Patel, lodged a complaint with the UN Security Council invoking Articles 34 and 35 of the UN Charter that called for a peaceful settlement of disputes between India and Pakistan, suspecting that it was behind the invasion. In the complaint, as it had already been pledged by Mountbatten in his letter to Hari Singh on October 26, India reiterated its pledge of its conditional aggressor was evicted — a pledge which India later regretted and which continues to haunt her until today.

On January 20, 1948, the Security Council established a three-member UN commission on India and Pakistan (UNCIP) to send them to Kashmir to investigate the situation and exercise mediation. On April 21, the Council expanded the commission to five and authorized it to restore peace and arrange for a plebiscite after the withdrawal of tribal troops.

Following Minister Sir Mohammed Zafrullah Khan's admission on July 7, 1948, that his country's regular troops were in Kashmir, the UNCIP on August 13, passed a resolution calling both on India and Pakistan to conduct a plebiscite after they agreed to a cease-fire and after Pakistan's regular troops and tribesmen were completely withdrawn. The cease-fire went into effect on January 1, 1949, while Pakistan was still in control of one-third of the state. Based on its resolution of August 13, 1948, the UNCIP sent a Monitoring Group for India and Pakistan (UNMGIP) to the region on January 24, to monitor the cease-fire line (CFL).

This line was renamed in 1972 as the line of control or line of actual control (LAC). The presence of the UNMIP was approved by India and Pakistan following by their agreement in Karachi on July 27, 1949. Fleet Admiral Chester Nimitz an American was appointed as the plebiscite administrator by the UN Secretary General, but he could not assume his functions as India and Pakistan objected to its implementation based on their varying interpretations of the UNCIP resolutions on the issue of demilitarization. In December 1949, the Security Council entrusted its President General A. G. L. McNaughton of Canada to negotiate a demilitarization plan in but India chose to ignore it by raising moral and legal issues about the plan. Without India's support the initiative failed. On March 14, 1950, the Security Council passed another resolution to follow up on McNaughton's proposals and appointed the noted Australian judge, Sir Owen Dixon, as UN representative to replace the UNCIP. In September 1950, Dixon suggested a proposal limiting the plebiscite only to the Kashmir Valley of the predominantly

Muslim population, which both countries rejected. In April 1951, the Council appointed Dr. Frank Graham, former US Senator, as UN representative. Between December 1951 and February 1953, Graham frantically tried to convince both India and Pakistan to accept his Secretary Council-supported demilitarization proposals that required the reduction of the military presence of both countries in Kashmir and Azad Kashmir preceding the conduct of a plebiscite but to no avail.

Against the backdrop of this stalemate, Nehru and Pakistan's Prime Minister, Mohammed Ali Bogra, met in June 1953 at the commonwealth conference in London. Following that meeting on August 20, 1953, both India and Pakistan temporarily agreed to take the issue out of UN's hands and resolve it directly. Subsequently in 1953, to the pleasant surprise of Pakistan, Nehru who had already informed Kashmir's new Prime Minister, Bakshi Mohammed Ghulam Mohammed of his intentions, told Bogra when he visited New Delhi that he would conduct a plebiscite in Kashmir. Bogra returned to Pakistan triumphantly. But Nehru's offer failed to materialize due to Bogra's procrastination reportedly brought about by the conspiratorial politics of General Ayub order to achieve his goal.

But following Pakistan's joining of the US-led Baghdad Pact in April 1954, and the South East Asian Treaty Organization (SEATO) in September 1956, Nehru reversed his position on plebiscite as he considered this decision by Pakistan as inimical to India's interest as a nonaligned state. He argued that Pakistan's alliance with the US, rendered all plebiscite agreements in Kashmir obsolete. Subsequently, following the February 1954 States' Constituent Assembly's declaration that Kashmir's accession to India was final; India took the position that the Assembly's action was equivalent to a plebiscite.

Based on that position it informed the Security Council that the issue of Kashmir was "finally settled" notwithstanding that Pakistan and the Council rejected that assertion. The Security Council met in January 1957 and reaffirmed its earlier resolutions that required a plebiscite. In February of that year, the council authorized its president Gunnar Jarring to mediate between India and Pakistan on the proposals of demilitarization and plebiscite. But like his predecessors, Jarring, did not have any success during his visit to the region and proposed to the Council in April that the issue be referred to arbitration, which Pakistan accepted, but India rejected. In September following Pakistan Prime Minister Sir Feroz Khan Noon's declaration that his country was willing to withdraw its troops from Kashmir to meet India's preconditions, the Security Council once again sent Frank Graham to the area. He tried to secure an agreement between India and Pakistan but to no avail as India again rejected it. In March 1958, Graham submitted a report to the Security Council (CSC) recommending that it arbitrate the dispute but as usual India rejected the proposal. From the mid-1950s issue practically died in the Security Council until it was again raised in 1963 and 1965. Surprisingly, the Indo-Pak borders remained mostly quiet during the period 1949-65, despite the non-resolution of the conflict. In 1965, however, India and Pakistan fought another war.

THE SUBSEQUENT KASHMIR WAR (SEPTEMBER 1965)

Pakistan became frustrated with India's increasing attempts to integrate Kashmir into its fold. Embolded by a presumed victory against India in the Rann of Kutch in April 1965, Pakistan made plans for "Operation Gibraltar" to recover Kashmir. As it did in 1947, it first sent Pakistani guerrillas into the Valley in August 1965 hoping that the Kashmiri Muslims would rise in rebellion against India. Instead, the guerrillas were apprehended and handed over to the Indian authorities. The situation worsened rapidly.

On September 1, when Indian troops crossed the international border, Pakistan launched an attack on Jammu. In response, India launched a series of attacks through the state of Punjab toward Lahore, Pakistan, and battled the Pakistani army. As the clashes continued, the UN Security Council, supported by the United States, Britain, and the USSR, called for an immediate cease-fire, which India and Pakistan accepted on September 6. Although the war was brief, it was a bitter one. Neither country was a winner. In January of 1966, at the invitation of Soviet Premier Alexsei Kosygin, both Shastri and Khan met in the city of Tashkent (Republic of Uzbesistan) and signed the agreement known as the Tashkent Declaration. On January 10, the agreement was formalized and the hostilities ended followed by the withdrawal of the Indo-Pakistani forces to the previous cease-fire lines. Shastri died of a heart attack in Tashkent right Pakistan fought a third war over Bangladesh's Independence in which the Kashmir dispute was only a peripheral issue.

On July 2, 1972, Mrs. Gandhi signed the Simla agreement with Mr. Zulfikar Ali Bhutto, the first President and later Prime Minister of Pakistan who had succeeded the military dictator General Yahya Khan in 1971. Under this agreement, India and Pakistan, among others, committed themselves to "settling their differences through bilateral negotiations or by any other peaceful means mutually agreed upon between them," and that the "basic issues and causes which bedeviled the relations between the two countries for the last 25 years shall be resolved by peaceful means." They also agreed that in "Jammu and Kashmir, the Line of Control (LOC) resulting from the cease-fire of December 17, 1971, shall be respected by both sides without prejudice to the recognized position of either side." The agreement became the basis for the renewal of official relations between the two countries both at political and economic levels, thus ending any role for either the UN or outside powers including the US. On July 24, 1973, they both signed another agreement in New Delhi agreeing to repatriate all POW's except for 195 who were held to be tried but were later released without trial.

While it demanded a plebiscite in the Indian-part of Kashmir, Pakistan unilaterally detached Gilgit Agency and Baltistan from Azad Kashmir in 1974, and integrated them into Pakistan. This move ignored the UN Security Council's longstanding resolutions in the same fashion that India did when it had integrated Kashmir into her union in 1956. Pakistan and India also renewed diplomatic recognitions in 1976.

In 1968, following the end of the third Indo-Pakistani war, India released Sheikh Abdullah and his colleague, Mirza Afzal Beg, from jail unconditionally. Abdullah became reconciled to accepting Kashmir's accession to India as final. For example, on March 10, 1972, in an interview with *The Times* (London), he said, "our dispute with the government of India is not accession but it is the quantum of autonomy" for Kashmir. In June of the same year, the state government headed by Side Mir Passim lifted the ban on Abdullah's entry into Kashmir as he dropped the demand for a plebiscite. Beginning in 1974, he and Beg joined India in a series of negotiations. The negotiations between Mrs. Gandhi's special representative G. Parthasarathi and Beg resulted in a six-point accord called the Kashmir Accord signed by Abdullah on February 12, 1975. Abdullah agreed to Kashmir's status as a part of India while being allowed to enjoy special provisions for the state under Article 370. On February 25, 1975, Abdullah became the Chief Minister of the state replacing Qasim of the Congress Party. In July 1975, his party, the National Conference finally came into existence again. He governed the state until he died on September 21, 1982. His son, Dr. Farooq Abdullah, succeeded him. But Farooq joined by the influential Cleric Maulvi Farooq of the Awami Action Committee demanded autonomy, the kind that had been promised in the 1952 Delhi Agreement to his father. During the 1983 legislative elections despite Mrs. Gandhi's anger and her manipulation of the elections, he stressed this theme and won the election. Upset by his demand for autonomy, Mrs. Gandhi intervened in the domestic politics of the state and dismissed Abdullah's government in 1984, by engineering defections from his party led by his brother-in-law, G. M. Shah. She brought the state under central control (Presidential violence increased under his leadership, in the Valley and Jammu, between Muslims and Hindus allegedly encouraged by him, he was dismissed in 1986. In the same year, in a surprisingly *volte face*, perhaps, as a matter of expediency, Abdullah signed a deal with Mr. Rajiv Gandhi, the new Prime Minister, who had succeeded his mother following her assassination in June 1984. In June 1986, a coalition of National Conference and Congress was formed. This coalition won a landslide victory in the March 1987 elections but it did not help Abdullah to keep power for long. The election of 1990 resulted in Abdullah downfall following the outbreak of a Muslim uprising in 1989.

THE NATIONALIST MUSLIM INSURGENCY 1989-PRESENT

The opposition party, the Muslim United Front (MUF) a party of disparate groups that had expected to do well, won only five seats. It branded the election victory as blatantly fraudulent and rigged. This perception alienated a large number of Kashmiris. They became unhappy with the national government of Mr. Rajiv Gandhi for its apparent disregard for the democratic procedures and for the principles of federalism. Besides, the Abdullah government's failure to promote economic development in the state further aggravated a sense of despair that existed among the college-educated Kashmiris whose anger and frustration turned against what they perceived to be a corrupt and insensitive government. Pakistan, on the sidelines, was ready to fish in troubled waters by supporting the secessionist groups with funds, weapons, and training, as it continued to make claims over Kashmir.

Three principal umbrella groups were involved in the uprising. One group, composed of Muslim fundamentalists, was pro-Pakistan and had links with the the Jammu and Kashmir Liberation Front (JKLF) established in 1965, and demanded an independent Kashmir. The third group was the Jammu and Kashmir Peoples' League that had a pro-Pakistan orientation. These groups demanded that a plebiscite as pledged by India and guaranteed by the UN Resolutions of 1948-49 be conducted so that the Kashmiris could exercise their right of self-determination. Their demands were supported by Pakistan. India, however, rejected their demands based on the argument that in 1956 the Kashmir constituent assembly acceded to India. It further contended that the plebiscite was outdated and that based on the July 1972 Simla agreement, Pakistan was obligated to resolve the Kashmir dispute bilaterally with her and not under the aegis of any international organization. Furthermore, India pointed out that Kashmir had been under a democratic Muslim leadership with an opportunity to rule itself, while Pakistan had been under a military dictatorship for more than twenty-five years since its independence in 1947. Therefore, India argued that for Pakistan to call for self-determination in Kashmir was disingenuous and hypocritical. Besides, India had to consider that 110 million Indians were Muslim, the second largest Muslim population in the world, and that Kashmir being a predominantly Muslim state (65% out of nearly 7 million population) stood out as a test case of India's commitment to secularism. In addition, India was also concerned with the Hindus and

Buddhists who live in Jammu and Ladakh respectively, represent 35% of the population and want to be part of the Indian Union. Hence, India rejected the demands of the secessionists. But the militants determined to realize their goal engaged the Indian security forces in armed struggle and terrorism. By intensifying their struggle they made the state ungovernable. As noted in paramilitary forces numbering more than 300,000 to help put down the militancy. It dismissed Abdullah's government in August 1990 and brought the state under central control. Under the July 1990 Jammu and Kashmir Disturbed Areas Act and Armed Forces Special Powers Act (AFSPA), repealed in May 1995, the security forces allegedly committed a series of human right abuses.

The abuses included the following: -Staged mock "encounters" with suspects to cover-up the deaths of victims who died in police custody, -Inhuman treatment of prisoners and suspects with beatings, burnings with cigarettes, suspension by the feet and electric shocks, -Arbitrary arrest and detention of the suspects for more than 12 months, albeit granting them right of habeas corpus, -Searching and arresting suspects without a warrant, and conducting the surveillance of their communications, and -Using excessive force against mass demonstrations and militants.

The encounter between the security forces and the militants resulted in more than 50,000 casualties. This number included many hundreds of innocent, civilian bystanders, as the militants used them as shields in their battles with the security forces. Militants have also been accused of committing many human rights violations. For example, they allegedly engaged in killing the moderate Muslim leadership, raping women (especially in Kashmir) and bombing and booby-trapping railway bridges, passenger buses, and public buildings.

By early 1996, the central government adopted a multi pronged approach to deal with the insurgency. It lifted direct rule over the state and restored state although the 30-disparate party coalition, known as the All-Party Hurriyat (Freedom) Conference (APHC), had denounced and boycotted the elections. It also created several Muslim counterinsurgency groups to fight the insurgents along with its security forces. In February 1996, the central government released from jail the four Pro-Pakistani separatist leaders, Imran Rahi of the Hiz-Ul-Mujahideen, Bilal Lodhi of the Al-Barq, Babbar Badr of the Muslim Janbaz Force (MJF), and Ghulam Mohiuddin of the Muslim Mujahideen, and initiated talks with them. They agreed to talks with the government with no preconditions and without Pakistan's involvement. On February 10, another pro-Pakistani Master Ahsan Dar, the founder of the Hiz-Ul-Mujahideen, who was in jail, joined them by endorsing their stand. The Indian government welcomed their offer and accused the Hurriyat Conference of "failing the people of Kashmir and breaching their faith."

The conference responded by denouncing them for excluding Pakistan and that its actions were "anti-movement," and asked that they be expelled from their organizations. The moderate separatist leader of the Peoples League, Shabir Ahmad Shah, also joined the conference by saying that the problem could not be solved without the inclusion of Pakistan in the talks.

Meanwhile, inter-group clashes began to increase, thus undermining their cause. For example, in 1995 alone, 167 clashes took place and 107 militants were killed. Even the leaders have been targeted for murder. This included Mohammed Yasin Malik, leader of the splinter group of the Jammu and Kashmir Liberation Front (JKLF) which espouses independence; Syed Ali Shah Geelani of the Jumat-I-Islami; and Abdul Ghani Lone of the Peoples Conference who are pro-Pakistani. In addition, many Kashmiris have not only grown tired of the long lasting violence and and Abdul Ghani Bhat is of the Muslim Conference party. The leaders came under increasing public criticism that questioned their commitment to the cause as they began to enrich themselves with foreign money. Consequently, it is not surprising that Ghulam Nabi Azad, leader of the Jammu and Kashmir Ikwan, accused the Hurriyat leadership as one who has "lost its relevance and has betrayed the people of Kashmir."

For quite some time, it seemed that the central government had put down the Muslim militancy in Kashmir. But given the Abdullah Government's inept attempts to address the socio-economic problems of the Kashmir Muslims, and given Pakistan's active role in fostering and promoting its home-based and mercenary outfits to fight in Kashmir, peace has become illusive and since 1997, the insurgency has intensified. Hoping to incite a sectarian violence, the militants began to indiscriminately kill scores of innocent Hindus and Sikhs since 1998. For example, the day that President Clinton arrived in New Delhi on March 20, 2000 for a visit, they killed 35 Sikhs in the Kashmir Valley. In July 2000, when the leader of the Kashmir-based Hiz-Ul-Mujahideen, Syed Salahuddin declared a unilateral cease-fire from Pakistan and called on India to engage Pakistan and Kashmir Muslims in trilateral talks, the Pakistan-based militant groups such as the Harkat-Ul-Ansar and Lashkar-E-Toiba, denounced his call and killed 100 people in one day to show their displeasure. Subsequently, Salahuddin withdrew his call as Pakistan also opposed it and India refused to talk to Pakistan until it had desisted supporting terrorism in the state. The persistent insurgency intensified conflict between India and Pakistan and increased the possibility of a nuclear encounter.

PAKISTAN RESOLUTION IN RETROSPECT

Pakistan owes her emergence to four outstanding leaders – Sir Syed Ahmad Khan (1817-98), Maulana Muhammad Ali (1878-1931), Muhammad Ali Jinnah (1876-1948), and Allama Muhammad Iqbal (1877-1938). These leaders provided intellectual and political leadership to Indian Muslims during the ninety years (1858-1947) of the British imperial dominance.

Surprisingly though, all of them were thorough-bred nationalists at one time or another. But, betimes, they got disillusioned and shied away willy-nilly from their Hindu compatriots, either because of Hindu ethnocentrism in the late 19th century or Congress's rather exclusive, unitary nationalism in the 1920s and 1930s. That makes Pakistan, in part, a product of these Hindu, myopic approaches, asymmetrical with the prime dictates of the ground realities in a multi-nation and multi-cultured subcontinent. In part it was, of course, a product of the Muslims' quest for an equitable share in power, a quest designed primarily to organise their society on the basis of their pristine value structure.

Interestingly, three of these four leaders – Sir Syed, Iqbal and Jinnah – had initially started out as full blooded nationalists, but were obliged to end up, finally, at threshold of Muslim "separatism". And that, of course, after a good deal of traumatised reappraisals. So did Maulana Muhammad Ali, who joined mainstream nationalist politics midway through his career. But he was the foremost "nationalist" leader along with Gandhi during the Khilafat and Non-Cooperation Movement (1920-22), and he also presided over the subsequent Cocanada Congress session (1923), a unique honour for a Muslim, an honour that was inexplicably denied to Jinnah, though he occupied the top echelon of Congress leadership for several years and was considered the embodied symbol of Hindu-Muslim unity. Yet, within seven years, Muhammad Ali would vehemently denounce Gandhi's much-trumpeted Civil Disobedience Movement, launched in April 1930. In his presidential address to the All India Muslim Conference at Bombay on April 23, 1930, he declared, "We refuse to join Mr Gandhi, because his movement is not a movement for the complete independence of India but for making the seventy millions of Indian Musalmans dependents of the Hindu Mahasabha". And he was cheered by over 20,000 Muslims that had gathered on the occasion.

Jinnah's postures and predilections during his long political life (1904-48) were a microcosm of Muslim India's during the period. For some seventeen years (1904-20), he had stood on the Congress's platform, pleading the Congress cause and envisioning a truly nationalist destiny for India. For another sixteen years (1921-37), though out of Congress for good, he was still working for a nationalist destiny; he was still striving for a Hindu-Muslim settlement and he was still collaborating with the Congress and its leadership. In pursuit of his mission, he devised several constitutional formulae, but all to no avail. At the Congress-sponsored All Parties National Convention at Calcutta in December 1928, called to consider and ratify the Nehru Report (1928) as the blueprint of India's future constitution, Jinnah had put forward the six minimum Muslim demands for acceptance. But all of them were outvoted one by one. In vain did Jinnah argue: "... what we want is that the Hindus and Muslims should march together until our object is obtained... I want you... to rise to that statesmanship which Sir Tej Bahadur describes. Minorities cannot give anything to the majority... If they are small points, why not concede? It is up to the majority and majority alone can give."

In aggregate terms, the most acrimonious and acerbic controversy in Indian politics in the late 1920s (since the Nehru Report) and all through the 1930s had hinged around the basic issue of Hindu "Unitarianism" vs Muslim Federalism. The difference in the approaches was sharply reflected in the formation of ministries in the Hindu and Muslim majority provinces in mid 1937. While the Muslim provinces went for coalition governments, the Hindu provinces under the Congress's aegis opted for exclusive, one party government.

Till early 1937, however, Jinnah was still his "nationalist" self; preaching his credo eloquently; trying to unite Hindus, Muslims and Sikhs. But, alas, Jinnah came to be caught on the wrong wicket. For one thing, at about this time, Pandit Nehru, the Congress Rashtrapathi (1936-38), began expounding his controversial "two-forces" formula, which counted Muslims out of India's politic body as a religio-political entity. He fired his first salvo in that direction on September 18, 1936, saying that "... the real contest is between two forces- the Congress representing the will for freedom of the nation and the British Government in India and its supporters who oppose this urge and try to suppress it. Intermediate groups, whatever virtue they may possess, fade out or line up with one of the principal forces. The issue for India is that of independence. He who is for it must be with the Congress and if he talks in terms of communalism he is not keen on independence."

To this formula Nehru returned, on January 10, 1937. Shorn of its sophistry and anti-imperialist tone, this represented a challenge to Muslim individuality in Indian politics, an individuality which they had nurtured and claimed since the times of Sir Syed Ahmad Khan. It also represented not only a challenge to the continued existence of the Muslim League (AIML), but also a moment of truth for Jinnah who had led that body continuously since 1919, except for his three years of self-exile (1931-34) in England.

Yet Jinnah's response was surprisingly conciliatory, if only because he still hoped for a rapprochement with the Congress. In his speech at Calcutta's Muhammad Ali Park, on January 4, 1937, he said "I refuse to line up with the Congress. I refuse to accept this proposition. There is a third party in this country and that is Muslim India.... We are not going to be camp followers of any party". (Italics for emphasis) Despite this timely rebuttal, he held out the olive branch, saying, "We are willing as equal partners to come to a settlement with our sister communities in the interest of India." And Jinnah reaffirmed this stance repeatedly for the next six months.

The deep divergence that characterised the Hindu-Muslim, Congress-League, thinking in 1937 stemmed from the basic dichotomy between Hindu "Unitarianism", a la the Nehru Report, and Muslim federalism, a la Jinnah's Fourteen Points (1929). In essence, it centred on the issue that whether India was uni-national or bi-national, whether it was uni-cultured or bi-cultured. In denying the "intermediate groups" the right to existence and in denying "all third parties' in the historical sense, Nehru was not only denying the AIML the right to exist or its due importance; more important: he was denying the Muslims the right to organize themselves politically on a platform of their own or on a platform other than that of the Congress. In other words, he was denying them their distinct individuality in India's body politic as a religio-political entity.

Jinnah, as opposed to this, felt that India was multinational and multi-cultured; that Muslims had the right to maintain their separate entity; that Muslim India represented the "third party" in India's body politic; that they should refuse to be "camp followers of any party" and that, above all, Muslims should organise themselves politically to make the third party claim a fait accompli. As a corollary to this claim, he demanded equality of status for Muslims. Of course, he repeatedly offered to coalesce with the Congress in the struggle for freedom, but only if the Muslims were "assured of their political freedom".

Thus, he told a meeting at the residence of Syed Ali Zaheer, presided over by the pro-Congress Syed Wazir Hasan, on May 9, 1937, "While we shall not knock at the Government House, we shall not also bow before Anand Bhawan", the Congress headquarters at Allahabad. Six weeks earlier, in late March 1937, he had told the AIML Council in categorical terms why he considered the Muslims' merger with the Hindus, and the AIML's with the Congress, almost impossible. It was impossible for Muslims to merge with Hindus because "their language, culture and civilization are quite different", he argued. National self-government, he said, was his creed; but Muslims "must unite as a nation and then live or die as a nation" (italics for emphasis).

The Muslims were considered a minority at this stage of India's political evolution. But "minorities", argued Jinnah in the Indian Legislative Assembly on February 7, 1935, while speaking on the Report of the Joint Parliamentary Committee on Indian Constitutional Reforms, "means a combination of things. It may be that a minority has a different religion from the other citizens of a country. Their language may be different, their race may be different, their culture may be different, and the combination of all these various elements – religion, culture, race, language, arts, music, and so forth – makes the minority a separate entity in the State, and the separate entity as an entity wants safeguards. Surely, therefore, we must face this question as a political problem; we must solve it and not evade it..."

Thus, what was at issue in the Congress-League, Nehru-Jinnah, controversy was, above all, the status of Muslims in Indian politics. Their status, in turn, depended upon whether India was uni-national or bi-national. The Congress's political conduct in 1937, remarked Penderel Moon in his Divide and Quit, meant that "there would be no room on the throne of India, save for Congress and Congress stooges". The developing Congress's policy, thus, gave Muslims a foretaste of what the Hindu un-remitted centralism and homogenic ambitions meant. Under the sort of nationalist dispensation envisaged by the Congress, Muslims would surely be relegated to a back seat.

Their values would be at a discount, their cultural identity in jeopardy. Above all, they would have no hope of shaping their spiritual, social, and cultural life according to their own ethos. All this meant culturicide, pure and simple. The Congress's conduct and rule were thus, in gross violation of 'minority' rights, civil society, and of adequate, if not good, governance – issues which, under the prevalent Westphalian Model (1648), with its overriding credo of the sovereignty of 'nations' and the 'sanctity' of borders, had not acquired the measure of importance and criticality which they have had since the demise of the Soviet Union (1991), the prime anti-Human Rights paradigm in the twentieth century. All this obviously posed a new and serious challenge to Muslims as a religio-cultural entity.

In immediate terms, it was this situation, at once despairing and agonising, that turned Muslim thinking towards Pakistan. If the Islamic way of life could not be preserved in an all-India set up, it should be saved wherever it was possible. Pakistan, or more accurately the demand for it, was thus a last-ditch attempt: an attempt to centralise, to quote Iqbal, "the life of Islam as a cultural force" in a specified territory, so that "the most living portion of the Muslims of India" could develop to the fullest in that territory, their "spiritual, cultural, economic and social life according to their own genius", to quote Jinnah, – a development which was practically impossible under the sort of dispensation envisaged by the Hindu-dominated Congress. Such, in short, were the urges and motivations that, in immediate terms, led to the formulation of the demand for Pakistan.

At another level, with the grim prospect of having been denied a place on the throne of India, what alternative did the Muslims have except for forging a throne for themselves in their majority provinces? And Pakistan simply meant only that much-and nothing more. Hence, in 1940, Muslims had no choice but to go to the Pakistan platform – unless they were prepared to be decimated as a religio-political entity in India's body politic.

RADCLIFFE LINE

The Radcliffe Line was announced on 16 August 1947 as a boundary demarcation line between India and Pakistan upon the Partition of India. The Radcliffe Line was named after its architect, Sir Cyril Radcliffe, who as chairman of the Border Commissions was charged with equitably dividing 175,000 square miles (450,000 km^2) of territory with 88 million people.

Background

On 15 July 1947, the Indian Independence Act 1947 of the Parliament of the United Kingdom stipulated that British rule in India would come to an end just one month later, on 15 August 1947. The Act also stipulated the partition of the Provinces of British India into two new sovereign dominions: the Union of India and the Dominion of Pakistan.

Before partition, some 40% of the area of India was covered by princely states. These states were in subsidiary allianceswith the British, who were responsible for their external affairs, but they were not British possessions and did not form part of British India. Thus, the British could not grant them independence, nor partition them. The Indian Independence Act abandoned the suzerainty of the British Crown over the princely states and dissolved the Indian Empire, so that the rulers of the states found themselves fully independent and were free to decide for themselves whether to accede to one of the new dominions or to remain independent. In the event, almost all decided quickly to join India or Pakistan. A small number did not.

Pakistan was intended as a Muslim homeland, while the new India was secular with a Hindu majority. Muslim-majority British provinces in the north were to become the foundation of Pakistan. The provinces of Baluchistan (91.8% Muslim before partition) and Sindh (72.7%) were granted entirely to Pakistan. However, two provinces did not have an overwhelming majority — Bengal in the north-east (54.4% Muslim) and the Punjab in the north-west (55.7% Muslim). The western part of the Punjab became part of West

Pakistan and the eastern part became the Indian state of East Punjab, which was later divided between a smaller Punjab State and two other states. Bengal was also partitioned, into East Bengal (in Pakistan) and West Bengal (in India). Following independence, the North-West Frontier Province (whose borders with Afghanistan had earlier been demarcated by the Durand Line) voted by a narrow margin in a controversial referendum to accede to Pakistan, despite a boycott by the most popular Pukhtun movement in the province at that time.

The Punjab's population distribution was such that there was no line that could neatly divide Hindus, Muslims, and Sikhs. Likewise, no line could appease the Muslim League, headed by Jinnah, and the Indian National Congress led by Jawaharlal Nehru and Vallabhbhai Patel, and by the British. Moreover, any division based on religious communities was sure to entail "cutting through road and rail communications, irrigation schemes, electric power systems and even individual landholdings." However, a well-drawn line could minimize the separation of farmers from their fields, and also minimize the numbers of people who might feel forced to relocate.

As it turned out, on "the sub-continent as a whole, some 14 million people left their homes and set out by every means possible — by air, train, and road, in cars and lorries, in buses and bullock carts, but most of all on foot — to seek refuge with their own kind." Many of them were slaughtered by an opposing side, some starved or died of exhaustion, while others were afflicted with "cholera, dysentery, and all those other diseases that afflict undernourished refugees everywhere". Estimates of the number of people who died range between 200,000 (official British estimate at the time) and two million, with the consensus being around one million dead.

Process and Key People

A crude border had already been drawn up by Lord Wavell, the Viceroy of India prior to his replacement as Viceroy, in February 1947, by Lord Louis Mountbatten. In order to determine exactly which territories to assign to each country, in June 1947, Britain appointed Sir Cyril Radcliffe to chair two Boundary Commissions—one for Bengal and one for Punjab.

The Commission was instructed to "demarcate the boundaries of the two parts of the Punjab on the basis of ascertaining the contiguous majority areas of Muslims and non-Muslims. In doing so, it will also take into account other factors." Other factors were undefined, giving Radcliffe leeway, but included decisions regarding "natural boundaries, communications, watercourses and irrigation systems", as well as socio-political consideration. Each commission also had 4 representatives—2 from the Indian National Congress and 2 from the Muslim League. Given the deadlock between the interests of the two sides and their rancorous relationship, the final decision was essentially Radcliffe's. After arriving in India on 8 July 1947, Radcliffe was given just 5 weeks to decide on a border. He soon met with his fellow college alumnus Mountbatten and travelled to Lahore and Calcutta to meet with commission members, chiefly Nehru from the Congress and Jinnah, president of the Muslim League.

He objected to the short time frame, but all parties were insistent that the line be finished by the 15 August British withdrawal from India. Mountbatten had accepted the post as Viceroy on the condition of an early deadline. The decision was completed just a couple of days before the withdrawal, but due to political manoeuvring, not published until 17 August 1947, two days after the grant of independence to India and Pakistan.

Problems in the Process

Boundary-making Procedures

All lawyers by trade, Radcliffe and the other commissioners had all of the polish and none of the specialized knowledge needed for the task. They had no advisers to inform them of the well-established procedures and information needed to draw a boundary. Nor was there time to gather the survey and regional information. The absence of some experts and advisers, such as the United Nations, was deliberate, to avoid delay. Britain's new Labour government "deep in wartime debt, simply couldn't afford to hold on to its increasingly unstable empire." "The absence of outside participants—for example, from the United Nations—also satisfied the British Government's urgent desire to save face by avoiding the appearance that it required outside help to govern—or stop governing—its own empire."

Political Representation

The equal representation given to politicians from Indian National Congress and the Muslim League appeared to provide balance, but instead created deadlock. The relationships were so tendentious that the judges "could hardly bear to speak to each other", and the agendas so at odds that there seemed to be little point anyway. Even worse, "the wife and two children of the Sikh judge in Lahore had been murdered by Muslims in Rawalpindi a few weeks earlier." In fact, minimizing the numbers of Hindus and Muslims on the wrong side of the line was not the only concern to balance.

The Punjab Border Commission was to draw a border through the middle of an area home to the Sikh community. Lord Islay was rueful for the British not to give more consideration to the community who, in his words, had "provided many thousands of splendid recruits for the Indian Army" in its service for the crown in World War I. However, the Sikhs were militant in their opposition to any solution which would put their community in a Muslim ruled state. Moreover, many insisted on their own sovereign state, something no-one else would agree to.

Last of all, were the communities without any representation. The Bengal Border Commission representatives were chiefly concerned with the question of who would get Calcutta. The Buddhist tribes in the Chittigong Hill Tracts in Bengal had no official representation and were left totally without information to prepare for their situation until two days after the partition.

Perceiving the situation as intractable and urgent, Radcliffe went on to make all the difficult decisions himself. This was impossible from inception, but Radcliffe seems to have had no doubt in himself and raised no official complaint or proposal to change the circumstances.

Local Knowledge

Before his appointment, Radcliffe had never visited India and knew no one there. To the British and the feuding politicians alike, this liability was looked upon as an asset; he was considered to be unbiased toward any of the parties, except of course Britain. Only his private secretary, Christopher Beaumont, was familiar with the administration and life in the Punjab. Wanting to preserve the appearance of impartiality, Radcliffe also kept his distance from Viceroy Mountbatten.

No amount of knowledge could produce a line that would completely avoid conflict; already, "sectarian riots in Punjab and Bengal dimmed hopes for a quick and dignified British withdrawal". "Many of the seeds of postcolonial disorder in South Asia were sown much earlier, in two centuries of direct and indirect British rule, but, as book after book has demonstrated, nothing in the complex tragedy of partition was inevitable."

Haste and Indifference

Had the Commission been more careful, gaffes in the division could have been avoided. For example, there were instances where the border was drawn leaving some parts of a village in India and some in Pakistan. Since he had just a month, Radcliffe saw little point in being careful to skirt villages. His border was drawn right through thickly populated areas instead of between them. There were even instances where the dividing line passed through a single house with some rooms in one country and others in the other.

Radcliffe justified such casual division with the truism that no matter what he did, people would suffer. The thinking behind this justification may never be known since Radcliffe "destroyed all his papers before he left India".

He departed on Independence Day itself, before even the boundary awards were distributed. By his own admission, Radcliffe was heavily influenced by his lack of fitness for the Indian climate and his eagerness to depart India.

The implementation was no less hasty than the process of drawing the border. On 16 August 1947 at 5:00pm, the Indian and Pakistani representatives were given two hours to study copies, before the Radcliffe award was published on the 17th.

Secrecy

To avoid disputes and delays, the division was done in secret. The final Awards were ready on 9 August and 12 August, but not published until two days after the partition.

According to Read, there is some circumstantial evidence that Nehru and Patel were secretly informed of the Punjab Award's contents on August 9 or 10, either through Mountbatten or Radcliffe's Indian assistant secretary. Regardless of how it transpired, the award was changed to put a salient east of the Sutlej canal within India's domain instead of Pakistan's.

This area consisted of two Muslim-majority tehsils with a combined population of over half a million. There were two apparent reasons for the switch: (1) the area housed an army arms depot and (2) contained the headwaters of a canal which irrigated the princely state of Bikaner, which would accede to India.

Likewise, it is not known how Radcliffe was persuaded to award the Chittagong Hill Tracts to Pakistan. This came as a shock to Patel and Nehru who had assumed the areas would be awarded to India since they were 98% non-Muslim. Similarly, the decision to award India the Muslim-majority districts of Murshidabad and Malda in Bengal was kept so secret that the inhabitants hoisted the Pakistani flag there till the award was made public on 17 August 1947.

The truth of how these decisions were made may never be known, since Radcliffe destroyed all of his records and Mountbatten expressly denied any special-knowledge or favouritism.

Implementation

After the partition, the fledgling governments of India and Pakistan were left with all responsibility to implement the border. After visiting Lahore in August, Viceroy Mountbatten hastily arranged a Punjab Boundary Force to keep the peace around Lahore, but 50,000 men was not enough to prevent thousands of killings, 77% of which were in the rural areas. Given the size of the territory, the force amounted to less than 1 soldier per square mile. This was not enough to protect the cities much less the caravans of the hundreds of thousands of refugees who were fleeing their homes in what would become Pakistan. Both India and Pakistan were loath to violate the agreement by supporting the rebellions of villages drawn on the wrong side of the border, as this could prompt a loss of face on the international stage and require the British or the UN to intervene. (This did not prevent them from getting into immediate conflict over the former princely state of Kashmir, as this territory was not a part of the Radcliffe agreement.)

Border conflicts led to three wars, in 1947, 1965, and 1971, as well as the May 1998 dual tests of nuclear weapons and the Kargil conflict of 1999.

Disputes along the Radcliffe Line

There were two major disputes regarding the Radcliffe Line, the Chittagong Hill Tracts and the Gurdaspur District. Minor disputes evolved around the districts of Malda, Khulna, and Murshidabad of Bengal and the sub-division of Karimganj of Assam.

Chittagong Hill Tracts

Chittagong Hill Tracts had a majority non-Muslim population of 97% (most of them Buddhists), but was given to Pakistan. The Chittagong Hill Tracts People's Association (CHTPA) petitioned the Bengal Boundary Commission that, since the CHTs were inhabited largely by non-Muslims, they should remain within India. Since they had no official representation, there was no official discussion on the matter, and many on the Indian side assumed the CHT would be awarded to India.

On 15 August 1947, many of the tribes did not know to which side of the border they belonged. On 17 August, the publication of the Radcliffe Award put the CHTs in Pakistan.

The rationale of giving the Chittagong Hill Tracts to Pakistan was that they were inaccessible to India and to provide a substantial rural buffer to support Chittagong (now in Bangladesh), a major city and port; advocates for Pakistan forcefully argued to the Bengal Boundary Commission that the only approach was through Chittagong.

Two days later, the CHTPA resolved not to abide by the award and hoisted the Indian flag. The Pakistani army dealt with the protest but its polemic somewhat remains with some of its non-Muslim majority arguing for its cessation.

Gurdaspur District

Under British rule, the Gurdaspur district was the northernmost district of the Punjab Province of British India. The district itself was administratively subdivided into four tehsils: Shakargarh, Gurdaspur, Batala, and Pathankot. Of the four, only Shakargarh Tehsil, which was separated from the rest of the district by the Ravi river, was awarded to Pakistan and became part of Sialkot District within the West Punjab province of Pakistan. The rest of the district, retaining the name Gurdaspur, became part of India's East Punjab state. The division of the district was followed by a population transfer between the two nations, with Muslims leaving for Pakistan and Hindus and Sikhs leaving for India. The entire district of Gurdaspur had a plurality of Muslims, which was a majority when counting the Ahmadiyya community as Muslim. Ahmadiyya were counted as Muslim even though they had been declared non-Muslim by Muslim clergy.

The district was home to a large concentration of Ahmadiyyas, their cultural centres, and their spiritual centre Qadian. In the 1901 census, the population of Gurdaspur district was 49% Muslim, 40% Hindu, and 10% Sikh. At the time of partition, the census showed the following distribution of Muslims and non-Muslims:

Part of district	*Majority*	*% Muslim (including Ahmadiyya)*
Shakargarh tehsil	Muslim	51%
Gurdaspur tehsil	Muslim	51%
Batala tehsil	Muslim	53%
Pathankot tehsil	non-Muslim	33%
Entire District (all four tehsils)	Muslim	50.6%
Area awarded to India	non-Muslim	less than 50%

It has been speculated that the following arguments were made before the boundary commission by Lord Mountbatten and others in favour of awarding much of Gurdaspur to India:

1. The territory would allow the kingdom of Kashmir to be contiguously accessible to India, so that its ruler could opt to integrate with the Indian Union.
2. Pathankot tehsil contained a direct railway link with the adjoining Hoshiarpur and Kangra districts of East Punjab.
3. Batala and Gurdaspur tehsils would provide a buffer to the Sikh holy city of Amritsar, whose district would otherwise be surrounded by Pakistani territories on three of its four sides.
4. If the area east of the Ravi river was considered as one block, it would have a slight non-Muslim majority. This block would consist of Amritsar and most of Gurdaspur district (excluding Shakargarh).

5. Also, by doing this, the majority of the Sikh population (58%) would fall into East Punjab; by doing the opposite, a slight majority would be left in Pakistan and this would increase the number of Sikh refugees.
6. This could help pacify the Sikh population who lost major tracts of lands in West Punjab.

Firozpur District

To counterbalance the relatively small share of Gurdaspur district awarded to Pakistan, Radcliffe attempted to instead transfer Firozpurand Zira tehsils in Firozpur district to Pakistan.

This was opposed by the Maharaja of Bikaner because Harike headworks on the confluence of the Satluj and Beas rivers, from where a canal originated, the only source of water for his desert state was in Ferozepore.

It was only after he threatened Mountbatten, that he would accede his state to Pakistan if Firozpur was awarded to West Punjab, that the award was changed at the last minute and all of Firozpur district was awarded to India.

Malda District

Another disputed decision made by Radcliffe was division of the Malda district of Bengal. The district overall had a slight Muslim majority, but was divided and most of it, including Malda town, went to India. The district remained under East Pakistan administration for 3–4 days after 15 August 1947. It was only when the award was made public that the Pakistani flag was replaced by the Indian flag in Malda.

Khulna and Murshidabad Districts

The entire Khulna District with a slight Hindu majority of 52% was also given to East Pakistan in lieu of the much smaller Murshidabad district with a 70% Muslim majority, which went to India.

Karimganj

Sylhet district of Assam joined Pakistan in accordance with a plebiscite. However, the Karimganj sub-division with a Muslim majority was severed from Sylhet and given to India. As of the 2001 Indian Census, Karimganj still has a Muslim majority of 52.3%.

KARGIL WAR IN THE ARTS

The brief conflict provided considerable dramatic material for filmmakers and authors in India. Some documentaries which were shot on the subject were used by the ruling party coalition, led by Bharatiya Janata Party (BJP), in furthering its election campaign that immediately followed the war. The following is a list of the major films and dramas on the subject.

- "Lord John Marbury (The West Wing)" (1999), 11th episode of the first season depicts a fictionalized representation of the Kargil conflict.
- Pentagram's single, 'Price Of Bullets', released in 1999 dealt with the Kargil War.
- *LOC: Kargil* (2003), a Hindi movie which depicts many incidents from the war was one of the longest in Indian movie history, running for more than four hours.
- *Lakshya* (2004), another Hindi movie portraying a fictionalised account of the conflict. Movie critics have generally appreciated the realistic portrayal of characters. The film also received good reviews in Pakistan because it portrays both sides fairly.
- *Sainika* (2002), the Kannada film directed by Mahesh Sukhdhare depicted the life of a soldier with Kargil war as one of the events. Starring C.P.Yogishwar and Sakshi Shivanand.
- *Dhoop* (2003), Hindi film, directed by national award winner Ashwini Chaudhary, which depicted the life of Anuj Nayyar's parents after his death. Anuj Nayyar was a captain in the Indian army and was awarded Maha Vir Chakra posthumously. Om Puri plays the role of S.K. Nayyar, Anuj's father.
- *Mission Fateh – Real Stories of Kargil Heroes*, a TV series telecast on Sahara channel chronicling the Indian Army's missions.
- *Fifty Day War* – A theatrical production on the war, directed by Aamir Raza Husain, the title indicating the length of the Kargil conflict. This was claimed to be the biggest production of its kind in Asia, budget of Rs. 1.5 crore, involving real aircraft and explosions in an outdoor setting.
- *Kurukshetra* (2008) – A Malayalam film directed by a former Indian Army Major Ravi (Retd) based on his experience of Kargil War.
- *Laag* (2000)— A Pakistani film-drama based on the armed intrusions and struggle of Pakistan army soldiers in the conflict.

Many other movies like *Tango Charlie* drew heavily upon the Kargil episode, which still continues to be a plot for mainstream movies with a Malayalam movie *Keerthi Chakra*.

The impact of the war in the sporting arena was visible during the India-Pakistan clash in the 1999 Cricket World Cup, which coincided with the Kargil timeline. The game witnessed heightened passions and was one of the most viewed matches in the tournament.

AFTERMATH OF WAR

India

From the end of the war until February 2000, the Indian stock market rose by over 30%. The next Indian national budget included major increases in military spending.

There was a surge in patriotism, with many celebrities expressing their support for the Kargil cause. Indians were angered by media reports of the death of pilot Ajay Ahuja, especially after Indian authorities reported that Ahuja had been murdered and his body mutilated by Pakistani troops. The war had produced higher than expected fatalities for the Indian military, with a sizeable percentage of them including newly commissioned officers. One month after conclusion of the Kargil war, the Atlantique Incident – where a Pakistan Navy plane was shot down by India – briefly reignited fears of a conflict between the two countries.

After the war, the Indian government severed ties with Pakistan and increased defence preparedness. India increased its defence budget as it sought to acquire more state of the art equipment. Media reported about military procurement irregularities and criticism of intelligence agencies like Research and Analysis Wing, which failed to predict the intrusions or the identity/number of infiltrators during the war.

An internal assessment report by the armed forces, published in an Indian magazine, showed several other failings, including "a sense of complacency" and being "unprepared for a conventional war" on the presumption that nuclearism would sustain peace. It also highlighted the lapses in command and control, the insufficient troop levels and the dearth of large-calibre guns like the Bofors. In 2006, retired Air Chief Marshal, A.Y. Tipnis, alleged that the Indian Army did not fully inform the government about the intrusions, adding that the army chief Ved Prakash Malik, was initially reluctant to use the full strike capability of the Indian Air Force, instead requesting only helicopter gunship support. Soon after the conflict, India also decided to complete the project – previously stalled by Pakistan – to fence the entire LOC.

The end of the Kargil conflict was followed by the 13th Indian General Elections to the Lok Sabha, which gave a decisive mandate to the National Democratic Alliance (NDA) government. It was re-elected to power in September–October 1999 with a majority of 303 seats out of 545 in the Lok Sabha. On the diplomatic front, Indo-U.S. relations improved, as the United States appreciated Indian attempts to restrict the conflict to a limited geographic area. Relations with Israel – which had discreetly aided India with ordnance supply and matériel such as unmanned aerial vehicles and laser-guided bombs, as well as satellite imagery – also were bolstered.

Kargil Review Committee

Soon after the war the Atal Bihari Vajpayee government set up an inquiry into its causes and to analyze perceived Indian intelligence failures. The high-powered committee was chaired by eminent strategic affairs analyst K. Subrahmanyam and given powers to interview anyone with current or past associations with Indian security, including former Prime Ministers. The committee's final report (also referred to as the 'Subrahmanyam Report') led to a large-scale restructuring of Indian Intelligence. It, however, came in for heavy criticism in the Indian media for its perceived avoidance of assigning specific responsibility for failures over detecting the Kargil intrusions. The Committee was also embroiled in controversy for indicting Brigadier Surinder Singh of the Indian Army for his failure to report enemy intrusions in time, and for his subsequent conduct. Many press reports questioned or contradicted this finding and claimed that Singh had in fact issued early warnings that were ignored by senior Indian Army commanders and, ultimately, higher government functionaries.

Pakistan

Faced with the possibility of international isolation, the already fragile Pakistan economy was weakened further. The morale of Pakistan forces after the withdrawal declined as many units of the Northern Light Infantry suffered heavy casualties. The government refused to accept the dead bodies of many officers, an issue that provoked outrage and protests in the Northern Areas. Pakistan initially did not acknowledge many of its casualties, but Sharif later said that over 4,000 Pakistani troops were killed in the operation. Responding to this, Pakistan President Pervez Musharraf said, "It hurts me when an ex-premier undermines his own forces," and claimed that Indian casualties were more than that of Pakistan. The legacy of Kargil war still continues to debated on Pakistan's news channels and television political correspondents, which Musharraf repeatedly appeared to justified the causes and preludes of the Kargil war.

Many in Pakistan had expected a victory over the Indian military based on Pakistani official reports on the war, but were dismayed by the turn of events and questioned the eventual retreat. The military leadership is believed to have felt let down by the prime minister's decision to withdraw the remaining fighters. However, some authors, including Musharraf's close friend and former American CENTCOM Commander General Anthony Zinni, and former

Prime minister Nawaz Sharif, state that it was General Musharraf who requested Sharif to withdraw the Pakistani troops. In 2012, Musharraf's senior officer and retired major-general Abdul Majeed Malik maintained that Kargil was a "total disaster" and gave bitter criticism to General Musharraf. Pointing out to the fact that Pakistan was in no position to fight India in that area; it was the Nawaz Sharif government that initiated the diplomatic process by involving the US President Bill Clinton and got Pakistan out of the difficult scenario. Malik maintained that soldiers were not "Mujaheddin" but an active-duty serving officers and soldiers of Pakistan Army.

In a national security meeting with Prime minister Nawaz Sharif at the Joint Headquarters, General Musharraf became heavily involved with serious altercations with Chief of Naval Staff Admiral Fasih Bokhari who ultimately called for a court-martial against General Musharraf. Taking participation in the arguments, Chief of Air Staff Air Chief Marshal PQ Mehdi quoted that "any intervention by the Navy and the PAF into disputed land of Indian-controlled Kashmir would be perceived as an escalation to all-out declared war". After witnessing Musharraf's criticism given to his fellow officers, ACM PQ Mehdi decided to give Musharraf a favor after issuing orders to PAF's F-16s for the patrolling missions near the Skardu Valley. The Pakistan Navy largely remains camouflaged during this entire conflict, only submarines were deployed for partrolling missions. With Sharif placing the onus of the Kargil attacks squarely on the army chief Pervez Musharraf, there was an atmosphere of uneasiness between the two. On October 12, 1999, General Musharraf staged a bloodless *coup d'état,* ousting Nawaz Sharif.

Benazir Bhutto, an opposition leader in the parliament and former prime minister, called the Kargil War "Pakistan's greatest blunder". Many ex-officials of the military and the Inter-Services Intelligence (Pakistan's principal intelligence agency) also believed that "Kargil was a waste of time" and "could not have resulted in any advantage" on the larger issue of Kashmir. A retired Pakistan Army's Lieutenant-General Ali Kuli Khan, lambasted the war as "a disaster bigger than the East Pakistan tragedy", adding that the plan was "flawed in terms of its conception, tactical planning and execution" that ended in "sacrificing so many soldiers." The Pakistani media criticized the whole plan and the eventual climbdown from the Kargil heights since there were no gains to show for the loss of lives and it only resulted in international condemnation.

Despite calls by many, no public commission of inquiry was set up in Pakistan to investigate the people responsible for initiating the conflict. The Pakistan Muslim League (PML(N)) published awhite paper in 2006, which stated that Nawaz Sharif constituted an inquiry committee that recommended a court martial for General Pervez Musharraf, but Musharraf "stole the report" after toppling the government, to save himself. The report also claims that India knew about the plan 11 months before its launch, enabling a complete victory for India on military, diplomatic and economic fronts.

A statement in June, 2008 by a former X Corps commander and Director-General of Military Intelligence (M.I.) that time, Lieutenant-General (retired) Jamshed Gulzar Kianisaid that: "As Prime minister, Nawaz Sharif "was never briefed by the army" on the Kargil attack, reignited the demand for a probe of the episode by legal and political groups.

Though the Kargil conflict had brought the Kashmir dispute into international focus – which was one of the aims of Pakistan – it had done so in negative circumstances that eroded its credibility, since the infiltration came just after a peace process between the two countries was underway. The sanctity of the LOC too received international recognition. President Clinton's move to ask Islamabad to withdraw hundreds of armed militants from Indian-administered Kashmir was viewed by many in Pakistan as indicative of a clear shift in US policy against Pakistan.

After the war, a few changes were made to the Pakistan armed forces. In recognition of the Northern Light Infantry's performance in the war – which even drew praise from a retired Indian Lt. General – the regiment was incorporated into the regular army.

The war showed that despite a tactically sound plan that had the element of surprise, little groundwork had been done to gauge the politico-diplomatic ramifications. And like previous unsuccessful infiltrations attempts, such as *Operation Gibraltar*, which sparked the 1965 war, there was little coordination or information sharing among the branches of the Pakistani Armed Forces. One U.S. Intelligence study is reported to have stated that Kargil was yet another example of Pakistan's (lack of) grand strategy, repeating the follies of the previous wars. In 2013, General Musharraf's close collaborator and confidential subordinate Lieutenant-General (retired) Shahid Aziz revealed to Pakistan's news televisions and electronic media, that "[Kargil] adventure' was India's intelligence failure and Pakistan's miscalculated move, the Kargil operation was known only to General Parvez Musharraf and four of his close collaborators."

Casualties

Pakistan army losses have been difficult to determine. Pakistan confirmed that 453 soldiers were killed. The US Department of State had made an early, partial estimate of close to 700 fatalities. According to numbers stated by Nawaz Sharif there were over 4,000 fatalities.

His PML (N) party in its "white paper" on the war mentioned that more than 3,000 Mujahideens, officers and soldiers were killed. Another major Pakistani political party, thePakistan Peoples Party, also says that "thousands" of soldiers and irregulars died.

Indian estimates stand at 1,042 Pakistani soldiers killed. Musharraf, in his Hindi version of his memoirs, titled "Agnipath", differs from all the estimates stating that 357 troops were killed with a further 665 wounded. Apart from General Musharraf's figure on the number of Pakistanis wounded, the number of people injured in the Pakistan camp is not yet fully known although they are at least more than 400 according to Pakistan army's website.

One Indian Pilot was officially captured during the fighting, while there were eight Pakistani soldiers who were captured during the fighting, and were repatriated on 13 August 1999;

India gave its official casualty figures as 527 dead and 1,363 wounded.

2

Siachen Conflict

The Siachen conflict, sometimes referred to as the Siachen War, was a military conflict between India and Pakistan over the disputed Siachen Glacier region in Kashmir. A cease-fire went into effect in 2003. The contended area is nearly 1,000 square miles (2,600 km^2) of territory. The conflict was started in 1984 by India's successful capture of the Siachen Glacier as part of Operation *Meghdoot*. India took control of the 70-kilometre-long (43 mi) Siachen Glacier and its tributary glaciers, as well as all the main passes and heights of the Saltoro Ridge immediately west of the glacier, including Sia La, Bilafond La, and Gyong La.

Pakistan controls the glacial valleys immediately west of the Saltoro Ridge. According to *TIME* magazine, India gained more than 1,000 square miles (3,000 km^2) of territory because of its military operations in Siachen.

CAUSES

The Siachen Glacier is the highest battleground on earth, where India and Pakistan have fought intermittently since 13 April 1984. Both countries maintain permanent military presence in the region at a height of over 6,000 metres (20,000 ft). More than 2000 people have died in this inhospitable terrain, mostly due to weather extremes and the natural hazards of mountain warfare.

The conflict in Siachen stems from the incompletely demarcated territory on the map beyond the map coordinate known as NJ9842 (35.008371°N 77.008805°E). The 1949 Karachi Agreement and 1972 Simla Agreement did not clearly mention who controlled the glacier, merely stating that the Cease Fire Line (CFL) terminated at NJ9842. UN officials presumed there would be no dispute between India and Pakistan over such a cold and barren region.

Paragraph B 2 (d) of Karachi Agreement

Following the UN-mediated ceasefire in the 1949, the line between India and Pakistan was demarcated up to point NJ9842 at the foot of the Siachen Glacier. The largely inaccessible terrain beyond this point was not demarcated, but delimited as thence north to the glaciers in paragraph B 2 (d) of the Karachi Agreement.

Paragraph B 2 (d) of 1949 Karachi Agreement states: (d) From Dalunang eastwards the cease-fire line will follow the general line point 15495, Ishman, Manus, Gangam, Gunderman, Point 13620, Funkar (Point 17628), Marmak, Natsara, Shangruti (Point 1,531), Chorbat La (Point 16700), Chalunka (on the Shyok River), Khor, thence north to the glaciers. This portion of the cease- fire line shall be demarcated in detail on the basis of the factual position as of 27 July 1949, by the local commanders assisted by United Nations military observers.

Later, following the Indo-Pakistani War of 1971, and the Simla Agreement in July 1972, the ceasefire line was converted into the "Line of Control" extending from the "*Chhamb sector on the international border [to] the Turtok-Partapur sector in the north.*" The detailed description of its northern end stated that from Chimbatia in the Turtok sector "*the line of control runs north-eastwards to Thang (inclusive to India), thence eastwards joining the glaciers.*" This vague formulation further sowed the seed for the bitter dispute to follow. The general description of CFL given in Section 1 of Karachi Agreement is further explained at Page 38 where it states:

"thence northwards along the boundary line going through Point 18402 up to NJ-9842"

The U.N. document number S/1430/Add.2. is the second addendum to the 1949 Karachi Agreement, and shows the CFL marked on the Map of the State of Jammu and Kashmiras per the explanation of CFL in paragraph 'B' 2 (d) of the Karachi Agreement.

U.N. map of ceasefire line

Title of U.N. document number S/1430/Add.2 which illustrates the CFL as per the Karachi Agreement reads:

Map of the State of Jammu and Kashmir showing the Cease Fire Line as Agreed Upon in the Karachi Agreement, Ratified by the Governments of India and Pakistan on 29 and 30 July Respectively.

Oropolitics

In 1949, a Cease-Fire Line Agreement (CFL) was signed and ratified by India, Pakistan and the UN Military Observer Group that delineated entire

CFL. In 1956–58, a scientific team led by the Geological Survey of India recorded its findings publicly including information about the Siachen and other glaciers.

After Pakistan ceded Shaksgam Valley to China in a boundary agreement in 1963, Pakistan started giving approval to western expeditions to the east of mountain K2. In 1957 Pakistan permitted a British expedition under Eric Shipton to approach the Siachen glacier through the Bilafond La, and recce Saltoro Kangri. Five years later a Japanese-Pakistani expedition put two Japanese and a Pakistani Army climber on top of Saltoro Kangri. These were early moves in this particular game of oropolitics.

In the 1970s and early 1980s several mountaineering expeditions applied to Pakistan to climb high peaks in the Siachen area due in part to US Defense Mapping Agency and most other maps and atlases showing it on the Pakistani side of the line. Pakistan granted a number of permits. This in turn reinforced the Pakistani claim on the area, as these expeditions arrived on the glacier with a permit obtained from the Government of Pakistan. Teram Kangri I (7,465 m or 24,491 ft) and Teram Kangri II (7,406 m or 24,298 ft) were climbed in 1975 by a Japanese expedition led by H. Katayama, which approached through Pakistan via the Bilafond La.

In 1978 a German Siachen-Kondus Expedition under the leadership of Jaroslav Poncar (further members Volker Stallbohm and Wolfgang Kohl, liaison officer major Asad Raza) entered Siachen via Bilafond La and established the base camp on the confuence of Siachen and Teram Shehr. The documentary "Expedition to the longest glacier" was shown on the 3rd channel of WDR (German TV) in 1979.

Prior to 1984 neither India nor Pakistan had any permanent presence in the area. Having become aware of the US military maps and the permit incidents, Colonel Narendra Kumar, then commanding officer of the Indian Army's High Altitude Warfare School, mounted an Army expedition to the Siachen area as a counter-exercise. In 1978 this expedition climbed Teram Kangri II, claiming it as a first ascent in a typical 'oropolitical' riposte. Unusually for the normally secretive Indian Army, the news and photographs of this expedition were published in The Illustrated Weekly of India, a widely circulated popular magazine.

Historic maps of Siachen Glacier

Maps from Pakistan, the United Nations and various global atlases depicted the CFL ending at NJ9842 until the mid 1960s. The United States Defense Mapping Agency (now National Geospatial-Intelligence Agency) began in about 1967 to show a boundary on their Tactical Pilotage Charts as proceeding from NJ9842 east-northeast to the Karakoram Pass at 5,534 m (18,136 ft) on the China border. This line was replicated on US, Pakistani and other maps in the 1970s and 1980s, which India believed to be a cartographic error.

AN EXERCISE REPLETE WITH CONSTANT AMENDMENTS

One of the most delicate issues faced by the British Government in India attributed to complex communal problems; the different communities residing in the vast continent of India, professing diverse faiths, inherited district social and political traditions, divided by the regional and geographical areas, always created a difficult task for the policy makers in their efforts to unite the people on a common platform. During the 20th century the British Government initiated efforts to establish a legal framework order to streamline the aims and objectives of different communities.

The Acts of 1909 and 1919 were designed to meet the ever-increasing needs of the educated Indians, who demanded substantial share in the management of public institutions. Imbibed with national spirit and driven by the dream of freedom from the foreign yoke, the Indian leaders, irrespective of their political affiliation, pressurised the British Government to introduce reforms in the public institutions of India. Realising the growing discontent among the Indian people, the British Government invited the prominent persons, representing various interests and classes, to England to participate in the Round Table Conferences held in 1930-32. The delegates deliberated on the basic issues and tried to evolve a viable constitution, catering to the needs of the rulers as well as the ruled. It was a unique exercise in the history of constitutional development. The British parliament passed the Government of India Act on August 2, 1935, providing a framework for the future development of a popular constitution. The Act was amended by the British parliament on July 18, 1947, as the Indian Independence Act, setting up in India, two Independent Dominions.

On August 14, 1947 Pakistan came into being as an independent country. The preparations for the constitution of the new dominion were commenced with the election of the Quaid-i-Azam Muhammad Ali Jinnah as the first president of the Constituent Assembly of Pakistan on August 11, 1947; it was a historic occasion. Addressing the Constituent Assembly the Quaid said, "The Constituent Assembly has got two main functions to perform. The first is the very onerous and responsible task of framing our future constitution of Pakistan and the second of functioning as a full and complete Sovereign body as the Federal Legislature of Pakistan."

Identifying the major problems to be confronted by the Legislature he pointed out, "The first observation that I would like to make is this: You will no doubt agree with me that the first duty of the government is to maintain law and order, so that the life, property and religious beliefs of its subjects are fully protected by the State. The second thing that occurs to me is this: One of the biggest curses from which India is suffering-I do not say that other countries are free from it, but, I think our condition is much worse-is bribery and corruption. (Hear, hear). That really is a poison. We must put that down with an iron hand and I hope that you will take adequate measures as soon as it is possible for this Assembly to do so."

Condemning the evil of black-marketing, he categorically stated, "A citizen who does black-marketing commits, I think, a greater crime than the biggest and most grievous of crimes. These black-marketers are really knowing, intelligent and ordinary responsible people, and when they are indulged in black-marketing, I think they ought to be very severely punished."

Another evil he described and which needed to be crushed in the new state was nepotism and jobbery. He declared, "I want to make it quite clear that I shall never tolerate any kind of jobbery, nepotism or any influence, directly or indirectly, brought to bear upon me. Wherever I find that such a practice is in vogue, or is continuing anywhere, low or high, I shall certainly not countenance it".

In this speech he laid down important guiding principles to be followed by the lawmakers and administrators. He briefly stated his ideas about the duties of the future state. Rejecting the criticism against the creation of Pakistan, he referred to the prevailing situation. He said, "Any idea of a United India could never have worked and in my judgment it would have led us to terrific disaster. Maybe that view is correct; maybe it is not; that remains to be seen."

The question of minorities remained a core issue in any political adjustment. In spite of countless efforts, both individual and collective and private and official, Hindu-Muslim unity became a dream, never to be realised. The partition of India conclusively decided the fate of the minorities in each dominion. The minority issue acquired a new dimension in parameters of Pakistan. In spite of the prevailing hatred and discontent, the Quaid assured the minorities that their rights and interests would be safeguarded. He laid down the noble principle for the posterity of Pakistan, "Now if we want to make this great State of Pakistan happy and prosperous we should wholly and solely concentrate on the well-being of the people, and especially of the masses and the poor. If you will work in cooperation, forgetting the past, burying the hatchet, you are bound to succeed.

If you change your past and work together in a spirit that every one of you, no mater to what community he belongs, no matter what relations he had with you in the past, no matter what is his colour, caste or creed, is first, second and last a citizen of this State with equal rights, privileges and obligations, there will be no end to the progress you will make."

Pakistan, being an ideological state, was demanded to establish an Islamic State which created fears in the mind of the minorities about the safety of their own religion and culture. To remove this misconception the Quaid declared: "You are free: you are free to go to your temples; you are free to go to your mosques or to any other places of worship in this State of Pakistan.

You may belong to any religion or caste or creed—that has nothing to do with the business of the State." He further stated that "in course of time Hindus would cease to be Hindus and Muslims would cease to be Muslims, not in the religious sense, because that is the personal faith of each individual, but in the political sense as citizens of the State."

Concluding his historic address, he pronounced his policy, reflecting his noble sentiments, "I shall always be guided by the principles of justice and fairplay without any, as is put in the political language, prejudice or ill-will, in other words, partiality or favouritism. My guiding principle will be justice and complete impartiality, and I am sure that with your support and cooperation, I can look forward to Pakistan becoming one of the greatest Nations of the world." The Quaid's speech was appreciated worldwide; even his opponents admired the liberal and secular ideas expressed in the speech. However, questions were repeatedly asked about the pattern of the constitution, which he articulated in his broadcast speech to the people of the USA in February, 1948.

"The constitution of Pakistan has yet to be framed by the Pakistan Constituent Assembly. I do not know what the ultimate shape of this constitution is going to be, but I am sure that it will be of a democratic type, embodying the essential principles of Islam. Today, they are as applicable in actual life as they were 1,300 years ago. Islam and its idealism have taught us democracy. It has taught equality of man, justice and fair play to everybody. We are the inheritors of these glorious traditions and are fully alive to our responsibilities and obligations as framers of the future constitution of Pakistan. In any case Pakistan is not going to be a theocratic state-to be ruled by priests with a divine mission. We have many non-Muslims-Hindus, Christians and Parsis-but they are all Pakistanis. They will enjoy the same rights and privileges as any other citizens and will play their rightful part in the affairs of Pakistan."

After his death Prime Minister Liaquat Ali Khan, inspite of the critical situation faced by the country, devoted his energies for the preparation of the constitution. On March 7, 1949 he moved in the Constituent Assembly, the Objective Resolution, embodying the main principles on which the constitution of Pakistan was to be based. The objective resolution became preamble of future constitutions.

"In the name of Allah, the Beneficent, the Merciful; Whereas sovereignty over the entire Universe belongs to God Almighty alone and the authority which He has delegated to the State of Pakistan through its people for being exercised within the limits prescribed by Him is a sacred trust;

This Constituent Assembly, representing the people of Pakistan, resolves to frame a constitution for the sovereign independent State of Pakistan. Wherein the State shall exercise its powers and authority through the chosen representatives of the people;

Wherein the principles of democracy, freedom, equality, tolerance and social justice as enunciated by Islam, shall be fully observed.

Wherein the Muslims shall be enabled to order their lives in the individual and collective spheres in accord with the teachings and requirements of Islam, as set out in the Holy Quran and the Sunnah; Wherein adequate provision shall be made for the minorities freely to profess and practise their religions and develop their cultures;

Whereby the territories now included in, or in accession with, Pakistan and such other territories as may be hereafter be included in or accede to Pakistan shall form a Federation wherein the Units will be autonomous with such boundaries and limitation on their powers and authority as may be prescribed;

Wherein shall be guaranteed fundamental rights including equality of status, of opportunity and before law, social, economic and political justice, and freedom of thought, expression, belief, faith, worship and association, subject to law and public morality;

Wherein adequate provision shall be made to safeguard the legitimate interests of minorities and backward and depressed classes;

Wherein the independence of the judiciary shall be fully secured; Wherein the integrity of the territories of the Federation, its independence and all its rights including its sovereign on land, sea and air shall be safeguarded; So that the people of Pakistan may prosper and attain their rightful and honoured place amongst the nations of the world and make their full contribution towards international peace and progress and happiness of humanity. The first constitution of Pakistan was prepared in eight years.

The Constant Assembly was dissolved by Governor General Ghulam Muhmmad in October, 1954. A new Assembly tackled the task vigorously and on February 29, 1956, presented the first constitution which was promulgated on 23rd of March, 1956 as the constitution of the Islamic Republic of Pakistan.

However, its life was very brief and on October 7, 1958, the first Martial Law was imposed in Pakistan and the constitution was abrogated. The Martial Law regime appointed a Constitution Commission which produced its report in 1961 and a new constitution was promulgated by President Ayub Khan based on the basic democracies and presidential system. This constitution was also abrogated by General Yahya Khan when he imposed Martial Law in 1969. The nation remained without a constitution till 1973 when a new Constituent Assembly adopted the present constitution unanimously.

The Constitution is considered a sacred document to be preserved and protected. It signifies the aspirations of a nation. However, in the case of Pakistan, the constitution was neither respected nor implemented in letter and spirit. The present constitution was amended on a number of occasions to serve the needs of the rulers. God knows how long the country would face this situation which is becoming alarming every day. God save Pakistan. (Ameen)

INDIA-PAKISTAN CEASEFIRE VIOLATIONS: THEORETICAL MOORINGS

It was done once again. In the last fortnight, we have seen one of the biggest ceasefire violations between India and Pakistan for the first time since the Kargil war took place in 1999. This was preceded after killing of five Indian soldiers who were on a patrol duty to guard the Indian borders, which were attacked by army personnel and supported by the non-state actors. This led to massive firing from across the border by the Pakistani army personnel to let infiltrate terrorists from their side of LOC. (Line of Control).

This vernacular media in India reacted actively and pent up the emotions across the nation. With election year round the corner, the Opposition party took the chance to attack the UPA government on the issue of national security and laxity in handling the ceasefire violations. The right wing party BJP leader Narender Modi saw this opportunity to attack PM Manmohan Singh and his lacksaidal attitude on dealing with issues of national security.

Negative peace is defined as absence of violence; on the other hand Positive peace is equated with harmony absence of structural or indirect violence. - *Johan Galtung*

As an observer of peace and conflict studies it really intrigues me to write on the recent cease fire violations on the LOC, which has marks of disrupting the peace process between both the countries.

We could fault either side for the cease-fire violation, but the sufferer in all this is the peace process, which takes a lot of time to reach a point and then one terrorist incident or ceasefire violation to bring it back to square one. These incidents happen on the backdrop of slated Manmohan Singh and Nawaz Sharif meeting to revive the composite dialogue on the side-lines of UN General Assembly meeting in September.

Theoretically speaking, ceasefire violation could be a classic case where in framework of positive and negative peace may find some relevance. As opined by Johan Galtung (Mathematician turned sociologist-peace theorist) who had devised the concepts of positive and negative peace. To apply these concepts in case of India and Pakistan remains a possibility. To quote from Galtung, negative peace is defined as absence of violence; on the other hand Positive peace is equated with harmony absence of structural or indirect violence. He goes on further to define four forms of positive peace which are; Direct positive peace; Structural positive peace; Cultural positive peace. In case of India and Pakistan, relevant form could be structural positive peace which includes; non-homocentric peace, intra-interpersonal peace, development, parity, equity, peace regions, governance, cultural co-existence and sustainability from above. (Galtung—1996-pp-33)

The relations between India and Pakistan may not have reached a complete circle in the context of negative and positive peace. There have been traces from the past, where attempts to make peace have been carried out by its political class, due to terrorist incidents or border skirmishes both nations have come back to status-quoist mode.

Efforts were on from both sides to bring back derailed peace process ever since the Mumbai terror attacks in 2008. Structural peace was constructed in the form of agreement on a composite dialogue slated for next month. After these skirmishes on the LOC, revival of peace process seems to be in limbo.

During the status quoist phase between both the countries, traces of positive peace could be seen; this could be gauged from the political statements from the political elites. With the present incident on the border, we have chance of positive peace dipping back to negative peace not in truly Galtungian sense, rather through firing along the border posts by respective armies and then ceasefire. These incidents will have a long term impact on the political peace process, due to change in public opinion and tendencies of retaliation and retribution amongst either of the communities.

It is a known fact there are various non-state actors in Pakistan which are working against India in Pakistan, which the former have taken up in discussions with their Pakistani counterparts. A big problem in this case remains a simple denial from the other party to accept presence of non-state actors. Rhetorical statements are issued every now and then to calm the nerves, but situation on the ground remains the same. In such a scenario, how do we construct peace?

Structural peace process does not come naturally in the case of India and Pakistan; it needs to be manufactured step by step. Similar attempts were being made by the political class; this could be seen from the positive vibes from newly anointed PM of Pakistan Mian Nawaz Sharif. Until the ceasefire violations began to take place in the summer months on the Line of Control making the process haywire and thus began the shifting of pendulum from positive structural peace to negative peace.

Media and political parties have been eyeing the head of soft spoken Defence minister Mr. A.K. Antony. Immense pressure from the Opposition parties in India as well as the media led him to give a strong statement in the Upper-house of Parliament. Antony blamed the Pakistan army for ceasefire violations as well killing of five Indian soldiers on the border post by the Pakistan army led Border Action Team (BAT) which contained mix of Pakistan military and non-state actors. This deadly cocktail of Pakistan army and non-state actors if sustains for longer period, we could see escalation of conflict between the two.

Although some optimism still remains on the Indian side for not shelving off the talks this can be read from no statement from the Prime Minister's Office (PMO) who have refused to comment on the ceasefire violations and left for the Ministry of Defence to do the hard talk.

Peace process has taken a hit up-teem times between both the countries in the past. They have come to square one from conflict prevention to conflict and vice versa. An account of this was given by Steve Coll in the New Yorker article, "The Back-channel" which described the manner in which representative from the Indian side Amb. Satinder Lambah and Pakistani representative Tariq Aziz practically went on to solve all the pending issues including Kashmir in back-channels talks held in Bangkok, Dubai, London. Then came the regime change in Pakistan and Musharraf was ousted from power and things went back to square one.

Are we entering another face of confrontation or freezing of peace talks? To take cognizance from independent Pakistan researcher Ayesha Siddiqua who has equated conflict between both the countries to the game theory model. In a sense she says, India may protest but has limited capacity to raise the cost for Pakistan due to the fear of nuclear mutual assured destruction in place. To perceive of this sort of connotation could be strategic in nature. At the base level it has to be understood peace needs to move on from conflict prevention to transformation stage and status –quoist position is not a way forward in all senses.

MILITARY EXPEDITIONS

In 1977, an Indian colonel named Narendra Kumar, offended by international expeditions venturing onto the glacier from the Pakistani side, persuaded his superiors to allow him to lead a 70-man team of climbers and porters to the glacier. They returned in or around 1981, climbed several peaks and walked the length of Siachen.

MAJOR COMBAT OPERATIONS

At army headquarters in Rawalpindi, the discovery of repeated Indian military expeditions to the glacier drove Pakistani generals to the idea of securing Siachen before India did. This operation was called Operation Ababeel. In the haste to pull together operational resources, Pakistan planners made a tactical error, according to a now retired Pakistani army colonel. "They ordered Arctic-weather gear from a London outfitters who also supplied the Indians," says the colonel. "Once the Indians got wind of it, they ordered 300 outfits—twice as many as we had—and rushed their men up to Siachen". The acquisition of key supplies needed for operations in glaciated zones marked the start of major combat operations on the glacier.

April 1984 Operation Meghdoot: Indian Army under the leadership of Lt. Gen. Manohar Lal Chibber, Maj. Gen. Shiv Sharma, and Lt. Gen. P. N. Hoon learned of the plan by Pakistan Army to seize Sia La, and Bilafond La, on the glacier. Indian Army launched an operation to preempt the seizure of the passes by the Pakistan Army. Men of the Ladakh Scouts and Kumaon Regiment occupy Bilafond La on 13 April and Sia La on 17 April 1984 with the help of the Indian Air Force. Pakistan Army in turn learned of the presence of Ladakh Scouts on the passes during a helicopter recon mission. In response to these developments Pakistan Army initiated an operation using troops from the Special Services Group and Northern Light Infantry to displace the three hundred or so Indian troops on the key passes. This operation led by the Pakistan Army led to the first armed clash on the glacier on 25 April 1984.

June – July 1987: Operation Rajiv: Over the next three years, with Indian troops positioned at the critical passes, Pakistan Army attempted to seize heights overlooking the passes. One of the biggest successes achieved by Pakistan in this period was the seizure of a feature overlooking Bilafond La. This feature was named "Qaid Post" and for three years it dominated Indian positions on the glacier. Pakistani Army held Qaid post overlooked Bilafond La area and offered an excellent vantage point to view Indian Army activities. On 25 June 1987 Indian Army under the leadership of Brig. Gen. Chandan Nugyal, Major Varinder Singh, Lt. Rajiv Pande and Naib Subedar Bana Singh launched a successful strike on Qaid Post and captured it from Pakistani forces. For his role in the assault, Subedar Bana Singh was awarded the Param Vir Chakra – India's highest gallantry award. The post was renamed Bana Post in his honour.

September 1987: Operation Vajrashakti/Op Qaidat: The Pakistan Army under Brig. Gen. Pervez Musharraf (later President of Pakistan) launched Operation Qaidat to retake Qaid peak. For this purpose units from Pakistan Army SSG (1st and 3rd battalions) assembled a major task force at the newly constructed Khaplu garrison. Having detected Pakistani movements ahead of Operation Qaidat, the Indian Army initiated Op Vajrashakti to secure the now renamed Bana Post from Pakistani attack.

March – May 1989: In March 1989 Operation Ibex by Indian Army attempted to seize the Pakistani post overlooking the Chumik Glacier. The operation was unsuccessful at dislodging Pakistani troops from their positions. Indian Army under Brig. R. K. Nanavatty launched an artillery attack on Kauser Base, the Pakistani logistical node in Chumik and successfully destroyed it. The destruction of Kauser Base induced Pakistani troops to vacate Chumik posts concluding Operation Ibex.

28 July – 3 August 1992: Indian Army launched Operation Trishul Shakti to protect the Bahadur post in Chulung when it was attacked by a large Pakistani assault team. On 1 August 1992, Pakistani helicopters were attacked by an Indian Igla missile and Brig. Masood Navid Anwari (PA 10117) then Force Commander Northern Areas and other accompanying troops were killed. This led to a loss of momentum on the Pakistani side and the assault stalled.

May 1995: Battle of Tyakshi Post: Pakistan Army NLI units attacked Tyakshi post at the very southern edge of the Saltoro defense line. The attack was repulsed by Indian troops.

June 1999: Indian Army under Brig. P. C. Katoch, Col. Konsam Himalaya Singh seized control of pt 5770 (Naveed Top/Cheema Top/Bilal Top) in southern edge of the Saltoro defense line from Pakistan troops.

GROUND SITUATION

In his memoirs, former Pakistani president General Pervez Musharraf states that Pakistan lost almost 900 square miles (2,300 km) of territory that it claimed. *TIME* states that the Indian advance captured nearly 1,000 square miles (2,600 km) of territory claimed by Pakistan.

Further attempts to reclaim positions were launched by Pakistan in 1990, 1995, 1996 and even in early 1999, just prior to the Lahore Summit.

The Indian army controls all of the 76 kilometres (47 mi) long Siachen Glacier and all of its tributary glaciers, as well as all the main passes and heights of the Saltoro Ridge immediately west of the glacier, including Sia La, Bilafond La, and Gyong La—thus holding onto the tactical advantage of high ground. Indians have been able to hold on to the tactical advantage of the high ground... Most of India's many outposts are west of the Siachen Glacier along the Saltoro Range. In an academic study with detailed maps and satellite images, co-authored by brigadiers from both the Pakistani and Indian military, pages 16 and 27: "Since 1984, the Indian army has been in physical possession of most of the heights on the Saltoro Range west of the Siachen Glacier, while the Pakistan army has held posts at lower elevations of western slopes of the spurs emanating from the Saltoro ridgeline. The Indian army has secured its position on the ridgeline."

The line between where Indian and Pakistani troops are presently holding onto their respective posts is being increasingly referred to as the Actual Ground Position Line (AGPL).

Views

Siachen is seen as a major military setback by the Pakistani Army. Pakistani generals perceives the Siachen glacier as their land that had been stolen by Indians. When India occupied the Saltoro Ridge in April 1984, Benazir Bhutto publicly taunted the Pakistan Army as "fit only to fight its own citizens". When, in June 1987, the Indian Army captured the 21,153 foot high "Quaid Post" and renamed it to "Bana Top", in honour of Naib Subedar Bana Singh, Bhutto once again publicly taunted the Pakistani generals, telling them to wear bangles if they cannot fight on the Siachen.

American observers say that the military conflict between India and Pakistan over the Siachen Glacier "made no military or political sense".

In the book *Asymmetric Warfare in South Asia: The Causes and Consequences of the Kargil Conflict*, Khan, Lavoy and Clary wrote:

The Pakistan army sees India's 1984 occupation of the Siachen Glacier as a major scar, outweighed only by Dhaka's fall in 1971. The event underscored the dilution of the Simla Agreement and became a domestic issue as political parties, led by Benazir Bhutto's Peoples Party, blamed an incompetent military government under Zia ul-Haq for failing to defend Pakistani-held territory — while Zia downplayed the significance of the loss.

General Ved Prakash Malik, in his book *Kargil from Surprise to Victory*, wrote:

Siachen is considered a military setback by the Pakistan Army. That the Indians dominate the area from the Saltoro Ridge and Pakistani troops are nowhere near the Siachen Glacier is a fact never mentioned in public. The perceived humiliation at Siachen manifests itself in many ways. It is synonymous with Indian perfidy and a violation of the Shimla Agreement... In Pakistan, Siachen is a subject that hurts, just like a thorn in its flesh; it is also a psychological drain on the Pakistani Army. Pervez Musharraf had himself once commanded the Special Services Group (SSG) troops in this area and made several futile attempts to capture Indian posts.

SEVERE CONDITIONS

A cease-fire went into effect in 2003. Even before then, every year more soldiers were killed because of severe weather than enemy firing. The two sides by 2003 had lost an estimated 2,000 personnel primarily due to frostbite, avalanches and other complications. Together, the nations have about 150 manned outposts along the glacier, with some 3,000 troops each. Official figures for maintaining these outposts are put at ~$300 and ~$200 million for India and Pakistan respectively. India built the world's highest helipad on the glacier at Point Sonam, 21,000 feet (6,400 m) above the sea level, to supply its troops. The problems of reinforcing or evacuating the high-altitude ridgeline have led to India's development of the Dhruv Mk III helicopter, powered by the Shakti engine, which was flight-tested to lift and land personnel and stores from the Sonam post, the highest permanently manned post in the world. India also installed the world's highest telephone booth on the glacier.

According to some estimates, 97% of the casualties in Siachen have been due to weather and altitude, rather than actual fighting. In 2012, an avalanche hit Pakistan's Gayari military base, killing 129 soldiers and 11 civilians.

KARGIL WAR

One of the factors behind the Kargil War in 1999 when Pakistan sent infiltrators to occupy vacated Indian posts across the Line of Control was their belief that India would be forced to withdraw from Siachen in exchange of a Pakistani withdrawal from Kargil. After the Kargil War, India decided to maintain its military outposts on the glacier, wary of further Pakistani incursions into Kashmir if they vacate from the Siachen Glacier posts.

Visits

On 12 June 2005, Prime Minister Manmohan Singh became the first Indian Prime Minister to visit the area, calling for a peaceful resolution of the problem. In 2007, the President of India, Abdul Kalam became the first head of state to visit the area. Indian Prime Minister Narendra Modi visited Siachen on 23 October 2014 to celebrate Diwali with the troops and boost their morale.

The Chief of Staff of the US Army, General George Casey on 17 October 2008 visited the Siachen Glacier along with Indian Army Chief, General Deepak Kapoor. The US General visited for the purpose of "developing concepts and medical aspects of fighting in severe cold conditions and high altitude".

Since September 2007, India has welcomed mountaineering and trekking expeditions to the forbidding glacial heights. The expeditions have been meant to show the international audience that Indian troops hold "almost all dominating heights" on the important Saltoro Ridge west of Siachen Glacier, and to show that Pakistani troops are nowhere near the 43.5-mile (70 km) Siachen Glacier.

Artistic depiction

The Siachen glacier and its conflict was depicted in a 48-page comic book, *Siachen: The cold war*, released in August 2012. Later its sequel, *Battlefield Siachen*, was released in January 2013.

LIST OF POST-CEASEFIRE AVALANCHES AND LANDSLIDES

2010–2011

On 11 February 2010, an avalanche struck an Indian army post in the Southern Glacier, killing one soldier. A base camp was also struck, that killed two Ladakh scouts. The same day, a single avalanche hit a Pakistani military camp in Bevan sector, killing 8 soldiers.

In 2011, 24 Indian soldiers died on the Siachen glacier from the climate and accidents. On 22 July, two Indian officers burned to death when a fire caught on their shelter.

2012–2014

In the early morning of 7 April 2012, an avalanche hit a Pakistani military headquarters in the Gayari Sector, burying 129 soldiers of the 6th Northern Light Infantry battalion and 11 civilian contractors. In the aftermath of the disaster, Pakistan's army chief General Ashfaq Parvez Kayani suggested India and Pakistan should withdraw all troops from the contested glacier.

On 29 May, two Pakistani soldiers were killed in a landslide in the Chorbat Sector.

On 12 December, an avalanche killed 6 Indian soldiers in the Sub Sector Hanif in Turtuk area, when troops of the 1st Assam regiment were moving between posts. In 2012, a total of 12 Indian soldiers died of hostile weather conditions.

In 2013, 10 Indian soldiers died due to weather conditions.

2015

On 14 November 2015, an Indian captain from the Third Ladakh scouts died in an avalanche in the Southern Glacier while 15 others were rescued.

2016

On 4 January 2016, four Indian soldiers of the Ladakh Scouts, were killed in an avalanche on the Southern Glacier while on patrol duty in Nobra Valley.

On the morning of 3 February 2016, ten Indian soldiers including one Junior commissioned officer of the 6th Madras battalion were buried under the snow when a massive avalanche struck their post in the Northern Glacier at a height of 19,600 feet, on the Actual Ground Position Line. Pakistani officials offered their help in search and rescue operations 30 hours after the incident, although it was declined by Indian military authorities. During the rescue operations, the Indian army found Lance Naik Hanumanthappa alive, though in a critical condition, after being buried under 25 feet snow for 6 days. He was taken to Army Research and Referral Hospital in Delhi. His condition became critical later on due to multiple organ failure and lack of oxygen to brain and he died 11 February 2016.

On 27 February, a civilian porter working with the Indian army in the Northern Glacier, fell to his death in a 130-foot crevasse.

On 17 March, two Indian soldiers from the Chennai-21 regiment were killed, and bodies recovered in 12-feet deep ice.

On 25 March, two Indian jawans died after they were buried in an avalanche in the Turtuk sector while on patrol.

On 1 April, Indian General Dalbir Singh and General D. S. Hooda of the Northern Command visited the Siachen glacier in order to boost morale after 17 of its soldiers died in 2016.

2018 - 2019

On 14 July 2018, 10 Indian Army soldiers were killed as result of Avalanche in Siachen. On 19 January 2019, 7 Indian Army soldiers soldiers were killed as result of avalanche in Siachen.

On 3 June 2019, Indian defence minister Rajnath Singh visited Indian army's forward posts and base camp in Siachen. He interacted with the Indian soldiers deployed on Siachen and commended their courage. He claimed that more then 1,100 Indian soldiers have died defending the Siachen glacier.

SIACHEN CONFLICT START BETWEEN INDIA AND PAKISTAN

To understand how Siachen conflict began, we first need to have some idea of the geographical positions of India, Pakistan and China in J&K as of now-the map of J&K basically. So, J&K is broadly divided into three areas: India-administered(shown in white here+ Siachen), Pakistan administered (which in India we call Pak Occupied Kashmir and comprises of two parts from Pakistani point of view: Northern Areas and Azad Kashmir) and China administered(Aksai Chin and Shaksgam Valley).

Having clarified the present map of J&K, let me now address the question asked. The present Line Of Control(LOC) between India and Pakistan has come about as a result of wars of 1948, 1965 and most recently 1971.The 1972 Shimla agreement between India and Pakistan delineated the LoC as it stands today but curiously the agreement did so only till a point called NJ9842 for everybody believed that the area beyond it is just too inhospitable.This point can be seen as the southern tip of Siachen0

India assumed that the line further stretches northwards along the Saltoro ridge(shown above as dotted line) while Pakistan assumed that the line goes further North East (shown above as black dashed lines).

Before the Shimla agreement, in 1963 itself, Pakistan had "ceded" a part of Pak Ocupied Kashmir called the Shaksgam valley to China(this lies immediately northwards of the Siachen glacier) and can be seen in the first image I showed.

In 1970s and early 80s, Pakistan began to issue visas to foreigners for mountaineering expeditions to the Siachen region. An Indian Army expert on mountaineering, then Major Narendra Kumar got to know of it. He brought this to the knowledge of Army high command.

Indian leadership was naturally concerned because:

1. It perceived(and continues to do so) Siachen and in fact the whole of J&K as its legitimate territory.
2. The occupation of Siachen would have connected the Pak Occupied Kashmir and Aksai Chin region therefore posing a strategic disadvantage to India.
3. Siachen was crucial for India as it overlooks the strategically located Shaksgam valley which is under Chinese occupation.

Therefore, India conducted Operation Meghdoot in 1984 and occupied the glacier. Pakistan has made several futile attempts since then to dislodge India from there.

As with so many long-running conflicts around the globe, it began with an undefined border dispute.

The roots of the conflict over Siachen (the place of roses) lie in the non-demarcations on the western side on the map beyond NJ9842. The 1949 Karachi agreement and the 1972 Simla agreement presumed that it was not feasible for human habitation to survive north of NJ9842. Prior to 1984 neither India nor Pakistan had any permanent presence in the area.

War at the Top of the World

The highest battleground on Earth, where India and Pakistan have fought intermittently since 1984. Both countries maintain permanent military personnel on the glacier at a height of over 7,000 meters. The site is a prime example of mountain warfare. The glacier's melting waters are the main source of the Nubra River, which falls into the Shyok River. The Shyok in turn joins the Indus River, crucial to both India and Pakistan.

Beginning of conflict

With its ally China to the north, Pakistan was first to see the potential for oropolitics in this strategic vacuum. In the 1970s and early 1980s Pakistan permitted several mountaineering expeditions to climb high peaks on this glacier. This was to reinforce their claim on the area as these expeditions arrived on the glacier with a permit obtained from the Government of Pakistan.

Once having become aware of this in about 1978, Colonel N. Kumar of the Indian Army mounted an Army expedition to Teram Kangri peaks as a counter-exercise.

In the late 1970s, a German mountaineer showed Col Kumar a US-drawn map of northern Kashmir marking the Indian-Pakistan ceasefire line much further to the east than he expected. It appeared the Americans had cartographically ceded a large chunk of the eastern Karakoram to Pakistan, including the Siachen glacier.

"I bought the German's map and sent it straight to the director general of military operations," says Col Kumar, then in charge of the Indian army's mountain warfare school. "I said I would organise an expedition to the area to correct the map!"

But when he got permission for a counter-expedition in 1978, it quickly leaked across the border. "As we reached the Siachen, Pakistani helicopters were flying over us," Col Kumar smiled, "and they were firing out coloured smoke."

This and rubbish left by previous climbing teams convinced him the Pakistanis were stealthily taking over. But at first, he complains, Indian generals would not take him seriously. Then in early 1981, Col Kumar was given the go-ahead to map the entire glacier, all the way to the Chinese border.

This time there were no leaks. And the following year he wrote up his expedition in a mountaineering magazine, in effect staking India's claim. With the Indian army now clearly involved, the Pakistanis were determined to entrench their claim. They might have succeeded if Indian intelligence had not learned of some interesting shopping in the UK in early 1984.

"We came to know the Pakistanis were buying lots of specialist mountain clothing in London," grins Col Kumar. A retired Pakistani colonel later admitted they had blundered by using the same store as the Indians.

India immediately dispatched troops to the Siachen, beating Pakistan by a week. By then they had already got control of the glacier and the adjacent Saltoro ridge, using Col Kumar's maps.

India launched Operation Meghdoot on 13 April 1984 when the Kumaon Regiment of the Indian Army and the Indian Air Force went into the Glacier. Pakistan, which had also gotten wind of it quickly responded with troop deployments and what followed was literally a race to the top. Within a few days, the Indians were in control over most of the glacier as Pakistan were beaten by just a week. The two passes due to Indian military pre-emption – Sia La and Bilfond La were secured by India while the Gyong La pass remained under Pakistan control. Since then both sides have launched several attempts to displace each others forces, but with little success.

A Pakistani counter-attack led by -Brig Gen Pervez Musharraf- a few years later was one of several that failed to dislodge the Indians. Since a ceasefire deal in 2003, the Pakistanis have given up trying

Current situation

The Indian Army controls a few of the top-most heights, holding on to the tactical advantage of high ground, however with Pakistani forces in control of Gyong La pass, Indian access to K-2 and other surrounding peaks has been blocked effectively and mountaineering expeditions to these peaks continue to go through with the approval of the Government of Pakistan. The situation is as such that Pakistanis cannot get up to the glacier, while the Indians cannot come down. Presently India holds two-thirds of the glacier and commands two of the three passes including the highest motorable pass – Khardungla Pass. Pakistan controls Gyong La pass that overlooks the Shyok and Nubra river Valley and India's access to Leh district.

Every year more soldiers are killed because of severe weather than enemy firing. The two sides have lost close to 4,000 personnel primarily due to frostbites, avalanches and other complications. Both nations have 150 manned mirroring outposts along the glacier, with some 3,000 troops each. Official figures for maintaining these outposts are put at ~$300 and ~$100 million for India and Pakistan respectively. The Indians rely on helicopters made indigenously, which are probably the only choppers that can reach such heights, whereas Pakistan has simplified the logistical nightmare by building roads and paths to all of its positions across the glacier. India has also built the world's highest helipad on this glacier at a place called Sonam, which is 21,000 feet above the sea level, to serve the area and ensure that her troops are kept supplied via helicopter support (adding to considerable cost).

India based Jet Airways plans to open a chartered service to the glacier's nearest airlink, the Thoise airbase, mainly to fly the soldiers. Pakistan's PIA flies tourists and trekkers daily to Skardu, which is the jumping off point for K2, although bad weather frequently grounds these scheduled flights.

Shocking waste

On average, one Pakistani soldier is killed every fourth day, while one Indian soldier is killed every other day. Over 1,300 Pakistani soldiers have died on Siachen between 1984 and 1999. According to Indian estimates, this operation had cost India over Rs. 50 billion and almost 2,000 personnel casualties till 1997. Almost all of the casualties on both sides have been due to extreme weather conditions.

"It's been a shocking waste of men and money", says a former senior Indian army officer and Siachen veteran. "A struggle of two bald men over a comb" is the verdict of Stephen Cohen, a US specialist on South Asia, dismissing the Siachen as "not militarily important".

This would perhaps be comforting if the two combatants did not both have nuclear weapons. Surrounded by photographs and memorabilia of his climbing exploits, Col Kumar, now in his 80s, says the struggle was critical to preventing Pakistani encroachment into northern Kashmir.

But though both sides are now better at coping with the extreme environment, it still claims the lives of dozens of soldiers each year. Because it occupies the harder-to-supply higher ground, India pays the heaviest financial price, currently estimated to be around $1m (£600,000) a day.

"With all the money we have spent in Siachen, we could have provided clean water and electricity to half the country," says the former Indian army officer. Both armies, he says, ensure their "heroic narratives" of the conflict dominate by limiting media access to the Siachen.

Any hints of a thaw, most recently when Pakistan lost 140 soldiers in an avalanche, have always faded away. The Siachen is just the coldest of several fronts in the frozen conflict over Kashmir, with neither India or Pakistan prepared to take the first step.

INDIA-PAKISTAN LOOK FOR BILATERAL SOLUTIONS SANS OUTSIDERS

There is a shifting discourse on India – Pakistan relations in the West holding rivalry between two nuclear armed neighbours as the root cause of current impasse in Afghanistan. The discourse runs on the lines that India – Pakistan are reaching a negative crest in their relationship underscored by growing economic and military asymmetry. This according to western analysts is enhancing the Pakistani insecurities that has resulted in three negative movements in Pakistani security discourse.

First is Pakistan's attempt to increase its nuclear arsenal both qualitatively and quantitative, making it the fastest growing arsenal in the world. Second and even more destabilising is development of battle field nuclear weapons by mounting them on short range and cruise missiles. What is most dangerous and destabilising is the attempt to link these tactical weapons with their conventional warfare doctrine in an attempt to deny India so called space for conventional war "under nuclear overhang".

The second perspective is the growing India – Pakistan rivalry and jockeying for strategic space in Afghanistan in a clear attempt to hyphen India once again. This perception is fuelled by nervous Pakistani military establishment which feels the future political discourse in Afghanistan including the Quetta Shura led Taliban may not be as favourable to them as indeed they have been able to perpetuate under the veneer of "TINA" factor and salience of Pakistan as logistic support hub. This is changing as the American and NATO forces begin their pull out and logistic route through Pakistan loses its relevance. What is more worrisome for Pakistani establishment is the fact even the Taliban in whatever form of reintegration it joins the political process they will also realise that for the future economic development and meting aspirational needs of "emirate" need to have good relations both with West and other major donor countries that puts India right in front.

So Pakistan is attempting to use its current leverages by creating post 2014 horror scenarios and draw on the shaken sensibilities of the west and cut a deal that ensures its post pull out relevance and curry favour with Taliban as an honest broker. In this melting pot they throw in the Haqqani group to provide further credibility to its strategic depth story.

However there is a change in the attitude of Pakistani interlocutors (Track II) over the past six months or so. Earlier they were dismissive about the West's ability to hold fast in Afghanistan leading to hasty pull out following which the afghan Army they believed was sure to collapse.

The import of both post 2014 scenario in terms of relative credibility of ANA seen in recent operational performance and feasibility of substantial presence of Western forces at least of counter insurgency and combat support operations including cross border drone attacks have made them to rethink their own position based on spoilers role?

So the attempt now is to use its current but fast diminishing leverages to create a space in post 2014 scenario that ensures Pakistan's interests are not harmed and use that as a base to leverage its position from thereon.

Third and last issue is improvement of relations with India and providing great publicity to these moves as a means to put pressure on India to help gain give both political and economic bargains as part of grand reconciliation brokered by the west.

The current discourse of India – Pakistan rivalry being central to the deteriorating situation in Afghanistan is part of this. Pakistani military establishment believes that as long as it can leverage both the cross border terrorism as also the conventional asymmetry through use of nuclear card it has little problem in managing relations with India. In fact Pakistan wants to use "regional stability" and "building bridges" with India card to extract maximum mileage in bilateral relations through Western pressure concerned with situation in Pakistan.

This is not the only game plan, it realises that there are enough constituencies in India that are keen to normalise relations with Pakistan at any costs, secure in the belief that the three aspects highlighted particularly the nuclear and growing internal instability in Pakistan will force Indian elites to seek early dialogue and concessions.

The Pakistani perspective needs to be seen from larger geo strategic perspective wherein cornered international forces are willing to make any compromises, accommodation and even arm twisting to ensure early and somewhat credible exit. It is this fear of pre pull out instability that Pakistan is attempting to leverage.

India, which wants stability on its Western borders with Pakistan and also in Afghanistan, is caught in a bind. What are the options? Will attempt to flag three possible courses;

- Clear message to Pakistan and international community that India reserves the right of acting in self defence and restoring deterrence credibility if another Mumbai 26/11 attack was to take place. As such an attack will cross the threshold of Indian tolerance leaving no option for Indian establishment to act.
- Second, India must look at its engagement in Afghanistan from the cold prism of national self interest. If these demand training of national security forces for security of national sovereignty or fight against subversive forces from within than it must support the Government of Afghanistan including developmental assistance as it has been doing all these years.

- Lastly any dialogue with Pakistan must be based on clear cut objectives. We must engage with Pakistan but must make clear both terms and redlines. Pakistan must address three important India concerns, stop cross border terror. The insidious comments such as no guarantees on Kashmir being disputed territory will not work. Second it must address the issue of bringing to quick justice perpetrators of 26/11 including Hafiz Saeed. The proposed dialogue with radical groups must address this issue with clear commitment of Army being on board in this political move.

Next Pakistan must move forward on normalising economic relations with India. This must be on reciprocal basis with India certainly offering greater concession provided Pakistan shows positive intent that could include, MFN and transit rights for India. Given the right atmospherics two suggestions can be considered. One rethink on IPI pipeline and second a Free Trade Zone around Lahore where large number of industries can participate and use Pakistani super highways as export routes from either Karachi or Gwadar. Despite US and other concerns both can be win-win options.

It is important that both India and Pakistan must remain committed in bilateral discourse sans external leverages. There is a need to try and shed baggage of the past and look for innovative solutions. What should be clear to Pakistani is the fact that India does not conflict but improved relations, having said that there can be no question of allowing Pakistan to exploit geo political scenario at India's behest. In the post 2014 scenario it will be better that both learn to sink their differences and move forward in resolving bilateral issues.

It is however important for Pakistan to understand that Indian state is resilient enough not to be undermined by cross border terrorism which must be discarded as instrument of state policy. Simultaneously India would like it to be internally strong to deal with its own challenges posed by radical and extremist ideologies.

PAKISTAN: SECURITY THREATS ARE DISCURSIVELY CONSTRUCTED FOR DOMESTIC POLITICAL LEGITIMACY

It is argued that, Pakistan's insecurities are constituted by the perceived threats from India. The representation of threats from India and insecurity discourses is largely political and military in nature. Pakistan has used its Islamic identity in order to project its insecurity perceived from India. The identity of Pakistani state and its national insecurities after partition have been shaped by an aggressive 'Hindu Psyche' of Indian state which is in many cases represented by the subsequent military and political leadership of Pakistan through their insecurity discourses.

It has been suggested that, the military rulers for their domestic consolidation of power and popular support often engaged in discursive construction of threats. In a complex structure of military-bureaucratic supremacy over national security especially nuclear security programs of Pakistan, civilian governments hardly have any role to play.

Before nuclear test, Pakistan's security choice was manipulated in favor of politico-military context. The representation of India-centric dangers by the subsequent political and military leaders and the realities constructed in the domestic politics by them largely shaped the (in)security culture or behavior of Pakistan. After the complete possession of destructive nuclear weapons Pakistani leadership made attempt to give a totalizing effect to its nuclear weapons program by intertwining it in the context of Islamic world and divine commandments. From the critical constructivist perspective, this articulative contours help us read the (in)security culture of Pakistan as culturally and socially constructed.

However, India's insecurity culture can be defined through the combined frames of modern political/territorial and cultural construction of insecurities. Pakistan's insecurity culture can be put in the context of politico-military parlance and religious and cultural construction of insecurities. From the critical constructivist point of view, leadership in both countries resorted to representation of threats from other.

They articulated insecurity discourses so as to suit their politico-military and social and cultural interests. Following a more interpretive analysis, Pakistan and India both for justification of their security behavior articulated (in)security discourses along the cultural lines.

Therefore, in keeping conformity with the critical constructivist claim that 'insecurities are cultural in the sense that they are produced in and out of "the context within which people give meanings to their actions and experiences and make sense of their lives" ...' (Weldes et al., 1999: 1), we can also claim that, the (in)security culture of Pakistan and India are grounded on social and cultural constructions.

CONCLUSION AND CONTRIBUTION

As Paul and Hogg note, mainstream international relations theories—particularly those that offer systemic explanations such as neo-realism—have limited application to the India-Pakistan conflict, which defies a narrow, parsimonious understanding.

On the other hand, the analyses of area specialists of the conflict tend to suffer from the opposite problem by offering accounts of the conflict which include a range of idiosyncratic causes without a coherent analytical framework. In this paper, I have sought to avoid both of these approaches and have produced a constructivist analytic framework of identity for analysing the enduring India-Pakistan conflict.

Engaging with constructivism in this way has allowed me to avoid conceptualising identity as one of many variables in an idiosyncratic or multivariate explanation of the conflict. Instead, I have drawn on the insights of constructivist analyses and produced a coherent analytic framework of identity for analysing the India-Pakistan conflict. The arguments that I have presented suggest that the role of identity in shaping the understandings, interests, preferences, and conflictual dynamics between India and Pakistan is central to understanding the enduring nature of the conflict.

Materialist and rationalist explanations which take identities and social structures for granted inhibit our understanding of the conflict, and international relations' in general, in serious ways, which has been demonstrated throughout this paper. Thus, it is time for scholars of South Asian international politics to engage more actively with constructivism, because it not only offers a profound critique of mainstream rationalist theories which still dominate India-Pakistan security studies and analyses, but also has terrific research potential and a far richer ontology than rationalism.

3

Background of Kargil War

After the Indo-Pakistani War of 1971, there had been a long period with relatively few direct armed conflicts involving the military forces of the two neighbours – notwithstanding the efforts of both nations to control the Siachen Glacier by establishing military outposts on the surrounding mountains ridges and the resulting military skirmishes in the 1980s. During the 1990s, however, escalating tensions and conflict due to separatist activities in Kashmir, some of which were supported by Pakistan , as well as the conducting of nuclear tests by both countries in 1998, led to an increasingly belligerent atmosphere.

In an attempt to defuse the situation, both countries signed the Lahore Declaration in February 1999, promising to provide a peaceful and bilateral solution to the Kashmir conflict.

During the winter of 1998 -1999, some elements of the Pakistani Armed Forces were covertly training and sending Pakistani troops and paramilitary forces, some allegedly in the guise of mujahideen, into territory on the Indian side of the LOC.

The infiltration was code named "Operation Badr"; its aim was to sever the link between Kashmir and Ladakh, and cause Indian forces to withdraw from the Siachen Glacier, thus forcing India to negotiate a settlement of the broader Kashmir dispute. Pakistan also believed that any tension in the region would internationalise the Kashmir issue, helping it to secure a speedy resolution. Yet another goal may have been to boost the morale of the decade-long rebellion in Indian Administered Kashmir by taking a proactive role.

Pakistani Lieutenant general Shahid Aziz, and then head of ISI analysis wing, has confirmed there were no mujahideen but only regular Pakistan Army soldiers who took part in the Kargil war. "There were no Mujahideen, only taped wireless messages, which fooled no one. Our soldiers were made to occupy barren ridges, with hand held weapons and ammunition," Lt Gen Aziz wrote in his article in the The Nation daily in January 2013.

Some writers have speculated that the operation's objective may also have been as a retaliation for India's Operation Meghdoot in 1984 that seized much of Siachen Glacier.

According to India's then army chief Ved Prakash Malik, and many other scholars, much of the background planning, including construction of logistical supply routes, had been undertaken much earlier. On several occasions during the 1980s and 1990s, the army had given Pakistani leaders (Zia ul Haq and Benazir Bhutto) similar proposals for infiltration into the Kargil region, but the plans had been shelved for fear of drawing the nations into all-out war.

Some analysts believe that the blueprint of attack was reactivated soon after Pervez Musharraf was appointed chief of army staff in October 1998. After the war, Nawaz Sharif, Prime Minister of Pakistan during the Kargil conflict, claimed that he was unaware of the plans, and that he first learned about the situation when he received an urgent phone call from Atal Bihari Vajpayee, his counterpart in India. Sharif attributed the plan to Musharraf and "just two or three of his cronies", a view shared by some Pakistani writers who have stated that only four generals, including Musharraf, knew of the plan. Musharraf, however, asserted that Sharif had been briefed on the Kargil operation 15 days ahead of Vajpayee's journey to Lahore on February 20.

War progress

There were three major phases to the Kargil War. First, Pakistan infiltrated forces into the Indian-controlled section of Kashmir and occupied strategic locations enabling it to bring NH1 within range of its artillery fire. The next stage consisted of India discovering the infiltration and mobilizing forces to respond to it. The final stage involved major battles by Indian and Pakistani forces resulting in India recapturing some territory held by Pakistani forces and the subsequent withdrawal of Pakistani forces back across the Line of Control after international pressure.

Occupation by Pakistan

During the winter season, due to extreme cold in the snow-capped mountainous areas of Kashmir, it was a common practice for both the Indian and Pakistan Armies to abandon some forward posts on their respective sides of the LOC and to reduce patrolling of areas that may be avenues of infiltration. When weather conditions became less severe, forward posts would be reoccupied and patrolling resumed.

During February 1999, the Pakistan Army began to re-occupy the posts it had abandoned on its side of the LOC in the Kargil region, but also sent forces to occupy some posts on the Indian side of the LOC. Troops from the elite Special Services Group as well as four to seven battalions of the Northern Light Infantry (a paramilitary regiment not part of the regular Pakistani army at that time) covertly and overtly set up bases on the vantage points of the Indian-controlled region. According to some reports, these Pakistani forces were backed by Kashmiri guerrillas and Afghan mercenaries.

Pakistani intrusions took place in the heights of the lower Mushkoh Valley, along the Marpo La ridgeline in Dras, in Kaksar near Kargil, in the Batalik sector east of the Indus River, on the heights above of the Chorbatla sector where the LOC turns North and in the Turtok sector south of the Siachenarea.

WAR IN KARGIL 1999

It is now fairly well established that the first physical contact with Pakistani troops and irregulars in the Kargil sector was established on the Jubbar heights, on May 3. Appropriately for a war characterised by the Indian security establishment's negligence, and on occasion incompetence, the contact had nothing to do with military reconaissance or patrolling.

Tashi Namgyal, Morup Tsering, and Ali Raza Stanba, three shepherds from the tiny village of Garkhun, had made their way up the Banju heights with their flocks of sheep. Shepherds in the Kargil mountains routinely pool their livestock together, assigning groups of two or three villagers by turn to graze the animals on the high meadows. Namgyal and his friends are a little coy about just what led them up towards the Jubbar heights quite so early in summer, but the most plausible explanation is that they hoped to use the time to engage in the region's favourite sport, poaching mountain goats. Tsering carried with him a pair of powerful field binoculars, purchased years earlier in Leh, a tool of particular use for hunting.

By the morning of May 3, Namgyal had moved some 5 kilometres up the Jubbar Langpa [*nullah* or mountain stream]. As he scanned the mountain with Tsering's binoculars, he saw groups of men in Pathan suits, digging earth and putting up makeshift bunkers. Although it was possible neither to establish their numbers nor strength, Namgyal promptly informed officers of the 3 Punjab Regiment, stationed locally. Initial reactions to Namgyal's story appear, by local accounts, to have been more than slightly *blasé*. According to 15 Corps Commander Lieutenant General Kishan Pal, two patrols subsequently despatched on May 4 and May 5 to Yaldor and Kha Baroro detected seven intruders on the Kukerthang ridge and two at Kha Baroro. Two further patrols were sent up in the night on May 7. The one sent to Kukerthang lost one man in an ambush, while the second patrol lost two soldiers and suffered several injured in a second ambush in the morning on May 10. Clearly, the patrols had not gone out expecting serious resistance.

Army officials have so far been less than forthcoming about just when patrols were sent out in other areas of Kargil, and what precisely their fate was. Lieutenant Saurabh Kalia's ill - fated patrol is now affirmed to have moved down the Kaksar Langpa on May 14 although officials had first claimed it had, in fact, left on its mission ten days earlier. There is as yet no verifiable account of what other patrols were sent out and just where they encountered or engaged Pakistani units. The scale and character of military response to the information first provided by Namgyal is just one of many issues that needs to be established through independent and rigorous inquiry. All that is known is that by the middle of May, the Army was discovering fresh Pakistan-held positions on an alarmingly regular basis, spanning the entire Kargil sector fry om the Mushkoh Valley in the west to Chorbat La in the east.

The 15 Corps Commander Lieutenant General Kishan Pal has given at least some indication of the conceptual framework that underpinned the Army's early responses. In his first press conference on the Kargil War, called before air strikes commenced, Pal described the territory occupied by Pakistan as "unheld areas". In a subsequent interview, he explained just what he meant by this novel formulation. "If I don't take notice of them", he said, "it will make no difference.... If they come off the heights in the summer, they will be slaughtered. And if they don't leave them in the winter, they will freeze to death". The true significance of these observations has been little understood. Evidently, the military leadership believed the intrusion at that stage to be little other than a very localised nuisance, an abortive enterprise to push in irregulars into an area of Jammu & Kashmir until then unaffected by insurgent activity.

The middle of May, however, saw at least some degree of unease set in. Pal ordered helicopters engaged in Wide Area Surveillance Operations [WASO] to fly lower, an effort to locate small Pakistan units entrenched on the mountains which would be undetectable from altitude. Three helicopters engaged in WASO were shot at with machine guns. Two were hit, but mercifully managed to return to base safely. Shortly afterwards, Cheetah helicopters used for WASO began to be equipped with machine guns mounted on their skids, a tactic first experimented with in Kupwara in spring.

By most accounts, this tactic was only of limited defensive utility. Given the lack of a broad appreciation of the strength and purpose of Pakistan's thrust into Kargil at this stage, small numbers of poorly-acclimatised troops with thin artillery support were pushed up the mountains in a desperate effort to vacate its positions. No weekly breakdown of casualties has so far been made available, but the figures may cast interesting light on the results of Army strategy during this first phase of its Kargil operations.

Both Union Defence Minister George Fernandes' glib pronouncements during the first phase of the Kargil War and the fact that the first meeting of the Cabinet Committee on Security (CCS) was not summoned until May 25 say not a little about the chaotic management and poor strategic appraisal that characterised this period.

The meeting of the CCS led to the commencement of the second phase of the Kargil War. The morning after, Indian combat jets bombed Pakistan-held positions throughout the arc from the Mushkoh Valley to Batalik. For much of the media and public opinion, this signalled the real begining of the Kargil War; but the initial air campaign provided less than illustrious results. The loss of a Mig-21 fighter flown by Squadron Leader A. Ahuja to a Stinger missile on May 27, minutes after a Mig-27 flown by Flight Lieutenant K. Nachiketa went down accross the Line of Control with engine trouble, was followed a day later by the destruction of a Mi-17 helicopter fitted with rocket pods in the Drass sub-sector, resulting in the death of all four crew.

Indian planners had clearly not anticipated the use of Stinger missiles by Pakistani air defence. In the wake of the losses, combat aircraft were compelled in general to fly at higher altitudes, using defensive measures to deflect the heat-seeking Stinger missiles. The use of Mi-17 helicopters as weapon platforms was subequently severely restricted. What uses, then, did the air offensive serve? Chief of Air Force Staff, Air Marshall A.Y. Tipnis, at a press conference in Srinagar, made it clear that "the consequences of the restricted use of air power had been made clear to the Government". By this, Tipnis presumably meant that combat aircraft were not being used for the tasks for which they were designated. Attacks on major Pakistan supply, bases and artillery positions were ruled out by the fact that such an offensive would have meant flying accross the LoC. None the less, the use of air power had two significant consequences. First, it signalled to Pakistan troops and irregulars on the Indian side of the LoC that the battle had been joined in earnest. Any expectations that an effette enemy could be held at bay until the winter began to set in were now dispelled. Second, and perhaps most important, sagging Indian troop-morale received not a little aid from the air strikes. Soldiers struggling up the mountains now moved in the knowledge that their adversaries, too, were facing sustained and lethal bombardment.

It is perhaps not coincidental that the first major Indian victory, the capture of the Tololing heights facing Drass, followed the use of air power. Troops of the Rajputana Regiment succeeded in pushing their way up this 4,950-metre summit, and further on to the highest summitt visible from Drass, Peak 4,510. The push, followed six weeks of sustained artillery bombardment, and demonstrated to poorly acclimatised and sometimes demoralised troops that the war in the high Himalayas, could in fact, be won. The subsequent assault on Tiger Hills west of Drass, and Peak 5,062 overlooking the Sando Langpa, the gateway to the LoC at Marpo La, proved similarly successful. These victories were the subject of considerable media hype. Officials claimed they had considerable strategic importance, since Pakistani forward observation posts overlooking the highway had now been vacated.

While there was some element of truth in this claim, the fact remained that much of the war remained to be fought. In early July, the picture in several other sectors was less comforting. The body of Major Mariappan Sarvanan, killed in a May 28-assault on a Pakistani position at Height 4,250 in Batalik, had yet, to be recovered. This made it clear that Indian troops had yet to move to higher positions, from where the enemy fire preventing Sarvanan's body from being collected could be engaged and neutralised. Mechanised Infantry officer Major Rajesh Adhikari, killed in the Mushkoh Valley at a height above 4,000 metres, was also listed as missing, a similar indicator of Indian progress. No significant success in India's efforts to regain its forward position on the LoC in Kaksar, Bajrang Post, had been reported at all. In some areas, the Indian attack had faced severe reverses. On June 10, troops of the 12 Jammu & Kashmir Light Infantry and the Desert Scorpions Paracommando unit who had taken a commanding position above the Yaldor Langpa found themselves sandwiched between two fresh lines of counter-attacking Pakistan troops. This established that, contrary to Army claims, Pakistan's resupply lines were still open.

Despite slow progress in several areas, however, India's formidable military machine was clearly at work. This second phase of the battle might best be described as one of consolidation. The 56 Brigade, brought in early in the battle to relieve the 121 Brigade in the Drass sub-sector, had begun to establish itself west of the Munar Langpa. Initial logistics problems, which had on more than one occaision left troops without adequate food, clothing and ammunition, had been resolved. West of Tingel Langpa, another new formation, the 79 Brigade, had taken charge of fighting in Mushkoh. Further troops were pouring in, and over five additional Brigades were in position before fighting was to conclude. At least some officials who were discredited in the early phase of fighting had been removed from their positions. Artillery positions had been reinforced with Bofors guns and Pinaka multi-barrel rocket launchers.

This phase of consolidation, mirrored by sustained air and ground bombardment, prepared the way for the final push that began in early July. Among the most spectacular victories were claimed by soldiers from the Garhwal Rifles, the Bihar Regiment, the Gurkha Rifles and the Grenadiers pushing their way along the flanks of the Batalik heights. The 5,287-metre summit of Khalubar, east of Yaldor, fell on July 2, and the entire mountain was cleared within three days by the Gurkhas. West of the Urdas Langpa, Peak 4,812, which Indian soldiers call Dog Hill, rapidly followed. Holding these flanks, troops could now begin to cut off Pakistani reinforcements making their way down from their rear base at Muntho Dalo, which had been hit by successive waves of air strikes through the previous weeks.

Luck played a significant role in the capture of Jubbar. Troops had succeeded in making their way up the Urdas Langpa to Banju, the minor peak which guards the Jubbar ridge line. The final assault up the ridge would have been murderous, had a shell not hit a massive Pakistani ammunition dump near the Jubbar peak. The route up Jubbar, on to Peak 4,924 and beyond, to Peak 4,927, was now clear. Progress had been rapid on the eastern side of the Garkhun Langpa as well. The push from the village of Yaldor, on the Yaldor Langpa, to Peak 4,821 on Kukerthang had been a protracted one, claiming heavy casualties. But the mountain was finally taken, and the 5,103-metre Tharu followed soon after. With the heights reclaimed, troops could now dominate the Garkhun Langpa, and the villages of Baroro and Kha Baroro. Further Pakistani movement to reinforce positions along the Gargurdu, Garkhun and Yadlor Langpas was now near-impossible.

Interestingly, progress in the Batalik area provided the first irrefutable evidence of Pakistan's military presence on the Indian side of the LoC. Naik Inayat Ali of the 5 Northern Light Infantry (NLI), captured on July 2, told interrogators that his entire unit of 200 had been wiped out in the course of fighting in the Batalik area. Earlier evidence of such involvement had emerged. The US-based magazine, *Time* reported that troops "from the northern light infantry were used because of their high-altitude experience and because they are from the region".

They were encouraged to look like *mujahideen*, and they discarded their uniforms for traditional *shalwar kameez*, or tracksuits, grew beards and wore traditional white religious skullcaps. The soldiers say that when they reached the heights in February, some genuine *mujahideen* were at the abandoned Indian positions. But these men left after a few days because they could not survive in the high altitudes. They are now used for reconnaissance and as porters.

In an interview, one Pakistani soldier provided a lucid account of his deployment in the Kargil sector, and of the Army's logistical support. Much of what he stated bears out Namgyal's account of his May 3-sighting in Jubbar.

At the time Pakistan troop withdrawals were announced on July 11, the battle for Batalik, and the third phase of the Kargil War in general, was, contrary to official claims, far from over. Pakistan troops retreating from Jubbar had been reinforcing at two heights over a kilometre inside the Line of Control, Peaks 5,121 and 5,327. Assaulting these heights could have proved costly. To the east of Yadlor lay Muntho Dalo, the 5,065-metre pyramid which acted as Pakistan's principal supply base for the Batalik sector. Although Muntho Dalo had come under sustained bombardment until at least July 9, the final physical occupation could again have taken time. In the event, Pakistan's withdrawal from Muntho Dalo allowed Indian troops to occupy the position almost without resistance. No counter attacks appear to have been encountered from the reinforcements that had begun to gather at Peaks 5,121 and 5,327.

Pakistan's movement out of the Drass area also prevented what could have been a series of small but bitter skirmishes along the Tiger Hills belt. At least one Pakistani position on the western face of Tiger Hills remained intact until the withdrawal, and there had been concerted counter-attacks on Peaks 5,100 and 4,875. Interestingly, the Tiger Hills area also appears to have received significant reinforcements of Pakistani regulars until July 8. On that day, the bodies of at least two Pakistani soldiers, Captain Imtiyaz Malik of the 12 NLI and Captain Karnal Sher of the 165 Mortar Regiment, were reported recovered from the hills. Pakistan continued to dispute claims that its soldiers were there in the first place, a proposition that, by this point, was somewhat ludicrous. But there is little doubt that the early withdrawal helped India retake positions like Marpo La. Somewhat mystifyingly, the Army announcement of the capture of Marpo La was preceeded weeks earlier by a signed official claim that its positions there were already occupied by Indian soldiers.

But it was in the Mushkoh Valley and Kaksar that the Pakistan withdrawal had its most significant impact. The assault down the Mushkoh valley that commenced on 7 July claimed 23 soldiers the next day, and heavy casualties were subsequently reported. Much of the worst fighting came along the Mun Thang, the stream that drains Peak 4,342 above the Mushkoh Valley.

The fighting was at an air distance of between five and six kilometres from the Line of Control, but Pakistan troops were not likely to be present at depth in the region since temperatures in the glaciers north of the Mushkoh Valley would rule out holding positions for any length of time. The counter attacks on Tiger Hills and Peak 5,100 appeared designed to relieve pressure on Pakistani positions in Mushkoh.

Kaksar was also certain to see bitter fighting. At least three attempts to storm the Pakistan-occupied Bajrang Post and Peak 5,299 which dominates the Kaksar stream, had been beaten back since fighting began. A major offensive that commenced on July 6 showed few results until the withdrawal from the area commenced, and while Indian troops had been engaged in virtual hand-to-hand combat a fortnight earlier, Pakistan succeeded in reinforcing its positions. Officials had been desperately petitioning New Delhi for a limited retaliatory incursion across the Line of Control in this area, since the only local ridge-line-route to Peak 5,299 and to India's lost forward-area Bajrang Post lies on the other side. The option was a succession of near-suicidal assaults up the mountain face, certain to claim large numbers of soldiers.

Pronouncements of unconditional victory are clearly problematic, made in the context of the ground situation at the time of Pakistan's withdrawal. Although Indian troops had made significant advances, and Pakistan troops and irregulars had sustained significant casualties, the fact remained that there was more than a little fighting still to be done. The withdrawal saved time for India, and, inevitably, significant economic and human costs.

Yet, I shall argue, the structure and conditions of the withdrawal have rendered what most likely would have been an unconditional military victory into a profoundly complex and problematic one. The war on the Kargil heights ended not as the triumph the Union Government would have us believe it was, but as punctuation in a larger conflict over the future of Jammu & Kashmir.

THE KARGIL WAR TIMELINE

The 1999 Kargil conflict between India-Pakistan is the conflict that came the closest to a nuclear exchange than any other conflict in the post-Cold War period. Following the conflict in which Pakistan was perceived to have lost, Pakistani prime minister Nawaz Sharif is overthrown by the Army under Pervez Musharraf leading to a very tense period in bilateral relations between India and Pakistan.

- May 8th-15th 1999: Pakistani troops cross the Line of Control in Kashmir and occupy Indian positions in the disputed territory– Indian Army patrols detect intruders atop Kargil ridges. Army errs in saying 100 infiltrators are occupying 25 km of Indian Territory. India realises Pakistan plans to cut Leh from Srinagar by taking key highway.

- May 25th 1999: Indian Army acknowledges that 600-800 Pakistani infiltrators are lodged in remote Kargil-Drass-Batalik sectors. India surprises Pakistan, ups ante with air strikes. India launches air strikes against militants in Indian-administered Kashmir for the first time in 20 years.India promises further raids.
- May 26th 1999: India launches Kashmir air attack/ Indian Air Force MiG-27 flames out and Indian officer K. Nachiketa is taken prisoner by Pakistan. MiG-21 on a rescue mission hovers over Line of Control, shot down. Squadron Leaderr Ajay Ahuja is killed in action. Srinagar airport closed. India mobilises its armed forces in response Operation Vijay puts 200,000 Indian troops on alert across the border almost overnight—sudden and massive escalation in tensions and military force available to both sides in the crisis/ Pakistani & Indian forces start exchanging fire/ quickly develops into brushfire war
- May 28th 1999: Mi-17 helicopter shot down. Four-man crew dead, Indian Army withdraws choppers. Fernandes goofs up, says Sharif and ISI have no hand in Kargil operations. Detecting the infiltrators by chance, the New Delhi admits it was caught unawares by intrusions

May 1999

India says it will continue to bomb militant infiltrators in Indian-administered Kashmir until it has driven them out.

- May 26th 1999: Pakistan army on high alert. Pakistan has called the Indian air strikes in Kashmir "very, very serious" and put its troops on high alert.
- May 27th 1999: India loses two jets over Kashmir. The Indian Government confirms that two of its aircraft are lost during a series of air strikes against militants in Kashmir.
- Pakistan proposes Delhi mission. Pakistan proposes sending foreign minister Sartaj Aziz to India to ease tensions in the disputed Kashmir region.
- May 30th 1999: Indian pilot 'killed in cold blood'. An Indian pilot whose plane was shot down by Pakistan forces died from bullet wounds suffered after he ejected, Indian officials say.
- May 31st 1999: Bid to defuse Kashmir tensions. India and Pakistan agree to hold talks over Kashmir in the first sign that the two sides might be trying to defuse escalating tensions.

June 1999

- 3rd June 1999: Kashmir peace hopes flounder. India slams 'dangerous' Kashmir claims. As India promises to continue ground and air strikes against infiltrators, a senior Indian minister warns there is little point in peace talks with Pakistan.
- 5th June 1999: India halts bombing. India hands over 'Pakistani bodies'. India announces a pause in bombing raids in Kashmir.
- 8th June 1999: Kashmir talks confirmed. Indian Prime Minister's address to the nation
- Pakistan and India fix a date for their first significant attempt to defuse the tension over Kashmir.
- 9th June 1999: New air strikes ahead of talks. India continues its assault on suspected infiltrators holed up in the Himalayas with fresh air strikes, ahead of talks with Pakistan.
- 11th June 1999: Pakistan denies mutilation claims. Pakistan strongly denies allegations that the bodies of six Indian soldiers in Kashmir were mutilated by its soldiers before being handed back.
- 13th June 1999: No deal at Kashmir talks. India and Pakistan end their talks on the fierce fighting in Kashmir without agreement on how to halt the conflict.
- 16th June 1999: India pushes on with offensive
- 17th June 1999: India claims successes in Kashmir. Thousands flee fighting. India presses ahead with its military offensive, a day after US President Clinton asked Pakistan to persuade them to pull out.
- 29th June 1999: Kashmir diplomacy hots up. Pakistan's Prime Minister Nawaz Sharif returns from China, as a flurry of diplomatic activity aimed at ending the ongoing Kashmir conflict gets underway in India and Pakistan.

July 1999

- 4th July 1999: Clinton urges India-Pakistan talks. Pakistan's Prime Minister Nawaz Sharif and US President Bill Clinton that "concrete steps will be taken" to restore the fragile Line of Control between Indian and Pakistani forces in Kashmir. India seizes strategic peak.
- India announces it has taken the key Tiger Hill peak following an all-out assault, as it prepares to respond to a joint statement by Pakistan's prime minister. Nawaz Sharif and US President Bill Clinton agree that "concrete steps will be taken" to restore the Line of Control.

- 11th July 1999: Kashmir pull-out agreed. Islamic militants are reported to be leaving the mountains of Indian Kashmir as both Pakistan and India claim victory in the two-month conflict.
- 12th July 1999: The Pakistani Prime Minister, Nawaz Sharif, appeals for a permanent settlement of the Kashmir.

American Diplomacy

With India and Pakistan exchanging artillery fire and both sides suffering casualties in Kargil—Pakistan in particular suffering losses to the Indians army/ on July 4th 1999 Bill Clinton meets Pakistani president Nawaz Sharif at Blair House, Washington D.C. – US intelligence assets over Pakistan begin seeing movement concerning Pakistan's nuclear arsenal—

The deployment alarmed President Clinton due to two key areas that differed from the US-Soviet nuclear confrontations—firstly the move was alarming due to Pakistan and India's apparent unawareness of each other's doctrines relating to nuclear weapons—thus a nuclear war could have started by accident—secondly a questions and concerns over command and control in Pakistan—that the army in Pakistan may have circumvented the civilian leadership and deployed the weapons without Nawaz Sharif's prior knowledge—more dangerous than Soviet-US confrontations

The prospect of a nuclear exchange on the Indian-subcontinent represented one of the gravest threats at the end of the 20th Century—greater threat in the 1990s than the collapse of Yugoslavia and risking more lives lost than even the 2nd Congo War in central Africa —a nuclear exchange would have been killed, injured and displaced millions of people—destroyed two great civilisations and forever damaged the Indo-Pacific as an economic area.

Indo-Pakistani relationship in Asia-Pacific: Long term effects

The Indo-Pakistani crises that occurred in the late 1990s & into 2000s represented a major threat to the economies and states of Asia-Pacific—key event in that Clinton diplomacy & dexterity with Pakistan & India prevented a crisis from escalating further—case of meeting at Blair House with Prime Minister Nawaz Sharif, India proved to be a key economic & security actor in the 2000s – providing large numbers of professionally trained troops to UN peacekeeping operations—the economic rise of India—creation of an Indian middle class– would have been forever halted if a nuclear exchange were to have had occurred—by 2050 India economy equal to US economy (Goldman Sachs figures) minimum larger than the United Kingdom, France and Japan.

India-Pakistan relations

India-Pakistan remains the most important flashpoint in Asia-Pacific in terms of danger to the region/ nuclear rivals that unlike the US-USSR have directly fought multiple conflicts/ every single one of these conflicts Pakistan has lost conventionally—hence the resort to violent non-state actors and a strategic nuclear deterrence/ Both the United States and China have a role to play in the Indian subcontinent—both command influence and hard power.

HOW INDIAN AIR FORCE MADE HISTORY WITH THE KARGIL WAR

Operation "Safed Sagar" commenced on May 26, 1999 and concluded on July 11, 1999 after all military objectives were achieved. This was the first time in the history of military aviation that air power was used at a height of upto 32,000 feet by the Indian Air Force. From April 1999, the Pakistan Army along with elements of Mujahadeen (irregulars) crossed the 168km Line of Control (LoC), along Kargil and occupied high ground and vantage points. The intrusion was announced by the Indian Army by May 7-8 and had come as a complete surprise to the military as well as intelligence agencies. The decision to induct the IAF was taken on May 24 after due deliberations at the highest levels of the Indian government and instructions were issued to jointly, with the Army, evict the intruders. It was emphasised that the IAF must not cross the LoC.

The targets were small sangars (shelters made of boulders) and isolated tents. This made close air force support to the army extremely difficult. Initially, the targets were not known to the Indian Army and little or no information was available to the Air Force. The stinger was also formidable. This shoulder fired the missile system, a Canberre aircraft, and managed to hit on a recce mission on May 21. Fortunately, the aircraft returned safely. An Mig 21 was lost on May 27 and an MI-17 Heptr the very next day due to stingers. Thereafter, a change of tactics and attack patterns was necessitated to stay above the stinger "bubble". This implied that weapon delivery would need to be above 26,000ft and upto 32,000ft. At such height, the aircraft performance reduces drastically due to less atmospheric density as also the ballistics of bombs. The piloting skills of the Indian Air Force overcame the difficulties and ensured discernable results.

The first phase of Air Force operations was to conduct a recce to identify the targets, the second was interdiction, which was to hit the logistics and administration camps that supplied ammunition, food, fuel, et al to the occupied posts in the higher mountain reaches. Then the Air Force moved to the final phase -of providing close air support after the target systems were clearly identified. All the phases were executed in close co-operation with the Army.

Credit must be given to the Mig 21 and Mig 27 pilots, who, with primitive navigation/attack systems, were very effective. The use of hand held GPS (Global Positioning System) was an innovation that produced great results when used for area targets. The constant bombardment had a tremendously demoralising effect on the adversary's psyche.

The terrain consisted of the Himalayas running in the northwest-southeast direction, with peaks reaching above 22,000 to 25,000 feet. On the northern side of LoC, the valleys were running in the north-south direction with gradual slopes to the peaks. Most targets were on the northern slopes. This made it rather difficult to evolve a strike pattern without crossing the LoC. Wind speeds were somewhere between 50-100 knots per hour. The sun rise cast shadows in the valleys from 8AM, when visibility was considerably reduced and targets could not be seen. The clouds engulfed the ridges and peaks by 11AM. Therefore, the window of opportunity was only the three-hour period between 8AM and 11AM.

The tide turned from the middle of June 1999. At this time, the areas of occupation became known. The Army was now in a position to make an attack plan versus the target systems. As a consequence, the Air Force was able to coordinate with the Army the "close Air support" requirements.

The Mirage 2000 aircraft, the pilots and engineers performed exceptionally well. In a very short period of time, the "Laser Guided Bombs" were made operational. No pilots or engineers and technicians were trained at the beginning of the campaign, but within a week they carried out trials and training. The accurate delivery of "Laser Bombs" on Tiger Hill - a command post in the Mashkoh sector - was devastating. Innovations like cheating the computers, for different than authorised weapon carriage, were commendable. The lasing time of the laser pods was altered manually with good results. There were no fuzes available for the 1000lb bombs, so pistol fuzes were modified and used effectively. Clearance for carriage of 1000lbs indigeneous bombs was done at Gwalior, the home base of the Mirage 2000 aircraft. There were other innovations like using the "laser designator pod" for recce. The largest logistics camps at Muntho Dalo in the Batalik sector and Pt 4388 in the Mashkoh sector were identified through this method and neutralised effectively. The Mirage 2000 aircraft flew a total of 500 missions with only three drops outs.

The IAF flew a total of 1,235 missions, striking 24 major target systems and ensuring air dominance over the area of operations through Air Defence Interceptor aircraft like Mirage 2000 and Mig 29s.

Significant air strikes that altered the course of the conflict:

1. June 13 1999 Tololing Ridge Complex in the Batalik Sector
2. June 17 1999 Muntho Dalo the Main Admin and Lgs camp in the Batalik sector
3. June 24 1999 Command and Control structure on Tiger Hill. Direction Centrefor forward artillery in the Dras Sector.
4. June 23 1999 Logistics Camp at Pt 4388 in Mashkoh Nallah

The Pakistan side's armed intrusion across the LoC during May to July 1999 at the Kargil sector was a misadventure with severe consequences. The Indian side had achieved its final objective of evicting the intruders with the successful Air Force-Army joint operation. The Kargil conflict was a limited Pakistani effort to internationalise the Kashmir issue, which was seen to be losing its momentum. They had assessed that a counter attack would only last a few days and, thereafter, a ceasefire through international pressure, would allow them to stay in their occupied positions and renew their supplies. The Pakistani planners failed to assess the involvement of air power, the capability of the IAF and the Indian Army's determination.

The hesitation, at the political and military leadership, for the use of air power, delayed the induction of the IAF for over two weeks. It was nearly a repeat of the 1962 Chinese conflict, where air power was not utilised with disastrous consequences. Perhaps a "declaratory policy" to confirm that there will be no hesitation to use air power for any willful violation of the LoC or the international border is warranted. This would have a deterrant effect.

Intelligence, surveillance and reconnaisance capability are of utmost importance to national security and the induction of two Pakistan Army battalions in the region should have been monitored. Gilgit, Skardu and Gulteri in Pakistan Occupied Kashmir (PoK) should have been under surveillance round the year. Strategic reconnaissance is a core competency of all Air Force and in India, it is included in external intelligence gathering under R&AW (Aviation Research Centre). The gap between satellite and tactical recce (UAVs, fighters, et al) is strategic recce, which must be with the IAF and resources provided.

The importance of technology cannot be overstated. Induction of technology would give us greater and sustainable capability, enhancing national security considerably. Do we need high tech, well trained and motivated defence forces in smaller numbers or superior forces in large numbers? Higher level military leadership must be selected through merit. During the Kargil War, it was the middle and junior level leadership that rose to the occassion. The Kargil operation would have never happened if the higher leadership had ensured realistic threat assessment and planning. There should be greater interaction between the political and military leadership. Thus far, it is non existent. Military leadership does not only include the chiefs of staff, but also the Air Force, Army and Navy commanders who formulate and execute the operational plans. This would expedite and rationalise the decision making process during conflict situations.

In the final analysis, Kargil was a military, diplomatic and political success for India. However, the loss of nearly 500 military men and over 1,100 serious casualties, subdues the success. During this Kargil Diwas, we should spare a moment for the great uniformed personnel who gave their today for our tomorrow. Jai Hind.

AIR FORCE TILTED THE KARGIL WAR IN INDIA'S FAVOUR

As India celebrates Kargil Divas and pays homage to martyrs of the war, it is time to recall the significant role of air power that actually tilted the balance in Operation Vijay, in July 1999, in India's favour. The Indian Army supported by Indian Air Force (IAF) evicted the infiltrators from Pakistan on July 26, 1999. Kargil is located 205 km from Srinagar. The area of action was near Drass, which is 160 km east of Srinagar. Drass is one of the coldest inhabited places in the world with winter temperatures ranging between -48 and -54 degrees. The military outposts on the ridge, that overlooks the Line of Control (LoC) on one side and the Srinagar-Leh highway on the other, were traditionally vacated during extreme cold weather. These outposts were quietly infiltrated and occupied by Pakistani troops in the spring of 1999. The infiltration was discovered by the Indian Army only in May 1999 and operations began to evict the intruders.

The military outposts in this region are at 16,000 to 18,000 ft. To regain the posts would mean an uphill climb against the enemy sitting on the top at vantage point. The conflict area included the Mushko Valley as well as the Batalik sector. This was the first war between the newly declared nuclear states. In February 1999, much to the dislike of Pakistan Army, the two countries had signed the Lahore declaration to move towards lasting peace. Pakistan intended to cut off the Srinagar-Leh highway and the blueprint for the attack was the brain child of the now infamous General Pervez Musharraf.

India's political leadership decided to restrict the military operation to the localised area with a clear objective of regaining territory. Involvement of the Air Forces normally escalates the war. Therefore, initially, the IAF was restricted only to logistics and aerial reconnaissance roles. Srinagar and Awantipur are the nearest big IAF air bases in the area of operation. However, the disadvantageous ground position was such that India could lose a large number of troops. On May 26, IAF was given the go ahead to strike enemy positions in an operation code-named 'Safed Sagar', but were not allowed to cross the LoC thus seriously curtailing the freedom to employ air power in a classic manner. 20 X 20 km area is a very small area for an air force to operate. For a very high-speed fighter, even when a target had been spotted, it would be difficult to attack with such restrictions. Jaguars and MiG 25's were used for reconnaissance sorties. Only about 25% of the total strike force of the Western Air Command was utilised.

On the second day IAF lost two fighter aircrafts, a MiG-21 to enemy missile fire, and a MiG-27, due to an engine failure. On the third day a Mi-17 helicopter was shot down by ground fire. IAF immediately reviewed its strategy and brought in Mirage 2000 fighters to drop high technology laser guided bombs from high altitude so as to remain above the ground fire lethal zone. These were escorted by MiG-29 air superiority fighters. Soon IAF was targeting individual bunkers atop the now famous Tiger hill with 1000 pound precision bombs. Air strikes on Pakistan's Northern Light Infantry battalion headquarters at Muntho Dhalo and the administrative base in the Batalik sub-sector were a spectacular success. Repeated bombing of Muntho Dhalo strangulated the Batalik sub-sector. Strikes along the Sando Nulla cut off Tiger hill. Nearly 12-14 strikes were flown every day. Fighters flew about 1,200 sorties. Another 650 sorties were undertaken for reconnaissance and air defence tasks. Helicopters and transport aircraft flew over 1200 sorties. Approximately 6,500 tons of load including ammunition, drinking water and other logistic requirements were air lifted. A major airlift was undertaken in the form of casualty evacuation and fresh reinforcements, in which the helicopters played a crucial role.

Laser head videos released to TV channels reinforced national morale and deeply demoralised the enemy. Heavy casualties from the air attacks and destruction of their fortified positions forced Pakistani soldiers to commence a hasty withdrawal.

Meanwhile, IAF also started targeting enemy logistics nodes and artillery gun locations in the valley behind the ridge. As a result, when the Indian Army launched its major offensive on June 6, they faced relatively lesser resistance and also reduced casualties. By June 13, India had recaptured Batalik sector, and Tololing in Drass. Tiger hill that dominates the NH-1D highway was finally captured on July 4.

On July 14, Operation Vijay was declared successful by Prime Minister Atal Bihari Vajpayee. On July 26, the operation was officially declared closed.

Around 30,000 troops were actively involved in combat. Official figured stated that 527 Indians were martyred and 1363 wounded. On Pakistan's side, General Musharraf's said that 665 soldiers were wounded while thousands died. India estimated around 1050 fatalities on Pakistan's side.

Several soldiers won four Param Vir Chakra among other gallantry awards. Squadron Leader Ajay Ahuja was awarded a Vir Chakra. Names of Param Virs Captain Batra and Lieutenant Manoj Pandey are part of military folklore.

With its significant war footage, Kargil was the first Indo-Pak War that impacted public opinion through mass media coverage. Pakistan faced international condemnation for this foolhardy adventure and once again exposed the strife between Pakistan's army and its political leadership. In October 1999, Musharraf ousted elected Prime Minister Nawaz Sharif in a bloodless coup.

Young Indian military officers and jawans made the country proud of their valour and initiative. Air power once again proved a clincher.

INITIAL AIR OPERATIONS

Less than a week before the start of Operation Vijay, on May 21, the IAF had launched a Canberra PR57 from 106 Squadron to conduct a reconnaissance of the besieged area that overlooked highway NH1A and the adjacent town of Kargil. While descending to 22,000 feet just two miles from the LoC, which put the aircraft as low as 4,000 feet above the highest ridgelines, the Canberra sustained a direct hit in its right engine by what was later determined to have been a Chinese-made Anza infrared surface-to-air missile. From that moment onward, the IAF leadership knew without doubt that it was nearing the brink of a major combat involvement.

The initial attacks marked the first time that the IAF had expended ordnance in combat in Kashmir since its early-generation Vampire jet fighters destroyed Pakistani bunkers in the Kargil sector in December 1971.

Kinetic air operations began in earnest at 0630 on May 26 with six attacks in succession by two-ship elements of MiG-21, MiG-23, and MiG-27 fighters against intruder camps, materiel dumps, and supply routes in the general areas overlooking Dras, Kargil, and Batalik. These initial attacks marked the first time that the IAF had expended ordnance in combat in Kashmir since its early-generation Vampire jet fighters destroyed Pakistani bunkers in the Kargil sector in December 1971. The IAF fighters that were pressed into these first-day attacks conducted 57mm rocket attacks and strafing passes against enemy targets. A second wave of air attacks began that afternoon, followed by high-altitude reconnaissance overflights by Canberra PR57s and subsequent low passes by MiG-21Ms to conduct near-real-time battle damage assessment.

Nearly all of the targets selected for attack in those initial strikes were on or near jagged ridgelines at elevations ranging from 14,000 to 18,000 feet. The stark backdrop of rocks and snow made for uncommonly difficult visual target acquisition, complicated further by the small size of the enemy troop positions dispersed against a vast and undifferentiated snow background. Inspired by the unique view from the cockpit of a fighter flying high over the rugged terrain, the IAF codenamed its contribution to the campaign Operation Safed Sagar—Hindi for "white sea."

During the second day of surface attack operations, the IAF lost two fighters in close succession. The first, a MiG-27 from 9 Squadron, experienced an engine failure while coming off a target after its pilot had just conducted a successful two-pass attack with 80mm rockets and 30mm cannon fire on one of the enemy's main supply dumps. The ensuing in-flight emergency resulted in the pilot ejecting safely after several unsuccessful airstart attempts, only to be captured by the Pakistani intruders almost as soon as he hit the ground. Air Chief Marshal Tipnis later reported that the pilot had fired his rockets well outside the operating envelope stipulated for the weapon, causing the engine to flame out. The sudden loss of power in the thin Himalayan air could have resulted from rocket exhaust gas having been ingested through the engine's air inlets on either side of the aircraft. (The MiG-27 was flying at an altitude well above that at which the rockets had been cleared to be fired.)

The second fighter loss, a MiG-21 from 17 Squadron flying top cover for the strikers, sustained an infrared surface-to-air missile hit while its pilot was flying over the terrain at low level to assist in the search for the downed MiG-27 pilot. The pilot, Squadron Leader Ajay Ahuja, also succeeded in ejecting safely but was executed shortly after he was captured following his landing. His body was subsequently returned bearing fatal bullet wounds and clear signs of brutalization.

The IAF's pilots quickly understood what the Israelis had learned at great cost during the Yom Kippur War of 1973, when Egyptian and Syrian surface-to-air missiles and antiaircraft artillery downed nearly a third of the Israeli Air Force's fighter inventory (102 aircraft) before the three-week war finally ended in victory for Israel. Demonstrating its adaptability, the IAF moved with dispatch to equip all of its participating fighters with flares in order to provide an active counter-measure against any enemy infrared-guided missiles. It also called a halt once and for all to any further use of slow-moving and vulnerable Mi-17 helicopters in an armed fire-support role and directed that all target attacks by IAF fighters be conducted from outside the lethal threat envelopes of enemy shoulder-fired surface-to-air missiles. In all, enemy forces fired more than 100 surface-to-air missiles at IAF aircraft throughout the conflict. After the service's first three days of combat operations, however, not a single one of its aircraft was downed or sustained battle damage.

Throughout the campaign, whenever IAF reconnaissance or ground attack operations were under way in the immediate combat zone, Western Air Command ensured that MiG-29s or other air-to-air fighters were also airborne on combat air patrol stations over the ground fighting on India's side of the LoC to provide top cover against any attempt by the Pakistan Air Force (PAF) to enter the fray in a ground attack role. PAF F-16s to the west typically maintained a safe distance of 10 to 20 miles on the Pakistani side of the LoC, although they occasionally approached as close as 8 miles away from the ongoing ground engagements. The PAF's director of operations during the Kargil War later reported that there had been isolated instances of IAF and PAF fighters locking on to each other with their onboard fire control radars, but that caution had prevailed on both sides and that "no close [air-to-air] encounters took place." IAF fighters never joined in aerial combat with the PAF F-16s due to the Vajpayee government's strict injunction that Indian forces not cross the LoC. Seven years later, however, Air Chief Marshal Tipnis recalled that he had personally authorized his escorting fighter pilots to chase any Pakistani aircraft back across the LoC in hot pursuit were those pilots to be engaged by enemy fighters in aerial combat.

In all, the IAF flew some 460 fighter sorties throughout the campaign dedicated exclusively to maintaining battlespace air defense. These medium- and high-altitude defensive combat air patrols and offensive fighter sweeps, typically entailing four-ship flights of MiG-29s, took place not only in the immediate area of ground fighting in the Kargil sector but throughout Western Air Command's area of responsibility. As Operation Vijay's air component commander later recalled, he was not just concerned about Kargil or the Kashmir region but had a potentially larger-scale war in mind: "I was working on a much bigger canvas.... I was fully conscious that as we hit and killed enemy soldiers, there was every possibility for escalation, possibly outside the immediate combat area, and it was my job to be ready with adequate remaining resources for that eventuality."

IAF strike aircraft operated primarily from three northern bases, Air Force Stations Srinagar, Avantipur, and Udhampur. The closest of those to the fighting, Srinagar, was more than 70 miles away from the war zone. Within just days after the full extent of the Pakistani incursion was confirmed and well before the formal start of Operation Safed Sagar, the MiG-21bis squadron permanently stationed at Srinagar was joined by additional MiG-21M, MiG-

23BN, and MiG-27ML squadrons, while additional squadrons of MiG-21Ms and MiG-29s deployed northward to Avantipur.

By the time Operation Safed Sagar had reached its full stride, the IAF had deployed some 60 of its frontline aircraft to support the war effort, making for about a quarter of Western Air Command's combined fighter inventory. As they awaited mission tasking, those squadrons committed to the campaign initiated special training aimed at better acclimating their pilots to conducting night attacks under moonlit conditions. Such combat operations by fighters over high mountainous terrain at night had never before been attempted in the IAF's history.

Because of their rudimentary bomb sights, the inaccuracy of their unguided weapons, and the ruling against crossing the Line of Control, MiG-21, MiG-23, and MiG-27 pilots typically achieved only limited effectiveness when attempting to provide close air support against enemy point targets.

Increasingly as the joint campaign unfolded, most Indian Army operations were preceded by preparatory air strikes, each of which was closely coordinated beforehand between 15 Corps planners and the AOC for Jammu and Kashmir. Because of their rudimentary bomb sights, the inaccuracy of their unguided weapons, and the ruling against crossing the LoC, MiG-21, MiG-23, and MiG-27 pilots typically achieved only limited effectiveness when attempting to provide close air support against enemy point targets.

Rapidly adapting to these constraints, on May 30, just four days after the start of Operation Safed Sagar, Air Chief Marshal Tipnis decided to take action to help correct the problem of inaccuracy. He chose to commit IAF Mirage 2000H fighters capable of delivering laser-guided bombs to ground attack operations in the Kargil sector. The fighters first had to be configured to deliver the bombs, so Air Headquarters launched an accelerated effort to do so at Air Force Station Gwalior, where the Mirage 2000Hs were principally based.

India's Aircraft System Testing Establishment (ASTE) in Bangalore was well along in a developmental program to integrate Israeli-made Litening electro-optical targeting pods onto the Mirage 2000H and Jaguar fighters. To support the accelerated effort at Gwalior, ASTE began a full-court press to prepare selected Mirage 2000Hs from 7 Squadron to be fitted with Litening pods for use over Kargil. At the same time, ASTE helped modify the Mirage 2000H's centerline weapons station to carry 1,000-pound U.S.-made Paveway II laser-guided bombs instead of the IAF's French-produced Matra precision munitions, which were prohibitively expensive. Concurrently, the IAF's elite Tactics and Air Combat Development Establishment located at Air Force

Station Jamnagar took the lead in developing and validating best tactics, techniques, and procedures for delivering the Paveway II. By June 12, the upgraded Mirage 2000Hs were ready to commence precision strike operations in anger for the first time in IAF history.

In the meantime, air operations against identified intruder positions and support facilities continued in the Jubar and Mashkoh Valley sectors between May 28 and June 1. Throughout the first week of June, inclement weather hindered such operations and persisted to a point where a cloud deck below the ridgelines precluded air attacks entirely on June 10 and 11. Fortunately, 15 Corps had no urgent target servicing requirements for the IAF during those two days.

INDIA ATTACKS PAKISTANI POSITIONS

The terrain of Kashmir is mountainous and at high altitudes; even the best roads, such as National Highway No. 1 (NH 1) from Leh to Srinagar, are only two lanes. The rough terrain and narrow roads slowed traffic, and the high altitude, which affected the ability of aircraft to carry loads, made control of NH 1A (the actual stretch of the highway which was under Pakistani fire) a priority for India.

From their observation posts, the Pakistani forces had a clear line-of-sight to lay down indirect artillery fire on NH 1A, inflicting heavy casualties on the Indians. This was a serious problem for the Indian Army as the highway was its main logistical and supply route. The Pakistani shelling of the arterial road posed the threat of Leh being cut off, though an alternative (and longer) road to Leh existed via Himachal Pradesh.

The infiltrators, apart from being equipped with small arms and grenade launchers, were also armed with mortars, artillery and anti-aircraft guns. Many posts were also heavily mined, with India later stating to having recovered more than 8,000 anti-personnel mines according to an ICBL report. Pakistan's reconnaissance was done through unmanned aerial vehicles and AN/TPQ-36 Firefinder radars supplied by the US.

The initial Indian attacks were aimed at controlling the hills overlooking NH 1A, with high priority being given to the stretches of the highway near the town of Kargil. The majority of posts along the Line of Control were adjacent to the highway, and therefore the recapture of nearly every infiltrated post increased both the territorial gains and the security of the highway. The protection of this route and the recapture of the forward posts were thus *ongoing objectives* throughout the war. The Indian Army's first priority was to recapture peaks that were in the immediate vicinity of NH1a. This resulted in Indian troops first targeting the Tiger Hill and Tololing complex in Dras, which dominated the Srinagar-Leh route. This was soon followed by the Batalik-Turtok sub-sector which provided access to Siachen Glacier.

Some of the peaks that was of vital strategic importance to the Pakistani defensive troops were Point 4590 and Point 5353. While 4590 was the nearest point that had a view of NH1a, point 5353 was the highest feature in the Dras sector, allowing the Pakistani troops to observe NH1A. The recapture of Point 4590 by Indian troops on June 14 was significant, notwithstanding the fact that Point 4590 resulting in the Indian Army suffering the most casualties in a single battle during the conflict. Though most of the posts in the vicinity of the highway were cleared by mid-June, some parts of the highway near Drass witnessed sporadic shelling until the end of the war.

Once India regained control of the hills overlooking NH 1A, the Indian Army turned to driving the invading force back across the Line of Control. The Battle of Tololing, among other assaults, slowly tilted the combat in India's favor. Nevertheless, some of the posts put up a stiff resistance, including Tiger Hill (Point 5140) that fell only later in the war. A few of the assaults occurred atop hitherto unheard of peaks – most of them unnamed with only Point numbers to differentiate them – which witnessed fierce hand to hand combat.

As the operation was fully underway, about 250 artillery guns were brought in to clear the infiltrators in the posts that were in the line-of-sight. The Bofors field howitzer (infamous in India due to the Bofors scandal) played a vital role, with Indian gunners making maximum use of the terrain that assisted such an attack. However, its success was limited elsewhere due to the lack of space and depth to deploy the Bofors gun.

It was in this type of terrain that aerial attacks were used with limited effectiveness. The IAF lost a MiG-27 strike aircraft which it attributed to an engine failure as well as a MiG-21 fighter which was shot down by Pakistan; Pakistan said it shot down both jets after they crossed into its territory and one Mi-8 helicopter to Stinger SAMs. During attacks the IAF used laser-guided bombs to destroy well-entrenched positions of the Pakistani forces.

In many vital points, neither artillery nor air power could dislodge the outposts manned by the Pakistan soldiers, who were out of visible range. The Indian Army mounted some direct frontal ground assaults which were slow and took a heavy toll given the steep ascent that had to be made on peaks as high as 18,000 feet (5,500 m). Since any daylight attack would be suicidal, all the advances had to be made under the cover of darkness, escalating the risk of freezing.

Accounting for the wind chill factor, the temperatures were often as low as “11 °C to “15 °C (12 °F to 5 °F) near the mountain tops. Based on military tactics, much of the costly frontal assaults by the Indians could have been avoided if the Indian Military had chosen to blockade the supply route of the opposing force, virtually creating a siege. Such a move would have involved the Indian troops crossing the LoC as well as initiating aerial attacks on Pakistan soil, a manoeuvre India was not willing to exercise fearing an expansion of the theatre of war and reducing international support for its cause.

Two months into the conflict, Indian troops had slowly retaken most of the ridges they had lost; according to official count, an estimated 75%–80% of the intruded area and nearly all high ground was back under Indian control.

OCCUPATION BY PAKISTAN

During the winter season, due to extreme cold in the mountainous areas of Kashmir, it was a common practice for both the Indian and Pakistan Armies to abandon some forward posts on their respective sides of the LOC and to reduce patrolling of areas that may be avenues of infiltration. When weather conditions became less severe, forward posts would be reoccupied and patrolling resumed.

During February 1999, the Pakistan Army began to re-occupy the posts it had abandoned on its side of the LOC in the Kargil region, but also sent forces to occupy some posts on the Indian side of the LOC.

Troops from the elite Special Services Group as well as four to seven battalions of the Northern Light Infantry (a paramilitary regiment not part of the regular Pakistani army at that time) covertly and overtly set up bases on the vantage points of the Indian-controlled region. According to some reports, these Pakistani forces were backed by Kashmiri guerrillas and Afghan mercenaries.

Pakistani intrusions took place in the heights of the lower Mushkoh valley, along the Marpo La ridgeline in Dras, in Kaksar near Kargil, in the Batalik sector east of the Indus river, the heights above of the Chorbatla sector where the LC turns North as well in the Turtok sector south of the Siachen area.

CASUALITIES IN KARGIL WAR

“Battalions of Northern Light Infantry (NLI) were wiped out by the Indian Forces in Kargil”, the deposed Prime Minister of Pakistan Nawaz Sharief told newsmen while in detention testifying to the ferocious counter attack launched by the Indian Army and Indian Air Force to evict the regular Pakistani intruders from Indian soil in the Drass, Batalik, Mushkoh sectors in June-July last year.

The nation gratefully commemorates the sacrifices made by 527 brave soldiers and airmen for the success of "Operation Vijay", which is being observed as *Kargil Vijay Diwas* on July 26, 2000. Indian forces had thus foiled Pakistan's politico-strategic motives to internationalise Kashmir as a nuclear flash point requiring urgent third party intervention, to alter the Line of Control (LOC) and disrupt its sanctity by capturing unheld areas in Kargil and to achieve a better bargaining position for a possible trade off against the positions held by India in Siachen.

Another tactical move on the part of enemy, was to interdict the Srinagar-Leh road by disrupting the vital NH-1A and to give fillip to militancy in J&K. The Indian political leadership and the various Ministries of Government of India worked in perfect synergy to meet the challenge.

The media coverage on the Kargil war, especially the electronic media, served as a force multiplier leading to a national upsurge of giant proportions and a feeling of oneness with our courageous *jawans.* Significantly, as the *15 Corps* mobilised its forces for the counter attack and elements of the *18 Mountain Division* poured into the various sectors of Kargil, the people of Jammu & Kashmir were steadfast against the enemy forces.

The gallantry displayed by *'Ladakh Scouts'* and *'J&K Light Infantry'* is testimony to that. The rapid Indian deployment was not reckoned by the Pakistanis.

The use of the Indian Air Force in support of the Army in Kargil had a strong impact on the course of the tactical battle in terms of the interdiction of Pakistani supply lines within Indian territory, the damage inflicted on the Pakistani defences and the lowering of the morale of the intruders.

In a skilful use of naval power in the form of *'Operation Talwar'*, the *'Eastern Fleet'* joined the *'Western Naval Fleet'* and blocked the Arabian sea routes of Pakistan. Apart from a deterrent, the former Prime Minister Nawaz Sharief later disclosed that Pakistan was left with just six days of fuel (POL) to sustain itself if a full fledged war broke out.

At the end of the day, it was the courageous deeds of soldiers from the *Jat Regiment, Rajputana Rifles,* the *Grenadiers, Madras Regiment, Sikh Regiment* and *Mahar Regiment* at the icy heights of Kargil mountains that overwhelmed the enemy.

The *'Artillery Regiments'* performed a splendid job by destroying enemy positions and pinning them down by continuous barrage of fire from 155 mm

Bofors howitzers and 130 mm field guns. When the strategic Tiger Hill fell on account of a brilliantly executed tactical plan, the Prime Minister of Pakistan Nawaz Sharief was blissfully unaware of the development. His wife Kulsoom Sharief heard the news on ZEE TV and rushed to inform Nawaz Sharief, who was then enjoying golf at his residence near Lahore.

Apart from sheer courage of forces fighting in very hostile and inclement weather conditions, the military leadership has to be given due credit for keeping up the great traditions of Indian Army namely, obedience to the civilian authority in letter and spirit. The situation was such and militarily so compelling that the Army Chief would have felt it absolutely necessary to violate the LOC and get behind the enemy and threaten its lines of withdrawal.

In doing so, the Indian side would have succeeded in driving out the enemy much earlier. While the Army considered this option, it also restrained itself to go by the Central Government decision, i.e. to avoid the escalation of the conflict. It is precisely because of this reason that the eviction of the enemy took a little over two months and resulted in heavy loss of life. Strangely, a war limited to a small area like Kargil sector had gone to highlight the Indian Foreign Policy that is principally directed towards world peace.

By deciding not to take the war with Pakistan, by deciding not to violate the LOC, by deciding to wily-nily accept high rate of casualties on its side and thus limiting the conflict on its side and in determining that these are small sacrifices in the larger cause of world peace – all this reflects India's innate love for peace and good neighbourly relations even if it meant at some cost.

This exemplary demonstration of restraint, in the face of provocations, India was able to project itself to the international community that it stood for peace and not war. This peaceful assertion turned the tables on Pakistan to the extent that America, once Pakistan's most dependable ally, not only chose to condemn it as an aggressor but build up fresh solid relations between India and itself. The result is Pakistan's isolation and General Musharaaf's regime left in lurch. For, this is the first military regime in Pakistan that has been disapproved by America and P-5 countries. Kargil war brought into sharp focus India's commitment to peace. While remembering the martyrs of Kargil war, let us also imagine what these martyrs were saying while dying, "go back and tell them that we are giving up our today for their tomorrow."

'INDIAN ARMY COULD'VE CROSSED LINE OF CONTROL DURING KARGIL WAR IN 1999'

Omar Abdullah, a former chief minister of Indian-held Jammu Kashmir and working president of the National Conference party, has defended his party leader and his father Dr Farooq Abdullah's remarks that India cannot take Azad Jammu Kashmir away from Pakistan, saying the Kargil war in 1999 provided an 'opportunity' to cross the Line of Control but India preferred to 'respect' its sanctity. "I understand there is a parliament resolution that authorises or pressurises the Indian government to bring back that part of Jammu Kashmir to India control. If that be the case, why didn't we do it in the Kargil war," he questioned in an interview to *The Hindu* newspaper. During the Kargil war, there were express 'instructions' that no man or machine would cross the Line of Control, he said.

Reflecting a change in earlier stand to convert the Line of Control into a border, Omar said that people of the two parts of Jammu Kashmir, which have been artificially divided, should be allowed to reunite. "Whether that reunification takes place under a sovereign arrangement or this sort of thing where the Line of Control is converted into a de-facto border and then is made softer and irrelevant border," he said.

"The Line of Control being the line on which solution can be drawn, these are not new views. These views expressed by my father even as chief minister between 1996 and 2002 and successively at functions and events after that. They are based on sound logic, which is that too much water has flown in the (river) Jhelum now for you to be able to start undoing that. For any solution in Kashmir to work you will have to arrive at some sort of arrangement where neither India nor Pakistan loses face, no one side claim victory," he said.

"Take the Ufa declaration, no sooner had the declaration been made public that India took the position that it was a victory on their part because Pakistan had sort of make no mention of Kashmir. Two days later, Pakistan took a completely different position and the whole process was unraveled. This is a small declaration. Imagine the same thing in the case of territory," he said, adding that the fact was that the gun was not a solution.

"Kashmir is also now increasingly under pressure from a version of Islam that was otherwise alien to the state. To what extent this will continue and how this change processes and thoughts in Jammu Kashmir, it is too early to tell," he said while commenting on prolonging the Kashmir issue. Calling for resumption of dialogue process on internal and external dimension of Kashmir, he said that his party would once again take to people the autonomy as a solution.

"Autonomy is the cornerstone of our political identity," he said. Omar also accused India's Prime Minister Narendra Modi of failing the legacy introduced by Atal Bihari Vajpayee, a former prime minister. "He (Vajpayee) never stood up and said he knows everything about Jammu Kashmir. He was willing to listen. Prime Minister Modi chose to interpret words of Vajpayee with limited application."

He also said that his grandfather Sheikh Muhammad Abdullah, founder of the party, was being demonised. "There were misunderstandings and misgivings about him, misplaced as they were. At that point in time, too much effort was made to sow the seeds of doubt in the minds of Jawaharlal Nehru. The Kashmir problem started from there. If he hadn't been unceremoniously dethroned or detained and after that autonomy was not tinkered with, who knows how different our history would have been today."

"You have a European like model where the free flow of people and goods and material is allowed and the PDP took it one step further and called for a free trade zone to be established. These are all various permutations and combinations of the same idea that if a border exists, it does not interfere in the day to day life of people," he said. "We have been supportive of a dialogue process. There were aspects in the four-point formula (introduced by former president Pervez Musharraf) that we found difficult to implement particularly joint control, which is difficult to manage at the best of times," he said.

"Other aspects which called for phased demilitarisation and greater people-to-people contact, no territorial give and take, these were workable ideas," he said. "We already have a clear cut sub-regional identifications like plains of Jammu, Chenab valley, Pir Panchal and the Valley etc. There is need to give adequate voice and space. A limited beginning was with the hill development councils in Leh and Kargil. This was internal autonomy that our party talked about. We didn't talk about just autonomy between New Delhi and the state," he said.

"We also talked about regional autonomy within the valley and Jammu. But our document was accused of being communal but there is a sort of religious differentiation in these regions. This is not something we have created but over the course of time it has come to be," Omar said. "Chief Minister Mufti Muhammad Sayeed tries to take credit for things that is not his doing, for example opening up of the Srinagar-Muzafarrabad bus. As the chief minister he was privy to developments that were happening so he came here and tried to sell as if he was architect of that. Whereas the actual architect were Vajpayee and Musharraf," he said.

"I have met Musharraf and leaders from Prime Minister Nawaz Sharif's party as well as the Pakistan People's Party. It is not true that as mainstream parties we have not reached out to political leaders in Pakistan. Given the right circumstances, we will continue to do that," he said. "We have seen to many knee jerk reactions on ceasefire violation and Hurriyat Conference," he said.

He also said that the meetings between Pakistan and the Hurriyat leaders were not new. "It has continued since the phase of 'militancy' started," he said.

"Pakistan will never allow a situation, as of now, where they will come to India and not meet Hurriyat leaders," the Kashmiri leader said. "Therefore to make these meetings a dialogue process to breakdown is tantamount to accepting that a dialogue will not take place at all in India. We need to recognise that the way we have internal compulsions so does Pakistan. To make Hurriyat Conference a reason for dialogue not to take place between Pakistan and India is giving them more importance than they require," he said.

"The Hurriyat has a stated position and have a constituency within Jammu Kashmir as much as we like to wish them away you can't do that. They are part of both the problem and the solution as well. This government (in New Delhi) has chosen to set this fact aside or ignore," he said. "For external dimension, we need to have concerted efforts. For example, you meet in Ufa and don't look at each other in Kathmandu and barely wave in New York and then you sit down and have cozy chat in Paris. This is confusing and doesn't help," he said.

"We need continuous process to talk and make it immune to external influences," Omar said. "Hurriyat has a point of view. The problem arises when they try to capitalise on unfortunate developments that take place in the state, particularly when people die. But I do not agree with the recent steps of the Mufti government to detain them and prevent them from meeting Foreign Affairs Adviser (Sartaj Aziz), which was unprecedented. No government in the past has taken steps like that but yes I guess that was the compulsion for the chief minister for allied with the BJP," he said.

4

Glacier Dangerous India and Pakistan Freeze

Caught up in the dynamics of nuclear brinkmanship, Indiaand Pakistan hold their entire region hostage to clear and present danger. But a recent impromptu meeting between two heads of state and a deadly glacial avalanche could be the start for thawing relations between the nuclear-armed arch rivals.

On April 8, Indian Prime Minister Manmohan Singh and Pakistani President Asif Zardari met in New Delhi, proffering a long-awaited opportunity to pursue stability in South Asia. Both their overtures signal a softening of attitudes. But will the meeting serve as symbolic kow-towing or will the statesmen open up space for future talks?

Since independence from British colonial rule in 1947, protracted territorial and political disputes have led India and Pakistan to engage in three full scale and three quasi-wars. Cross-border skirmishes are common. Indian allegations concerning Pakistan's involvement in a number of terrorist attacks inside its territory complicate relations further.

One such issue is the dispute over the Siachen Glacier, a territorial tussle with substantial economic and human costs for the two states. Tragically, on the eve of the meeting between the two heads of state, Siachen experienced a deadly avalanche killing 135 Pakistani soldiers and civilians.

Known as the world's highest battleground, Siachen is located at an elevation ranging between 11,000 to 22,000 feet. Since April 1984, when India and Pakistan deployed troops in a tit-for-tat competition for territory, both militaries have lost an estimated 5,000 and 3,000 soldiers respectively, primarily due to adverse climate and treacherous terrain.

While an unofficial cease-fire at the Siachen Glacier remains in force since 2003, both India and Pakistan continue an armed standoff in the region. Exclusive territorial claims stem from ambiguities in agreements defining the cease-fire line, or the Line of Control to the northeast of Kashmir following the wars of 1948 and 1971. India has approximately 7,000 troops deployed in the region, and Pakistan about 4,000.

It is estimated that fewer than a thousand lives have been lost in combat during the past 28 years. More men here die due to harsh weather, high altitude illness, and other hazards. On average, one Pakistani soldier is killed every third day in Siachen, with a higher Indian average of one soldier every other day.

Siachen is sometimes regarded as a by-product of the Kashmir conflict. But unlike their hardened positions on Kashmir, both states have demonstrated a willingness to explore a negotiated settlement on the Siachen dispute, with 12 rounds of talks already held between 1985 and 2011. Regrettably, none have reached fruition.

Now in the wake of the avalanche, Pakistan Army Chief General Ashfaq Parvez Kayani is calling for demilitarization, an opportunity that must not be missed by India. The cost of deploying battalions in the region runs in millions of dollars each year for the two impoverished nations.

Yet both states maintain their military status quo to defend a 50-mile long icy wasteland. India and Pakistan have each recognized that defense expenditure in Siachen does not justify its lack of strategic advantage. But they also need to account for the financial, social, and psychological costs for the families of the snow warriors, most of them junior soldiers, in the calculus.

While settling the claims on Siachen may not happen very soon, demilitarization is an actionable option. In 2005, Indian Prime Minister Singh had expressed hope for turning the glacier into a peace mountain. Indian and Pakistani mountaineers and environmentalists have also called for the possibility of converting the region into a civilian zone or peace park.

Such an initiative could potentially transform the battlefield into a jointly managed conservation area serving a threefold purpose: to preserve the environment, to help build peace, and to generate revenue through ecotourism.

Settlement of inter-state territorial disputes present challenges, but the dividends of cooperation for India and Pakistan would be immense, particularly in terms of greater regional and global stability. There is also a strong precedent for joint military disengagement: One took place at the Chumik Glacier in 1989, close to Siachen.

Another hopeful sign is that the two militaries have largely upheld the 2003 cease-fire. Joint aerial and on-site inspections could make demilitarization a viable option especially if facilitated by the UN, sponsor of the 1949 cease-fire agreement.

Unresolved territorial disputes have led India and Pakistan to conventional warfare in the past. But the addition of nuclear weapons in the security landscape makes their standoff more precarious than ever.

Given the implications of their tenuous relationship, it is time for a paradigm shift in strategic thinking in India and Pakistan. And Siachin could help break this deadlock.

ABOUT THE SIACHEN GLACIER

The roots of the conflict over Siachen (the place of roses) lie in the non-demarcations on the western side on the map beyond NJ9842. The 1949 Karachi agreement and the 1972 Simla agreement presumed that it was not feasible for human habitation to survive north of NJ9842. Piror to 1984 neither India nor Pakistan had any permanent presence in the area.

Time Magazine: War at the Top of the World

The Siachen Glacier is located in the East Karakoram/Himalaya, at approximately 35.5° N 76.9° E. It is one of the five largest glaciers in the Karakoram, situated at an average altitude of 5,400 meters (~17,700 feet) above sea level. Most of the Siachen Glacier as is the LoC, a hotly contested territory between Pakistan and India.The Siachen glacier lies South of the great watershed that separates Central Asia from the Indian subcontinent, and Pakistan from China in this region. The 78 km long Siachen glacier lies between the Saltoro ridge line to the west and the main Karakoram range to the east. The Saltoro ridge originates from the Sia Kangri peak in the Karakoram range and the altitudes range from 5500 to 7300 m (18,000 to 24,000 feet). The major passes on this ridge are Sia La at 6100 m (20,000 ft) and Bila Fond La at 5800 m (19,000 ft).Understand Kashmir through these books I Siachen Glacier Satellite Image

War at the Top of the WorldThawing relations between India and Pakistan have brought a cease-fire to the strife-torn Siachen Glacier.Will hostilities remain on ice?

Conflict Zone

The glacier is located in the disputed Kashmir region and is claimed by India and Pakistan. In spite of the severe climate, the word 'Siachen' ironically means 'the place of wild roses', a reference some people attribute to the abundance of Himalayan wildflowers found in the valleys below the glacier, but specifically refers to the thorny wild plants which grow on the rocky outcrops. The glacier is also the highest battleground on Earth, where India and Pakistan have fought intermittently since 1984. Both countries maintain permanent military personnel on the glacier at a height of over 7,000 metres. The site is a prime example of mountain warfare. The glacier's melting waters are the main source of the Nubra River, which falls into the Shyok River. The Shyok in turn joins the Indus River, crucial to both India and Pakistan.The roots of the conflict over Siachen lie in the non-demarcation of the cease-fire line on the map beyond a map coordinate known as NJ9842. The 1949 Karachi agreement and the 1972 Simla Agreement presumed that it was not feasible for human habitation to survive north of NJ9842. Prior to 1984 neither India nor Pakistan had any permanent presence in the area.

Fighting

In the 1970s and early 1980s Pakistan permitted several mountaineering expeditions to climb high peaks on this glacier. This was to reinforce their claim on the area as these expeditions arrived on the glacier with a permit obtained from the Government of Pakistan. Once having become aware of this in about 1978, Colonel N. Kumar of the Indian Army mounted an Army expedition to Teram Kangri peaks as a counter-exercise. The first public mention of a possible conflict situation was an article by Joydeep Sircar in The Telegraph newspaper of Calcutta in 1982, reprinted as "Oropolitics" in the Alpine Journal, London,in 1984. India launched Operation Meghdoot (named after the divine cloud messenger in a Sanskrit play) on 13 April 1984 when the Kumaon Regiment of the Indian Army and the Indian Air Force went into the Glacier. Pakistan, which had also gotten wind of it quickly responded with troop deployments and what followed was literally a race to the top. Within a few days, the Indians were in control over most of the glacier as Pakistan were beaten by just a week. The two passes due to Indian military pre-emption – Sia La and Bilfond La were secured by India while the Gyong La pass remained under Pakistan control. Since then both sides have launched several attempts to displace each others forces, but with little success.

ENVIRONMENTAL IMPACT OF SIACHEN CONFLICT

The Siachen glacier has long been a source of conflict between India and Pakistan, and now ecological problems are causing concern for the whole of South Asia. The glacier is melting and putting millions of South Asians at risk of catastrophic floods, droughts and food shortages, environmentalists warn.

Siachen is the planet's second largest glacier apart from the polar caps and also the world's highest battleground at some 6,000 metres above sea level. Soon, it could win the title of the world's filthiest glacier. In Siachen, the decade-long conflict between India and Pakistan is perpetuated by bullets that whistle over the wild roses and snow leopard dens, endangering the fragile environment.

The intense activity of more than 30,000 soldiers along the 70-kilometre-long glacier, a headwater for major rivers in India, Pakistan and Bangladesh is causing great concern to environmentalists.

Human presence is aggravating situation

Professor Syed Iqbal Hasnain, from India's Energy and Resources Institute (TERI), believed that the human presence was aggravating the situation, which is already critical because of global warming. "There is an additional input of warming by the presence of huge armed forces, their machines and their garbage, which goes into the glacier itself," he said.

The conflict at Siachen is also a "death sentence" for other Himalayan glaciers, said Arshad H Abbasi, a researcher at the Sustainable Development Policy Institute in Islamabad.

He explained that India and Pakistan's armies have used chemicals to melt and cut through the age-old glacial ice to construct bunkers, helipads and airfields.

"When you cross the actual line of demarcation there are so many troops on the glacier and so many base camps. India has laid a 165-km long kerosene oil pipeline. You would be amazed to see satellite images of these glaciers – it's just as if the armed forces have converted them into slums."

This ecological deterioration is gradually poisoning the health of the Himalayan glaciers, which are also known as the "third pole". Environmentalists also worry about the impact on low-lying countries such as the Maldives and Bangladesh.

GOVERNMENTS SHOULD ACT WISELY

Professor Shahnaz Huq Hussain from Dhaka University warned that the governments of both countries should act wisely: "We have to preserve the natural balance. Whatever they have done cannot be rectified, but no more harm should be done." Peace activists and environmentalists from both India and Pakistan have called for the region to be demilitarised and converted into a peace park.

Shekhar Gupta, the editor-in-chief of the national Indian Express daily, thought that a Siachen peace park "would be a wonderful idea". He believed it would be great "if the two countries were able to restore faith because Siachen is such an exclusive and rare place and there are not so many glaciers at that altitude that are accessible."

"Both sides have now set up base camps on either side, which are today used to launch troops, but tomorrow they could be used to launch expeditions."

In the aftermath of the Mumbai attacks in November 2008 and attempts by India and Pakistan to resolve the problems of terrorism, activists hope that there might be progress towards preserving the natural balance in Siachen in 2010.

UNITED STATES' ROLE AND INFLUENCE ON THE INDIA-PAKISTAN CONFLICT

Although the Soviet Union played a critical role in formally ending the second India-Pakistan war in 1965—through the Tashkent Declaration—its close military and security relationships with Delhi during much of the Cold War years decreased its influence over Islamabad, which became increasingly linked to the United States for the supply of arms. China's discreet missile and nuclear linkages with Islamabad, along with memories of the India-China border war of 1962, precluded Beijing's influence over the India-Pakistan dispute. Despite an apparent shift in Beijing's position since 1996 (especially during the Kargil conflict in 1999 when it refrained from publicly supporting Pakistan, and due to its concerns over Islamist extremists in Xinjiang province), elements of future India-China competition make it difficult for Beijing to influence Delhi. While French, European Union or Japanese influence appear limited, a potential British role exists only alongside the United States, with the latter doing much of the 'heavy lifting'. Notwithstanding Washington's unprecedented and simultaneous influence over both Delhi and Islamabad, the nature and extent of its future engagement in the India-Pakistan conflict remains unclear.

Kashmir Dispute

In view of India's asymmetrical relationship with Pakistan—population, size, economic strength and relative military power—Delhi has invariably resisted the role of a third party or the United Nations in its conflict with Pakistan; it is precisely for these reasons that Islamabad has favoured such a role, with the hope that 'internationalization' would provide a favourable resolution of the Kashmir dispute. India's disillusionment with the international community over Kashmir began soon after Independence, when Prime Minister Jawaharlal Nehru took Pakistan's aggression against India in Kashmir to the United Nations on 1 January 1948.

Instead of being seen as the aggrieved party, losing Indian territory to an armed attack by Pakistan—following the signing of the Instrument of Accession by the Hindu ruler of the predominantly Muslim province of

Jammu and Kashmir on 26 October 1947— India became a party to the dispute.

Subsequent UN Security Council resolutions advocating the future of Kashmir on the basis of a UN-mandated plebiscite—after the withdrawal of armed forces by both countries from divided Kashmir—were ignored by Delhi, as was the United Nations force, the UN Military Observer Group in India and Pakistan (UNMOGIP). Since the UN-sponsored ceasefire to the first India-Pakistan war over Kashmir on 1 January 1949, UNMOGIP has been deployed to monitor the ceasefire line—currently, the Line of Control (LoC) (the *de facto* border dividing Indianand Pakistan-administered Kashmir).

For Islamabad, however, the UN Security Council resolutions on Kashmir boosted its position on Kashmir, and justified its stance that it was a territorial dispute between the two sides. This contradicted Delhi's view that Kashmir was 'not a disputed territory', with the only point of contention being Pakistan's 'illegal occupation of a portion of the state', fortified by a Parliamentary resolution to this effect in the early 1990s. Even though it was clear that neither Pakistan nor India were inclined to withdraw forces from divided Kashmir, Islamabad was not averse to using UN Security Council resolutions on a plebiscite in Kashmir for political purposes.

However, Indian and Pakistani positions on a plebiscite and the status of Kashmir appeared to change in December 2003-January 2004. In an interview with Reuters in mid-December 2003, Pakistan's President Musharraf, in a bold move, publicly offered to drop Pakistan's traditional demand for a UN plebiscite in Kashmir, and meet India 'half-way' in a bid to resolve the Kashmir dispute. Musharraf reportedly stated, '... we are for the United Nations Security Council resolutions whatever it stands for. However, now we have left that aside'. Although this was subsequently denied by Pakistani officials, it was clear that this was simply a recognition that a UN plebiscite could never have been implemented, in view of Indian and Pakistani intransigence. Yet, it had been a major irritant to Delhi, which welcomed Musharraf's statement. Subsequently, in the joint press statement of 6 January 2004, following the meeting between Indian Prime Minister Vajpayee and Musharraf, on the sidelines of the twelfth South Asian Association for Regional Cooperation (SAARC) Summit in Islamabad, Delhi implicitly agreed that Kashmir was disputed territory, by explicitly agreeing that Kashmir was to be settled 'to the satisfaction of both sides'.

'Third Party' Involvement in War

Notwithstanding India's aversion to a 'third party' (including UN) role in its dispute over Kashmir, this did not apply to assistance in formally ending wars, or in the 1990s, preventing the outbreak of full-fledged conventional war. The second India-Pakistan war in 1965, for example, ended with a UN Security Council-sponsored ceasefire on 23 September 1965. Three months later, Indian Prime Minister Lal Bahadur Shastri and Pakistani President Mohammed Ayub Khan met in Tashkent and signed an agreement to formalize the end of the war and the withdrawal of their armed forces to positions held prior to 5 August 1965. The erstwhile Soviet-brokered 'Tashkent Agreement' of 10 January 1966 also pledged continued negotiations and the observation of ceasefire terms on the ceasefire line.

During this period, American policy towards South Asia remained fairly ambivalent, although an attempt at engagement on the Kashmir dispute had been made during the Eisenhower Administration in the 1950s. Although the Kennedy Administration was able to initiate direct negotiations between India and Pakistan—in the aftermath of the 1962 India-China war, the talks failed; by the mid-1960s the United States had virtually given up on Kashmir. During the 1971 India-Pakistan war, the United States 'tilt' towards Pakistan—through the deployment of an aircraft carrier task force in the Bay of Bengal in the midst of the war—whatever its intent or purpose—made it difficult for India, among other reasons, to develop a satisfactory 'comfort level' with the United States on security issues. Despite American economic and military sanctions on Pakistan in 1979 in an attempt to stem its covert nuclearweapons programme, Pakistan's role as a front-line state against the Soviet occupation of Afghanistan in the 1980s alleviated this situation. The demise of the former Soviet Union, along with India's economic liberalization in the aftermath of the 1991 economic crisis, began to lead to more favourable Indo-American relations.

In the late 1990s, high publicity American engagement with South Asia took place on nuclear issues, sparked off by multiple Indian and Pakistani nuclear tests in May 1998. On 11 and 13 May 1998, India carried out a series of five underground nuclear tests, twenty-four years after its first 'peaceful nuclear explosion' on 18 May 1974. This was promptly followed by six Pakistani nuclear tests on 28 and 30 May 1998. Although the immediate American reaction was to impose economic and military-related sanctions on both India and Pakistan, their respective importance in United States foreign policy soon generated less coercive measures to counter proliferation. In a significant development, within the Lahore Memorandum of Understanding (MoU), both countries agreed to develop confidence-building measures (CBMs) in the nuclear and conventional fields aimed at the avoidance of conflict within nine months of the nuclear tests. The Lahore documents—signed at the Summit between Vajpayee and Pakistani Prime Minister Nawaz Sharif in Lahore—

appeared to provide the momentum towards enhanced and formalized nuclear stability in South Asia.

American Facilitation in the Kargil Conflict, 1999

Unfortunately, the Lahore framework remains unimplemented, with the single exception of advanced notification of ballistic missile flight tests on a unilateral basis—in the 'spirit' of the Lahore MoU—although this has generated its own share of controversy over the years. Pakistan's military intrusion across the LoC, allegedly at the time of the Lahore Summit, effectively ended all moves towards regional nuclear stability. Instead, India and Pakistan were involved in an armed conflict with each other for the first time after their nuclear tests; the Kargil conflict of May-July 1999 formally ended with United States facilitation.

In early 1999, Pakistan's regular and irregular forces crossed the LoC and occupied positions in the Kargil sector of Indian-administered Jammu and Kashmir, for reasons that are as yet unclear. When this was detected in early May 1999, Delhi's response was swift and comprehensive, involving the use of land and air forces to evict the intruders from the Indian side of the LoC.

After several weeks of increasingly bloody conflict, Indian forces captured the key heights of Tololing (14 June) and Tiger Hill (early morning on 4 July). With Pakistani forces suffering critical defeats, it was expected to be only a matter of time before they were pushed back across the LoC; but, undoubtedly this would have raised Indian casualties further.

Meanwhile, the United States was urging Pakistan to respect the LoC and withdraw its forces across the LoC, while at the same time, urging India to restrain itself from crossing the LoC to open another front in the conflict. Notwithstanding Delhi's public statements on not using force across the LoC, the potential for escalation into a full-scale conventional war raised fears in the international community of the risk of inadvertent nuclear escalation.

In early July, the Pakistani Prime Minister flew to Washington, concerned over Pakistan's increasing international isolation. At a hastily organized meeting with President Clinton on 4 July, Sharif requested American intervention to stop the fighting and resolve the Kashmir issue. But Clinton came down heavily on Sharif, and told him that a clear Pakistani withdrawal to the LoC was essential. Clinton also told Sharif that Pakistan was preparing its nuclear arsenal for possible deployment at the instructions of the Army Chief, General Musharraf, which was apparently taking place without Sharif's knowledge.

Amidst considerable American pressure, Sharif finally agreed 'to take concrete and immediate steps for the restoration of the LoC', which was accepted by Vajpayee when it was conveyed to him prior to its publicization. In effect, the United States facilitated a formal end to the Kargil conflict, which shortly afterwards saw the withdrawal of all Pakistani forces to its own side of the LoC without many additional Indian casualties. American facilitation on the Kargil conflict—in Delhi's favour— came as quite an unexpected surprise to many in India's Ministries of External Affairs and Defence. This was, in effect, the first time in fifty years that the United States had sided with India against Pakistan 'openly and firmly'. This soon led to a greater 'comfort level' with the United States, followed by Clinton's successful visit to India in March 2000, followed by Vajpayee's visit to the United States in the final days of the Clinton Administration.

American Facilitation in the India-Pakistan Border Confrontation, 2001–2002

Even though the United States became involved in resolving the Kargil conflict, it is the Americanled war on terror in South Asia and the subsequent India-Pakistan border confrontation that has brought about a significant change in American engagement in South Asia. Following the American attack against Afghanistan in October 2001—targeting the terrorist Al-Qaeda leadership responsible for the attacks on the United States and their Taliban hosts—Pakistan became a frontline state for American logistics support and intelligence facilities in Afghanistan. A number of American military personnel and equipment also remain deployed in Pakistani military bases in support of the ongoing war on terror in Afghanistan.

However, the attack on the Indian Parliament on 13 December 2001—allegedly by Pakistanbased Jaish-e-Mohammed terrorists—threatened to disrupt the ongoing American-led military campaign in Afghanistan. As part of its 'coercive diplomacy' against Pakistan, Delhi launched 'Operation Parakram' ('valour') on 19 December 2001, which constituted the largest mobilization of the Indian armed forces. This was a deliberate move, taking place amidst the war on terror, to threaten military action against Pakistan if its demands to end alleged Pakistan-sponsored cross-border terrorism were not met. This included the deployment of India's three strike corps (comprising armoured and mechanized formations) at forward positions on the international border with Pakistan. With Pakistan's countermobilization, nearly one million armed personnel were deployed across the India-Pakistan borders. In view of the nuclear-armed status of both states, there appeared to be considerable risk of nuclear escalation—by misperception or miscalculation—following the break-out of a conventional war. On 20 March 2002, the Director of the Central Intelligence Agency (CIA), George Tenet, warned the United States Senate

Armed Services Committee that the chances of a war in the region were the highest since 1971.

Having repeatedly stressed the sanctity of the LoC during the Kargil war, India's prospective actions—threatening the use of force across the LoC—set off alarm bells in Washington and London. Meanwhile, Pakistan appeared equally determined to counter an Indian military attack with conventional and nuclear forces. With the deliberate disruption of normal diplomatic communication, Delhi and Islamabad were communicating with each other on nuclear and conventional matters on a public basis during much of the ten months of the 2001–2002 border confrontation. These nuclear signals were multiple in nature, carried out at multiple levels, and addressed to multiple constituencies—internal, regional and international. For both India and Pakistan, the most important constituencies were the domestic public, each other and the United States, which had the most influence in the region. For Delhi, the United States could help put pressure on Pakistan to cease cross-border infiltration of militants into Indian-administered Kashmir; for Islamabad, the United States could restrain Delhi from military action.

With tensions heightening following the terrorist attack on an Indian Army residential camp in Kaluchak, Jammu, on 14 May 2002, and Delhi's subsequent nuclear signalling, a flurry of high-level American and British choreographed visits took place to Delhi and Islamabad. The contours of a possible easing of India-Pakistan tensions began to emerge from Jack Straw's visit at the end of May. On 28 May, Straw visited Islamabad, where he urged Musharraf to take action on the ground to counter cross-border 'terrorism' in Indian-administered Kashmir. In Delhi the next day, Straw urged India to exercise restraint and prevent its armed forces from using force across the LoC. He also told Delhi that Musharraf had promised to curb infiltration into India and to close down 'terrorist' camps in Pakistan-administered Kashmir by the time of Armitage's visit to the region in early June. On his return to London on 31 May, Straw publicly expressed his concern over the 'dangerous situation' in the region, 'when you have one million men under arms on either side of the LoC, all in a high state of alert and readiness, both countries have nuclear weapons, and one of them—Pakistan— has said they reserve the right to use them first'. This essentially signalled the issue of travel advisories on 1 June by the Governments of the United States, the United Kingdom, Canada, France, Japan, Australia, New Zealand and others, urging their citizens to leave India and Pakistan immediately, and warned others from travelling to either country. The travel advisories led to an exodus of business visitors, tourists, diplomatic personnel and their dependants, largely from India, as they had already pulled out from Pakistan earlier. Ostensibly ordered for fear of an outbreak of war, this unprecedented step caused much annoyance in Delhi, which perceived it as an attempt to pressure it against launching an attack across the LoC.

On 31 May, United States Secretary of State Colin Powell publicly criticized Pakistan for the 'continuing' infiltration across the LoC, despite Musharraf's assurances that it would be ended. The following day, in an interview with the BBC, Musharraf indicated that 'instructions' had been given by Pakistan to cease such activity. Although it was still too early to say that it had stopped, Powell emphasised that '... when, and if, it does stop, it must also stop permanently'. On 6 June, United States Deputy Secretary of State Richard Armitage arrived in Islamabad to build on Straw's visit, and hammer out a deal between India and Pakistan. After a tough meeting, Musharraf gave Armitage a commitment that he would end cross-border infiltration 'permanently'. This was a considerable improvement on his pledge to Straw a week earlier to curb infiltration into India. While Delhi formally welcomed this development, it expressed caution in terms of implementation. Consequently, Armitage described India-Pakistan tensions as 'a bit down on both sides'. Within days of Armitage's departure from Delhi, the thaw in India-Pakistan tensions was evident. In effect, American facilitation successfully eased India-Pakistan tensions, and ended the ten-month border confrontation—the longest period of military mobilization between the two countries.

India-Pakistan Joint Press Statement, 6 January 2004

In a dramatic development on the sidelines of the twelfth SAARC Summit in Islamabad in January 2004, India and Pakistan agreed to resume an official-level dialogue after a three-year hiatus. The Joint Statement of 6 January 2004 also noted that Delhi agreed to settle Kashmir 'to the satisfaction of both sides', and that Islamabad would not permit 'any territory under Pakistan's control to be used to support terrorism in any manner'. On 18 February 2004, after three days of official-level 'talks on talks' in Islamabad, India and Pakistan agreed to resume their bilateral 'composite dialogue' in May– June 2004, soon after the Indian general elections. This is to take the form of a 'composite dialogue' on eight issues, including two—on 'peace and security, including CBMs' and 'Jammu and Kashmir'— at the Foreign Secretary-level. The two foreign ministers are to meet in August 2004 to review progress. Both Delhi and Islamabad had strong motivations to reach an accord during the SAARC Summit. For Vajpayee, a personal desire for a stable bilateral relationship with Pakistan—his third and final peace effort—had been initiated with his 'hand of friendship' speech in Srinagar in April 2003, and buttressed by approaching general elections in April 2004; for Musharraf, two assassination attempts within eleven days in December 2003 had led to a renewed vigour to fight terrorism of all kinds, along with the increasing radicalization of domestic politics. Vajpayee's rising popularity, seen by the results of the Indian assembly elections in November 2003, also boosted Islamabad's view that it would be advisable to deal with Vajpayee himself.

In addition, American pressure on Islamabad to end cross-border infiltration into Indianadministered Kashmir, and to a lesser extent on India— to begin an official-level dialogue with Pakistan— may also have played a part in the success of bilateral diplomacy on the sidelines of the multilateral summit. Even if the United States had facilitated such a dialogue, it would have been advisable to have maintained this in a low-key manner, for fear of undermining the fledgling peace process.

THE SIACHEN IMPASSE

V.R. Raghavan is highly qualified to write on the Siachen issue. He was Director-General of Military Operations (DGMO) at the Army HQ till 1992; was Commanding General of the Siachen sector and was involved in negotiations with Pakistan on the Siachen dispute. After retirement he earned high repute as an analyst on strategic affairs.

This is by far the most comprehensive work on the subject. It is now 18 years since armed conflict between India and Pakistan erupted in 1984 in that forbidding region. Excellent maps designed by the author himself, rare photographs, and appendices containing texts of pertinent documents enhance the value of the book.

Pakistan intended to acquire a permanent presence in the Siachen. India sensed it and moved in first. "There is a growing body of military opinion that the strategic value of holding defences in the Saltoro is not matched by the effort required for it."

Lt.-Gen (retd) I.S. Gill, Director of Military Operations during the 1971 war with Pakistan, observed: "The amounts of money wasted by both sides is very large indeed. There is nowhere that either side can go in this terrain. You cannot build roads on glacier, which are moving rivers of ice. We have no `strategic-tactical advantage' in this area and nor can Pakistan. Ask any officer who has been on the glacier what Pakistan will do if we pull out, and he will tell you at once that Pakistan will do the same. We must withdraw immediately and unilaterally and save wastage of money which we cannot afford — estimated at Rs.30,000 crores since 1985" (*The Hindu*, March 5, 1997).

It is on the diplomatic aspect that the book disappoints us. The author skirts the issue of responsibility for the failure and maintains studied even-handedness in what is otherwise a very sound work, indeed. He carefully traces the origins of the problem in its historical and geographical setting. Unfortunately, both the July 27, 1949 agreement defining the ceasefire line and the December 11, 1972 agreement defining the Line of Control (LoC) stopped at grid point NJ 9842. They trusted the glaciers to keep the peace.

Once Pakistan's map stretching the LoC to the Karakoram Pass gained currency and it began granting permits to mountaineering expeditions, Indian fears were rightly aroused. It decided to move into the area before Pakistan could. Shortly before his assassination in May 1991, Rajiv Gandhi told the Foreign Correspondents Association in New Delhi: "We don't want to sell out, we want to be friendly. I was friendly with Zia, we almost signed a treaty on Siachen with Zia. The only reason it wasn't signed was that he died (in August 1988). At no time were we soft with Pakistan, but we got our work done" (`A role for India', *Frontline*, May 11, 1991, page 116). Note the fear of being accused of a "sell-out" and of being "soft". Granted the failure in 1988, he offered no explanation for the failure to conclude an accord with Benazir Bhutto in June 1989.

We swear by the Simla Agreement but merrily imply that it does not apply to Siachen since the LoC does not cover that region (it stops at NJ 9842). *The impression is utterly wrong.* Para 1 (ii) of the Agreement embodies an overriding commitment, independently of respect for the LoC. It says "neither side shall unilaterally alter the situation," in regard to "any of the problems between the two countries".

Rajiv Gandhi tacitly acknowledged breach of the Simla Agreement when he said on November 16, 1989 in Kolkata: "`We have *recovered* about 5,000 square kilometres of area *from occupied Kashmir* in Siachen. We will not forgo one square kilometre of that." It was this mindset that wrecked the June 1989 understanding. There have been seven rounds of talks between representatives of the two countries from January 1986 to November 1998. "There seemed no urgency on either side to seek an end to the conflict or to be ready to make the concessions needed to obtain a positive overall outcome."

The even-handedness is laboured. The last three rounds of talks between the Defence Secretaries reflect poorly on India's leaders — the fifth (June 1989), sixth (November 1992) and the seventh (November 1998).

The joint statement issued on June 17, 1989 recorded: "There was *agreement* by both sides to work towards a comprehensive settlement, *based on redeployment of forces* to reduce the chances of conflict, avoidance of the use of force and determination of future positions on the ground *soas to conform with the Simla Agreement* and to ensure durable peace in the Siachen area. The army authorities of both sides will determine these positions" (emphasis added, throughout).

The fact of an "agreement" was explicitly mentioned, so also the two basic principles on which it was based — "redeployment of forces" (that is, withdrawal) and "determination of future positions on the ground so as to conform with the Simla Agreement". In sum, return to positions held by the parties at the time of the Simla Agreement.

This was in striking contrast to all previous joint statements. The next day, separate talks between the Foreign Secretaries concluded. At a joint press conference, Pakistan Foreign Secretary Humayun Khan referred to the Defence Secretaries' meeting. According to the Voice of America's tape, he called it "a significant advance" and spoke of a joint commitment to *"relocation of forces to positions occupied at the time of the Simla Agreement*. The exact location of these positions will be worked out in detail by military authorities of the two countries." Foreign Secretary S.K. Singh said: "I would like to thank the Foreign Secretary, Dr. Humayun Khan, and endorse everything he has said."

The very next day Aftab Seth, Joint Secretary and official spokesman of the Ministry of External Affairs (MEA) in New Delhi, said that no agreement had been reached on troop withdrawals. "There was no indication of any such agreement in the joint press statement issued at the end of the talks." This statement was palpably untrue. The two meetings of military representatives during July 11-13 and August 17-18, 1989 did not help.

In the sixth round held in New Delhi from November 2 to 4, 1992, India proposed (a) the demarcation of the LoC in the area as a matter of priority; (b) redeployment of troops on both sides to agreed positions, but *after recording existing positions*; (c) definition of a Zone of Disengagement which would come into being consequent on the redeployment and (d) undertakings by both sides not to 1. reoccupy vacated positions; 2. occupy new positions "across the alignment determined by the vacated positions", 3. undertake any military or mountaineering activity in the zone.

The Zone and the alignment of existing positions marked a clear retreat from the June 1989 agreement to India's former position. The monitoring would have been along the existing positions. The zone itself was defined to accord with the existing Actual Ground Position Line.

Pakistan's riposte was to propose a triangle whose points were Indira Col in the west and the Karakoram Pass in the east, both joined to NJ 9842. Troops of both countries would be withdrawn from the area within this triangle. The *status quo* would be maintained pending demarcation of the LoC by a Joint Commission.

Both proposals were non-starters. Put off by the Indian proposal, Pakistan made one that India could not possibly have accepted. However — *and this is to fact which has not been publicised* — confronted by the deadlock, Pakistan sought to revive the 1989 agreement by *formally making a proposal which was a major concession to India; namely, that existing positions would be recorded, albeit in an annexure* and on the understanding that it would not constitute a basis for a claim to the area legally, morally or politically. The annexure would mention the points at which the troops will "redeploy" (read, retreat). Demarcation of the LoC will follow thereafter. *India did not respond to the proposal, and the talks ended.*

However, in the technical talks in November 1992 it was agreed that: (a) India would withdraw to Zingrulma and Pakistan to Goma at the base of the Bilafond Glacier, and (b) surveillance would be undertaken by helicopter.

On November 6, an MEA spokesman acknowledged that "there was a certain progress made in terms of technical details of the disengagement". He claimed that the 1989 talks foundered on this point but that was not the case this time. He did not claim that any accord had been reached. Thereafter reports appeared in the press that India's concessions would not go beyond "minor adjustments" on the Saltoro Range.

A year later, K.K. Katyal reported in *The Hindu* of January 25, 1994: "As regards Siachen, India has *veered to the view taken by Pakistan towards the end of 1992.* There is an element of frankness in New Delhi's explanation that the *domestic political environment of that period came in the way of acceptance.* In doing so, India may have exposed itself to criticism that decisions on crucial issues were allowed to be influenced by narrow domestic considerations."

The Non-Paper India gave Pakistan on January 24, 1994 unctuously claimed: "1. During the discussions between India and Pakistan at the Sixth Round of Talks held at New Delhi, 1992, on Siachen, *a broad understanding had been reached* on disengagement and redeployment, monitoring, maintenance of peace and implementation schedule. 2. It was agreed that immediate focus should be on restoring peace and tranquillity in Siachen. Towards this end, without prejudice to the positions taken by either side in the earlier rounds of talks (India's position: Point NJ 9842 should extend to Sia Kangri; Pakistan's position; Point NJ 9842 should join with Karakoram Pass), both sides agreed that the delineation of the LoC beyond NJ 9842 shall be examined by a Joint Commission later. 3. Both sides agreed that to reduce tension in Siachen, the two sides shall disengage *from authenticated positions* they are presently occupying and shall fall back to positions as under: ... ." This was sent with Foreign Secretary J.N. Dixit's approval, obviously. He retired from service on January 31, 1994. India was to disengage from its positions on the Saltoro Ridge to those east and north of Zingrulma. Pakistan was to withdraw from its positions to a defined line to the west. The area so vacated was to constitute a Zone of Complete Disengagement. Pakistan's Non-Paper of February 19, 1994 flatly denied that any such agreement was reached in 1992 and relied on the 1989 accord. It sought, obviously, to whittle down its major concession in 1992 — recording the existing positions in an annexure.

No sooner did George Fernandes become Defence Minister in March 1998 than he decided to wipe out the fundamental principle on which the talks had proceeded for over a decade; namely, disengagement based on mutual withdrawal. He declared on July 18, 1998 that "India needs to hold on to Siachen, both for strategic reasons and wider security in the region". Lt.-Gen. Raghavan's book ably refutes this absurd view. Fernandes adopted it to secure political mileage and to court the hardliners in the Bharatiya Janata Party as well as the Army. He left the seventh round of talks held on November 6, 1998 doomed to certain failure. The four-point proposal made by India on November 6 was crafted to ensure its rejection — comprehensive ceasefire based on a freeze of "present ground positions", discussions on the modalities for implementing the ceasefire within an agreed time-frame, a "bilateral monitoring mechanism" and authentication of existing ground positions. Earlier, inspired press reports had it that the talks would be "dominated by one issue — the control of strategic positions along the Saltoro Range". In short, the *status quo* should be preserved.

Having resiled from the 1989 agreement and aborted an accord in 1992, India itself made an offer in 1994 based on the fundamentals of 1989 and 1994. In 1998 it abandoned all these and insisted on preserving the *status quo.* At the end of the talks, on November 6, 1998, the DGMO, Lt.-Gen. Inder K. Verma, claimed that the area north and east of grid point NJ 9842 where the LoC ended, had been under India's control even before the Simla Agreement was signed on July 3, 1972. The claim was as novel and belated as it was utterly untrue. It flew in the face of the incontrovertible facts about the 1984 Operation Meghdoot and of Rajiv Gandhi's statement on November 16, 1989.

The author grapples with the record on these three episodes of 1989, 1992 and 1998 with remarkable delicacy. In 1989 "there had been some informal contacts established between the two Prime Ministers. These had led to the understanding that a mutual pullback by the two militaries from the Saltoro would not be difficult to accomplish. *The Indian delegation had therefore been given a mandate to work for a disengagement by both armies.*" But Pakistan sought "to retain its position unchanged". He blames it for the failure and deals thus with S.K. Singh's remarks in endorsement. "He had in fact only endorsed the sentiment that there had been progress during the bilateral talks. Confronted with Pakistan's interpretation of the talks as amounting to an Indian pullback, the Indian government denied that there had been any such agreement." This is contrary to the joint statement as well as the record of the 1989 episode.

On the 1992 talks the author does little better. "It was now the turn of the Indian side to *find* (sic.) a stumbling block to progress on the Zone of Disengagement idea. Senior members of the Indian team briefed the top political leadership about the outcome of the talks. The outcome had been on lines which had been discussed during pre-talk sessions at the highest levels. The Zone of Disengagement, which had been approved, was *now* found to be unacceptable. Either the support of major political parties to the outcome had not been forthcoming, or the political executive had second thoughts in view of the violence that was being instigated by Pakistan in Jammu and Kashmir. Relations between the Congress government and the BJP were also beginning to harden due to differences on the Babri Masjid issue. These developments had not been anticipated." This defensive explanation is followed by an assertion that is untrue.

"*The Pakistanis were in any case unwilling to concede the need for marking the current deployment*, and were extremely hesitant about a Zone of Disengagement which even remotely indicated the ground reality before the pullback commenced." This is grossly misleading. The truth is that, true to form, Prime Minister P.V. Narasimha Rao went back on the brief he had given the Indian team. Pakistan's delegation was kept waiting only to be told that — *despite its vital concession on recording the existing positions* — no further talks would be held. This, incidentally, was repeated by Vajpayee in Agra in July 2001. The author remarks: "In India, it was essential that the major political parties in Parliament agreed to the disengagement plan. It would *as such be unfair to entirely blame the government of the day in New Delhi* for the failure of negotiations in the sixth round." Who else should share the blame, pray? Public opinion, apparently, does not exist in Pakistan or China. The author, likewise, puts a gloss on India's stand in the Seventh Round (1998). He notes, *but does not criticise,* the fact that India's proposal "indicated a significant shift in positions taken earlier". Yet, he criticises Pakistan for rejecting a ceasefire based on the rejection of the decade-old agreed principle of withdrawal by both sides.

Raghavan asserts that the "new dimension to these (Indian) proposals was that they referred to the Saltoro Range. There was no mention of the Siachen glacier". The official press note, which he cites in support, however, said: "We have proposed an agreement on ceasing fire *in Siachen*." He ends, predictably, with Kargil. His solution is simple. "A freeze on fighting through an agreed ceasefire, a commitment to stop changing the status quo on ground, and reducing some forces over an agreed period after informing each other, can provide the basis for a deliberate and carefully planned exercise."

Nationalism triumphs over objectivity. Raghavan misses the point that India wants to freeze the *status quo* it altered militarily to its advantage in 1984. Pakistan the revisionist, cannot accept that, either on the LoC or in Siachen. As always, even the best of us, like Raghavan himself, refuse to look beyond our own narrow interests whether on Siachen, Kashmir or the boundary dispute with China and despite the fact that compromise will be in India's larger, long-term interests.

J.N. Dixit was India's High Commissioner to Pakistan in 1989 and Foreign Secretary in 1992. His versions are tabulated below:

1. "The fifth round of talks on Sir Creek and the sixth round of talks on Siachen were held in Delhi between 2 and 6 November (1992). Both the meetings were resultless because Pakistan refused to budge from its highly technical stance on the issues involved" (Dixit's book, *Anatomy of a Flawed Inheritance* 1995; page 168).
2. Asghar Ali Engineer in *The Hindu* of February 24, 1996 reported Dixit's claims at a seminar. In 1992, he along with his then Pakistani counterpart had evolved an agreed draft to solve the Siachen issue. However, the Prime Minister had said that though it was good he could not accept it as he was not sure whether Parliament would support him."
3. Dixit's *Memoirs of a Foreign Secretary* (1996, page 125): "The sixth round of talks between the Defence Secretaries of India and Pakistan regarding Siachen had been held from 2 to 5 November 1992. My colleague, Defence Secretary N. N. Vohra and Pakistan's Defence Secretary Syed Salim Abbas Jallani almost finalised an agreement for the redeployment of Indian and Pakistani forces. I expected that this would put an end to a strategically futile and economically costly confrontation. Three factors prevented the agreement from getting governmental approval from India and Pakistan. First, for its part, Pakistan continued to harp on the precondition that India should agree to the line of control notionally being accepted as running north-eastwards from the grid reference point known as NJ 9842. Secondly, Pakistan continued to express reservations about finalising *a joint cartographic document* which would pinpoint positions from which troops of both countries should pull back. Thirdly, our own government had reservations at the political level about approving the agreement reached at that point of time, because of increased levels of Pakistan-sponsored violence in Jammu and Kashmir and also because of the intensity of the hostile diplomatic and publicity activities against India in which Pakistan was engaged. It was felt that Indian public opinion and Parliament would not be supportive of any positive move forward on Siachen at that point. At

the official level, we felt if this was the case, we need not have got into the very detailed discussion which we had with Pakistan in November 1992."

The first two assertions are untrue. Pakistan had agreed to record existing positions. Narasimha Rao's refusal to ratify the understanding was not due to the factors Dixit cites but due entirely to the unworthy ones that Katyal mentioned.

4. Dixit's article in *Outlook* of November 2, 1998 put forth a totally different version altogether. "One wonders why both countries do not implement the agreement already arrived at and *initialled* on Siachen and the Tulbul navigation project finalised between 1990 and 1994." A professional diplomat, he used the word "initialled" advisedly, one would think. However it is untrue. No accord on Siachen was reached let alone reduced to writing and — *"initialled"*. This novel assertion is contradicted by his own earlier accounts. The Non-Paper of January 23, 1994, given after the Foreign Secretaries' talks from January 1 to 3, 1994 in Islamabad made no such claim.
5. Dixit's book *India, Pakistan in War and Peace* (2002) repeats (page 288) what he wrote in his memoirs in 1996; *not the claim of initialling*. Dixit, no doubt, considers his versions from 1995 to 2002, to be consistent with one another. Others may be forgiven for holding a different view.

   Pakistan's version of the May 1989 understanding is set out in Benazir Bhutto's National Security and Foreign Affairs Adviser Iqbal Akhund's memoirs *Trial and Error* (Oxford University Press, 2000; pages 99-112). During his visit to Pakistan in June 1989, Rajiv Gandhi remarked: "If only your Foreign Secretary had not mentioned the 1972 positions in talking of redeployment, we would not be having all this trouble." Akhund remarks that this was "a confirmation that he was having problems with the Opposition and, probably, with the Army". The year 1989 was an election year. In 1992, Narasimha Rao had no such excuse. He lacked leadership, a quality that did not grace any of his successors either — H.D. Deve Gowda, I.K. Gujral, or Atal Behari Vajpayee of the Agra fame.

Akhund confirmed Rajiv's version (page 105). His able aide, Ronen Sen, now High Commissioner in London, proposed splitting the difference. The LoC would have "run due north, that is, up to the Chinese border in a ruler-straight line"; between Indira Col in the west and Karakoram Pass in the east.

Thanks to Narasimha Rao's attitude in 1992, Pakistan withdrew its concession in 1994 and linked Siachen to the 'K' issue. It must be delinked now. Both sides must withdraw from the Siachen.

SIACHEN GLACIER

The Siachen Glacier is a glacier located in the eastern Karakoram range in the Himalayas at about 35.421226°N 77.109540°E, just northeast of the point NJ9842 where the Line of Control between India and Pakistan ends. At 76 km (47 mi) long, it is the longest glacier in the Karakoram and second-longest in the world's non-polar areas. It falls from an altitude of 5,753 m (18,875 ft) above sea level at its head at Indira Col on the China border down to 3,620 m (11,875 ft) at its terminus.

The entire Siachen Glacier, with all major passes, is currently under the administration of India since 1984. Pakistan controls the region west of Saltoro Ridge, far away from the glacier, with Pakistani posts located 3,000 ft below more than 100 Indian posts on Saltoro Ridge.

The Siachen Glacier lies immediately south of the great drainage divide that separates the Eurasian Plate from the Indian subcontinent in the extensively glaciated portion of the Karakoram sometimes called the "Third Pole". The glacier lies between the Saltoro Ridge immediately to the west and the main Karakoram range to the east. The Saltoro Ridge originates in the north from the Sia Kangri peak on the China border in the Karakoram range. The crest of the Saltoro Ridge's altitudes range from 5,450 to 7,720 m (17,880 to 25,330 feet). The major passes on this ridge are, from north to south, Sia La at 5,589 m (18,336 ft), Bilafond La at 5,450 m (17,880 ft), and Gyong La at 5,689 m (18,665 ft). The average winter snowfall is more than 1000 cm (35 ft) and temperatures can dip to "50 °C ("58 °F). Including all tributary glaciers, the Siachen Glacier system covers about 700 km^2 (270 sq mi).

Etymology

"Sia" in the Balti language refers to the rose family plant widely dispersed in the region. "Chun" refers to any object found in abundance. Thus the name Siachen refers to a land with an abundance of roses. The naming of the glacier itself, or at least its currency, is attributed to Tom Longstaff.

DISPUTE

Both India and Pakistan claim sovereignty over the entire Siachen region. US and Pakistani maps in the 1970s and 1980s consistently showed a dotted line from NJ9842 (the northernmost demarcated point of the India-Pakistan cease-fire line, also known as the *Line of Control*) to the Karakoram Pass, which India believed to be a cartographic error and in violation of the Shimla Agreement. In 1984, India launched Operation Meghdoot, a military operation that gave India control over all of the Siachen Glacier, including its tributaries.Between 1984 and 1999, frequent skirmishes took place between

India and Pakistan. Indian troops under Operation Meghdoot pre-empted Pakistan's Operation Ababeel by just one day to occupy most of the dominating heights on Saltoro Ridge to the west of Siachen Glacier. However, more soldiers have died from the harsh weather conditions in the region than from combat. Pakistan lost 353 soldiers in various operations recorded between 2003 and 2010 near Siachen, including 140 Pakistani personnel killed in 2012 Gayari Sector avalanche. Between January 2012 and July 2015, 33 Indian soldiers lost their lives due to adverse weather. In December 2015, Indian Union Minister of State for Defence Rao Inderjit Singh said in a written reply in the Lok Sabha that a total of 869 Army personnel have lost their lives on the Siachen glacier due to climatic conditions and environmental and other factors till date since the Army launched Operation Meghdoot in 1984. Both India and Pakistan continue to deploy thousands of troops in the vicinity of Siachen and attempts to demilitarise the region have been so far unsuccessful. Prior to 1984, neither country had any military forces in this area.

Aside from the Indian and Pakistani military presence, the glacier region is unpopulated. The nearest civilian settlement is the village of Warshi, 10 miles downstream from the Indian base camp. The region is also extremely remote, with limited road connectivity. On the Indian side, roads go only as far as the military base camp at Dzingrulma at 35.1663°N 77.2162°E, 72 km from the head of the glacier.The Indian Army has developed various means to reach the Siachen region, including the Manali-Leh-Khardung La-Siachen route. In 2012, Chief of Army Staff of the Indian Army General Bikram Singh said that the Indian Army should stay in the region for strategic advantages, and because a "lot of blood has been shed" by Indian armed personnel for Siachen. According to the present ground positions, relatively stable for over a decade, India maintains control over all of the 76 kilometres (47 mi) long Siachen Glacier and all of its tributary glaciers, as well as all the main passes and heights of the Saltoro Ridge immediately west of the glacier, including Sia La, Bilafond La, Gyong La, Yarma La (6,100m), and Chulung La (5,800m). Pakistan controls the glacial valleys immediately west of the Saltoro Ridge.According to *TIME* magazine, India gained over 1,000 square miles (3,000 km^2) in territory because of its 1980s military operations in Siachen. In February 2016, Indian Defence Minister Manohar Parrikar stated in Parliament that India will not vacate Siachen as there is trust deficit with Pakistan and also said that 915 people have lost their lives in Siachen since Operation Meghdoot in 1984. As per official records, only 220 Indian soldiers have been killed by enemy bullets since 1984 in Siachen area. India has categorically stated that India will not pull its army from Siachen until the 110-km long AGPL is first authenticated, delineated and then demarcated.

The 1949 Karachi agreement only carefully delineated the line of separation to point NJ9842, after which, the agreement states that the line of separation would continue "thence north to the glaciers."

According to the Indian stance, the line of separation should continue roughly northwards along the Saltoro Range, to the west of the Siachen glacier beyond NJ9842; international boundary lines that follow mountain ranges often do so by following the watershed drainage divide such as that of the Saltoro Range. The 1972 Simla Agreement made no change to the 1949 Line of Control in this northernmost sector.

DRAINAGE

The glacier's melting waters are the main source of the Nubra River in the Indian region of Ladakh, which drains into the Shyok River. The Shyok in turn joins the 3000 kilometre-long Indus River which flows through Pakistan. Thus, the glacier is a major source of the Indus and feeds the largest irrigation system in the world.

ENVIRONMENTAL ISSUES

The glacier was uninhabited before 1984, and the presence of thousands of troops since then has introduced pollution and melting on the glacier. To support the troops, glacial ice has been cut and melted with chemicals. Dumping of non-biodegradable waste in large quantities and the use of arms and ammunition have considerably affected the ecosystem of the region.

Glacial retreat

Preliminary findings of a survey by Pakistan Meteorological Department in 2007 revealed that the Siachen glacier has been retreating for the past 30 years and is melting at an alarming rate. The study of satellite images of the glacier showed that the glacier is retreating at a rate of about 110 meters a year and that the glacier size has decreased by almost 35 percent. In an eleven-year period, the glacier had receded nearly 800 meters, and in seventeen years about 1700 meters. It is predicted that the glaciers of the Siachen region will be reduced to about one-fifth of their 2011 size by 2035. In the twenty-nine-year period 1929–1958, well before the military occupation, the glacial retreat was recorded to be about 914 meters. One of the reasons cited for the recent glacial retreat is chemical blasting, done for constructing camps and posts. In 2001 India laid oil pipelines (about 250 kilometres long) inside the glacier to supply kerosene and aviation fuel to the outposts from base camps. As of 2007, the temperature rise at Siachen was estimated at 0.2 degree Celsius annually, causing melting, avalanches, and crevasses in the glacier.

Waste dumping

The waste produced by the troops stationed there is dumped in the crevasses of the glacier. Mountaineers who visited the area while on climbing expeditions witnessed large amount of garbage, empty ammunition shells, parachutes etc. dumped on the glacier, that neither decomposes nor can be burned because of the extreme climatic conditions. About 1000 kilograms of waste is produced and dumped in glacial crevasses daily by the Indian forces. The Indian army is said to have planned a "Green Siachen, Clean Siachen" campaign to airlift the garbage from the glacier, and to use biodigestors for biodegradable waste in the absence of oxygen and freezing temperatures. Almost forty percent (40%) of the waste left at the glacier is of plastic and metal composition, including toxins such as cobalt, cadmium and chromium that eventually affect the water of the Shyok River (which ultimately enters the Indus River near Skardu.) The Indus is used for drinking and irrigation. Research is being done by scientists of The Energy and Resources Institute, to find ways for successfully disposing the garbage generated at the glacier using scientific means. Some scientists of the Defence Research and Development Organisation who went on an expedition to Antarctica are also working to produce a bacterium that can thrive in extreme weather conditions and can be helpful in decomposing the biodegradable waste naturally.

Fauna and flora

The flora and fauna of the Siachen region are also affected by the huge military presence. The region is home to rare species including snow leopard, brown bear and ibex that are at risk because of the military presence.

BORDER CONFLICT

The glacier's region is the highest battleground on Earth, where Pakistan and India have fought intermittently since April 1984. Both countries maintain a permanent military presence in the region at a height of over 6,000 m (20,000 ft). Both India and Pakistan have wished to disengage from the costly military outposts. However, after the Pakistani incursions during the Kargil War in 1999, India abandoned plans to withdraw from Siachen without official recognition of the current line of control by Pakistan, wary of further Pakistani incursions if they vacate the Siachen Glacier posts without such recognition.

Prime Minister Manmohan Singh became the first Indian Prime Minister to visit the area, during which he called for a peaceful resolution of the problem. After that present Prime Minister Narendra Modi also visited this place. President of Pakistan Asif Ali Zardari also visited the area during 2012 with Pakistan Army Chief Gen. Ashfaq Parvez Kayani. Both of them showed their commitment to resolve Siachen conflict as early as possible. In the previous year, the President of India, Abdul Kalam became the first head of state to visit the area.

Since September 2007, India has opened up limited mountaineering and trekking expeditions to the area. The first group included cadets from Chail Military School, National Defence Academy, National Cadet Corps, Indian Military Academy, Rashtriya Indian Military College and family members of armed forces officers. The expeditions are also meant to show to the international audience that Indian troops hold "almost all dominating heights" on the key Saltoro Ridge and to show that Pakistani troops are nowhere near the Siachen Glacier. Ignoring protests from Pakistan, India maintains that it does not need anyone's approval to send trekkers to Siachen, in what it says is essentially its own territory. In addition, the Indian Army's Army Mountaineering Institute (AMI) functions out of the region.

PEACE PARK PROPOSAL

The idea of declaring the Siachen region a "Peace Park" was presented by environmentalists and peace activists in part to preserve the ecosystem of the region badly affected by the military presence. In September 2003, the governments of India and Pakistan were urged by the participants of 5th World Parks Congress held at Durban, to establish a peace park in the Siachen region to restore the natural biological system and protect species whose lives are at risk.

Italian ecologist Giuliano Tallone terming the ecological life at serious risk, proposed setting up of *Siachen Peace Park* at the conference. After a proposal of a transboundary Peace Park was floated, the International Mountaineering and Climbing Federation (UIAA) and the International Union for Conservation of Nature (IUCN) organised a conference at Geneva and invited Indian and Pakistani mountaineers (Mandip Singh Soin, Harish Kapadia, Nazir Sabir and Sher Khan). The region was nominated for inclusion in the United Nations' World Heritage List as a part of the Karakoram range, but was deferred by the World Heritage Committee. The area to the east and west of the Siachen region have already been declared national parks: the Karakoram Wildlife Sanctuaryin India and the Central Karakoram National Park in Pakistan.

Sandia National Laboratories organised conferences where military experts and environmentalists from both India and Pakistan and also from other countries were invited to present joint papers. Kent L. Biringer, a researcher at Cooperative Monitoring Center of Sandia Labs suggested setting up *Siachen Science Center*, a high-altitude research centre where scientists and researchers from both the countries can carry out research activities related to glaciology, geology, atmospheric sciences and other related fields.

SIACHEN: THE STALEMATE CONTINUES

Engagement over Siachin glacier has remained a dilemma for both India and Pakistan. Are the two fighting only for military prestige' Since 1984, the snow-warriors of India and Pakistan have been locked in supremacy for the control of Siachin glacier. Its inhospitable terrain has taken heavy toll of men and resources on both sides. Fiction and folklore have become mingled with Siachin warfare. Siachin being world's largest non-polar glacier is also sometimes referred to as the third pole. It is 78 kms long and situated at an altitude of 5,472 metres above sea level. Siachin glacier is the great Himalayan watershed that demarcates central Asia from the Indian sub-continent. It also separates Pakistan from China in this region.

ROOTS OF THE CONFLICT

The roots of the conflict over Siachin lie in the non-demarcations on the western side on the map beyond NJ9842 1949 Karachi agreement and 1972 Shimla agreement presumed that it was not feasible for human habitation to survive north of 9842. In 1949 after the ceasfire line agreement was signed between India and Pakistan, cease-fire line was delineated to a point north of Shyok river. A similar indeterminate Line of Control exists north east of Siachin glacier on the border with China.

Under 1963 Sino-border agreement, Pakistan ceded the 5000 sq. km Shaksgam valley to China. It lies to the north east of Siachen glacier. Article six of this agreement mentioned that the 'two parties have agreed that, after the settlement of Kashmir dispute between India and Pakistan, the sovereign authority concerned will reopen negotiations with the government of People's Republic of China on the boundary, so as to sign a formal boundary treaty to replace the present agreement, provided that, in the event of that sovereign authority being Pakistan, the provisions of the present agreement and the aforesaid protocol be maintained.' Intriguingly, this clause was dropped by China in 1987.

To the east beyond the Shaksgam valley lies China's vulnerable Sinkiang region. As nothing was demarcated on the map beyond point NJ9842, Shaksgam valley was a no-main's land. China also stands in possession of forcible grab of 37,555 sq. kms of Ladakh territory-Aksai Chin. It built a motorable road from Gartok in Tibet via Rudok through Aksai Chin to Sinkiang in 1958.

Since 1984, India and Pakistan have been claiming the Siachin wasteland as their territory and engaged in grabbing the more advantageous position along the line. In early eighties Karakoram ranges became special destination for many western Army expeditions. Subsequently, this area came to be shown as part of Pakistan in the maps issued by western countries. This alerted India. Pakistan claims that Siachin is part of country's northern areas. It says that this area has remained under its administrative control since 1947.

India's contention is that this undemarcated area was never under the control of Pakistan and cites Shimla agreement as a proof.

The 78 km long Siachin glacier is hemmed in between the Saltoro ridge line to the west and the main Karakoram range to the east. The Saltoro ridge originates from the Sia Kangri in the Karakoram range and the altitudes range from 18,000 to 24,000 ft.

The major passes on this ridge are Sia La at 20,000 ft and Bila Fond La at 19,000 ft. India's position on Line of Control is based on the terrain configuration, which runs along the Saltoro ridge line upto Sia Kangri. Pakistan claims that the Line of Control is a straight line joining NJ9842 to Karakoram pass north of the Indian Dault Bag Ouldi outpost. The Pakistani claim does not relate to the accepted principles of frontier demarcation. It cuts across the river valleys Nubra and Shyok of Indian Ladakh, 10,000 sq km of Indian territory, which includes Siachen glacier.

Presently India holds two-thirds of glacier and commands two of the three passes. Pakistan controls Gyong La pass that overlooks the Shyok and Nubra river Valley and India's access to Leh district. Indian imperatives are that if Pakistan is allowed to control the glacier, it would endanger the security of Ladakh and also of J&K. With Chinese already in control of Aksai Chin, it is argued that the whole of northern Ladakh would be imperilled if Pakistan is allowed unfettered movement through Siachen. In long-term perspective, Indian strategists also feel that this Himalayan watershed can yield it access to resource rich Central Asian republics through the Afghan panhandle.

Through its control of the glacier, Pakistan intends not only to threaten Leh-Ladakh but also to take her border to meet that of China. It believes then it can find an alternate route to the treacherous Karakoram highway. On the face of it, Pakistan argument looks simply ridiculous. Indian occupation of Siachen can hardly threaten Sino-Pak Karakoram highway, as the highway is nearly 200 km of broken mountainous terrain away from Siachen.

Of and on Pakistan activates Siachen prior to any formal talks with India and links Siachen to the Kashmir issue. Its purpose being to focus the 'core' issue of Kashmir. By making key Siachen as a potential flash point, especially now in a nuclearised environment, it seeks third party intervention in its favour.

Confrontation

By the begining of 1984, Pakistani plans for occupying Saltoro ridge and Siachen glacier were ready. India pre-empted this by launching Operation Meghdoot in April 1984. An advance unit from Kumaon Regiment was airlifted, which established Indian posts on Siachen. India gained control of the two passes Sia La and Bilfond La, which overlook the strategic Karakoram highway. Pakistan vainly tried to recapture these passes in late 1984 and 1985.

In 1986, Pakistani army received another setback. In an extraordinary act of valour and skill, Subedar Bana Singh captured 21,000 ft high Qaid Post from Pakistanis. India renamed the post as Bana Post and this earned Bana Singh India's first and only Paramvir Chakra after 1971. After this defeat, Benazir Bhutto tauntingly told late General Zia-ul-Haque to wear a burqa.

To dislodge India from Bilfond La, Pakistan raised an elite Special Service Group (SSG) commandos in 1987. It built up Khapalu garrison with eight thousand troops. General Pervez Mushraff, then incharge SSG, and now Pak Army Chief, spent his first soldier's night with SSG at Siachen. Pakistan launched the assault in September 1987 and suffered a crushing defeat.

Though Pakistan failed in its attempt to capture the Bilfond La pass but Indian also lost the strategic initiative. It failed to appreciate that takeover of Khapalu rather than the control of either Siachen or the Saltoro-ridge line was strategic to Indian security interests in the area.

Distance between Khapalu and Saltoro passes is only forty kms as crow flies. Defence strategists believe that any attack on Leh from Pakistan via Saltoro and Siachen would be logistically and humanly difficult. The likely route can be only along the Shyok river to Khardong La, which leads on to Leh. Obviously, it would have made sense strategically, if Indian army had taken over Khapalu before Pak build up in 1987, using Shyok river route, which is militarily, viable. But then, this is the sad story of India's repeated failures in appreciating strategic security interests.

In 1990 there were again skirmishes on the periphery of the glacier. In 1995 Pak SSG suffered forty casualties in an attack on an outpost by Sikh battalion. An IAF MI-17 helicopter was shot down in 1996. In 1998 there were five abortive attacks in fifteen days by Pakistan on Ashok, Malon, Fateh 5770 and other posts. Last Pak attack was on March 10,1999 some three weeks after the Lahore summit. of and on artillery fire is exchanged intermittently. Pakistan's elite commandos and soldiers of 36 Baluch Regiment have failed to gain a toehold on Saltoro crestline, Indira Col, to an anonymous benchmark NJ9842. This has forced Pakistan to shift its strategy from one of offensive to containment by forcing huge expenditure on India.

Currently Pakistan maintains three battalions, while India has seven battalions defending Siachen. Pakistan spends Rs 10 million a day, which amounts to Rs 3.6 billion a year. Indian expenditure is Rs 14.40 billion a year. So far Pakistan has spent Rs 50.2 billion, a huge drain on financial resources for a small poor country like Pakistan.

On an average, one Pakistani soldier is killed every fourth day, while one Indian soldier is killed every second day. 1344 Pak soldiers have died on Siachen since 1984. Ninety five percent casualties have been due to extreme and intolerable weather conditions. The number of wounded is nearly twenty times more, while the number is in thousands of those traumatized.

Dialogue

The huge drain on resources have forced India and Pakistan to open a dialogue for a disengagement on Siachen, without prejudice to either side's actual ground position locations or its interpretation of the extension of LoC beyond NJ9842, where it was terminated in 1972.

As per India the line follows the Saltoro crestline to Indira Col, while Pakistan draws a straight line from NJ9842 to Karakoram pass. This triangle of dispute is made up of NJ9842, Indira Col and Karakoram pass.

The zone of disengagement, however, would require the Indian troops to move east of Siachen glacier around its snout in the Nubra valley, while the Pakistani troops would have to pull back west to fall back positions around Goma-NJ9842. The Indian Himalaya brigade is based in Pratapur, while Pakistan's Frontier Controlled Northern Areas (FCNA) functions from Skardu. Pakistan's compulsions for talks on Siachen stem from a reality that India commands higher and more commanding posts on Sia La and Bilfond La passes.

These two passes provide access across the Saltoro ridge into Siachen from Pakistan side. As it has been unable to dislodge India, Pakistan army has settled for containing it to the Saltoro, while strengthening its build-up in adjoining Skardu, facing Kargil sector of Ladakh.

In June 1990, Pakistan after deploying additional troops close to the glacier, called for 'talks'. Army brass in Northern Command prevailed upon VP Singh, the then Prime Minister not to fall into the Pak trap on settlement of glacier. It warned that army can do little if the two strategic mountain passes, Sia Lal and Bilfond La were handed to Pakistan.

Pakistan subsequently mounted pressure through its patrons. In March 1993 in its report titled 'India and America after the cold war', prepared by U.S. think tank Carnegie Endowment Study Group called upon Indian Prime Minister to unilaterally withdraw from the contested Siachen glacier as a stimulus to 'broaden' the dialogue on confidence building measures. Earlier, two UN military observers, who had sneaked incognito into the Siachen area were pushed out by the Indian Army.

The Prospect

Pakistan has been sending contradictory signals on disengagement in Siachen. Prior to Lahore talks, Pak army Chief, Parvez Mushraff went in the company of Mr Nawaz Sharif to Siachen and said that the challenge to Pakistan security was from within. He ruled out any threat from India. But soon after the Lahore summit he backtracked on delinking Siachen from Kashmir issue and Okayed attack on an Indian post. This has raised doubts about Pakistan's real intentions. India proposes six-point formula, which includes cessation of cartographic aggression and culminating in the withdrawl of forces by both sides. Pakistan opposes it and calls for first withdrawing forces and then delineating an extension of LoC beyond NJ9842.

Meanwhile, Siachen demili-tarisation, has been included in the agenda for dialogue in the forthcoming foreign secretaries meet between India and Pakistan. Only time will say whether the two will agree on de-escalation over Siachen, given the political ramifications of dis-engagement

5

Siachen Dispute: India and Pakistan's Glacial Fight

Virtually hidden from public view, the world's highest conflict is moving into its fourth decade. The struggle between India and Pakistan over the Siachen glacier has even spawned a new term: "oropolitics", or mountaineering with a political goal. The word is derived from the Greek for mountain, and Indian army colonel Narendra Kumar can justly claim to be the modern father of oropolitics because his pioneering explorations paved the way for India to take the glacier in early 1984.

But what started as a battle with crampons and climbing rope has turned into high-altitude trench warfare, with the two rival armies frozen - often literally - in pretty much the same positions as 30 years ago.

THE SIACHIN GLACIER DISPUTE

Siachin glacier is about 75 km long and 2 to 8 km wide. This glacier has the distinction of being the largest glacier outside the Polar or sub-Polar regions. It covers an area of about 450 sq km at an altitude of about 5,800 metre above sea level in Ladakh region near Karakoram Range.

The Karakoram highway between China and Pakistan is very close which enhances its strategic value. India occupies about two-third area of the glacier in its south-eastern part. Here Nubra river emerges from Karakoram glacier and meets the Shyok river which is a tributary of the Indus river. Indian troops use the Nubra valley to reach the glacier. The glacier has four passes. Of these Gasherbrum, Saltoro and Vilafondala are in India and Gyongla is in Pakistan.

It is worth mentioning that LoC demarcated in 1972 after the Shimla agreement stopped dead at the grid reference NJ. 9842, with no indication as to how it would run along the 70-odd km left to the Chinese border in the north.

While Pakistan decided to extend this line eastward to Karakoram Pass, thus claiming an area two-thirds the size of Sikkim, India's decision was to go by the wording of 1949 Karachi agreement that was superseded by LoC of 1972 which spoke of line "thence northwards joining the glaciers". Further, India wants Pakistan to officially recognise the Actual Ground Position Line (AGPL) begin NJ. 9892 grid point as a pre-requisite to de-militarisation of the Siachin glacier.

Pakistani troops established an observation post on Saltoro range. To counter this, India launched Operation Meghdoot on April 13, 1984. Since then both the countries are maintaining troops in this inhospitable environment at a very high altitude. A number of skirmishes have taken place making it the highest battlefield in the world.

Sending men and material in such an area is a very expensive affair. On an average India spends about Rs. 4 crore per day for maintaining troops in this hostile area. Pakistan also spends about Rs. 1 crore for the same purpose. Casualties on both sides of the border are also very high.

Even in normal circumstances, Indian troops suffer one casualty every second day while Pakistani troops suffer one casualty every fourth day. Besides there are psychological disorders, frostbite, high altitude pulmonary and cerebral edema and snow blindness. Such heavy losses can be avoided if both the countries start living in peace as friendly neighbouring countries.

SIR CREEK

Sir Creek forms the boundary between Gujarat state of India and Sind Province of Pakistan. This creek is extremely rich in marine life and both the countries desire to include it in their respective territories. While India claims that the middle point of Sir Creek should be demarcated as the international boundary, Pakistan wants the eastern bank of the Creek as the border between India and Pakistan.

As such Sir Creek has become a contentious issue between the two countries as Pakistan has been claiming a 40 km region inside India's territory.

Pakistan has responded positively to the goodwill gesture initiated by India since early 2004 to ease tension on the border. This can lead to friendly relations between the two countries if the concerned countries take necessary positive steps for normalisation of relations.

Some of the steps taken/proposed are:

(i) Srinagar-Muzaffrabad has survice.

(ii) Kargil-Skardu bus link and routes into Poonch-Rajouri sector.
(iii) Amritsar-Lahore bus and rail link.
(iv) Meeting points for divided families across LoC at Poonch, Mendhar,
(v) Suchetgarh, Uri, Tangdar and Kargil.
(vi) Rail link between Munnabao (Rajasthan) and Khokrapar (Sind).
(vii) Link between Ferozpur and Sahiwal.
(viii) Trade across the LoC/border.
(ix) Mechanisms to permit two-way religious pilgrims.
(x) Promotion of cultural interaction and cooperation.
(xi) Joint efforts to promote tourism.

PAKISTAN'S POLICY IN THE CHANGING SCENARIO

The events of 9/11, the attack on the Indian parliament, and the following war-like situation between India and Pakistan not only greatly impacted the Kashmiri resistance movement but also compelled Islamabad to change its track on Kashmir. Moreover, the unfriendly international environment and Pakistan's deep involvement in Afghanistan forced Islamabad to rethink its relations with India and its Kashmir policy. The decision of General Pervez Musharraf to join the US-led War on Terror was also a factor in changing Islamabad's strategic position on Kashmir, particularly in terms of its ideological foundation. The economic condition of the country, unrest in the tribal areas, and — allegedly externally sponsored — violence in some parts of Balochistan, and the growing engagement along the Afghan border also played an instrumental role in bringing about a paradigm shift in Islamabad's thinking towards India. It is also said that Pakistan's trusted friends, like China and Saudi Arabia, advised it to seek an unconventional way out for a lasting deal with India over the Kashmir issue and bilateral relations; besides, constant persuasion from the United States also continued.

Pakistan's capacity to protract the low cost conflict in Kashmir is beyond any doubt. Although the likely spillover effects of this on Pakistan's polity are obvious, they will be, to a great degree, manageable. On the other hand, despite its conventional military superiority and strong diplomatic backing from the world, India could not subdue the resolve of Pakistan to support Kashmir's right to self-determination and its demand for sovereign equality with India. Pakistan's ties with the United States, and its role as an ally of the West, are considered advantageous for seeking a settlement of the Kashmir issue. As the country's former Foreign Secretary Shamshad Ahmad observed:

We cannot deny the post-9/11 reality that our "friends," the Americans, now have deeper than ever stakes in India-Pakistan rapprochement as a factor of stability for regional and global peace. The 'covert' US engagement with Islamabad, Delhi and Kashmiris is no longer a secret. Washington has expressed its desire at a number of times to help settle the Kashmir issue within the existing territorial parameters but with minor realignment. It views India as a potential rival to China, not only in the region but also in global affairs. Siddharth Srivastava, a New Delhi-based journalist, observes: The US is striving to build India as a strategic counterweight to China, along with Japan and Australia.

Termed as naïve by critics, Pakistan's calculations of the ground realities are optimistic, being based on the belief that India will never be able to bring normalcy into Kashmir because Kashmiris are highly skeptical towards it, and that India will need Pakistan's support and will ultimately make tangible transformations in its current stance over Kashmir. The majority of Kashmiris do not trust the Indian government and, ever since the eruption of the resistance, their aspiration for the right of self-determination has multiplied manifold and now cuts across even the hardcore pro-India circles in the Kashmir Valley. India's carrot and stick tactics and the brutalities of its forces have alienated the local population and invoked armed resistance, which may not die down easily. It is this assessment of the situation that emboldened Islamabad to make tangible concessions on Kashmir and bring India to the table for talks. Some also believe that the personal ambition of the President Musharraf — his wish to be regarded in history as a statesman who settled one of the world's most complicated disputes — is a driving factor that has brought essential changes in Islamabad's policies.

Besides various other factors that caused India and Pakistan to change their policies on the Kashmir issue, back channel diplomacy led by the US played a major role in alleviating the crisis and creating a viable atmosphere for initiatives towards a comprehensive normalization process.

Change in India's Approach

For a long time, India's approach for dealing with Pakistan had revolved mainly around zero tolerance in any concerns related to India's security or political ideology. However, its inability to 'punish' Pakistan and to break its back economically (by creating a war-like environment in the region) had a sobering impact on the Indian mindset and led New Delhi to conclude that its conventional policies vis-à-vis Pakistan and Kashmir were getting nowhere. In the past, New Delhi had publicly pronounced several times that it would take punitive action and destroy what it alleged were militant training camps inside Azad Jammu and Kashmir (AJK) by air strikes. However, its hostile attitude did not yield the desired results and Islamabad did not succumb to its pressure. At the same time, economic tycoons and multinational companies were pressuring the Indian government to normalize relations with Islamabad as hostile relations between the two neighbors and the constant fear of war had a negative impact on business activity and international investment.

New Delhi needed peace in the region and internal stability to continue its current annual growth rate of 8-10 percent and obtain further foreign investment. As one researcher on the peace process put it:

Improved relations would lead to improved trade: there was money to be made, and this had become a strategic objective for both Islamabad and New Delhi.

India realized that its successful economic journey would cease if it did not settle disputes with Pakistan.

It had to think about the immense potential in bilateral trade and in trade with landlocked Afghanistan and Central Asia via Pakistan.

Besides, India aspires for a permanent seat in the UN Security Council for which it had to ensure friendly relations with neighbors and settle the Kashmir issue in the context of which India is regarded among those countries that did not comply with the UNSC resolutions. Moreover, the Kashmir resistance poses a huge financial burden on the Indian treasury. It is also acknowledged that the Indian security forces do not have the capacity to fix the problem; rather, they invite anger by frequently committing severe human rights violations that aggravate the already complex situation.

After the withdrawal of Indian forces from the Pakistani borders, Pakistan made a chain of unilateral concessions pronounced by President General Musharraf himself.

It began with a unilateral ceasefire on LoC announced by Prime Minister Zaffarullah Khan Jamali in November 2003. In the following month, speaking to *Reuters*, General Musharraf said he had "left aside" the 55-year-old demand for a UN mandated plebiscite on Kashmir and wished to meet India "halfway" in a bid for peace in the subcontinent.

These multiple pulls created a sense of obligation among the Indian ruling elite to at least take some measures to show that they were serious about settling the problems. Eventually, the Indian Prime Minister Atal Behari Vajpayee went to Kupwara in the south of the Kashmir Valley and offered a hand of friendship to Pakistan in April 2004. This was regarded a departure from the conventional Indian thinking on Kashmir and Pakistan, and paved the way for further initiatives on Kashmir. It also created a palatable environment for Vajpayee to visit Islamabad to attend the South Asian Association for Regional Cooperation (SAARC) summit.

Musharraf's 'Out of the Box' Thinking

Islamabad has consistently said that it supports the resistance in IHK diplomatically and politically, and has nothing to do with the armed struggle. It has also invariably linked talks with India with progress on the Kashmir settlement. But it relinquished both of these stands in the quest to find a compromised solution. Pakistan accepted the responsibility to rein in militants operating from areas under its control. It also pledged to stop all kinds of cross-border activities from Azad Kashmir. Pakistan had never acknowledged the armed resistance in IHK as terrorism, but astonishingly, it ceded even this stance and conceded to the Indian interpretation of the movement. As a retired former Ambassador aptly commented:

This amounted to an admission of its guilt and was unprecedented in that Pakistan unilaterally took on a responsibility that was not only almost impossible to honor, but even more importantly, it was given without any reciprocal obligation by the other side.

To further the shift in policy, the Pakistani President articulated his ideas on Kashmir for the first time while speaking to journalists during an *iftar*dinner held in Islamabad in October 2004. Although he said these were "off the cuff" ideas, the nature of the proposals on the Kashmir settlement that he forwarded suggests that he had in mind a well-conceived and thought-out plan, on which he was gauging feedback. The crux of the proposals is outlined below:

- Identify seven regions, demilitarize them, and change their status before looking for possible options to resolve the dispute.
- The status quo in Kashmir is unacceptable and the LoC cannot be a solution to the lingering dispute.
- As a starting point for a step-by-step approach on the option of demilitarization, the regions on both sides of the LoC need to be analyzed for local culture and demographic composition. After identifying these regions, there could be gradual demilitarization, following which the two sides could discuss who should control these areas.
- Pakistan and India could also have joint control of these areas or the United Nations could be asked to play a role.

Later, Musharraf dilated upon his ideas with the *CNBC* anchorperson, Karan Thapar, on January 8, 2006. He suggested the concept of self-governance and joint management of the entire Kashmir area. In his words, "self-governance is more than autonomy but less than independence. In other words, both India and Pakistan will keep the parts of Kashmir they control but under their joint management. Self-governance is devolved to the Kashmiris, independence being firmly ruled out." The interviewer, Karan Thapar, afterwards elaborated this concept in his article, saying, "...The self-governance would apply to the full state of Jammu and Kashmir as it existed in 1947. This means it would be implemented in Northern Areas (Gilgit Baltistan). Additionally, the border within old Kashmir state would be open and thus irrelevant."

Subsequently, Musharraf had a comprehensive discussion on his proposals with the noted Indian lawyer and journalist, A. G. Noorani, who published it in the Indian magazine *Frontline* on August 12-25, 2006. Later on, President Musharraf also spoke to *NDTV* on similar ideas, going further to clearly articulate his position as follows:

- Kashmir will have the same borders but people will be allowed to move freely back and forth in the region;
- The region will have self-governance or autonomy, but not independence;
- Troops will be withdrawn from the region in a phased manner
- A joint supervision mechanism will be set up with India, Pakistan and Kashmir represented in it.

The proposals offered by Musharraf sent clear signals that: a) Islamabad was ready to compromise its traditional stance that the people of Kashmir will decide their destiny through free and fair plebiscite; b) Indian and Pakistani sovereignty would remain as it currently was at the end of the day; c) The LoC would be irrelevant, except as a line on a map to demarcate both parts of the state; d) Self-governance or self rule would be granted to both parts of Kashmir and joint management established.

Pakistan's proposals paved the way to move forward on a slightly faster track as India did not view them as being against its strategic or political interests. Previously, Pakistan had banked on the UNSC resolutions that guaranteed the right of self-determination to the Kashmiris, besides recognizing Pakistan as a principal party to the dispute. Musharraf relinquished these positions unilaterally without seeking any quid pro quo. In other words, he came close to almost acknowledging the Indian claim that Kashmir could not be receded from the Union. India also tactfully rephrased its traditional stance that "J&K is its integral part" in more acceptable language, now asserting that "Borders cannot be redrawn but any kind of solution could be acceptable to India." Musharraf agreed to this proposition while rejecting the status quo and showed willingness to embrace some kind of joint management of the state.

Moreover, Pakistan accepted the pro-Indian Kashmiri leadership's role in the future dispensation and changed its position that only the All Parties

Hurriyat Conference (APHC) should be the representative of Kashmiri people in the negotiation process. President Musharraf said that the President of the National Conference, Omer Abdullah, and Mahbooba Mufti had a role to play in the Kashmir political landscape. This gesture comforted the Indian establishment as Pakistan's demands were in line with their own views and interests.

These major departures from the traditional stance made Musharraf a good bet for India to deal with Pakistan on Kashmir and settle other issues broadly allied to Pak-India trade and access to markets in Central Asia and Afghanistan.

A Review of the Composite Dialogue

The dialogue process between Islamabad and New Delhi is slowly progressing despite several ups and downs. It is often said that the continuation of the process is in itself a success because, in the past, the two countries have been unable to remain engaged in a sustainable dialogue. However, the substance of the process and prospects of its success need to be analyzed.

Until February 1994, India and Pakistan were engaged in sporadic dialogues that always ended with zero progress. This is why both countries formally suspended dialogue in 1994.

Islamabad's approach was to settle the Kashmir issue first, after which the other problems would get settled almost automatically, whereas India was interested in dilating first on other issues, such as trade and travel. Eventually, to bridge the gap between the two positions, both governments agreed to address all political and territorial issues simultaneously, including Jammu and Kashmir. Consequently, the foreign secretaries of the two countries met in Islamabad and resumed the stalled dialogue process in June 1997. They institutionalized the process by identifying eight areas to deliberate upon and established working groups to make progress on each issue separately but simultaneously.

This entire process was called off when the Kargil confrontation occurred. As discussed earlier, post-9/11 events also contributed in the stalemate between the two countries. Later, in 2004, India and Pakistan launched a renewed peace process aimed at resolving all their longstanding disputes. However, the Kashmir dispute still dominates over other issues. Even after voicing his new approaches, President Musharraf said that if progress on Kashmir could not make headway, the entire process would be back to square one. Recently, Prime Minister Shaukat Aziz has underscored the settlement of Kashmir as a precondition for further progress on other related disputes as well as for offering trade and business opportunities to India.

Since January 2004, both neighbors have been engaged on two different levels. The first is the official level, at which concerned officials from both sides meet periodically and report their progress to foreign secretaries, who meet to review the outcome and discuss the Kashmir, peace and security issues, before, finally, the foreign ministers meet to take stock of developments and set the rules for further dialogue. The second level of engagement is back-channel diplomacy. Pakistan's National Security Secretary, Tariq Aziz, who is known to be a close aide of President Musharraf, and India's S. K. Lamba, former High Commissioner to Pakistan, are engaged in a serious dialogue. However, it has been said that only five people in Pakistan are truly in the loop on the actual state of bilateral negotiations. Therefore, no one can really assess the behind-the-curtains activities or predict the contours of solutions.

So far, at the official level, both countries have completed four rounds of a composite dialogue. This process received a dent when the Mumbai train blasts on July 11, 2006 caused a postponement in the foreign secretary-level talks. India blamed elements from Pakistan for their involvement in the blasts but no evidence was provided by the Indian government to Pakistan. This decision was in violation of the joint statement, issued on April 18, 2005, by the leaders of Pakistan and India, which states that, "Terrorist acts would not be allowed to derail the peace process." Eventually, sanity prevailed and the stalled process was resumed in November 2006. Likewise, in February, the Lahore-bound Samjhauta Express became a target of bomb blasts that killed 68 passengers, most of whom were Pakistani. Islamabad reacted with caution and did not allow the peace process to derail, despite the immense loss of its citizens' lives. The question does arise how New Delhi would have reacted had Indian citizens been the victims.

The fourth round of composite dialogue was held in Islamabad on March 13-14, 2007, with a focus on the Jammu and Kashmir dispute and peace and security. In the context of peace and security, the two sides discussed a wide range of issues relating to their conventional and nuclear military capabilities and reviewed the entire process. The Pakistani team sought India's response to President Musharraf's "ideas" on the resolution of the Kashmir issue and emphasized the need for forward movement on Jammu and Kashmir, saying it was time to move from confidence-building measures to dispute resolution.

Among related issues, Pakistan pushed for early finalization of the agreements on speedy return of inadvertent line crossers; quarterly flag meetings of the sector commanders at the LoC; and liberalization of the visa regime. Pakistan also proposed some new cross-LoC confidence building measures, including allowing sports activities and launch of helicopter and postal services between Srinagar and Muzaffarabad.

In addition, Pakistan tabled a new proposal on anti-ballistic missiles. Siachen, Sir Creek and economic cooperation were among the other issues discussed.

Following are the significant consensus points of the fourth round of foreign secretary-level talks:

- After years of reluctance, Pakistan agreed to the Indian proposal of launching a bus service between Kargil and Skardu in the Northern Areas.
- It was agreed that a truck service between Srinagar and Muzaffarabad would be launched in a few months;
- It was agreed that the Joint Committee of Retired Judges, set up to look into the prisoners issue, would begin its work soon and suggest ways to ensure the humane treatment of Indian prisoners in Pakistani jails and Pakistani prisoners in Indian jails;
- The two countries agreed to conclude an agreement on "No Development of New Posts and Defense Works" along the LoC and proposed drafts for new border control guidelines along the International Border;
- The two sides agreed to work on finalizing a liberalized visa regime, including a proposal for group tourism.

Although the meeting could not settle the problem of demilitarizing Siachen, it was able to narrow down differences on some elements. The political leadership of both countries appears optimistic about resolving this issue in the days ahead.

Likewise, the formation of a Joint Counter-Terrorism Mechanism is also a significant development. India has long blamed Pakistan for any terrorist activities occurring on its territory. The Mechanism offers an opportunity for thorough investigation of incidents prior to the pronouncements of conclusions. However, it was reported in sections of the Pakistani and Indian press that Islamabad seeks to keep the armed resistance in J&K out of the ambit of the Joint Anti-Terrorism Mechanism. At a joint press conference with the Indian Foreign Secretary Shivshankar Menon, his Pakistani counterpart, Riaz Mohammad Khan, said that Jammu and Kashmir was "disputed" and should not be "mixed" with the initiatives that are between India and Pakistan only. The visible achievement of the four rounds of foreign sectaries' level dialogue is the initiation of a Srinagar-Muzaffarabad bus service and, of late, the opening of entry points along the LoC for civilian crossing. Although the 42-month dialogue process has not yielded the desired results, both the governments seem to be closer to agreements on a number of issues.

Besides, the two countries have also exchanged some proposals through the back channel on the settlement of the Jammu and Kashmir dispute. However, very few people of the two governments are fully aware of what is going on behind the scene. Concerned citizens and the general public on both sides know virtually nothing. This makes the back channel process vulnerable: nobody knows how stakeholders and the public will react when the solution is finally made public.

India's Mixed Response

Initially, the Indian leadership was quick to turn down President Musharraf's proposals on Kashmir, making it clear that sharing the sovereignty of Jammu and Kashmir with Pakistan was out of the question. However, due to the host of factors outlined above, it eventfully realized that it had to reciprocate and take the proposals into serious consideration.

The Indian Prime Minister made some reconciliatory remarks that encouraged pro-settlement forces in Kashmir and Pakistan. India resumed the negotiation process with APHC's Mirwaiz faction and also held meeting with Sajjad Ghani Lone, Chairman of the People's Conference and to the leader of Jammu & Kashmir Liberation Front (JKLF), Yasin Malk. The Indian Prime Minster held three Kashmir-related roundtables with the pro-India leadership of IHK and formed five working groups to seek recommendations on various issues.

The pro-independence leadership was also invited but it did not participate, demanding that a separate meeting be held with it instead of a joint sitting with pro-India politicians. Notably, President Musharraf personally encouraged the pro-independence APHC leadership to join talks with India and Pakistan separately, as this would be a step in the direction of trilateral talks. There is a feeling in a large section of the Indian establishment and public opinion that Pakistan has narrowed down its position and come closer to that of India's, despite its use of different jargon and nuances.

It is interesting to note that, in the last two years, Indian Prime Minister Manmohan Singh has spoken on his vision of how to settle the Kashmir issue several times. On March 24, 2006, in Amritsar, he argued for a step-by-step approach and commencement of dialogue with the people "in their areas of control" to improve the quality of governance. Regarding the future status of the LoC, he said that it might eventually become a mere line on a map, and that people might be able to visit and trade freely. He made a departure from his government's earlier stated position by acknowledging that the "the two parts of Jammu and Kashmir can, with the active encouragement of the governments of India and Pakistan, work out cooperative consultative mechanisms so as to maximize the gains of cooperation." He also offered a treaty of friendship between India and Pakistan.

Subsequently, at the Second Round Table Conference held in Srinagar in May 2006, the Indian Prime Minister indicated that he might take some institutional arrangements to bring people from both sides of the LoC closer to each other. While meeting with a APHC Conference delegation in New Delhi, he said India might create an environment in which a person could live in Srinagar or Muzaffarabad without any legal restriction. He reiterated that India was willing to move beyond its stated position, and expressed his openness to any ideas that might contribute to the ongoing thought process.

Finally, speaking to a meeting of Indian businessmen in New Delhi, Prime Minister Manmohan Singh repeated his hope for a treaty of peace and friendship with Pakistan and emphasized the need for linkage among South Asian states for economic development. This was the second time he had spoken of such a treaty in the period of about a month.

Just one month earlier, he had initiated his idea of a treaty of peace and friendship at a public rally in Amritsar. Echoing the same line a few days earlier, the Indian External Affairs Minster Paranab Mukarjee had said that India had to be prepared for some give and take in the border talks with China and Pakistan and should be prepared to shun rigid claims of national sovereignty if the talks were to be meaningful.

These pronouncements indicate that the Indian leadership is willing to have a phased-out formula for the resolution of the Kashmir issues. Nevertheless, it is neither relinquishing Indian sovereignty over Jammu and Kashmir, nor ready to trade off territory. At the end of the day, the people of Jammu and Kashmir may have de facto reunification of the state, which will give them psychological satisfaction. Apart from Monmohan Singh's reconciliatory remarks, a number of other key political stakeholders, such as Mufti Muhammad Sayyed's People's Democratic Party (PDP), National Conference, and APHC's Mirwaiz faction all support the Islamabad approach on Kashmir with slightly varied interpretations.

In this context, the Indian government has adopted a policy of engaging both Kashmiris and Pakistan in the dialogue process, separately but simultaneously. It suggests that New Delhi has attached huge expectations to an internal agreement with the people of Kashmir, giving relatively less importance to the external factor. However, it recognises the significance of people-to-people contacts across the LoC and, therefore, agreed to initiate the Srinagar-Muzaffarabad bus service and allowed Kashmiri leaders to travel on it to Muzaffarabad in July 2005. It has also given relatively better political space to the Mirwaiz faction of APHC and frequently facilitated its travel outside the country.

On the other hand, a number of Indian officials and commentators are restlessly following the beaten track of bitterness, continuing to hurl accusations at Pakistan with no regard for the emerging environment. Officials in India's top echelons quite frequently use isolated events to accuse Pakistan of terrorism without offering any substantial evidence. At times, Islamabad's sincerity is questioned. For instance, according to Satish Chandra, former Deputy National Security Advisor to the Indian government:

Is the military in Pakistan sincere in wanting good relations with India? Pakistan's engagement in the current dialogue process is due to compulsion of external pressures and military exigencies which have tied up substantial Pakistani forces on the West.

In April 2005, when Musharraf visited New Delhi, both the gov-ernments made announcements that the peace process was irreversible and no incident would be permitted to derail it. But immediately after the Mumbai bomb blasts, New Delhi called off the dialogue process and stalled the foreign secretary-level talks for almost three months. Indeed, New Delhi left no stone unturned to prove that Pakistan was a haven for terrorists and was involved in promoting terrorist networks inside India, particularly in the occupied Jammu and Kashmir. Satish Chandra observed:

Pakistan's involvement in terrorism is well-known. It is not limited to Jammu and Kashmir, but extends to several parts of India, including the northeast. One of my major concerns was that in many parts of India, including New Delhi, we are a hair's breadth away from a major terrorist attack.

In view of such contradictions, it may be assumed that either opinion within the Indian establishment is divided on the future course of action, or New Delhi has a well-defined, official double-edged policy of conducting talks with Islamabad and, at the same time, continuing its blame game to keep the latter under pressure. It is possible that New Delhi wishes to maintain tactical ambiguity to keep both pro- and anti-peace process forces confused with mixed signals. Such an approach also allows the Indian government to drag its feet on the peace process whenever it desires.

It appears that India does not care if its stance sends negative signals to the people of Pakistan, or if it reinforces the argument before them that Delhi is not responding to Musharraf's flexibility, even in diluted form. On the other hand, Musharraf has consistently applauded Vajpayee and Manmohan Singh, calling them statesmen, but the Indian leadership has never reciprocated the gesture. Musharraf has earned a lot of appreciation across the world for his efforts to solve the Kashmir problem but this too has made little impression on the Indian establishment.

Some leading Indian opinion makers believe that Pakistan had no option but to comply with Indian demands. This view has been echoed by former Indian Prime Minister Inder Kumar Gujral in the following words:

What options does he [Musharraf] have? His country faces innumerable problems. He also finds India growing taller and taller. His friends, the Americans, have told him not to rock the boat.

Thus, the process of reconciliation and the blame game are continuing simultaneously, indicating that the Indian establishment has yet to enter true reconciliation mode. Naturally, several questions arise about this complex Indian attitude. The answer primarily lies in the changed ground realities; for instance, back and forth movement across LoC has admittedly gone down, while militants are no longer a major threat to the security forces. Moreover, with the tacit approval of Islamabad, the fencing of the LoC has been completed without any real hassle. The unfaltering commitment on the part of Pakistan to respect the ceasefire along the LoC is a further encouraging factor. Inside Kashmir, the APHC stands divided into two factions and one of them, headed by Mirwaiz Omer Farooq, is in touch with Indian interlocutors, seeking a compromised settlement of the issue within the Indian Union.

New Stakeholders

Recently, Kashmiri domestic politics took a dramatic turn when the President of the pro-India National Conference, Omar Abdullah, made a striking demand. He said that no solution for Kashmir was possible without the involvement of Hizbul Mujahideen (HM) in the dialogue process. He urged India and Pakistan to hold talks with the United Jihad Council and HM's chief, Syed Salauddin.

Besides Omer Abdullah, the PDP chief Mehbooba Mufti has also consistently advised New Delhi to bring HM on board. JKLF leader Yasin Malik, known as the pioneer of militancy, also sets dialogue with HM as a precondition to a peaceful resolution of the Kashmir dispute. Moreover, a number of intra-Kashmir dialogue conferences organized by the Centre for Dialogue and Reconciliation, Delhi, have persistently been arguing for a seat for militants in the ongoing process.

HM has welcomed the suggestion for the first time in its 17-year armed resistance. Its inclusion in the dialogue has become a bipartisan demand of the Kashmiri stakeholders, cutting across the political divide. However, several questions arise regarding HM's future course of action. It is a fact that HM has played an instrumental role in highlighting the Kashmir issue by rendering huge sacrifices. It commands immense respect and credibility among the masses. Its chief, Syed Salauddin, is a household name in Kashmir and is regarded as one of the most trusted leaders of the state.

CBMs: A Blank Cheque for HR Violations

Despite a number of Confidence Building Measures (CBMs), the articulation of positive statements in the top echelons of the two countries, and several rounds of high level tête-à-tête between Indian and Pakistani officials, there has not been even a slight decline in the level of human rights violation in Indian-held Kashmir. Fake encounters and disappearances are still staged. The violations are so high that even the pro-Indian mainstream, along with the "separatist parties" — as India calls them — are up in arms against the government and security forces on this issue.

In the context of the ongoing peace process, it was not a misplaced expectation that, at least to improve its democratic image, the Indian government would take special measures to ensure respect for human rights and stop indiscriminate killings of civilians in the state. It was also necessary to get public support for the ongoing dialogue process. But events show that human rights abuses have actually doubled and random killings continue as a routine matter in IHK. It is quite surprising that the world community does not let a single opportunity slip to condemn human rights violations by resistance outfits but is silent on the acts of barbarism committed by the forces.

The Indian brutalities fuel feelings of vengeance among Kashmiris and invite more violence, which helps in providing fresh blood to the dissidents. It should be borne in mind that, in the initial years, the character of the resistance movement was not violent or communalized as it later became. However, even peaceful protests were dispersed with gunfire. The Indian forces imprisoned all renowned political figures and ceased all avenues for the peaceful and non-violent components of the struggle. Eventually, not only the youth but also professionals and the political leadership were dragged into armed struggle. These views were echoed in the editorial comments of the Jammu-based *Kashmir Times* on January 5, 2005:

> The poor track record of Indian forces on human rights front, which includes not just physical torture but also the mental trauma and agony of being looked upon with suspicion and subjected to every day humiliation in one's own home by a man in uniform who is for all practical purposes an outsider, thus becomes a major source of spread of militancy in its fanatic form, as is evident today.

Given, Kashmiri leaders often say that the current Indian strategy is aimed at crushing the Kashmiri struggle for self-determination under the disguise of parlays with Pakistan. This is why Indian forces are vigorously pursuing their military operations in the state. Secondly, as long as the two sides remain engaged in talks, the international community and human rights organizations will not voice any concerns lest it derail the dialogue process and spoil the atmosphere.

Besides, Pakistan is consciously avoiding making human rights a point in the talks, fearing that it might annoy India to the extent that it backs out of the negotiations.

India is taking undue advantage of this deliberate silence. On the other hand, it has practically given India a soft opportunity to suppress all the significant voices in the state.

It is also a known fact that the Indian armed forces have developed stakes in the J&K conflict. Over a period of time, they have developed a huge infrastructure and extract immense benefits from the festering wounds of Kashmir. They are entrusted with several draconian powers and prerogatives to conduct arbitrary operations and commit custodial killings. It is a proven fact that the security forces take money from local people through intimidation and threats.

Therefore, the huge military set-up in J&K has itself become a bottleneck in the peace process. Several Kashmir watchers believe that it was the military and intelligence establishment that compelled the Congress-led government to not budge from the Indian stated position on the issue. The ruling class in Delhi today also believes that Islamabad is on the receiving end and its game plan has been exhausted. So, eventually, the Indian writ on Kashmir shall be fully reestablished.

Dissident voices

Syed Ali Gilani, Chairman of his own faction of APHC, has emerged as a leading critic of the current peace process. He believes that the process is going to bury the Kashmir issue rather than settling it according to the people's wishes. His views have a strong following of politically aware lawyers, intellectuals, youth and women inside Kashmir. Apart from his political and religious ideology, he commands respect from all segments of Kashmiri society because of his firm stand on resolution of Kashmir according to the wishes of its people. Militant outfits, too, regard him as a source of aspiration. Hizbul Mujahideen, the largest indigenous militant outfit, has been especially under his influence since its inception. Armed groups, such as Lashkar and Jaish, have also expressed great respect for him. Because of his position within these outfits, he has emerged as one of the key influential leaders of the Valley. It is often said that he holds the key to the peaceful settlement of Kashmir.

On January 17, 2007 a strike was observed in the Valley to mark a protest against the visit of Mirwaiz Omer Farooq and his colleagues to Islamabad. Interestingly, however, public response to his recent strike call had been overwhelming, with the calling it a near to complete strike. This signifies the failure of the moderate APHC factions to take people into confidence. Mirwaiz visited Islamabad in January 19-27, 2007. He had meetings with President Pervez Musharraf twice and other government functionaries, besides sitting with a large number of political entities and Kashmiri parties. However, he could not get in touch with Syed Salahudin, the Hizbul Mujahideen commander-in-chief, as he declined to meet him. Likewise, in Azad Kashmir, apart from the ruling Muslim Conference, no other political party or civil society group supported the current formulation of the Kashmir settlement. Evidently, within Kashmiri opinion, the current moves do not enjoy reasonable support, which makes the entire process vulnerable and weak.

INDIA AND PAKISTAN'S GLACIAL FIGHT AT SIACHEN

Virtually hidden from public view, the world's highest conflict is moving into its fourth decade. The struggle between India and Pakistan over the Siachen glacier has even spawned a new term: "oropolitics", or mountaineering with a political goal.

The word is derived from the Greek for mountain, and Indian army colonel Narendra Kumar can justly claim to be the modern father of oropolitics because his pioneering explorations paved the way for India to take the glacier in early 1984. But what started as a battle with crampons and climbing rope has turned into high-altitude trench warfare, with the two rival armies frozen - often literally - in pretty much the same positions as 30 years ago.

SIACHEN AVALANCHE

Ten army soldiers, including a junior commissioned officer, are feared dead after an avalanche ripped off their post at 19,600ft in one of the world's highest battlefield between India and Pakistan, Saichen in the northern glacier sector of the Ladakh region on Wednesday. The army, late on Thursday, ruled out any possibility of missing soldiers being alive, although search operations will continue until the dead bodies have been extracted from the snow.

"It is a tragic event and we salute the soldiers who braved all challenges to guard our frontiers and made the ultimate sacrifice in the line of duty," The defence ministry's spokesperson in Jammu, Colonel SD Goswami, said in a statement.

"The glacier gets 35 feet of snow every season temperatures plumes to 60°C. Rescue teams are braving adverse weather and effects of rarified atmosphere to locate and rescue survivors. However, it is with the deepest of regret that we have to state that chances of finding any survivors are now very remote," the statement, added.

However, from the minute the army found out about the avalanche burying the post, there was little hope about the survivors. The question, senior army officers, pondered was not whether anyone was alive, but about the challenge of finding the dead bodies.

A senior army official based in Jammu and Kashmir told *Firstpost,* late on Thursday that even to reach the spot, rescuers would need to spread ropes, and then stairs, so that people could walk on it. At 19,600 feet, soldiers can't walk for more than 10 steps, "you need rest for five minutes, and than carry forward because the oxygen content is very low."

"There are pickets, (like this one) that remains closed for five months in areas like these — we call them winter posts. If someone is sick, you have to bring him back in a helicopter. When an avalanche comes, it destroys the helipad too. If the troops are not alive, who will set up that helipad?" he asked.

The army says that reaching the post also puts "someone else's life at risk", and that is the reason rescue operations are conducted during the night, mainly because the threat of avalanches is lower at night.

"The worst time to go there is between 11 am and 12 pm, but now the threat is reduced, because the area has already suffered one avalanche.

In any case, the army will be operating at night, because the snow is harder and the threat of avalanches is lower. But I'm afraid for them that even after reaching there, finding the dead bodies in these extreme circumstances will be a challenge," another officer said.

This is not the first time soldiers have lost their lives in Siachen — on both sides — and it won't be the last time. The deadly mountains buried 129 Pakistani soldiers and 11 civilians on 7 April, 2012, when a massive avalanche struck the Pakistani military headquarters at Gayari, 30 kilometres west of the glacier terminus. The operation, to rescue the dead bodies, lasted for months and Pakistan was forced to invite international experts to help them in the rescue mission — which also failed to extract dead bodies for a long time. There are many dead bodies of Pakistani soldiers still missing in these mountains.

INDIA AND PAKISTAN DEMILITARIZE THE SIACHEN GLACIER

Naik Hanamanthappa Koppad's story gripped India last week. The country mourned the death of the soldier, who survived for six days under 35 feet of snow after an avalanche at the Siachen Glacier. He was miraculously found alive with a pulse, but died later of multiple organ failure in New Delhi last Thursday. With his death, Koppad was thrust from anonymity at the icy glacier, some 20,000 feet above sea level, to the top of India's national consciousness. The avalanche claimed the lives of nine of his colleagues last week; the bodies of most of those soldiers remains buried under the snow.

The sheer scale of tragedy adds to the number of human casualties that India and Pakistan suffer with regular frequency in the inhospitable terrain of northern Kashmir. The ordeal their soldiers face raises the question of the feasibility of protecting this icy terrain. Koppad's tragedy brings into focus the need to demilitarize the area, which has claimed and maimed more lives than the actual fighting between India and Pakistan.

In 2012, more than 100 Pakistani soldiers and some civilians lost their lives in an avalanche. According to an estimate, more than 1,500 soldiers from both countries have lost their lives since 1984, when New Delhi captured Siachen from its western neighbor after a small skirmish. Since then, however, maintaining control of this difficult terrain has not been easy.

Experts differ on the strategic importance of the glacier, but they agree that the icy terrain has become more of a prestige issue for both India and Pakistan rather than a security issue. The non-delineation of a formal border between the two countries prevents the demilitarization of Siachen. This will not happen unless both nations demonstrate foresight and vision in handling the issue. Furthermore, as *The Hindu* noted in an editorial:

The demilitarization of Siachen is definitely doable. This is not only because it is diplomatically possible, but also because there is a critical mass of opinion in both India and Pakistan that neither can sacrifice, or put in harm's way, so many lives on the inhospitable glacier. If the initiative is not seized by both sides now, the vagaries of nature will continue to exact a toll on forces deployed in Siachen, even if peace holds.

Several initiatives were made in the past to solve the Siachen issue, but the deep seated mistrust between New Delhi and Islamabad always came in the way. India is concerned about Pakistani and Chinese designs in the region and is wary of losing the strategic advantage of the Saltoro ridge in Siachen, lest its enemies capture Leh. Pakistan meanwhile sees India as an occupying force on the icy terrain and, therefore, fears reputational costs if it compromises with India.

Amid the ongoing dispute, the real victims are the soldiers. Is it worth losing so many lives for this terrain?

The death of ten Indian soldiers last week should serve as a rude awakening for both nations to move beyond their past perceptions and begin a serious process to demilitarize the Siachen Glacier. Koppad's death has stirred India and has led to calls to do just this.

REASONS BEHIND THE DISPUTE

The Kashmir Conflict arose from the Partition of British India in 1947 into modern India and Pakistan. Both countries subsequently made claims to Kashmir, based on the history and religious affiliations of the Kashmiri people.

The princely state of Jammu and Kashmir, which lies strategically in the north-west of the subcontinent bordering Afghanistan and China, was formerly ruled by Maharaja Hari Singh under the paramountcy of British India.

In geographical and legal terms, the Maharaja could have joined either of the two new countries. Although urged by the Viceroy, Lord Mountbatten of Burma, to determine the future of his state before the transfer of power took place, Singh demurred. In October 1947, incursions by Pakistan took place leading to a war, as a result of which the state of Jammu and Kashmir remains divided between India and Pakistan.

Two-thirds of the former princely state of Jammu and Kashmir, comprising Jammu, the Kashmir Valley, and the sparsely populated Buddhist area of Ladakh are controlled by India while one-third is administered by Pakistan. The latter includes a narrow strip of land called Azad Kashmir and the Northern Areas, comprising the Gilgit Agency, Baltistan, and the former kingdoms of Hunza and Nagar.

Attempts to resolve the dispute through political discussions have been unsuccessful. In September 1965, war again broke out between Pakistan and India. The United Nations called for another cease-fire, and peace was restored following the Tashkent Declaration in 1966, by which both nations returned to their original positions along the demarcated line.

After the 1971 war and the creation of independent Bangladesh under the terms of the 1972 Simla Agreementbetween Prime Minister Indira Gandhi of India and Zulfiqar Ali Bhutto of Pakistan, it was agreed that neither country would seek to alter the cease-fire line in Kashmir, which was renamed as the Line of Control, "unilaterally, irrespective of mutual differences and legal interpretations".

Numerous violations of the Line of Control have occurred, including incursions by insurgents and Pakistani armed forces at Kargil leading to the Kargil war. There have also been sporadic clashes on the Siachen Glacier, where the Line of Control is not demarcated and both countries maintain forces at altitudes rising to 20,000 ft (6,100 m), with the Indian forces serving at higher altitudes.

Indian view

India has officially stated that it believes that Kashmir to be an integral part of India, though the then Prime Minister of India, Manmohan Singh, stated after the 2010 Kashmir Unrest that his government was willing to grant autonomy to the region within the purview of Indian constitution if there was consensus on this issue.

The Indian viewpoint is succinctly summarised by Ministry of External affairs, Government of India —

- India holds that the Instrument of Accession of the State of Jammu and Kashmir to the Union of India, signed by Maharaja Hari Singh (erstwhile ruler of the State) on 25 October 1947 and executed on 27 October 1947 between the ruler of Kashmir and the Governor General of India was a legal act and completely valid in terms of the Government of India Act (1935), Indian Independence Act (1947) as well as under international law and as such was total and irrevocable.
- The Constituent assembly of Jammu and Kashmir had unanimously ratified the Maharaja's Instrument of Accession to India and adopted a constitution for the state that called for a perpetual merger of Jammu and Kashmir with the Union of India. India claims that the constituent assembly was a representative one, and that its views were those of the Kashmiri people at the time.
- United Nations Security Council Resolution 1172 tacitly accepts India's stand regarding all outstanding issues between India and Pakistan and urges the need to resolve the dispute through mutual dialogue without the need for a plebiscite in the framework of UN Charter.
- United Nations Security Council Resolution 47 cannot be implemented since Pakistan failed to withdraw its forces from Kashmir, which was the first step in implementing the resolution. India is also of the view that Resolution 47 is obsolete, since the geography and demographics of the region have permanently altered since it adoption.The resolution was passed by United Nations Security Council under Chapter VI of the United Nations Charter and as such is non-binding with no mandatory enforceability, as opposed to resolutions passed under Chapter VII.
- India does not accept the two-nation theory that forms the basis of Pakistan's claims and considers that Kashmir, despite being a Muslim-majority state, is in many ways an "integral part" of secular India.
- The state of Jammu and Kashmir was provided with significant autonomy under Article 370 of the Constitution of India.

- All differences between India and Pakistan, including Kashmir, need to be settled through bilateral negotiations as agreed to by the two countries under the Simla Agreement signed on 2 July 1972.

Additional Indian viewpoints regarding the broader debate over the Kashmir conflict include –

- In a diverse country like India, disaffection and discontent are not uncommon. Indian democracy has the necessary resilience to accommodate genuine grievances within the framework of India's sovereignty, unity, and integrity. The Government of India has expressed its willingness to accommodate the legitimate political demands of the people of the state of Kashmir.
- Insurgency and terrorism in Kashmir is deliberately fuelled by Pakistan to create instability in the region. The Government of India has repeatedly accused Pakistan of waging a proxy war in Kashmir by providing weapons and financial assistance to terrorist groups in the region.
- Pakistan is trying to raise anti-India sentiment among the people of Kashmir by spreading false propaganda against India. According to the state government of Jammu and Kashmir, Pakistani radio and television channels deliberately spread "hate and venom" against India to alter Kashmiri opinion.
- India has asked the United Nations not to leave unchallenged or unaddressed the claims of moral, political, and diplomatic support for terrorism, which were clearly in contravention of United Nations Security Council Resolution 1373. This is a Chapter VII resolution that makes it mandatory for member states to not provide active or passive support to terrorist organisations. Specifically, it has pointed out that the Pakistani government continues to support various terrorist organisations, such as Jaish-e-Mohammad and Lashkar-e-Taiba, in direct violation of this resolution.
- India points out reports by human rights organisations condemning Pakistan for the lack of civic liberties in Pakistan-administered Kashmir. According to India, most regions of Pakistani Kashmir, especially Northern Areas, continue to suffer from lack of political recognition, economic development, and basic fundamental rights.
- Karan Singh, the son of the last ruler of the princely state of Kashmir and Jammu, has said that the Instrument of Accession signed by his father was the same as signed by other states. He opined that Kashmir was therefore a part of India, and that its special status granted by

Article 370 of the Indian Constitution stemmed from the fact that it had its own constitution.

In 2008, the death toll from the last 20 years was estimated by Indian authorities to be over 47,000.

Pakistani view

Pakistan maintains that Kashmir is the "jugular vein of Pakistan" and a currently disputed territory whose final status must be determined by the people of Kashmir.

Pakistan's claims to the disputed region are based on the rejection of Indian claims to Kashmir, namely the Instrument of Accession. Pakistan insists that the Maharaja was not a popular leader, and was regarded as a tyrant by most Kashmiris. Pakistan maintains that the Maharaja used brute force to suppress the population.

Pakistan claims that Indian forces were in Kashmir before the Instrument of Accession was signed with India, and that therefore Indian troops were in Kashmir in violation of the Standstill Agreement, which was designed to maintain the status quo in Kashmir (although India was not signatory to the Agreement, which was signed between Pakistan and the Hindu ruler of Jammu and Kashmir).

From 1990 to 1999, some organisations reported that the Indian Armed Forces, its paramilitary groups, and counter-insurgent militias were responsible for the deaths of 4,501 Kashmiri civilians. During the same period, there were records of 4,242 women between the ages of 7–70 being raped. Similar allegations were also made by some human rights organisations.

In short, Pakistan holds that –

- The popular Kashmiri insurgency demonstrates that the Kashmiri people no longer wish to remain within India. Pakistan suggests that this means that Kashmir either wants to be with Pakistan or independent.
- According to the two-nation theory, one of the principles that is cited for the partition that created India and Pakistan, Kashmir should have been with Pakistan, because it has a Muslim majority.
- India has shown disregard for the resolutions of the UN Security Council and the United Nations Commission in India and Pakistan by failing to hold a plebiscite to determine the future allegiance of the state.
- The reason for India's disregard of the resolutions of the UN Security Council was given by India's Defense Minister, Kirshnan Menon, who

said: "Kashmir would vote to join Pakistan and no Indian Government responsible for agreeing to plebiscite would survive."

- Pakistan was of the view that the Maharaja of Kashmir had no right to call in the Indian Army, because it held that the Maharaja of Kashmir was not a hereditary ruler and was merely a British appointee, after the British defeated Ranjit Singh who ruled the area before the British conquest.
- Pakistan has noted the widespread use of extrajudicial killings in Indian-administered Kashmir carried out by Indian security forces while claiming they were caught up in encounters with militants. These encounters are commonplace in Indian-administered Kashmir. The encounters go largely uninvestigated by the authorities, and the perpetrators are spared criminal prosecution.

Human rights organisations have strongly condemned Indian troops for widespread rape and murder of innocent civilians while accusing these civilians of being militants.

- The Chenab formula was a compromise proposed in the 1960s, in which the Kashmir valley and other Muslim-dominated areas north of the Chenab river would go to Pakistan, and Jammu and other Hindu-dominated regions would go to India.

Former Pakistani president General Pervez Musharraf on 16 October 2014 said that Pakistan needs to incite those fighting in Kashmir, "We have source (in Kashmir) besides the (Pakistan) army...People in Kashmir are fighting against (India). We just need to incite them," Musharraf told a TV channel.

In 2015 Pakistan's outgoing National Security Advisor Sartaj Aziz said that Pakistan wished to have third party mediation on Kashmir, but it was unlikely to happen unless by international pressure. "Under Shimla Accord it was decided that India and Pakistan would resolve their disputes bilaterally," Aziz said. "Such bilateral talks have not yielded any results for the last 40 years. So then what is the solution?"

Chinese view

China states that Aksai Chin is an integral part of China and does not recognise the inclusion of Aksai Chin as part of the Kashmir region.

- China did not accept the boundaries of the princely state of Kashmir and Jammu, north of Aksai Chin and the Karakoram as proposed by the British.
- China settled its border disputes with Pakistan under the 1963 Trans Karakoram Tract with the provision that the settlement was subject to the final solution of the Kashmir dispute.

THE DISPUTE OVER THE SIACHEN GLACIER

The battle for the Siachen glacier has been rightly described as "the world's most cruel, highest altitude war". So whenever India and Pakistan resume their bilateral dialogue, a solution on the Siachen Glacier dispute would be high on the agenda. But, while Pakistan wants a complete withdrawal of Indian troops to the pre-1984 positions – the year the conflict was initiated- this suggestion carries little enthusiasm amongst India's armed forces, that wants the Pakistanis to acknowledge India's military gains in the region, along what is called the Actual Ground Position Line (AGPL)that runs along the Soltoro ridge, west of the Siachen glacier. Because, capturing and retaining control over those icy heights has been tough enough for the Indian soldier, and if these were to be vacated now – as is being advocated by some then one cannot possibly get it back by the Indian Army, that has held on to the Siachen Glacier at great human cost. The AGPL runs along treacherous heights, as high as 20,000 feet, and temperatures there range from minus 35 to minus 70 degree Celsius. For the Indians, this is a line that defines a national policy; it is not a stand that India's Army brass has taken on its own.

The dispute is essentially about the alignment of the Line of Control (LoC) that separates India's Kashmir from Pakistan occupied Kashmir- beyond its terminal point north of NJ 9842. Pakistan insists that the LoC should run northeastwards – from NJ 9842 to the Karakoram pass- and therefore, in Islamabad's view, the Siachen glacier lies in Pakistani territory; while India says that the LoC must follow a geographical feature, like most international boundaries,- i.e., the Soltoro ridge which Indian troops dominate – and so Siachen glacier should lie within Indian territory. The current debate centres around India's insistence that Pakistan must acknowledge the gains that Indian troops have made beyond the glacier and along the 110 kilometer long AGPL before any troop withdrawal takes place – to prevent Pakistan making any future claim on the Siachen glacier, as it did with intrusions around Kargil (near Ladakh) leading to the Indo-Pak conflict in 1999. But this is a requirement that Pakistan's generals are unlikely to accept, because the Pakistan army has led Pakistanis to believe that their army is in control of the Siachen glacier, while in reality it is the Indian army that dominates the glacial battlefield. Therefore any peace agreement would eventually require a Pakistani acknowledgement that their military establishment and their politicians have misled their people about their role at Siachen!

The origins of the dispute therefore lie in a cartographic controversy. In the 1970's and the 80's several international maps had begun to depict the Siachen Glacier as part of Pakistan. This included the National Geographic

Society's Atlas of the World, University of Chicago's A Historical Atlas of South Asia and The Times Atlas of the World, published in London. All of these showed the Cease Fire Line (later re-designated in 1972 as the LoC) clearly extending from NJ 9842 in a northeasterly direction right up to the Karakoram Pass and onto the Chinese border. This, until then, not even the Pakistani maps had done! And in 1985, Pakistan published the official Atlas of Pakistan – the first such publication in Pakistan – that removed the Giligit Agency from the status of a disputed territory, as it had been hitherto always shown , and gave it an entirely separate standing. It left only Baltistan's status untouched (on whose eastern edge, Pakistan claims, stands the Siachen glacier) as a disputed territory. But some Indian writers cannot be absolved of the responsibility of adding to this confusion, either. Two books by Indian authors- The Fourth Round: Indo-Pak War in 1984 by Ravi Rikhye and Lt. Gen. KP Candeth's The Western Front: Indo- Pakistan War in 1971 – had maps, that only strengthened Pakistan's claim.

The source of this cartographic encroachment is said to be some maps that were initially produced by the US Defence Mapping Agency, which depicted the LoC running from the vicinity of NJ 9842 northeast to the Karakoram Pass, in the 1970's and the 80's. The best explanation for this error by America's map makers, appears to lie in the possible "translation" of Air Defence Information Zone (ADIZ) markings, which provides zoning boundaries for air controllers in civil/military aviation, into an extension of the LoC from NJ 9842 to the Karakoram Pass. These have become articles of faith for the Pakistanis. However, there can be several ADIZ's that could pass through one country, and these do not necessarily identify a boundary line. But the publication of such maps by many of the world's leading atlases further encouraged the Pakistani army to contest the sanctity of the LoC.

And so, General Zia-ul-Haq decided to occupy Siachen glacier in the 1980s, as a means to alter the status quo of the LoC. But being understandably sensitive to the implications of cartographic ambiguity after the 1962 Sino Indian conflict, the Indian Army took preemptive action, and in April 1984 it occupied the Soltoro Ridge which marks the western wall of Siachen glacier. As Lt Gen Chibber, formally India's northern army commander and now an author, who initiated the Indian presence on the glacier has admitted, "the strategic importance of the area was not a major consideration, nor was our purpose to capture any territory. It was simply to ensure that we were not presented with a fait accompli like that in Aksai Chin in the early fifties". The Government of India approved this action on the clear understanding that the definition of the Cease Fire Line (now the LoC) from the original Karachi Agreement of 1949 to the Simla Agreement of 1972, places the Siachen Glacier on the Indian side of the alignment from NJ 9842, as the LoC runs "thence north to the glaciers". Further east, the International Boundary (IB) gives way to the Line of Actual Control (LAC) between India and China in Ladakh. And given its interpretation of the Simla Agreement, it is no surprise that Pakistan subsequently stepped up its efforts to internationalise the Kashmir issue and seek third party intervention, projecting the LoC as a temporary arrangement.

The LoC, which is essentially a political variant of the 1949 UN ceasefire line – that defines the positions of Indian and Pakistani troops in J&K – ends abruptly at NJ 9842, a point on the map, south of the Siachen glacier. The dispute however, is based on the interpretations of India and Pakistan on whose territory the glacier lies. And as the control of the glacier has strategic implications for each country, but as the conflict has been fought along jagged peaks at rarefied heights, holding on to each post is now a matter of national pride. However, that has been left, in some instances, in the hands of just a section of ten men, since steep cliffs on the Soltoro ridge line can accommodate only that many, as infantrymen fight on heights ranging from 17 to 20000 feet in icy weather and sub zero temperatures, where few armies in the world would dare to venture.

An Indian General once said to me "decorated or not with a gallantry award, every man who has served at Siachen, is a hero". How true! But over the past two decades, casualties – which in any case are essentially weather related and not due to enemy fire – amongst Indian troops have been minimized with training and the implementation of stringent preventive measures. Moreover, the infantrymen who have braved isolation and cold, could not have done so without the tenacity and professionalism of the helicopter pilots, who in their small Cheetah helicopters have lifted troops to the highest posts, evacuated casualties and most importantly braved it all to provide rations and medicines that keep our soldiers going.

India's initiative however, at the glacier has become Pakistan's military nightmare. Several Pakistani commanders- including General Musharraf – have been unable to come to terms with the ability of the Indian soldier to hold out despite their repeated attempts to dislodge Indian troops from the Soltoro ridge, where most of the troops are deployed. And on being asked to explain by Pakistani journalists, as to how Indians had been able to capture posts from the Pakistani army in such a difficult terrain, Pakistan's officers had to resort to unconvincing excuses as answers. And their defeat in Kargil, has only strengthened Pakistan's resolve to link to a resolution of Siachen to the Kashmir issue. Perhaps the reason for Pakistan's adventure in Kargil in 1999 probably lay in General Musharraf's desire to avenge his own humiliation at Siachen – as a brigade commander in that region in 1987 he too was unable to push Indian troops out of the Soltoro ridge – but the Kargil conflict, has ironically for the Pakistanis, given the LoC sanctity. In fact, an eminent Pakistani writer, Altaf Gauhar, has suggested that the contingency plan for a Kargil-type operation was formulated as far back as 1987 during the period of General Zia-ul-Haq. The plan was however vetoed by the then Foreign Minister Sahibzada Yakub Khan as being militarily untenable and internationally and politically indefensible.

What then, ask some people, is the importance of the Siachen Glacier that started the conflict in 1984? Most importantly, the Glacier holds 100 million acres of fresh water resources, which both India and Pakistan dearly need. It is perhaps the desire to harness this essential resource, that had led the Prime Minister Manmohan Singh to indicate that we must make the Glacier a "Peace Park".It was not about the cost of keeping the Army on those icy peaks. That India can afford. At about Rs. 700 crore (a crore is about 120,000 Pounds Sterling) this takes up a small part of India's defence budget. In fact keeping troops at the heights around Kargil costs double the amount of what the deployments around Siachen glacier costs. Moreover, hasn't New Delhi subsidized almost everything in Jammu & Kashmir for decades now?

However, if we are eventually going to have a Peace Park in that region, so that we can all utilize the resources there, without disturbing the ecology, then India must ask for the inclusion of the Baltoro glacier that is now under Pakistan's control (and lies north west of AGPL), in the northern territories. Pakistan has for instance harnessed two glaciers (though small) north of Sia Kangri, in the Shaksgam Valley, by diverting them to the Indus. This was in an area illegally seceded by Pakistan to China (ie, the Shaksgam valley), but Pakistan's actions have so upset China that Beijing has stopped any further Pakistani expeditions K2, without Chinese permission.

Of late however, a number of articles have mushroomed in the media expressing concern over the degradation of the fragile eco system of the Siachen Glacier region. Most of these articles make out the Indian Army to be the 'villains of the piece'. It is, therefore, time that such fears were allayed and cognizable facts brought to the fore. Global warming has come to stay. The Indian Metrological Department has reported an increase in temperature by 40 Celsius in the Antarctica over the last 15 years. All Himalayan glaciers are known to be receding at the rate of 10 metres to 23 metres per year. Compared to these figures, the recession rate of the Siachen glacier is steady at 10.5 metres per year only. This low recession figure is paradoxically strongly indicative of the ecological conservation measures being successfully adopted by the Indian Army! The Gangotri glacier in Himachal Pradesh is receding at the rate of 23.5m a year.

To understand environmental issues relating to the Siachen Glacier, one must first, be familiar with its geography. The glacier flows between the Soltoro Ridge to the West and the Karakoram Range to the East. These mountain ranges are offset from the Siachen Glacier by a considerable distance. Though all talk is based on the occupation of the "Siachen Glacier" by the Army, there are no troops on the Glacier per se. The deployment of the Army is on the Soltoro Ridge 'not' on the Glacier. And the Soltoro ridge is 15 to 20 kilometers west of the Glacier.

Next we need to factor in the statistics of waste generation on the Soltoro Ridge and not, as is generally presumed, on the Siachen Glacier. Of the total waste generated per day, 90% is biodegradable. This waste is spread over a length of 85 km along the Soltoro Ridge, in small posts occupied by troops. The biodegradable waste is spread off in situ by incineration. The heat generated by this incineration, approximately 5 x 109 Kilo-Joules, is effectively utilized for heating of water and cooking, there by minimizing the heat dispersion into the environment, making the warming effect negligible. As far as human and kitchen waste is concerned, which forms 11% of the biodegradable waste, it is first bio-digested and the residue incinerated. For this, state of the art equipment is being provided by India's Defence Research and Development Organisation, which maintains a permanent presence in the region. The 10% residual non biodegradable waste is collected at Mother Waste Collection Baskets by means of porters, snow scooters and helicopters and brought out of the Siachen Glacier region and disposed off suitably as per international norms.

Having assimilated these facts, to say that the presence of the Indian Army in the Siachen Glacier is detrimental to the environment does not hold water. On the contrary it is the Indian army's conscious efforts in preserving the fragile environment and biosphere of the Ladakh region in general and of the Northern Glaciers in particular. Incidentally further south of the Glacier lies the Ladakh plateau, with its enormous, natural mineral resources that are yet to be exploited.

Centuries ago, historians say that, "Herodititus found... gold digging ants in the upper Indus Valley – ants that are smaller than dogs but larger than foxes...that throw up golden sand...and Indians rifle, the gold in the heat of the day when these ants hide from the heat...a similar story is told by Megathenes..." But the Buddhist have however, given that land a religious hue that limits efforts to mine the region. The reality is that the geo-strategic importance of the Siachen glacier, is a essentially non-military one, regardless of what some people might insist.

Some military commanders are of the view that, if a pull out from the Siachen Glacier helps us seal a deal over the 'LoC' as a permanent border with Pakistan after all you have to give something to get something – then let's pull out troops from Siachen. After all, not all of India's border with China is physically manned, so maybe we could go back to the pre-1984 days at Siachen also. But then, the Indian government must accept that the Indian Army cannot possibly regain those icy heights that define India's reach in that region, if withdrawn. The government must therefore publicly assure the Indian Army that it shall not be asked to send its soldiers back on top of the Soltoro Ridge, at a later date. They did so in 1984 when there were no Pakistani troops, to stall their efforts. They cannot do it now, as General Musharraf would himself agree. His failure to dislodge Indian troops in the mid 1980's in the region, led him into initiating the Kargil intrusions and then the conflict in 1999.

But the romance of battle apart, the central issue is, is there a way forward? Efforts to de-militarize the Glacier in 1989 and in 1992 were set-aside after long rounds of Indo-Pak negotiations it was politicians then – Rajiv Gandhi and Benazir Bhutto – and not soldiers, who had made the fight over the glacial region a matter of national honour and prestige and were in no mood to compromise and suffer a loss of face domestically. Today, a military solution to the Siachen dispute can be found, if only, both sides agree to a formal demarcation of their positions, as it exists today – called the AGPL – as was done with the LoC, with joint patrolling by sides. This could include first a disengagement and not withdrawal, for a reasonably long period that would take the Siachen dispute away from the public eye. And eventually to either convert the region into a Peace Park or to establish a Siachen Science Centre to be operated by scientists from India and Pakistan so that the conflict can be put to an end.

FUTURE OPTIONS FOR DECLARATION OF THE DISPUTE

Over the past fifty years, besides the UN resolutions, observers and intellectuals have proposed various other options for resolving the Kashmir dispute time and again at the UN fora and at the bilateral India-Pakistan levels. These proposals are examined below.

UN Resolutions: The Plebiscite Option

The UN Security Council resolutions of August 13, 1948 and January 5, 1949, proposed the plebiscite option for resolving the Kashmir dispute. However, it is important to note that the Government of India itself accepted *plebiscite* or *referendum* as a right of the Kashmiri people, when it filed the initial complaint against Pakistan before the United Nations on January 1, 1948, as pointed out in Part I of this paper. Beginning with Governor General Mountbatten, Indian leaders like Prime Minister Nehru also repeatedly made the commitment to 'the will of the Kashmiri people'.

After India filed its initial complaint, the UN Security Council passed the two important resolutions of August 13, 1948 and January 5, 1949. These resolutions laid down the principles and procedures for a free and impartial plebiscite under UN auspices. Broadly, the resolution of January 5, 1949, stated: '(a) the question of the accession of the State of Jammu and Kashmir to India and Pakistan, would be decided through the democratic method of a free and impartial plebiscite after the cease-fire and truce agreement provided for in the Resolution of August 13 had been carried out; (b) the Secretary General of the UN would nominate a Plebiscite Administrator, who would be appointed by the government of Jammu and Kashmir and given powers which he considers necessary for holding a free and impartial plebiscite; (c) on implementation of the ceasefire and the truce agreement, the Commission and the Plebiscite Administrator would determine, in consultation with the Government of India, the final disposal of Indian and State Armed Forces, as well as the Forces in Azad Kashmir (in consultation with the local authorities); (d) persons who had entered the State since August 15, 1947 would be required to leave the State, and citizens of the State who had left the State on account of disturbances would be allowed to return.'

Both India and Pakistan accepted the above UN Resolutions. However, later, differences arose over the interpretation of various clauses of the resolutions, especially on the issues of demilitarisation and disbandment/ disarming of the 'Azad Kashmir' forces. India gave its own interpretation to the agreement and suggested that the Azad Kashmir forces be disbanded and the defence and administrative responsibility of the region be given to India and Indian Kashmiri authorities.

Pakistan, on the other hand, was in favour of a complete and simultaneous withdrawal of armed forces personnel by both the countries. On this issue, the President of the Security Council, General McNaughton, in his proposal of December 22, 1949, in para 2, clarified that the Resolutions of 1948 and 1949 called for demilitarisation of the whole State of Jammu and Kashmir and not merely Azad Kashmir: that 'demilitarisation should include the withdrawal from the State of Jammu and Kashmir of the regular forces of Pakistan; and the withdrawal of the regular forces of India not required for purposes of security or for the maintenance of local law and order.'

The UN Security Council passed Resolution 80 on March 14, 1950, which called upon the Governments of India and Pakistan 'to prepare and execute within a period of five months from the date of this resolution a programme of demilitarisation on the basis of the principles of paragraph 2 of General McNaughton's proposal, or of such modifications of those principles as may be mutually agreed.' Pakistan accepted that Resolution as well, but India maintained its position as regards the demilitarisation issue.

The UN Security Council passed Resolution 98, in December 1952. The UNSC Resolution, regarding demilitarisation issue clarified that: (Article 4) 'the Governments of India and Pakistan to enter into immediate negotiations under the auspices of the United Nations representative for India and Pakistan in order to reach agreement on the specific number of forces to remain on each side of the cease-fire line at the end of the period of demilitarisation, this number to be between 3,000 and 6,000 armed forces remaining on the Pakistan side of the cease-fire line and between 12,000 and 18,000 armed forces remaining on the India side of the cease-fire line.'

Though during the discussions Pakistan's representative to the UN, Mr. Zafrulla Khan, pointed out that the number of forces proposed was not fair, yet he said that Pakistan 'is prepared to go forward on the basis of this resolution.'

The Indian representative, Mrs. Pandit, in her speech, however, categorically said, 'I should like to repeat that we reject the proposal in it and we are not prepared to enter into any talks on the basis suggested.'

Regarding the question of plebiscite, Pakistan was in favour of giving complete authority to the UN for holding, organising and supervising the plebiscite. India, on the other hand, only wanted the non-binding advice of the UN.

Various UN mediators were appointed to resolve this issue, but no one was successful in convincing India on a compromise. Sir Owen Dixon, the UN mediator, in his report submitted in 1950, wrote: 'In the end I became convinced that India's agreement would never be obtained to demilitarisation in any such form, or to provisions governing the period of plebiscite of any such character, as would in my opinion, permit of the plebiscite being conducted in conditions sufficiently guarding against intimidation and other forms of influence and abuse by which the freedom and fairness of the plebiscite might be imperilled.'

Dr. Frank P. Graham, appointed UN representative for India and Pakistan in 1951, submitted five reports, up to March 1953, but his efforts at mediation also proved to be unsuccessful as India would not agree on the size of the forces to be left on either side of the cease-fire line after demilitarisation.

India, therefore, consistently refused to take recourse to all proposals of various statesmen and UN representatives for the holding of a plebiscite in

Jammu and Kashmir. On the other hand, it is on record that Pakistan supported all such international mediation and UN efforts.

Defending the Indian position on plebiscite, Sisir Gupta, an Indian scholar, wrote: 'it became obvious even at the early stages of the Kashmir dispute that a plebiscite -an "ideal" solution according to some – because of the complexities in Kashmir was difficult to accomplish. Even as a democratic solution, it had loopholes.

Kashmir, clearly, is not composed of one people: in religion, it has three major groups; in language, four. If there is a section which wants to secede from India, there are others who do not.'

However, the fact of the matter is that, right from the beginning, India feared that if a plebiscite was held it would lose what it had already occupied.

According to a Kashmiri activist, Prof. Mrs. Shamim Shawl, 'plebiscite is the most plausible solution of the problem.

This has been accepted in the Resolutions of August 48 and January 1949. It is these resolutions, which confirm the disputed character of the problem and negate the Indian position that says Kashmir is an irrevocable part of India.

India is in fact challenging the rightful and legal authenticity of the United Nations by delaying the implementation of UN resolutions.'

Keeping in view the basic genesis and nature of the dispute, the option incorporated in the then UN resolutions is still valid. The UN resolutions are not time-barred, as observed in 1956, by the UN Secretary General, Dag Hammarskjold, who clarified the important principle that 'the UN decision is valid until it has been invalidated by the organ which took it.'

The UN Trusteeship Option

Generally, this option proposes that Kashmir should be placed under UN Trusteeship and then plebiscite may be held for the final resolution of the dispute.

It is argued that this will provide a face-saving for India, and will also give Kashmiris, on both sides of the Line of Control, enough time to come up with a joint option. The JKLF Chairman, Ammanullah Khan in December 1993, proposed: (1) complete, simultaneous withdrawal of Indian and Pakistani troops and civil administration, non-Kashmiri personnel from Jammu and Kashmir; (2) the reunification of Indian and Pakistani-controlled parts of Kashmir; (3) placement of the State under UN control for five to ten years; and (4) holding of a plebiscite.

Well-known Pakistani economist, the late Dr. Mahbubul Haq, in an interview he gave to an Urdu Weekly *Hurmat,* in 1994, proposed that only the Kashmir Valley be placed under UN Trusteeship for ten years and then plebiscite be held in the Kashmir Valley.

As India regards Occupied Kashmir as its integral part, it is obvious that it will never voluntarily agree to the placing of the State, or the Kashmir Valley under UN trusteeship. *Secondly,* both the above trusteeship options support the plebiscite option under the UN auspices, an option that has been rejected by India even though in the early years of the dispute India committed itself to holding of the plebiscite.

As regards Pakistan and the Kashmiris, since the above proposals support a UN role and the option of plebiscite, in view of the already existing UN resolutions which provide the plebiscite option under UN auspices, the above proposal would mean unnecessarily prolonging the solution beyond five or ten years.

Moreover, according to Article 76 of Chapter XII of the UN Charter one of the basic objectives of the trusteeship system is 'to promote the political, economic, social, and educational advancement of the inhabitants of the trust territories, and their progressive development towards self-government or independence, as may be appropriate to the particular circumstances of each territory and its peoples...' The case of Jammu and Kashmir does not require placement under UN trusteeship as the Kashmiris have, over the years, demonstrated their political will by waging an indigenous movement in Occupied Kashmir for their right of self-determination, underscoring the fact that their preferred option is self-determination.

The Independence Option

An option gradually evolved as a result of the impasse on the Kashmir issue is that of independence, generally known as the 'Third Option'. Under this option, the pre-Partition status of the Jammu and Kashmir State is to be restored and an independent state established. The proposal is mainly advocated by the JKLF.

Its Chairman, Amanullah Khan, in one of his articles says, 'the future independent Kashmir is to be neutral, like Switzerland, with friendly and trade relations with all its neighbours.'

According to Amanullah Khan's proposal, 'Independent Kashmir is to consist of five federating units: Kashmir Valley, Jammu province, Ladakh, Azad Kashmir and Gilgit-Baltistan, each enjoying considerable internal autonomy, having its own elected provincial government. At the centre there will be a bicameral parliament.' He further says, 'the re-unification and independence of the state can be brought about without making any drastic changes in the existing socio-economic, political and administrative structures of any of the present three units i.e. Indian occupied areas, Azad Kashmir and Gilgit-Baltistan.'

According to Indian scholars 'independence, either for part or all of J&K, is equally unrealistic.

They maintain that although an artificial product of war, the Line of Control does follow a rough and ready ethno-cultural divide in some measure.

Further, "self-determination" within the two parts of J&K could result in the Balkanisation of a mosaic put together by history, with every new 'self-determined' minority being assailed for a newly-created majoritarianism, which lesser minorities refuse to accept.

Such an unravelling would be a recipe for strife, insecurity, and destabilisation of the region.'

The option for an independent Jammu and Kashmir state does not seem to be a viable solution, as the State would be land-locked and, therefore, permanently dependent on its neighbours. For India the proposition would be unacceptable because it could lead to a similar unravelling in other areas where separatist movements are going on in India.

As regards Pakistan, the 'third option' can be advantageous. An independent Jammu and Kashmir state would have a preference for good relations with a neighbour that has consistently extended its support to the principles of self-determination. Pakistan's position on the 'third option' has been that it should not confound the existent problems further, and, therefore, it stresses the need to address the issue in the light of the Security Council Resolutions, as a first step in the resolution of the dispute.

The Irish Model

Recently, various scholars have suggested the Irish model, based on the 'Good Friday Agreement' signed in April 1998 between the Governments of the United Kingdom of Great Britain and Northern Ireland and the Government of Ireland, as a possible option for resolving the Kashmir dispute between India and Pakistan.

The main features of the 'Good Friday Agreement' are: (a) it recognises the consent principle: that change in the status of Northern Ireland can only come about with the consent of the majority of its people.

It acknowledges that while a substantial minority in the North and a majority on the island want a united Ireland, the majority in the North currently wishes to maintain the Union.

However, it says that if that situation changes, there is a binding obligation on both governments to give effect to whatever wish the people of the North express; (b) it recognises 'the birthright of all the people of Northern Ireland' to identify themselves and be accepted as Irish, British or both; (c) it proposes concrete legislative and constitutional changes; such as, the Government of Ireland Act, claiming British jurisdiction over all of Ireland is to be replaced, future polls in the North on its status are to be held on the order of the Secretary of State for Northern Ireland. Such polls must be at least seven years apart; (d) it proposes a 108-member Assembly elected by proportional representation; (e) it establishes a North-South Ministerial Council under legislation at Westminister and the Oireachtas, to bring together ministers from the North and the Republic; (f) it establishes a British-Irish Council consisting of representatives of the British and Irish Governments, devolved in situations in Northern Ireland, Scotland and Wales, the Isle of Man and the Channel Islands; (g) it establishes a new British-Irish Conference; (h) reaffirms commitment to the total disarmament of all paramilitary organisations, and confirms intention to work constructively with the Independent Commission on Decommissioning; and, (i) establishes an independent commission to make recommendations for future policing arrangements in the North.

Based on the Irish model, some Indian scholars have made suggestions supporting autonomy for various regions of Jammu and Kashmir. For example, Amit A. Pandya, an Indian scholar, has proposed the following steps:

(1) An India-Pakistan commission to discuss boundary issues in Jammu and Kashmir, and to engage in joint monitoring of the LOC;

(2) Phased demilitarisation at the LOC, contingent first on substantial cessation of 'cross-border' terrorism;

(3) Three-way (Indian, Pakistani, Kashmiri) commission on internal law and order. Kashmiris to be chosen from Pakistan-occupied Azad Kashmir and all Indian-occupied segments—Valley, Jammu and Ladakh.

(4) Indian and Pakistani commitments to proceed with a scheme of local government reform and strengthening of local institutions and local autonomy in respective areas of Kashmir.

(5) Issue-specific consultative bodies (water, power, tourism, finance) comprising such local units, and Indian Jammu & Kashmir State and Azad Kashmir governments.

(6) Regularly scheduled and publicity-free consultative mechanism for

Indian government's talks with all parties, and with non-party civil society institutions, within Indian Kashmir on political issues.

(7) Corresponding mechanism for Azad Kashmir.

(8) Consultative mechanism for talks among all parties on ethnic and religious minority protections.

(9) Consultative mechanism for dialogue between these processes on the Indian and Pakistani side of the LOC.

(10) Indian commitment to allow free access, consistent with security requirements, to independent and credible Indian human rights monitoring organizations, and to Indian, and Pakistani press.

Corresponding commitment by Pakistan for Azad Kashmir. Another Indian scholar, Professor Sumantra Bose, basing his suggestions on the Irish model proposes three dimensions.

Dimension one: the New Delhi-Islamabad axis, involving the 'establishment of a permanent India-Pakistan Intergovernmental Conference to promote the harmonious and mutually beneficial development of the totality of relationships between the two countries.'

As suggested by Professor Bose, this body is to be chaired by the respective prime ministers, and its twice-yearly meetings to be rotated between Indian and Pakistani cities.

Dimension two: the New Delhi-Srinagar and Islamabad-Muzaffarabad axis, here the 'objective in Kashmir would be the gradual, incremental normalisation of politics within Kashmir in both Indian-and Pakistani-controlled zones, and the devising and implementation of political frameworks which can foster a working degree of internal accommodation and cooperation between the representatives of communities holding radically different basic political allegiances.'

Dimension three: the Srinagar-Muzaffarabad axis, proposes 'along with the progressive normalisation of the overall framework of India-Pakistan relations and the gradual normalisation of life and politics in both sides of the Kashmir border', that there is greater need to make the border porous.

He further suggests 'the establishment of a cross-border Jammu and Kashmir Council for Cooperation, with representatives from inclusive, elected and autonomous governments from both sides of the line of control.'

These Indian proposals, selectively use the Irish model, but basically support autonomy for the regions of Jammu and Kashmir under the supervision of India and Pakistan.

The central aspects focusing on self-determination and total disarmament after implementation of the agreement are ignored. The Indian proposals are similar to the idea of a condominium with dominant Indian influence. Also, the LoC has been proposed as the dividing line and a soft border.

This is against the genesis of the Kashmir dispute, which is not for greater autonomy or 'self-government', as proposed, but for the right of self-determination to be expressed by the Kashmiris.

However, as Dr. Mazari has suggested, it is the central aspects of the Irish model, which are relevant in case of the Kashmir dispute and could be used as guiding principles for a resolution of the conflict. For instance the underlying principle is *recognition of the right of the people as of Northern Ireland* to choose their political future through a referendum. Also, the principle of deweaponisation is linked to it, as following the implementation of the Agreement.

6

Pakistan and India War over Kashmir in 1999

Within weeks, the troop concentration along the LoC and the international border has increased manifold, and the naval fleets of the two countries have sailed out into the open seas to position themselves against each other. And as thousands of villagers living on the two sides of the border start to move out to safer areas, India and Pakistan once again appear to be at the brink of another more disastrous war.

This situation deteriorated further in recent weeks when the Indian administration, embarrassed at its army's failure to flush out the militants from Kargil and Dras, looked for a military solution to the conflict. The Indian government's snub to Pakistan's proposal for talks, and its refusal to hold any dialogue until the withdrawal of the "Islamabad-backed infiltrators" from Kargil, and Pakistan's categorical rejection of its direct involvement, has led to a new level of jingoism in India.

Although the Indian government did try to clarify that the American visit did not amount to third-party mediation, Delhi's frustration over the prolonged conflict in Kargil had ultimately sucked it into accepting some kind of US role in this affair.

As more and more bodies of Indian soldiers from the conflict zone reach their respective towns, the most popular war cry in Delhi now is to "teach Pakistan another lesson." On the other hand, Pakistan's army chief, General Pervez Musharraf has made it absolutely clear that the Pakistani armed forces are fully prepared to counter any aggression.

Already, the so-called 'bus diplomacy', which only a couple of months ago had created a fresh atmosphere of optimism in the region, looks like a thing of the past. Now there is renewed talk on both sides of settling the outstanding dispute through military means. Yes, despite all the official denials from Delhi and Islamabad about the possibility of a direct engagement on the battlefield, a war between the two proud nuclear powers does look imminent.

As war clouds started to hover over the subcontinent, matters were made worse by the role of the media, particularly in India. Almost the entire battery of newspaper and satellite television networks in India appears to have fallen in line with the policy of the Indian ministry of external affairs and their military establishment, thus creating a tangible war-like atmosphere. There were statements, not only from politicians, but also journalists, wherein Pakistan was called a "rogue state", and demands were made to inflict "lasting punishment" on Pakistan.

Of course, the Pakistani media has also not lagged far behind. State-run television (PTV) and the right-wing conservative press continue to project these few hundred militants as the true liberators of Kashmir. The press has also kept up constant pressure on the government against any "peace deal". Some newspapers and analysts are now ridiculing the Indian army for its failure in Kargil, and are describing the present situation as "the most opportune time" to declare full-fledged war for the liberation of Kashmir.

These moves have been given further substance by statements and speeches made by members of the hard line Islamic parties. For instance, speakers at a rally in Rawalpindi, attended by several thousand supporters of the Pakistan-based militant group, Lashkar-e-Taiba, did not mince words in giving a warning to Prime Minister Nawaz Sharif against pulling out of the conflict. And then there are the likes of the former ISI chief, Lt. General (retd.) Hamid Gul, who went to the extent of saying that any deal with Delhi at the cost of the militants offensive would amount to putting the last nail in the coffin of the present government. So, if anything was lacking in creating an atmosphere to start a greater conflict, the hawks amongst the politicians and the media on the two sides have done their bit to justify an all-out war.

With both sides locked in one of the worst conflicts since the 1971 war, it soon started to dawn on the international community that developments in South Asia were getting out of hand. When Pakistan downed two Indian combat aircraft which had crossed into its territory, and Delhi started to show signs of crossing the LoC in a counter-offensive, the international community responded with alarm and panic. The United States and other G-8 countries, despite their heavy involvement in the Kosovo crisis, were compelled to take time out and turn their attention towards the conflict in South Asia.

It did not take them long to realise that the possible escalation in the region could have catastrophic consequences. A resolution passed by G-8 leaders not only took notice of the long-standing dispute over Kashmir, it also expressed serious concern over the escalation in the Kargil region.

US President Bill Clinton went a step further and telephoned both the Indian and Pakistani prime ministers, asking them to show restraint. But both these developments signalled diplomatic setbacks for Pakistan. The G-8 and President Clinton clearly sided with the Indian version of cause and blame. In fact, President Clinton even asked the Pakistani prime minister to use his influence to withdraw the militants from Kargil — thus directly implying that Pakistan not only had the means to pull out these fighters but that it had in fact put them there in the first place.

The United States did not stop just there. Realising the seriousness of the Kargil conflict, which by all means had the potential of snow-balling into all-out war, Washington immediately rushed its senior most military commander in the region and a senior State Department official to Islamabad. General Anthony Zinni and the State Department official held extensive discussions with top Pakistani officials, including the prime minister and the army chief.

Although there were no positive statements from either side, the meetings did produce enough ground for the State Department official to undertake a trip to Delhi to hold talks with the Indian authorities. And although the Indian government did try to clarify that the visit did not amount to third-party mediation on Kashmir, Delhi's frustration over the prolonged conflict in Kargil had ultimately sucked it into a situation where it had been forced to accept some kind of US role in this affair.

However, even as a small conflict in a remote mountainous region has resulted in a situation where a bloody war between the two known South Asian adversaries looks like a reality, very little is known about the circumstances which led to this development. Amidst allegations and counter-allegations, and claims and counter-claims by Islamabad and Delhi, the truth about the events of Kargil remains shrouded in secrecy.

The Indian establishment has directly blamed Pakistan's armed forces for carrying out the present offensive, accusing the Light Infantry Battalion of being actively involved with the Pakistani and Afghan militants in Kargil. Pakistan's foreign office and military establishment still maintain they have no active role in the Kargil conflict. But, does this also mean that they were unaware of the militants' plans? There have also been strong suggestions in Delhi that perhaps Prime Minister Nawaz Sharif was not even aware of the army's decision to launch this operation, and many Western diplomats in Islamabad tend to agree with this theory.

Despite the repeated claims by India about the active presence of Pakistani troops in the Kargil mountains, so far very little concrete evidence has been produced to substantiate such allegations. However, the Pakistan-based leadership of the various militant groups have not missed any opportunity to embarrass Islamabad. Their attempts to boost the activities of their comrades in Kargil and reports of sending in reinforcements belie the government's claim about the indigenous nature of the present conflict.

If a former head of the ISI, Lt. General (retd) Javed Nasir is to be believed, the preparations for the Kargil operation started several months ago. The Kargil region has been traditionally used by the Kashmiri militants to enter the valley. However, this time the militants had more ambitious plans. They decided to move into the area and try to capture the strategically located mountains and ridges that overlook the Kargil-Srinagar road. The idea was to try and block the supply route for the Indian troops based at the Siachen glacier. Towards the end of last year, several hundred volunteers from four well-known militant groups began vigorous training sessions in mountainous areas to prepare themselves to brave rough, wintry conditions.

They were mainly from Tehrik-e-Jihad, an organisation that draws its cadres from Kashmir, Al-Badr, whose members include both Kashmiris and Pakistanis, Harkatul Mujahideen, which has in its fold a few Kashmiris but many Pakistanis and Afghans, and Lashkar-e-Taiba, whose members largely hail from Pakistan. Later on, when the conflict intensified in Kargil, two more groups, Hizbul Mujahideen and Harkat-e-Jihad, also joined to provide reinforcements. But according to a number of western diplomats, it is hard to believe that these militant groups could have launched such a major offensive without the active help and support of the Pakistan army.

By now, it has been established beyond doubt that this time the militants have completely shaken the entire Indian establishment. Many senior Indian journalists admit that the belligerency presently being witnessed in India is not only because the militants have badly bruised the Indian claim of being a mighty regional power; the sheer number of casualties from the present conflict have shaken the entire country. Television images beamed by Indian satellite net¬works, showing the arrival of the dead and wounded from the battle front, and the reactions from the family members and the local population capture the real mood of depression and anger in India.

A recent report by the French news agency AFP from Indian-held Kashmir gave a graphic account of the way the dead and wounded are being brought to Srinagar from the battle front, before being sent to Delhi. According to the report, the Indian Airline's flight from Srinagar to Delhi these days has turned into an air ambulance service. Almost every day, it carries to the Indian capital dead bodies and injured soldiers from the battle front in Kargil in greater numbers than normal passengers. The passenger seats in the air¬craft are often removed to accommodate stretchers carrying the wounded, and a special section of the Delhi airport has been designated to accommodate the coffins arriving from the battle zone.

A few journalists covering the Kargil conflict who managed to get on the flight describe the atmosphere on the flight as a true reflection of the events in Kargil. According to Abu Maaz, who is a sector commander of the Tehrik-e-Jihad in Kargil, even now several bodies of Indian soldiers are lying decomposing on the mountains, and Indian troops dare not lift them for fear of coming in the line of fire. Abu Maaz, who recently came to Skardu for reinforcements, told journalists the number of casualties on the Indian side have been much higher that what is being claimed by New Delhi.

Rough estimates indicate that the Indian army has lost more officers and men in these few weeks of fighting in Kargil than it lost in the last full-fledged war with Pakistan in 1971. And according to a senior Indian journalist, this time the bodies are going to some of the remotest towns and villages in India, thus creating a nation-wide mood of anger, and encouraging hawks to go for an all-out war against Pakistan.

However, the question being asked by many senior observers is that can either India or Pakistan afford to engage in a full-scale war, even if it is limited to the use of conventional forces? Some Western diplomats in Islamabad are of the view that, even if there is a war, it will be fought along the LoC, and will remain confined to Kashmir. But are there any guarantees that the losing side is not going to launch an offensive on the international border? In either case, the level of destruction on the two sides will be immense, and despite Indian claims of military superiority, there is little chance that India can win a war against Pakistan in a decisive manner.

A report titled "South Asian Military Balance", submitted by the US Deputy Secretary of Defence Bruce Riedel before the American Senate's foreign relations sub-committee last year, clearly stated that while India enjoys a numerical advantage over Pakistan in conventional military capability, it is most unlikely that it would score a decisive victory over Pakistan. Recently reproduced excerpts from the report suggest that the internal security problems faced by India in Kashmir and East Punjab may also hamper India's quantitative advantage over Pakistan.

While analysing comparative conventional forces in detail, the Riedel report argues that because of its more developed industrial capability and greater geographical expanse which provides strategic depth not available to the much smaller Pakistan, India could fight a longer war than Pakistan — thus a longer war would favour India. However, many analysts say that such a war would be a major blow to economic and social development in the two countries and may push them back to where they started more than 50 years ago.

But is there really a way to prevent the present conflict from snowballing into an all-out war? Many analysts and western diplomats believe the key to ending the present conflict lies with Prime Minister Nawaz Sharif.

However, it mainly depends on what the government's real objectives, both strategic and diplomatic, are and the extent to which it wants to use the situation in Kargil to internationalise the Kashmir dispute. Some government leaders in favour of ending the present crisis believe the diplomatic advantage that Pakistan had in the initial stages of the conflict has gradually slipped away with the international community turning against Pakistan. This is precisely what the opposition leader, Aitzaz Ahsan, said in the Senate during the debate on the Kargil situation, and accused the government of isolating the country on the diplomatic front.

However, even if Prime Minister Nawaz Sharif wants to end the present impasse in an attempt to prevent a major escalation, his choices are quite limited, argue analysts. As things stand at the moment, the government is just one of the three elements in the entire conflict — the other two being the army and the militants and their parent political parties.

It is not clear how the army leadership will react if there is a serious proposal from Premier Sharif to try and end the present conflict by asking the militants to withdraw. There is another, equally important question: even if the militants' initial offensive was launched with the active support from this side of the LoC, is it possible to force them into withdrawal? Militant leaders, both in Muzaffarabad and Pakistan, say they are fully committed to the present phase of the Kashmir struggle, and their sacrifices in the present fighting make it incumbent upon them not to agree to any diplomatic settlement.

Those close to the prime minister say he is certainly aware of these complications, but this has not deterred his desire to use the process of dialogue to settle outstanding issues with India. Following the failure of his peace initiative, whereby foreign minister Sartaj Aziz was sent to Delhi for talks, Sharif now appears to be employing back-channel diplomacy to try and defuse the situation. Recently, former foreign secretary Niaz Naik was quietly sent to Delhi to hold talks with Indian leaders. During his brief stay, he met both Indian Prime Minister Atal Bihari Vajpayee and Foreign Minister Jaswant Singh.

The visit was supposed to be kept secret as apparently it was a serious attempt to try and find a way out of the current impasse without drawing any media attention. However, some Indian officials deliberately leaked it to the local press, thus prompting Islamabad to also leak the move by Delhi to send senior Indian journalist, Mishra along with a ministry of external affairs official, to meet Prime Minister Nawaz Sharif.

Senior analysts in Islamabad say it is not only domestic problems that are creating difficulties for Sharif in his search for an agreeable solution to the current crisis. The level of belligerency being displayed by Delhi is also being described as a major factor in preventing a real diplomatic break¬through. However, some Pakistani analysts and Western diplomats in Islamabad are convinced that, since the visit by the US military and State Department officials to the region, things appear to be moving in the right direction. If this optimism is not misplaced, it is quite possible that the war, which at the moment appears to be imminent, may eventually be averted through diplomacy.

INDIA DISCOVERS INFILTRATION AND MOBILIZES

Initially, these incursions were not detected for a number of reasons: Indian patrols were not sent into some of the areas infiltrated by the Pakistani forces and heavy artillery fire by Pakistan in some areas provided cover for the infiltrators. But by the second week of May, the ambushing of an Indian patrol team led by Capt Saurabh Kalia, who acted on a tip-off by a local shepherd in the Batalik sector, led to the exposure of the infiltration. Initially, with little knowledge of the nature or extent of the infiltration, the Indian troops in the area assumed that the infiltrators were jihadis and claimed that they would evict them within a few days. Subsequent discovery of infiltration elsewhere along the LOC, and the difference in tactics employed by the infiltrators, caused the Indian army to realize that the plan of attack was on a much bigger scale. The total area seized by the ingress is generally accepted to between 130 km^2 – 200 km^2;

The Government of India responded with Operation Vijay, a mobilisation of 200,000 Indian troops. However, because of the nature of the terrain, division and corps operations could not be mounted; subsequent fighting was conducted mostly at the regimental or battalion level. In effect, two divisions of the Indian Army, numbering 20,000, plus several thousand from theParamilitary forces of India and the air force were deployed in the conflict zone. The total number of Indian soldiers that were involved in the military operation on the Kargil-Drass sector was thus close to 30,000. The number of infiltrators, including those providing logistical backup, has been put at approximately 5,000 at the height of the conflict. This figure includes troops fromPakistan-administered Kashmir who provided additional artillery support.

The Indian Air Force launched Operation Safed Sagar in support of the mobilization of Indian land forces, but its effectiveness during the war was limited by the high altitude and weather conditions, which in turn limited bomb loads and the number of airstrips that could be used.

The Indian Navy also prepared to blockade the Pakistani ports (primarily Karachi port) to cut off supply routes. Later, the then-Prime Minister of Pakistan Nawaz Sharif disclosed that Pakistan was left with just six days of fuel to sustain itself if a full-fledged war had broken out.

India attacks Pakistani Positions

The terrain of Kashmir is mountainous and at high altitudes; even the best roads, such as National Highway 1D from Leh to Srinagar, are only two lanes. The rough terrain and narrow roads slowed traffic, and the high altitude, which affected the ability of aircraft to carry loads, made control of NH 1D (the actual stretch of the highway which was under Pakistani fire) a priority for India. From their observation posts, the Pakistani forces had a clear line-of-sight to lay down indirect artillery fire on NH 1D, inflicting heavy casualties on the Indians. This was a serious problem for the Indian Army as the highway was its main logistical and supply route. The Pakistani shelling of the arterial road posed the threat of Leh being cut off, though an alternative (and longer) road to Leh existed via Himachal Pradesh.

The infiltrators, apart from being equipped with small arms and grenade launchers, were also armed with mortars, artillery and anti-aircraft guns. Many posts were also heavily mined, with India later stating to having recovered more than 8,000 anti-personnel mines according to an ICBL report. Pakistan's reconnaissance was done through unmanned aerial vehicles and AN/TPQ-36 Firefinder radars supplied by the US. The initial Indian attacks were aimed at controlling the hills overlooking NH 1D, with high priority being given to the stretches of the highway near the town of Kargil. The majority of posts along the Line of Control were adjacent to the highway, and therefore the recapture of nearly every infiltrated post increased both the territorial gains and the security of the highway. The protection of this route and the recapture of the forward posts were thus *ongoing objectives* throughout the war.

The Indian Army's first priority was to recapture peaks that were in the immediate vicinity of NH 1D. This resulted in Indian troops first targeting the Tiger Hill and Tololing complex in Dras, which dominated the Srinagar-Leh route. This was soon followed by the Batalik-Turtok sub-sector which provided access to Siachen Glacier. Some of the peaks that were of vital strategic importance to the Pakistani defensive troops were Point 4590 and

Point 5353. While 4590 was the nearest point that had a view of NH 1D, point 5353 was the highest feature in the Dras sector, allowing the Pakistani troops to observe NH 1D. The recapture of Point 4590 by Indian troops on June 14 was significant, notwithstanding the fact that it resulted in the Indian Army suffering the most casualties in a single battle during the conflict. Though most of the posts in the vicinity of the highway were cleared by mid-June, some parts of the highway near Drass witnessed sporadic shelling until the end of the war.

Once India regained control of the hills overlooking NH 1D, the Indian Army turned to driving the invading force back across the Line of Control. TheBattle of Tololing, among other assaults, slowly tilted the combat in India's favor. The Pakistani troops at Tololing were aided by Pakistani fighters from Kashmir. Some of the posts put up a stiff resistance, including Tiger Hill (Point 5140) that fell only later in the war. Indian troops found well-entrenched Pakistani soldiers at Tiger Hill, and both sides suffered heavy casualties. After a final assault on the peak in which 10 Pakistani soldiers and 5 Indian soldiers were killed, Tiger Hill finally fell. A few of the assaults occurred atop hitherto unheard of peaks – most of them unnamed with only Point numbers to differentiate them – which witnessed fierce hand to hand combat.

As the operation was fully underway, about 250 artillery guns were brought in to clear the infiltrators in the posts that were in the line-of-sight. The BoforsFH-77B field howitzer played a vital role, with Indian gunners making maximum use of the terrain that assisted such an attack. However, its success was limited elsewhere due to the lack of space and depth to deploy the Bofors gun.

It was in this type of terrain that aerial attacks were used with limited effectiveness. French made Mirage 2000H of the IAF were tasked to drop laser-guided bombs to destroy well-entrenched positions of the Pakistani forces. However, The IAF lost a MiG-27 strike aircraft which it attributed to anengine failure as well as a MiG-21 fighter which was shot down by Pakistan; initially Pakistan said it shot down both jets after they crossed into its territory. One Mi-8 helicopter was also lost, due to Stinger SAMs.

On May 27, 1999, Flt. Lt. Nachiketa developed engine trouble in the Batalik sector and bailed out of his craft. Sqn Ldr Ajay Ahuja went out of his way to locate his comrade but was shot down by a shoulder-fired Stinger missile. According to reports, he had bailed out of his stricken plane safely but was apparently killed by his captors as his body was returned riddled with bullet wounds.

In many vital points, neither artillery nor air power could dislodge the outposts manned by the Pakistani soldiers, who were out of visible range. The

Indian Army mounted some direct frontal ground assaults which were slow and took a heavy toll given the steep ascent that had to be made on peaks as high as 18,000 feet (5,500 m). Since any daylight attack would be suicidal, all the advances had to be made under the cover of darkness, escalating the risk of freezing. Accounting for the wind chill factor, the temperatures were often as low as "15 °C to "11 °C (12 °F to 5 °F) near the mountain tops. Based on military tactics, much of the costly frontal assaults by the Indians could have been avoided if the Indian Military had chosen to blockade the supply route of the opposing force, virtually creating a siege. Such a move would have involved the Indian troops crossing the LoC as well as initiating aerial attacks on Pakistan soil, a manoeuvre India was not willing to exercise fearing an expansion of the theatre of war and reducing international support for its cause.

Two months into the conflict, Indian troops had slowly retaken most of the ridges that were encroached by the infiltrators; according to official count, an estimated 75%–80% of the intruded area and nearly all high ground was back under Indian control.

Withdrawal and Final Battles

The outbreak of armed fighting, Pakistan sought American help in de-escalating the conflict. Bruce Riedel, aide to then President Bill Clinton reported that the US intelligence had imaged Pakistani movements of nuclear weapons to forward deployments for fear of the Kargil hostilities escalating into a wider conflict between the two countries. However, President Clinton refused to intervene until Pakistan had removed all forces from the Indian side of the Line of Control. Following the Washington accord on July 4, where Sharif agreed to withdraw Pakistani troops, most of the fighting came to a gradual halt, but some Pakistani forces remained in positions on the Indian side of the LOC. In addition, the United Jihad Council (an umbrella for extremist groups) rejected Pakistan's plan for a climb-down, instead deciding to fight on.

The Indian army launched its final attacks in the last week of July; as soon as the Drass subsector had been cleared of Pakistani forces, the fighting ceased on July 26. The day has since been marked as *Kargil Vijay Diwas* (Kargil Victory Day) in India. By the end of the war, India had resumed control of all territory south and east of the Line of Control, as was established in July 1972 as per the Simla Agreement.

World Opinion

Pakistan was criticised by other countries for instigating the war, as its paramilitary forces and insurgents crossed the Line of Control. Pakistan's primary diplomatic response, one of plausible deniability linking the incursion to what it officially termed as "Kashmiri freedom fighters", was in the end not successful. Veteran analysts argued that the battle was fought at heights where only seasoned troops could survive, so poorly equipped "freedom fighters" would neither have the ability nor the wherewithal to seize land and defend it.

Moreover, while the army had initially denied the involvement of its troops in the intrusion, two soldiers were awarded the Nishan-E-Haider (Pakistan's highest military honour). Another 90 soldiers were also given gallantry awards, most of them posthumously, confirming Pakistan's role in the episode. India also released taped phone conversations between the Army Chief and a senior Pakistani general where the latter is recorded saying: "the scruff of [the militants] necks is in our hands," although Pakistan dismissed it as a "total fabrication". Concurrently, Pakistan made several contradicting statements, confirming its role in Kargil, when it defended the incursions saying that the LOC itself was disputed. Pakistan also attempted to internationalize the Kashmir issue, by linking the crisis in Kargil to the largerKashmir conflict but, such a diplomatic stance found few backers on the world stage.

As the Indian counter-attacks picked up momentum, Pakistani prime minister Nawaz Sharif flew to meet U.S. President Bill Clinton on July 4 to obtain support from the United States. Clinton rebuked Sharif, however, and asked him to use his contacts to rein in the militants and withdraw Pakistani soldiers from Indian territory. Clinton would later reveal in his autobiography that "Sharif's moves were perplexing" since the Indian Prime Minister had travelled to Lahore to promote bilateral talks aimed at resolving the Kashmir problem and "by crossing the Line of Control, Pakistan had wrecked the [bilateral] talks." On the other hand, he applauded Indian restraint for not crossing the LoC and escalating the conflict into an all-out war.

G8 nations supported India and condemned the Pakistani violation of the LOC at the Cologne summit. The European Union also opposed Pakistan's violation of the LOC. China, a long-time ally of Pakistan, insisted on a pullout of forces to the pre-conflict positions along the LoC and settling border issues peacefully. Other organizations like the ASEAN Regional Forum too supported India's stand on the inviolability of the LOC.

Faced with growing international pressure, Sharif managed to pull back the remaining soldiers from Indian territory. The joint statement issued by Clinton and Sharif conveyed the need to respect the Line of Control and resume bilateral talks as the best forum to resolve all disputes.

Gallantry Awards

A number of Indian soldiers earned awards for gallantry during the campaign.

- Grenadier Yogendra Singh Yadav, 18 Grenadiers, Param Vir Chakra
- Lieutenant Manoj Kumar Pandey, 1/11 Gorkha Rifles, Param Vir Chakra, Posthumous
- Captain Vikram Batra, 13 JAK Rifles, Param Vir Chakra, Posthumous
- Captain Anuj Nayyar,17 JAT Regiment, Maha Vir Chakra, Posthumous
- Major Saravanan, 1 Bihar, Vir Chakra, Posthumous
- Squadron Leader Ajay Ahuja, Indian Air Force, Vir Chakra, Posthumous
- Rifleman Sanjay Kumar, 13 JAK Rifles, Param Vir Chakra
- Major Rajesh Singh Adhikari, 18 Grenadiers, Maha Vir Chakra, Posthumous

Two Pakistani soldiers received the Nishan-e-Haider.

- Captain Karnal Sher Khan, Nishan-e-Haider, Posthumous
- Havaldaar Lalak Jan, Northern Light Infantry, Nishan-e-Haider, Posthumous

Impact and Influence of Media

The Kargil War was significant for the impact and influence of the mass media on public opinion in both nations. Coming at a time of exploding growth in electronic journalism in India, the Kargil news stories and war footage were often telecast live on TV, and many websites provided in-depth analysis of the war. The conflict became the first "live" war in South Asia; it was given such detailed media coverage that one effect was the drumming up of jingoistic feelings. The conflict soon turned into a news propaganda war, in which press briefings given by government officials of each nation produced conflicting claims and counterclaims. The Indian government placed a temporary news embargo on information from Pakistan, banning the telecast of the state-run Pakistani channel PTV and blocking access to online editions of the *Dawn* newspaper. The Pakistani media criticized this apparent curbing of freedom of the press in India, while India media claimed it was in the interest of national security. The Indian government ran advertisements in foreign publications including *The Times* and *The Washington Post* detailing Pakistan's role in supporting extremists in Kashmir in an attempt to garner political support for its position.

As the war progressed, media coverage of the conflict was more intense in India than in Pakistan. Many Indian channels showed images from the battle zone in a style reminiscent of CNN's coverage of the Gulf War (one of the shells fired by Pakistan troops even hit a Doordarshan transmission centre in Kargil while coverage continued). Reasons for India's increased coverage included the greater number of privately owned electronic media in India compared to Pakistan and relatively greater transparency in the Indian media. At a seminar in Karachi, Pakistani journalists agreed that while the Indian government had taken the press and the people into its confidence, Pakistan had not.

The print media in India and abroad was largely sympathetic to the Indian cause, with editorials in newspapers based in the west and other neutral countries observing that Pakistan was largely responsible for the conflict. Some analysts believe that Indian media, which was both larger in number and more credible, may have acted as a force multiplier for the Indian military operation in Kargil and served as a morale booster. As the fighting intensified, the Pakistani version of events found little backing on the world stage. This helped India gain valuable diplomatic recognition for its position.

WMDs and the Nuclear Factor

Since Pakistan and India each had weapons of mass destruction, many in the international community were concerned that if the Kargil conflict intensified, it could lead to nuclear war. Both countries had tested their nuclear capability in 1998 (India conducted its first test in 1974 while it was Pakistan's first-ever nuclear test). Many pundits believed the tests to be an indication of the escalating stakes in the scenario in South Asia. When the Kargil conflict started just a year after the nuclear tests, many nations desired to end it before it intensified. International concerns increased when Pakistani foreign secretary Shamshad Ahmad made a statement on May 31 warning that an escalation of the limited conflict could lead Pakistan to use "any weapon" in its arsenal. This was immediately interpreted as a threat of nuclear retaliation by Pakistan in the event of an extended war, and the belief was reinforced when the leader ofPakistan's senate noted, "The purpose of developing weapons becomes meaningless if they are not used when they are needed." Many such ambiguous statements from officials of both countries were viewed as warnings of an impending nuclear crisis where the combatants would consider use of their limited nuclear arsenals in 'tactical' nuclear warfare in the belief that it would not have ended in mutual assured destruction, as could have occurred in a nuclear conflict between the United States and the USSR. Some experts believe that following nuclear tests in 1998, the Pakistani military was emboldened by its nuclear deterrent to markedly increase coercion against India.

The nature of the India-Pakistan conflict took a more sinister turn when the U.S. received intelligence that Pakistani nuclear warheads were being moved towards the border. Bill Clinton tried to dissuade Pakistan prime minister Nawaz Sharif from nuclear brinkmanship, even threatening Pakistan of dire consequences. According to a White House official, Sharif seemed to be genuinely surprised by this supposed missile movement and responded that India was probably planning the same. In an article in May 2000 Dr Sanjay Badri-Maharaj claimed that India too had readied at least five nuclear-tipped ballistic missiles, but could not back up this claim with any official proof.

Sensing a deteriorating military scenario, diplomatic isolation, and the risks of a larger conventional and nuclear war, Sharif ordered the Pakistani army to vacate the Kargil heights. He later claimed in his official biography that General Pervez Musharraf had moved nuclear warheads without informing him. Recently however, Pervez Musharraf revealed in his memoirs that Pakistan's nuclear delivery system was not operational during the Kargil war; something that would have put Pakistan under serious disadvantage if the conflict went nuclear.

The threat of WMD included chemical and even biological weapons. Pakistan accused India of using chemical weapons and incendiary weapons such as napalm against the Kashmiri fighters. India, on the other hand, showcased a cache of gas masks as proof that Pakistan may have been prepared to use non-conventional weapons. US official and the Organisation for the Prohibition of Chemical Weapons determined that Pakistani allegations of India using banned chemicals in its bombs were unfounded.

THE 1999 KARGIL WAR: NOT A GENERALS' VICTORY

Much has been written about the event, including by the Chief of Army Staff at that time, Gen V P Malik, as also by the then Home Minister L K Advani. There was an official inquiry by India's renowned strategic affairs analyst, K Subrahmanyam, but he has pointed out to this writer that he did not go into operational details and accordingly, could not comment on certain weaknesses some top Indian commanders displayed. The mid-level and younger officers and men though fought well, and even though many of them perished, the victory actually belonged to them.

The Pakistani military leadership as well as its Inter Services Intelligence (ISI) have always been indulging in nasty manoeuvers against India. But that they dared to infiltrate troops into India and tried to capture a part of Kashmir yet again was possible because we were negligent, partly because we generally are so by temperament and partly because the government of the day, led by Mr A B Vajpayee, had ordered the forces to be "soft" on Pakistan because of the "positive" talks between him and his Pakistani counterpart, Nawaz Sharif towards maintaining peace and building friendship.

While opportunities for peace must be seized by politicians, there was no reason for the armed forces – the Army in particular – to be lax. In fact, the Pakistani move as it happened had been debated in the Indian Army for years and had been taken up as a strong possibility in periodic exercises. Yet, when it was happening, we were blind to it.

In the foreword to Brig Gurmeet Kanwal's book, Indian Army Vision 2020, Gen Malik says: "The Fact is that even after 60 years of independence, knowledge and experience of defence and military issues is lacking in most of our political leaders and civilian bureaucrats."

But the General has not shared the lapses and neglect of responsibilities of the Army leadership, particularly of the sector commanders, and to an extent, his own. Some of these are by now, well known, including the mindset of the 15 Corps Commander, Lt Gen Krishan Pal, who insisted that there were only a handful of infiltrators – 60 to 80 – and that none of them was a Pakistani soldier. He committed troops without allowing them adequate weapons and strength, and if facts given by Lt Gen Y M Bammi in a book are taken into account, he punished an officer, Brig Devinder Singh, who wanted better preparations insisting that there were a large number of Pakistani soldiers inside the Indian territory.

The officer had eight battalions under his charge, and by all accounts, he fought very well, leading the troops from the front. Gen Malik himself has been seen and heard praising this officer at various fora. Yet, Brig Devinder Singh's career was cut short to save those who were wrong.

To recall, the biggest players of the Kargil War were:

a. The Government at the highest echelon of the Political Leadership;
b. The top rung of the military leadership – The Army Chief, GOC-in-C Northern Command, 15 Corps Cdr , and the 3 Div Cdr;
c. The intelligence agencies, primarily the Intelligence Bureau (IB) and Research and Analysis Wing (RAW);
d. The Indian Air Force (IAF) and its exercise of Air Power.
e. The dedicated and committed soldiers and the middle and junior level officers.

The Role Of The Political Leadership

The NDA government was at its pinnacle in May 1998, having successfully conducted the nuclear test that month and having put India in the list of Nuclear Weapon States (NWS). The aim now was to resolve the Kashmir issue by seeking wellmeaning diplomatic and economic relations with Pakistan. Mrs Indira Gandhi had also attempted that, after the 1971 Bangladesh Liberation

War, by trying to tell the then Pakistani leader Z A Bhutto that only peace between the two neighbours would ensure their long-term economic prosperity and growth. In fact, she went out of the way to ensure a comfortable stay for Bhutto, personally choosing even the tapestry of the room he was to stay in Simla during the 1972 summit between them, and by telling Indian officers that the Pakistani leader must be given the respect due to a visiting head of government or state, and not that of a country which had lost war. She agreed to Bhutto's request to release nearly 96,000 Pakistani POWs, and Bhutto promised to work for peace with India.

Needless to say that he backed out. Mrs Gandhi did what was right in those circumstances. But the lesson for the Indian leadership was to understand that Pakistan is never to be trusted. Islamabad built a network of nuclear capability and missiles by smuggling and deceit, lying even to Washington which gave it liberal aid as a friend and mentor.

Prime Minister Vajpayee and his deputy, Advani, tried to establish a political dialogue with Pakistan. Coupled with the nuclear tests, a success with Islamabad would give them respect in the history books forever.

Intelligence organizations were told to be easy, and the armed forces stopped looking for periodic information from them. There was the February 1999 Bus Yatra (journey) by Vajpayee to Lahore to meet with his counterpart, Nawaz Sharif. It was a goodwill mission, seemingly wellresponded by Sharif.

But the fact that the then Pakistani Chief of Army Staff, Gen Parvez Musharraf, did not pay due respects to the visiting Indian leader during the visit, should have been an indication of the Pakistani army's intentions; that it had no intention to accommodate the rapprochement that the political leadership in Islamabad perhaps then wanted.

It may be noted that as a Brigadier on assignment with a think tank in London, Musharraf had written in a thesis that Pakistan must capture Kashmir to secure water from the Himalayan rivers for itself. As a Chief of Staff, he would certainly try to realize his thoughts.

It is a well known fact that the Srinagar-Leh axis runs closest to the Line of Control (LOC) in the Dras–Kargil Sector. Also, the terrain on the Indian side is hostile to defend, whereas the terrain on the Pakistan side is favorable to launch an offensive. Strategically, Pakistan has always intended to block, disrupt or permanently dislocate it.

My first posting after being commissioned into the IAF in 1963 was to Jammu in Squadron 43, flying Dakotas. The main task was to operate to Kargil and Thoise to provide logistic support to the troops deployed in forward areas. I was fortunate to be deputed as the Base Commander of Air Force clement at Kargil from Feb to May 1964, working along with 121 (Ind) Infantry Brigade.

It was an education. Brig Chopra, an Armoured Corps officer who was the Brigade Commander, always used to say that the Dras-Kargil Sector was the most sensitive because of its close proximity to the LOC as well as the terrain factors.

Much later, during a course in 1980-81 at the Army's prestigious College of Combat at MHOW, now renamed Army War College, this lesson was repeated by none other than the Commandant, Lt Gen K Sunderji.

He became the Chief of Army Staff later, and had a sand-model exercise conducted, visualizing exactly what the Pakistanis did to occupy Kargil. A counteroffensive plan was discussed at the 15 Corps Headquarters. I was privy to that along with Lt Gen B C Nanda, Army Commander Northern Command, Air Marshal M M Singh, AOC-in-C Western Command and some other officers.

That in 1998 and 1999, the top brass in the same sector was oblivious to the risk from the Pakistani Army, is absolutely un-understanable.

Raw's Aviation Research Centre (ARC)

Till mid-1997, a user could approach ARC only through the RAW HQ for its operational tasks. This used to delay the process by a week. The legendary Billy Bedi, who headed ARC for several years, initiated userfriendly steps, and a required mission could be launched within hours. Analytical reports were delivered ASAP, within hours if required.

Top 3-star officers from the services were invited and informed of the ARC's capabilities in airborne electronic intelligence, and the then Chief of Air Staff, Air Chief Marshal A Y Tipnis, commended the ARC.

The Kargil Surprise

In May 1999, once reports of Pakistani infiltration had come in, Army's Directorate General of Military Intelligence (DGMI) sought Air Reconnaissance Mission in the Dras-Kargil sector. I personally flew missions beginning May 13 and soon, on May 18, we had pictures of six Pakistani Army MI-17 helicopters parked in the Mushok Valley area on the Indian side. These photographs were shown to the then Defence Minister George Fernandes, who was aghast and observed that this could have happened only after months of planning and preparation.

Gen Malik also praised ARC for the inputs but strangely, till some three weeks after this input, Lt Gen Krishan Pal still seemed to believe that there were only a few infiltrators on the Indian side. He himself said in a TV statement that he revised his opinion only after India lost many lives in the Battle of Tololing (June 13).

Did the Army HQ fail to convey him the confirmation of the Pakistani helicopters, and presence, inside India? Or he just insisted on ignoring reality?

Perhaps, the Army should come out with the truth after an honest introspection. For record, Gen Malik had told ARC that he had no hesitation in admitting that its inputs enabled the Army to correlate its operational plans and that otherwise the causality figures could have been much higher. The gap between this statement and Lt Gen Krishanpal's observation is glaring, and led to a tragic loss of lives.

The Indian Air Force

IAF does not have combat helicopters for high altitude offensive operations, and on May 25, it was decided to commit aircraft to neutralize the Pakistan-occupied positions on the Indian side. Initially, IAF lost two aircraft and one Mi 17 helicopter.

An IAF spokesman pointed out that the air operations in Kargil had taken place in an environment that was totally new in the history of world military aviation. The IAF had to unlearn what had been taught before, as it was operating with a new set of paradigms such as the ballistic trajectory of weapons in high altitude operations. A well-respected Air Marshal Vinod Patney, Air Officer Commanding in-Chief (AOC-in-C) Western Air Command, conducted the air operations after a short course to his officers in precision bombing.

The Subrahmanyam Committee

The Subrahmanyam Committee did not attribute any intelligence failures to RAW or ARC, but highlighted equipment inadequacies like the lack of high resolution, all-weather and sub-meter imaging capability. Lack of UAVs and better coordination between the security agencies was also mentioned but it acknowledged that the IB Director did convey certain inputs on activities in areas under the Gilgit-based FCNA (Force Commander orthern Areas) of Pakistan to the Prime Minister, the Home Minister, the Cabinet Secretary, the Home Secretary and the Director-General Military Operations (DGMO).

There is apparently a general lack of awareness of the critical importance of, and the need for, assessed intelligence, at all levels. Joint Intelligence Committee (JIC) reports do not receive the attention they deserve at the political and higher bureaucratic levels. One officer in a listening post mentions that a senior bureaucrat asked him about some entertainment programmes only in a span of one year.

It is clear that a Kargil-type situation could have been avoided either by plugging gaps as in Siachin, or by a credible declaratory policy of swiftly punishing wanton and willful violation of the sanctity of the LOC, as the Committee observed.

The Nuclear Tangle

Kargil was a stupid adventure for Pakistan. Threats from Islamabad about using nuclear weapons were considered but dismissed as Pakistan would not have been more stupid to invite destructive retaliation. The Kargil War has also helped strengthen India's doctrine that while India would not first use nuclear weapons, it would retaliate by inflicting massive destruction.

Conclusion

There is much evidence available to suggest that the intelligence agencies, RAW and IB, had in fact provided their political masters and military commanders with ample warning about Pakistani intentions and activities. In any case, lack of strategic intelligence could have been made up by the observation on the ground through scouts and patrolling. One did not have to get basic inputs about the Pakistani infiltration from shepherds, which as a matter fact, happened. After all, the Pakistani infiltration was spread over a large front. India deliberately limited its response to the eviction of Pakistani soldiers. But many of our officers and men died needlessly as we were neither prepared for the war nor ready to absorb the inputs towards efficient and better coordination between the security forces. The victory indeed belonged to those officers and men who fought, died or survived, but won.

INDIA AFTER KARGIL : DIPLOMACY & POLITICS

India is generally recognized to have won both diplomatically and militarily in the limited Kargil war, with Western nations and media expressing open or indirect concern at Pakistan's provocation and support to militant Islamic elements. Privately, the US has taken a lead in labeling Pakistan as the aggressor nation and has quietly encouraged US media to write about Pakistan's direct army role in the Kargil incursion. The Clinton administration is also reported to have provided India with a secretly taped phone conversation between the Pakistan army chief and his local army commanders, a tape which India was able to successfully use in its global information campaign. India also won much support on Capitol Hill: a resolution asking for withdrawal of "Pakistan supported forces" was introduced in the US House of Representatives, and the House International Relations Committee has passed a resolution by a margin of 22 to 5 for suspension of World Bank loans to Pakistan.

The private and public stance of many Asian and European countries has also been pro-India, though less vocally so than the US. France has quietly suspended delivery of previously contracted military hardware supplies to Pakistan, which included 32 upgraded Mirages and a brand new Agosta-class submarine, and senior German and British officials have urged Pakistan to "respect the LOC" China and Islamic bloc nations have remained largely neutral despite intense lobbying by Pakistan, and this in itself is seen as a plus for India. Even the international media, particularly from the US and UK has supported India's claim that the Kargil war was inspired and supported, if not implemented, by the Pakistan army.

This is perhaps the first time in many years that India has not been on the diplomatic defensive over Kashmir, and most people here are somewhat surprised by, and unprepared for, this unexpected show of international support. Reactions among Indian policy makers and analysts have mirrored this confusion: there are either strong misgivings of having been finessed into allowing outside mediation in the Kashmir dispute, or optimism over a "new chapter" in relations with the US.

What happens from here ? What will be the implications on Indian diplomacy, public opinion and politics ? And what will be the impact of all this on foreign investors ? Some trends are already clear:

Fundamental Changes in Western Perception of Pakistan

Continuing Indo-Pak skirmishes over Kashmir, and their mutual incessant battle of wits and words in international fora, have often warped and obfuscated the larger dynamics of each country's changing relations with the outside world. And if viewed separately from Kashmir, Pakistan has lost much of its Cold War strategic value and has been unable to cultivate strong economic interests, institutional linkages or favourable public opinion within western nations. Pakistan may even be in danger of emulating India of the 70s and 80s: isolated from the global mainstream and able to draw support only from a single international bloc, that too a bloc which has peaked in clout or cohesion. In India's case it was NAM, in Pakistan's it is OIC.

- US is genuinely upset at Pakistan's continuing support to Taliban and other Islamic extremists, and the adverse impact this may have on regional stability, specially on weak Central Asian republics where large US economic interests in hydrocarbons are at stake. Pakistan did allow use of its air space and army bases in last year's US bombing of Osama bin Laden's training camps, but that was then. There was a quantum jump in anti-American sentiment after the bombing, Pakistan has turned more Islamic and Nawaz Sharif has stalled further cooperation with the US in tracking Bin Laden.

- Both the State and Commerce Departments in the US are angry at Pakistan over abrupt changes in telecom licenses, frequency allocations and forex repatriation rules, changes which have hurt American firms. And, even though US interests were not directly involved in the cancellation of a large infrastructure contract by the Sharif regime, this unprecedented act of reneging on a sovereign promise has caused deep concern over Pakistan's credibility.
- EU nations and US have been publicly unhappy with the Sharif regime over its crackdown on NGOs, media and political freedom. Many Pakistani journalists have been harassed on false charges of tax evasion or drug trafficking, some have even been beaten by the police, nearly 2000 NGOs have been banned, and a non-partisan governor of Sind province has been sacked and replaced with a business crony of Nawaz Sharif.. The Clinton administration has called to "terminate immediately this crackdown against journalists and other elements of civic society," and the EU has postponed signing a treaty on trade and investment. Both Karl Inderfurth (Assistant Secretary of State for South Asia) and Strobe Talbott (Deputy Secretary) are former journalists who are unlikely to be happy with Sharif for muzzling the domestic press.
- Nawaz Sharif has lost personal credibility and respect among many Western scholars, liberal thinkers and journalists who cover South Asia, and is slowly becoming quite a hate target. In recent months the western media has carried many reports of his overarching political methods and corruption, more than any negative story on India, and British and American newspapers have given prominent coverage to Benazir Bhutto's claims of political persecution and physical torture (her husband, Asif Zardari, is in jail in Pakistan). In stark comparison to Sharif, India's Vajpayee is seen as an elder statesman with strong moral values, even if his political party is suspect.

Western Media Reaction

"Pakistanis are plainly to blame for having started the fighting....In an evident act of provocation, hundreds of Islamic guerrillas and perhaps also some Pakistani soldiers infiltrated across the line of control."

The Economist (Editorial, July 1)

"Isolated diplomatically, Pakistan faces a choice between continuing its offensive in Kashmir at the risk of provoking a catastrophic war or finding a face-saving way out."

The Times, London (News report, July 3)

"While Pakistan army officials and politicians are denying that its troops crossed into Indian territory, there is little doubt about Pakistan's involvement"

NY Times (News report, July 5)

"In public, the Clinton Administration says Pakistan is supporting the forces, but less publicly, officials assert that the forces are a mix of guerrillas and Pakistani soldiers"

Christian Science Monitor (Editorial, July 7)

"It's apparent that guerrillas demanding independence for Kashmir are not simply "morally" backed by Islamabad, as Pakistan maintains, but are actually equipped by independent units of the Pakistani Army...It is a provocation to India."

Asiaweek (News report, July 9)

"According to Western military sources in Islamabad, the Pakistan-backed assault on Kargil is a joint operation undertaken by members of the Special Services Group, a top-secret commando wing of the army, and Muslim rebels"

Boston Globe (Commentary by director of the South Asia Program, Johns Hopkins University, July 12):

"...Pakistan's action in initiating the misadventure in Kargil is indeed mind-boggling....Loose statements by political leaders in Pakistan that the nuclear option remains open have appeared reckless against the measured response of the Indian government that the LOC will be respected"

TIME Asia (Feature Article, July 19)

"Pakistani soldiers, along with recruits from Islamic fundamentalist groups, took control of Indian-held territory in the Kargil region of Kashmir....Pakistan's adventure may cost it a lot more than a loss of face, it may hasten Western rethink of Pakistan's value as an ally"

But Also Global Concern On Kashmir

NY Times (Editorial, June 20):

"In the wake of the Kosovo campaign, awareness is growing in Washington and other capitals that the world pays a high price for waiting too long to address growing crises. The one in Kashmir is among the most combustible, and the fact that both contending nations are armed with nuclear weapons lends it an apocalyptic urgency.....few international summits are likely to pass now without discussion of the possibility of assertive action in places like Kashmir."

Washington Post (Editorial, June 28)

"If the Kargil crisis is calmed there must come a serious address to the Kashmir question. Pakistan needs to stop blowing on the fires of armed revolt in India-held Kashmir; this is basic. But India has its own responsibilities. The Indians want it both ways: to keep a tight grip on Kashmir and at the same time to deny Pakistan's effort to internationalize the issue."

The Economist (Editorial, July 1)

"India should not confuse a triumph in Ladakh, if it happens, with victory in Kashmir"

Christian Science Monitor (Editorial, July 7):

"Current worrisome developments have further internationalized the Kashmir issue, and the argument for breaking the military deadlock on a bilateral basis seems less convincing....The international community should recognize that defusing today's military crisis is only a part of the larger problem and a lasting Kashmir settlement is to be found....The time has come to heal the Kashmir crisis before a massive collapse destabilizes the entire region."

NY Times (Commentary by William Safire, July 9)

"Kashmir is like a fault in the political earth....The answer may well take the form of protectorate as it has in Kosovo and Kurdistan — but in this case, the intercession would be invited by all three parties."

Yomiuri Shimbun, Japan (News report, July 21)

"It is only natural for Indians to enjoy their "victory" this time. But resentment of the Indian military runs deep among local residents. In addition, the operation did not bring a fundamental solution to the Kashmir problem."

- Even before Kargil, newspapers in the US and UK had begun to report on Pakistan's complicity in supporting militancy in Kashmir. The Times (London) reported in December '98 that "there are no longer effective Kashmiri militant groups left in the Valley and foreign mercenaries are firmly in control....Pakistan's influence in spreading Islamic extremism in Kashmir is pivotal, and fundamental groups in Pakistan admit to training Pakistanis and Afghans for guerrilla warfare in the region." This was the first time that any reputed Western source had supported Indian contention on Kashmir, and was an indication of a shift in overall western thinking on South Asia.
- Pakistan has slowly lost much of its early support in the US, and the decline has been rapid since the departure of Robin Raphael from the South Asia bureau at State. Even the Defense Department, a key ally in earlier times, has reduced army cooperation and joint exercises, and did not help Pakistan in getting delivery of F-16 fighter jets. Senator Tom Harkin (Iowa) is the last key Pakistani friend and can be expected to push for pro-Pakistan proposals, such as US mediation in Kashmir,

but his ability to help Pakistan is limited because he has lobbied far too often on Pakistan's behalf in recent times without obtaining a desired quid pro quo for American power, pharma and telecom companies.

Kargil Aside, India-US Relations Have Picked Up Momentum

It is perhaps ironical that India's nuclear tests have actually been a trigger for both countries to carry out a more concentrated dialogue and mutual discovery than ever before, and both have come out with less rigid perceptions. The US is now taking a more long-term view of India, removed from the Kashmir dispute, and public opinion in India is also becoming more pro-US, or at least *less* anti-US, especially after Kargil. India-US ties are moving forward, but the onus is on India to provide real depth by addressing specific concerns over CTBT, tariff cuts and market access. However, India does have breathing time till 2000 and only then will a new US administration (Republican or Democrat) or a new US Congress begin to act strongly over these issues.

- US firms are unhappy with hassles and slow pace of reforms in India, but many have also realized that India is relatively safer in the long term because of its legal and financial structures. Whether India does it willingly or under force of WTO agreements, market access for US exporters and manufacturers will probably be given even in the remaining areas in the next 5 years, and the next round of reforms will cover housing, healthcare, insurance and banking sectors, areas where US firms have a global edge. Many existing US investments in India will by that time, in all likelihood, also start showing profits. US economic exposure in India will inevitably become stronger in the medium term, even if the exact path is long and tedious.
- US firms have lobbied on behalf of India in the past, notably when economic sanctions were imposed after India's nuclear tests, and have done so now during the Kargil crisis. In a recent article in the International Herald Tribune, titled "Pakistan Ought to Concentrate on Pulling Itself Together," a leading US business executive, not a diplomat or academic, openly commented on Pakistan's role in Kargil and criticized its "obsession with India." The expanding overlap between American diplomacy and business in respect to India now includes many former US diplomats acting as advisors to US firms in India, from Henry Kissinger down to a few Ambassadors to countless mid-level officials. There is little of this trend in Pakistan's case. This 'parallel diplomacy track' between India-US is providing more access for the Indian viewpoint.

- American think tanks and policy institutes have changed in character and focus since the end of the Cold War— this change is reflected in their staff and research — and many have now added economic and social dimensions to their analysis, especially the unstated mission to promote democratic institutions abroad. Though interest in India is still low, many have now begun to notice India as a relatively attractive market, open society and viable democracy. Reputed organizations such as the Brookings Institute, CSIS, Cato Institute, Asia Society, Center for International Private Enterprise, Rand Institute, Heritage Foundation and Council on Foreign Relations have shown more attention and favourable treatment to India than earlier.
- The diplomatic corps in both Europe and America has slowly changed in the past two decades in demography and culture. There are many more women, business executives, social workers, journalists and ethnic minorities in the service, and most of these new groups do not have the typical 'big power diplomacy' mindset. If anything, they have neutral-to-positive feelings towards India. Similar changes are happening on the Indian side as well, and the younger generation of Indian diplomats is less dogmatic or preachy. It is important not to exaggerate US fondness for India, but these cultural and attitudinal shifts *have*injected a greater personal ease in the relationship — the current US Ambassador normally even avoids wearing a suit when meeting Indian leaders — and less inclination to dwell on an estranged past.
- India's cyberspace triumph was perhaps even more convincing than its diplomatic or military victory, courtesy an active Indian community in America which is becoming more organized and effective in lobbying. Internet polls by CNN/TIME brought forth overwhelming support for India, hundreds of bulletin boards decrying Pakistan were set up, newspapers and Congressmen were sent a deluge of emails and letters, and a full-page ad was issued in The Washington Post detailing Pakistan's role in supporting militancy in Kashmir. Growing activism by Indian Americans, and their increasing profile in the US economy, has been noticed by US legislators: one of out four US Congressmen is now a member of the India Caucus.
- Repeated assertions of a no-first-use nuclear policy and its demonstrated restraint in respecting the LOC have been important factors in India getting Western support during Kargil, in comparison to Pakistan which has been severely criticized for even hinting at the possibility of a nuclear war. To a large degree, western nations no longer view

India as guilty of the 'original sin,' and it is Pakistan which is now seen as the bigger problem on the nuclear question, both in terms of the CTBT and sale of nuclear technology to a third party. In the minds of many western analysts is the unstated fear, and this is perhaps overplayed by India, of an unstable Pakistan selling N-bombs to Islamic terrorist groups.

- Leftist intellectuals are still well entrenched in key institutions in India, but their voice is increasingly in a minority. Anti-US mood has declined since the emergence of the middle class, and has visibly abated after Kargil. Even criticism of NATO's bombing of Serbia has vanished almost overnight. In an internet poll taken after Kargil by The Times of India, a majority voted to offer generous terms to the US in WTO negotiations and to provide bases to US army to fight Islamic guerrillas in Afghanistan. The significance is not in the result of this rather unscientific poll, but that a newspaper known to reflect establishment and left-of-centre views should even ask these questions. Indians are prone to quick changes in mood, and Indian gratitude to the US over Kargil could easily wane, but for the first time there is a feeling here that the US has acted as a friend. This allows the BJP some latitude in speeding economic reforms. At a minimum, the tone of India's foreign policy under Jaswant Singh, who is likely to continue as foreign minister, will become more friendly towards the US.
- There has also been a maturing of western perception of the BJP. The BJP's connection to the hard-line RSS still draws occasional negative comments in the western press, but the party has moved a long distance in international credibility since the days when it was viewed only as a party of 'Hindu fanatics.' In fact, as US officials privately acknowledge, America would prefer to deal with BJP rather than with Congress. For India, and for BJP, a valuable lesson which has been learnt is that restraint and going along with world opinion wins friends. Signing the CTBT is still politically risky in India, but the BJP/RSS leadership is now more willing to go along than ever before, just as long as they can get parliamentary approval. Ironically, the treaty now faces serious legislative opposition in Russia and the US, and is unlikely to be ratified by either country. This will provide some breathing space to India, at least for a while.

Instability and Anti-US Mood Will Grow in Pakistan

Both warring nations have indulged in huge propaganda, but Pakistan much more than India. The general public in Pakistan has been fed an overdose of anti-India stories and distorted media reports of developments surrounding the Kargil conflict. Consequently, a majority of people are still not reconciled to the end result, and blame the US. The dominant public mood is a combination of disbelief, confusion, anger and betrayal. It is difficult to predict the outcome of this heady mix of emotions, or to speculate on whether Prime Minister Sharif will ride out the current wave of protests against him, but trends in Pakistan strongly favour anti-western, Islamic tendencies. Pakistan is very likely headed towards extreme social and political instability.

- There is an air of unreality in the Pakistani version of events. Most Pakistanis believe they were winning the war "until the US stepped in and saved India." Daily news reports in the local press have been full of stories of how the "mujahideen are whipping the better-armed Indians," and how "Indian forces are on the run." In the last week of June most independent western news media, such as AFP and Reuters were reporting major Indian military gains. For example, The Economist said at that time "With its army gaining ground against the intruders, India has now eliminated most of the threat to a crucial road that links Srinagar to the main city in Ladakh. Faced with setbacks, Pakistani-backed forces have tried to open new fronts." At the same time, the Pakistani media was giving quite another picture. Pakistan News Agency reported that "Indian army suffers setbacks at many places," and The News, one of Pakistan's most influential newspapers, reported that "Muslim freedom fighters of Kashmir are consolidating their hold on the Kargil mountains." General Hamid Gul, ex head of the ISI, even predicted "Indian troop surrender" and this was headlined in The Pakistan Observer on June 27. Post-Kargil, the most comment lament among Pakistani commentators is that Pakistan has succumbed to US pressure and that this is a glaring example of "how a fight won on a battlefield is lost on the table."
- Extreme anger at the US is now visible in almost all sections of Pakistani society, specially among Islamic groups who have threatened to attack US targets in the event of an American raid on Osama bin Laden. The leader of the influential Jamiat Ulema-i-Islam party, has been reported by western news agencies as saying that "If there is an attack on Afghanistan then there will be war, not against America but against Americans...neither the ambassador nor any American diplomat in Pakistan will be safe." This threat is being taken seriously, and the US Embassy in Islamabad has already evacuated more than 75 dependents of diplomatic personnel in the first week of August. The US has also issued a travel advisory on Pakistan.

- Anti-US sentiment is growing not just on the street but also within the armed forces who are perhaps feeling the maximum sense of shame and betrayal. Daily, there are many articles or emotional press interviews by retired Pakistani officers, full of hate towards the US for its purported "anti-Muslim, anti-Pakistan and pro-India" stance. Two instances of this are "An Analysis of American Terrorism" and "Defeat Made in USA," both published in The Nation, a newspaper which represents the thinking of the ruling Punjabi elite.
- Ironically, senior generals are themselves feeling pressure from lower ranks. Pakistan's diplomatic postures and military setbacks (against a larger Indian force) in Kargil have deprived the army a glorious role, unlike in India where war heroes and even whole regiments have been beatified by the media. TV images of India burying unclaimed bodies of Pakistani soldiers has caused enrage. Clearly worried by this mood, both Sharif and General Musharaff have now begun to publicly commend the regiments involved in the Kargil incursion, and the government has announced generous financial compensation to those dead or wounded. But it may already be too late to curb a growing sense of alienation in the army. In light of the fact that middle and lower ranks of the army are already quite 'Islamicized,' this could well lead to a serious rupture in civilian-army balance of power in the future. Whether or not the Pakistan army steps in again to govern the country, it is now more likely that the next Army Chief will be tougher on the whole Kashmir issue and less willing to accept any compromise.
- There is no alternate leader to Nawaz Sharif in sight. Unlike India, Pakistan does not have many national-level leaders who command respect across the country. Benazir Bhutto comes the closest, but memories of her corruption are still fresh. And both the army and Islamic groups will now be less inclined to serve under a woman, non-Punjabi politician, unless she enters a tacit understanding on allowing them the final say on Kashmir policy. Socially, there has been an Islamic resurgence for some time — more than 15,000 new 'madrassas' have opened in the past decade — and even educated people are turning to religion, though this is still at the personal level. The overall political landscape is unclear, but Kargil may now bring Islamic forces to power. At the very least, it will distort the domestic political agenda in the short term and delay decisions on market liberalization and fiscal reforms which are vital to earning badly needed foreign exchange and international credibility.

India Is Realizing the Value of Moderation & Public Opinion

Both India and Pakistan have played extensively to the public gallery to score diplomatic and psychological points, and thanks to technology Kargil has been much more of a media and information war than any other recent geo-political conflict in Asia. As a matter of fact, Indian commentators are more excited about India's diplomatic and media success than victory on the ground. A sure lesson learnt by both countries is the importance of world public opinion, a lesson which has perhaps sunk deeper and more naturally in India. But even Pakistani diplomats privately admit that a single interview on BBC Television by Pakistan's hawkish Minister for I&B may have cost the country much international goodwill. India can now be expected to become more pro-active in its 'media diplomacy,' but this will also open it to greater western scrutiny over domestic issues, including economic policy and human rights. India is still in the grey zone, between a new imperative to join the global mainstream and a historical aversion to follow what many here consider 'western dictates,' but recent events may encourage moderation in social and economic views.

- Earlier noises and demands over Article 370, Common Civil Code, WTO, etc do not figure in the national debate any more. A proposal by the RSS for deploying nuclear weapons in Kashmir was followed by strong editorials across the board, and Vajpayee himself called top RSS leaders to keep them quiet. The leader of the hard-line Shiv Sena party, normally not one to give up a fight, has stayed away from the limelight after public backlash on his remarks against a respected Indian Muslim actor. And Left parties, opposed to the new telecom policy, have avoided references to "pressure from US multinationals," a standard argument. There is now more sensitivity to guarding India's international image, at least among senior politicians.
- The western press has provided India a big edge by establishing and documenting Pakistan's direct role in the Kashmiri secessionist movement. Previous Indian complaints about a 'western media bias' have now largely died out, and it is likely that opposition to the entry of foreign newspapers in India will now be visibly less, at least if the BJP comes back to power.
- India is better positioned than Pakistan to leverage its media, and this advantage will continue and grow in the medium term. The Indian media has greater experience, reach and credibility than in Pakistan where one section of the press is very hostile towards Sharif while the rest has suffered a serious erosion of credibility after Kargil. For instance,

a Pakistan News Service story that "India is using chemical weapons," a serious charge in any other circumstance, was largely ignored by most western news agencies even though PNS carried this story for many days.

- Most western journalists in South Asia are generally quite disdainful of Indian officials and politicians, and this attitude has not changed with Kargil. And so, future media diplomacy is not going to be as easy as imagined by India. Also, many diplomatic experts in India lack practical understanding of how international perceptions are shaped. The defense minister was criticized by almost the whole Indian press and many former diplomats for weakening India's case by offering 'safe passage' to Pakistan-backed insurgents, whereas this offer actually won India many points in western capitals.

China Factor Will Continue To Help India

Even though China's refusal to support Pakistan was guided by practical self-interest — China neither wants to set a precedent for Tibetan independence nor encourage Islamic separatism in the vicinity of its own Muslim province — Kargil may have speeded up the thaw in Indo-China relations by providing a common purpose. Both India and China now have a mutual interest in containing regional instability, even if the mechanics and extent of any formal cooperation in this regard are uncertain.

- US-China relations are more tenuous and uncertain than in a long time. The early-90s excitement among foreign firms over business opportunities in China has faded to a large degree, and the evolution of recent events, including Chinese threats over Taiwanese independence, have underscored the possibility of future confrontation on vital issues. Many of these contentious issues, such as WTO, nuclear spying and human rights, are unlikely to be resolved before US elections in 2000. Congressional Republicans led by Senator Jesse Helms, one of Taiwan's strongest supporters, have introduced 11 anti-China bills, and even though none of these bills is particularly worrying China has already queered relations between Democrats and Republicans. The possibility exists that China will become a major election campaign issue in the US.
- Meanwhile, in China, the top leadership is trying to appease restive government and military officials who believe that too much has already been given away to the West. China has taken a series of measures in recent months which have made it unpopular all around. MNCs are upset over the withdrawal of concessions in

telecommunications, banking and insurance sectors. Human rights activists are protesting China's denial of citizenship rights to many Hong Kong-born children. Asian nations are worried about China's deferment of arms controls talks and a new mood of confrontation. And China has inflamed pro-Tibet demonstrations in major western capitals by recently imposing its own hand-picked Panchen Lama, the second most important religious figure for Tibetans. Anti-China stories have increased in the international media, specially after US journalists were viciously attacked by Chinese protesters. All told, western honeymoon with China has peaked.

- Foreign diplomats, including those who have served in Beijing, confirm that China is genuine about its neutrality between India and Pakistan. Even in 1991, during Premier Li Peng's visit to India, China had categorically stated that Kashmir was purely a bilateral dispute. Indo-China relations have thawed in recent months, an Indian delegation in March was warmly received and, what is significant, was given appointments with all the top people. Keeping Chinese sensitivity in mind India also did not allow the Dalai Lama to speak at an international democracy conference in New Delhi early this year.
- Given the above trends and equations, a number of implications can be drawn. First, neither China nor any G7 government, and specially the Clinton administration, wants to rock the boat by activating Kashmir as a burning global issue and, in the process, opening the Tibet question. And it also does not suit China to allow US a primary space in Asian geopolitics, especially in light of Kosovo. Second, China's stance on Kargil should really not have come as a surprise to India, and the fact it did is a reflection of continued Indian insecurity and confusion vis-à-vis China. There is no unanimity in Indian policy circles on whether India should ally with China to stop US predominance, or the other way around. Indo-China relations will continue to be ambiguous at a higher geopolitical level, but in the short to medium term, and certainly in the immediate context, the China factor will help India in multiple ways.

Kashmir Has Been Internationalized, But So Has The LOC

Kashmir has been internationalized, but in a context which is favourable to India. First, Kargil has brought about a slight pro-India change of heart around the world. Second, and even more significantly, western countries are now less concerned by finer points of law and history, and want a *practical* and *quick* solution which can stop this conflict from spiraling out of control.

There is growing international opinion, quietly but surely, on converting the current Line of Control into an international border, an idea which India would gladly accept but which Pakistan vehemently opposes. Ironically, it is India's own opposition to international mediation which is becoming a barrier to public endorsement of this formula by western nations.

- One subtle side-effect of the Kargil conflict is that the Line of Control has become a psychological reference point for many western nations to judge who has been the aggressor and who the victim. The LOC is identified both with the beginning and the end of the Kargil war, and words such as "incursion across the LOC" and "respect for the LOC" were among the most frequently used phraseology in international press reports and official statements. In some ways, the LOC has already been sanctified as an international border.
- India's defensive and ducking attitude over the years on Kashmir have frustrated most western diplomats, and if anything have only added to western doubts over India's moral and legal claim to Kashmir. The Indian case looks more shaky every time Amnesty International reports on human rights violations in the province, and even during the Kargil war many international agencies and editorials were demanding a greater say for the local population, if not for a final solution to Kashmir under UN auspices. But whatever the international press might say, western nations in reality have few choices after Kargil, and neither independence nor plebiscite are attractive options from the western perspective. Both would only strengthen militant Islamic forces, at least in the immediate context, which is the least desired outcome. The LOC formula appears the most sensible to western diplomats, but no country is willing to take an open stand unless India accedes to international mediation, something which the current public mood and politics in the country will not allow.
- Kashmir does not offer any clear strategic gains to the West, and it is important only because of the risk of nuclear escalation or regional instability. Already, Islamic groups have intensified their fight for independence in the southern Russian republic of Dagestan. With elections around the corner and far more important issues on hand, President Clinton is likely to assign a lower priority to this dispute as long as another India-Pakistan clash does not erupt. The US*will* prefer that India re-starts dialogue with Pakistan, even if only to offer the latter a face-saving way out and to avoid further escalation, but it will not push India to the negotiating table. And after Kosovo, Arab or Muslim sentiment is now less likely to be a factor in US policy in South

Asia. America has already won diplomatic points with a majority of the Arab world by helping the Muslim population of Kosovo, allowing the US to adopt a tougher and independent line against Islamic militancy.

- Events in Kosovo favour India in yet another way. Despite NATO's success in that operation, western unity has actually been stretched to the brink and EU nations have lost enthusiasm for any costly military or diplomatic intervention around the world, much less in a messy dispute (Kashmir) which offers no attractive choices. Some EU nations, specially those who have a history of diplomatic activism, had been quietly working to push the Kashmir dispute higher on the global agenda, but that was before Kosovo and before Kargil. These initiatives have now been stalled. In fact, recent developments in Brussels favour a more accommodating European view of Indian sensibilities: both Mario Soares, the newly elected Speaker of the EU Parliament, and Romano Prodi, the new head of the EU Commission, are known to be very fond of India.
- India may have gained diplomatically from Kargil, but it is now more committed and constrained militarily. Pakistan has shown that it can easily create another Kargil-like situation, and *has* been successful in raising India's cost of defending Kashmir by tying down a large body of Indian troops and equipment.
- Kashmir will continue to fester as a problem and there are chances of another limited escalation — Pakistan's army generals will not sit by quietly, and pressure on them to avenge for Kargil will grow — but a full-fledged war between India and Pakistan is unlikely. This is because of a couple of reasons. First, India has learnt a valuable lesson about moderation, and knows that it risks losing both its moral high ground and economic recovery if it overreacts to any Pakistani provocation. Second, irrespective of their brash rhetoric in the press Pakistani generals have privately been quite surprised and taken aback by India's strong military response, and are acutely aware of Indian superiority in conventional forces, specially in the air. Border skirmishes will continue but the risk of war is low, at least in the short term.

Indian Foreign Policy Will Focus More On US & Europe

One of the expected consequences of Kargil is that Indian foreign policy will now increasingly focus on Europe and the US, and disparate diplomatic initiatives of recent years, such as the 'Look East' policy, the Indian Ocean Rim Initiative etc, will now assume lesser importance, at least in the purely diplomatic, non-economic sense. Already, there is increasing mention among Indian officials and intellectuals that what matters most for India is not G15 or G7, but G1, that is to say, the US. This may perhaps be typical Indian hyperbole, but recent events do support the view that at least in the context of Kashmir, which still remains its primary diplomatic concern, India's success or failure will be shaped by its relations with the US.

- Islamic-bloc nations, perhaps Pakistan's last remaining friends, have lost clout in the past few years. Various developments of the nineties, such as globalization, satellite TV, internet and the Arab-Israeli peace accords, have put Islamic nations on the defensive, forced them to turn to domestic issues and have taken away their earlier sense of cohesion and international zeal. Indonesia and Malaysia are going through a painful process of political change, and are now anyway more anchored to Asia than Islam. Oil producing Arab states are threatened by new petroleum discoveries in Central Asia, and oil prices have been stayed at historically low levels in recent months. Militant Islamic movements pose a serious problem for Turkey, Egypt and Algeria, so much so that Pakistani lobbying on Kargil at the recent OIC summit was overshadowed by Algeria's attempts to discuss laws for extradition of terrorists. And the emergence of the Taliban has been a divisive and destructive development, causing a PR problem for all Islamic nations. Even Iran is unhappy with the Taliban, and the two sides almost went to war last year after Taliban kidnapped nine Iranian diplomats. Also, very importantly, forex repatriation from overseas Indians working in Gulf nations is no longer as important an economic lifeline as it once was. Given this background, Islamic countries will become a lesser consideration for Indian foreign policy. Many Indian analysts have already started paying less attention to OIC resolutions on Kashmir, and a recent ban by the UAE government on import of South Asian labour, which would have become a major issue in earlier times, was only routinely reported by the local media.
- During most of this conflict both Australia and Japan have stayed relatively aloof, and their response ran along neutral lines of wanting "peaceful settlement of all disputes." Same was the case with the media in both countries. However, well after Pakistan's role in Kargil was already exposed by the western press, the Australian Financial Review came out with a hard hitting article, titled "Islamabad Pays High Price for Kashmir Incursion." At the recent ARF summit in Singapore the Australian Foreign Minister also commended India for showing "great restraint." Japan, whose initial offer to mediate in the

Kashmir dispute irked India no small amount, has in recent days tried to make amends. Its ambassador to India, departing from Japanese media shyness, has given many interviews to the local press obliquely apologizing for Japan's mishandling, and the Japanese Prime Minister has written to both Vajpayee and Sharif stressing "the need to resolve the Kashmir issue in the spirit of the Simla Agreement and the Lahore Declaration." The conclusion drawn by the Indian foreign office and many analysts is that neither Australia nor Japan are very important since they take their cue from the US.

- Indian officials are quite frustrated with Japanese reluctance to invest, and with their frequent complaints about various regulations on import, indigenization, royalty payments and the like. South Korea has in recent months overtaken both Japan and Germany in total foreign investment in India, and is now beginning to be seen as a much more valuable Asian ally than Japan. South Korean firms have also done a good public relations job in India in recent months, including sponsoring foreign travels of key Indian economists and editors. Early this year, Indian authorities fined a large number of Japanese firms for non payment of tax, and despite high level lobbying by these MNCs the government did not bend. Unless there is a jump in foreign investment from Japanese companies in the future, emotional and diplomatic ties between the two countries will stay cool. India is no longer very interested in wooing Japan.

Domestic Mood & Politics: Kargil Will Help BJP, But Only Slightly

Because of better media, and also some clever manipulation of public sentiment by the government, Indians have been more emotionally involved in this fight than Pakistanis, and there has been a resurgence of nationalism and anti-Pakistan sentiment. To some degree, though not much, there is a feel-good factor in the country which is due as much to positive economic news as to India's victory in Kargil. But there is also a growing sense of uncertainty and disquiet at the course of future events in Kashmir, and over the possibility of war, at least among the educated classes. Public memory in India is also notoriously short, and already, just a few weeks after Kargil, the BJP has come under some pressure from opposition parties over accusations of an "intelligence lapse" and "unnecessary deaths of Indian soldiers," charges which are beginning to bite. Kargil will clearly favour the BJP, but it will be not be a dominant factor in these elections. The positive impact on the BJP will perhaps be felt more in the long term. Whether support for the BJP will increase or not in these elections, *anti-BJP* sentiment has certainly come down.

- The way Vajpayee has handled this crisis has been appreciated by a majority of people. Even BJP's critics have noted that the hard-liners were kept on a tight leash and, except for a local incident in Gujarat, there were no anti-Muslim incidents. But nothing succeeds like success, and more than the way Kargil was handled is the end result, which is now a major feather in the BJP's cap. Intense media coverage of the war has also given party leaders more publicity than to the opposition, and has also helped build new bridges between the party and the English-language press. Most editorials and articles, even from long-time critics of the BJP, have largely been positive towards the BJP government.
- In comparison, the Congress party has appeared ungracious and petulant at what many consider its needless criticism of the government at a time of war. Even though the BJP has been put on the defensive on the question why Kargil was allowed to happen in the first place, Congress has probably lost some support in northern India where anti-Pakistan feelings run high. Congress party's insistent demand for an emergency session of the Upper House, denied by the BJP, has not had any impact because legislative process is an obscure and irrelevant point with the masses. Kargil has limited Sonia Gandhi's visibility in the media and has brought the Sonia v/s Vajpayee debate into sharper focus, both developments being to the disadvantage of the Congress party.
- Another political consequence of Kargil is that the Bhagwat incident has now been pushed into distant memory. Admiral Bhagwat, who was fired by the BJP government last year as the Naval chief, was reportedly ready to join politics as a Congress candidate in these elections, a development which could have turned potentially embarrassing for the ruling party.
- The BJP government on the whole has acted with restraint, but there have been a few incidents where the government has vied with the private media in going overboard on patriotism. For instance, huge advertisements issued by the Indian government in many national newspapers carried the following lines: *"We, the people of India, affirm that we are with our brave soldiers as they go about giving the enemy a bloody nose,"* and *"The nation salutes you, brave Indian soldiers, for your decency and big-heartedness in announcing that the Pakistani soldier captured will be treated as per Geneva conventions, and for giving Pakistani soldiers killed in battle whose bodies are turned away by their motherland at the LOC a decent burial."* In any other circumstance, Left intellectuals in India

would have lambasted this display of jingoism, and the fact they did not is a telling reminder that Kargil so highly consumed the nation that no major political group in India could afford to be seen as being soft on Pakistan.

- Despite all this, Kargil *has* genuinely touched a nerve in every part of the country. Whole villages and localities have turned up for cremations of dead soldiers, strong passions for rushing to the country's defense have echoed in rural areas, school children have sent cards and poems to soldiers by the bagful, celebrities have volunteered to visit border troops to raise morale, and Indian companies have donated generously to various Defense funds. The Indian Red Cross, which normally has to all but beg for blood donations, received so many potential donors during the Kargil war that it had to publicly request people to stop coming. Body bags of dead soldiers have arrived in almost every province, and Kargil is perhaps the first India-Pakistan war which is really pan-Indian in an emotional sense, and not just restricted to the northern states. In fact, Tamil Nadu has collected the maximum private donations for war widows. In a perverse way, Kargil has perhaps been good for national integration. It may also have arrested the growth of regional political parties in India, though it is perhaps still too early to judge.

INDO-PAK SECURITY RELATIONS IN THE COMING DECADE LESSONS FROM KARGIL FOR THE FUTURE

In February 1999, when Atal Behari Vajpayee, Prime Minister of India, journeyed by bus to Lahore at the invitation of Prime Minister Nawaz Sharif of Pakistan, most people on the sub-continent hailed it as a bold and courageous political act of the two leaders. It was felt that with nuclear weapons capability out of their respective closets in May 1998, India and Pakistan would be less suspicious and more transparent with each other. The conducive strategic environment and common peoples' desire would enable their political leaders to work genuinely for confidence building measures and improvement of relations between the two nations, which, since Independence in August 1947, had fought four wars and seen several minor actions.

But that was not to be. Even as Prime Ministers Vajpayee and Nawaz Sharif hugged and talked with each other, and then signed the Lahore Declaration, the Pakistan Army had already initiated a deliberate and well-planned intrusion across the Line of Control (LoC), delineated on maps as part of Simla Agreement in 1972 (Annexure 1). In May 1999, within three months of the Lahore Declaration, a limited conventional war broke out between India and Pakistan in the Kargil Sector. In the preceding winter months, Pakistan Army personnel, dressed as jihadi militants, infiltrated through gaps between Indian defences, in one of the world's most rugged terrain, to occupy several dominating heights between the LoC and the Road (National Highway 1-A) connecting Srinagar-Kargil and Leh. The Pak Army's initiative, taking advantage of the terrain and the extreme climatic conditions, achieved a tactical surprise but could not cope up with subsequent Indian military reaction.

It failed at operational and strategic levels and thus ended with adverse politico-military consequences for Pakistan. The outbreak of war in Kargil also showed that the Pak political leadership was working out of sync with the thinking and plans of its military brass. As two former Prime Ministers of Pakistan put it, the Kargil War was Pakistan's biggest blunder and disaster.

For the Government in India, the Pak intrusion after its Lahore initiative was a serious political setback. Prime Minister Atal Behari Vajpayee's National Democratic Alliance had lost its majority in the Parliament in April 1999. It was now governing the country as a 'caretaker' Government till the next elections, which were due any time before September 1999.

The Indian military had the formidable challenge of getting the Pak intrusion vacated under the most adverse conditions of terrain. This adversity was further compounded by the political mandate that the LoC should not be violated. Nuclear India's political leadership, despite being stabbed in the back, had decided to act with restraint and maturity.

The War in Kargil

It is now fairly certain that the decision to launch Operation Badr (Pak codename for the operation) across 160 km of the LoC in Kargil Sector was taken soon after General Pervez Musharraf took over as the Pak Army Chief in October 1998. The new Chief made some quick changes in the top echelons of the Army. He brought in Lieutenant General Mohammad Aziz Khan from the Inter Services Intelligence (ISI) to take over as Chief of General Staff, without commanding a Corps, as was the usual practice. An old contingency plan was updated, and after carrying out detailed preparations during winter, the operation was launched to coincide with the melting of snow and the opening of India's National Highway 1A linking Srinagar to Leh via Kargil. The military objectives were to:

- Occupy approximately 700 sq km area on the Indian side of the LoC in Kargil-Turtuk Sector.
- Interdict Srinagar-Kargil-Leh Road.

- Capture Turtuk and cut off Southern and Central parts of Siachin Glacier Sector, and
- Intensify militants' activities in J&K, which had received a setback after the State Assembly and National Parliament elections in 1997-98.

About 1,700 men of the Northern Light Infantry (four battalions) supported by Special Forces, artillery, engineers and other combat support personnel, in the garb of militants and under a well executed cover plan, infiltrated through gaps into Indian territory and occupied mountain tops between the LoC and the Highway at several locations.

As already stated, the Indian military was mandated to get the intrusion vacated without crossing the LoC. However, it had to maintain a strategic balance and a deterrent posture all along the Indo Pak front - on the ground, air and sea - should there be a sudden escalation. A deliberate decision was taken to continue the political and military level dialogue.

The politico military strategy made it clear that although India was a victim of intrusion, and exercising maximum restraint, it was determined to get the intrusion vacated. India employed about two divisions (including about 250 artillery guns) on the Kargil front, and mounted 1,200 fighter and 2,500 helicopter sorties. By the time Pakistan sued for peace and withdrawal of its troops from the area of intrusion, nearly 75 per cent intruded area, including all high features dominating the Highway, had been retaken. The War ended on 26 July 1999 when all Pakistani troops were finally evicted from our side of the LoC. During the War, 473 Indian soldiers were killed: Pakistani casualties were estimated to be over 700.

The Kargil War, fought at the turn of the century, has been a major turning point in Indo-Pak security relations. It has left a deep impact. Its lessons are indeed important and are a useful input when we discuss future Indo-Pak relations, or peace and stability in South Asia.

Lesson No 1

A proxy or sub-conventional war in the Indo-Pak security scenario can easily escalate into a conventional war.

Pakistan, since its very inception, has built considerable expertise in militancy and use of irregulars; on their own or as an extension of the Pak Army, for war. It made its first attempt to force accession of J&K with irregular forces, supported by the Pak Army in 1947-48. The same strategy was followed in 1965, when it infiltrated irregulars and some Pak Army personnel dressed as irregulars into the Rajouri-Poonch Sector. On both occasions, however, this strategy led to a conventional war between regular forces of India and Pakistan.

Three significant developments took place thereafter. First, the successful use of irregular forces and political legitimacy to organise and conduct Jihad in the Afghan War. This was an extremely useful experience for the Pak military. Second, the acquisition of nuclear capability by Pakistan in late 1980s, which remained covert till May 1998. This capability encouraged the Pak military to conclude that a conventional war with India was not possible hereafter, and therefore, the sub-conventional could be stretched further. Third, loss of initiative to India in the occupation of Siachin Glacier. All these developments prompted Pakistan to make fresh attempts to annex J&K through a proxy war, on the lines of the Afghan War. During the Kargil War, the Pakistan Army took an additional step forward. Regular Army personnel shed their uniforms and dressed themselves as irregulars to intrude and fight on Indian territory. It made use of the ongoing irregular Jihadi militant-centred armed conflict in J&K as a deception to launch a war with regular forces.

It is a well-known fact that during the Afghan War, Pak ISI siphoned off a plethora of arms, equipment and funds, meant for Afghan rebels. With several million dollars of unaccounted funds, the ISI had at its disposal a large well-oiled machinery for churning out Jihad-oriented trained irregulars to be inducted into J&K. The first wave comprised infusion of extreme Islamic teachings and literature, which was followed by training to Kashmiri locals in the art of guerrilla warfare. A large number of young Kashmiris were covertly exfiltrated to Pakistan Occupied Kashmir (POK) through a porous LoC for arms training. The period from 1987 to 1989 saw an increase in violence and prolonged strikes in the Kashmir Valley and attacks on political leadership, police and para military forces. The kidnapping and subsequent release of Dr Rubaiya Sayeed, daughter of the Union Home Minister of India, Mr Mufti Mohammed Sayeed – a Kashmiri - in December 1989, in exchange for five top militants proved to be the last straw. The elected J&K Government under Dr Farooq Abdullah resigned in January 1990. The proxy war had truly arrived.

In April-May 1990, due to increased tension, the Armed Forces of India and Pakistan were mobilised and deployed all along the LoC and International Border (IB). A conventional war between the two countries was averted due to efforts of the US Deputy National Security Advisor, Robert Gates, who flew between Islamabad and New Delhi to reduce tension and restore some confidence.

The history of proxy war, since then, is best observed through the statistics. As can be noted, the proxy war has had its ups and down. The downward trend, which commenced in 1994, enabled India to hold State Assembly and Parliamentary elections in the State in 1996-97. The situation had improved considerably when Pakistan decided to launch the intrusion in Kargil in 1999. This initiative was taken because the Pak military felt confident of its success. The brief story and result of the Kargil War has already been covered. Unfortunately, since then, there has been a renewal of effort to fuel proxy war. The area covered by it has also been enlarged.

Despite 'war against terror' launched by the US and its coalition partners after 11 September 2001, India has continued to face Jihadi terrorists' attacks on its people and its institutions. On 13 December 2001, suicide terrorists - all from Pakistan - unsuccessfully attacked India's most venerated democratic institution, the Parliament. These terrorists were stopped and killed very close to the office of the Indian Vice President and other political leaders. This incident, once again, resulted in full-scale mobilisation and deployment of the Armed Forces of both countries. Operational readiness to go to war this time was at the highest level, since the all out war fought by them in 1971.

My aim here is not to go into the details of the decade old proxy / sub-conventional war in J&K or elsewhere in India but to establish its linkage with a conventional war. A proxy war or a sub-conventional war is part of the spectrum of conflict, which can easily escalate into a conventional war; nuclear capability notwithstanding. There may be several situations where both the 'initiator' (of the proxy war) and the 'affected' nation, are tempted to use conventional weapons and forces. The 'initiator' is tempted to give it a greater push with conventional forces to achieve the desired results. Such a situation occurred in 1947-48, 1965, and again in the Kargil War in 1999. On the other hand, the 'affected' nation, when pushed to the wall, may use its conventional forces to bring the proxy war into the open rather than fight with all the limitations of a 'no war no peace situation'. Pakistan did so in 1971, and India was prepared to do so in 1990, and after the terrorists' assault on its Parliament on 13 December 2001.

Lesson No 2

State sponsored terrorism, due to the nature of socio-politics on the sub-continent, is a double-edged weapon. It is like a wicked dog, which often bites the hand that feeds it.

Here, I would also like to add that state sponsored terrorism, due to the nature of social divides across the boundary on the sub-continent is a double-edged weapon. It is like a wicked dog, which sooner or later bites the hand that feeds it. India experienced it with Bhindranwale, a Sikh cleric who took to politics, and later joined hands with the Pak ISI to collect weapons and equipment in 1983-84. Militancy spawned by him in India's Punjab with the assistance of Pak ISI lasted nearly a decade. India had a similar experience with the LTTE of Sri Lanka in 1980s. After obtaining training from India, the LTTE went against the Indian forces when, at the request of the Sri Lankan Government, they were inducted for peace keeping in Sri Lanka. Pakistan is facing that situation now after sponsoring Afghan Mujahideen and Taliban in the 1980s and 90s.

These organisations were raised during the military government of General Zia-ul-Haq. Since then, elements from these organisations have been sponsored and used by the ISI for proxy war or covert actions in Afghanistan and India. This genie has now grown so big that the Pak Government is finding it difficult to rein it in and reform the Madrassas that are a breeding ground for extremists and terrorists.

Lesson No 3

Acquisition of nuclear weapons by India and Pakistan has not reduced / eliminated the probability of a war between them. A limited conventional war remains possible.

In May 1998, India and Pakistan became overt nuclear states. Indian compulsions had more to do with China than with Pakistan. Although in its security paradigm, Pakistan has been accepted as a nuclear capable state since late 1980s, it is always China that looms large over the Indian security scenario because of the humiliating Sino-Indian 1962 War defeat, the rapidly growing defence, economic capability and political clout of China, and the slow progress on settling the Sino-India border issue. Notwithstanding improvement in Sino-Indian relations, people in India perceive China to be the bigger, long term challenge.

The Pakistani nuclear weapons programme has been Indo-centric from the beginning. Pakistan has sought and acquired nuclear weapons and missiles essentially to neutralise India's conventional military superiority.

Many Pakistani leaders have said in the past that the Indian conventional superiority can be neutralised, and Afghanistan type militancy in J&K initiated and nurtured, under a nuclear umbrella. As Pakistan's nuclear weapons capability grew, the sub-conventional war in J&K kept escalating. Its military strategy since late 1980s has been to escalate proxy war, and brandish the likelihood of a conventional war and a nuclear 'flashpoint', whenever India threatened to make use of its conventional force. It may be recalled that when tension between the two countries was high after the escalation of proxy war in Kashmir in 1990, Pakistan was reported to have cautioned the US Deputy National Security Advisor, Robert Gates that, in the event of a war with India, nuclear weapons might be used. During the Kargil War too, a Federal Minister of Pakistan. and some others spoke about the possible use of nuclear weapons. The international community condemned these statements.

In November 1998, looking at Pakistan's renewed attempts to escalate proxy war in J&K and recalling the Sino-Russian border confrontation in 1969, in a talk at the National Defence College, New Delhi, I stated that 'space existed between the proxy war and Indo-Pak nuclear umbrella, wherein a limited conventional war was a distinct possibility'. This statement generated a strong reaction in Pakistan as it contradicted their prevailing military wisdom. Even in India and elsewhere, not many people took my statement seriously, till Kargil happened.

The lesson that I wish to draw from this part is that leading from a proxy war, a limited conventional conflict between nuclearised India and Pakistan cannot be ruled out. In such a situation, there will be a risk of escalation and a testing of patience, nerves and rationality on both sides. The risk is enhanced when one takes into account the lack of safety and robustness of the nuclear command and control structure on the sub-continent. Most political leaders in India do not trust General Pervez Musharraf's military regime in Pakistan - which has already displayed its mindlessness in the Kargil War, and towards terrorism - in the handling of its nuclear weapons.

Lesson No 4

The imbalance in civil-military relations and lack of strategic culture on the sub-continent has an impact on Indo-Pak security relations.

There was a serious misreading of Pakistani nuclear tests in response to Indian nuclear tests at Pokhran in May 1998 in the political establishments of Pakistan as well as in India.

In India, Pakistani reaction to go overt was anticipated, and to some extent even welcomed by some strategists. The Indian establishment generally felt that an overt and transparent nuclear capability is better than a covert or translucent capability. The former would lead to a more stable Indo-Pak security relationship. Perhaps this was also the impression in the Pakistani political establishment. This common impression led to the Lahore Summit and Declaration.

What the political and a large part of the strategic community on the sub-continent failed to perceive was that the overt and neutralised nuclear parity on the sub-continent would lead to unbridling and early escalation of the Indo-Pak proxy war by the military establishment in Pakistan. The changeover of military leadership in October 1998 in Pakistan, from a moderate to a hardliner, led to such a manifestation and launching of Operation Badr within months of the May 1998 nuclear tests.

Why did such a misreading of overt Pak nuclear weapon capability take place in India, and even in Pakistan? For this, I hold the imbalance in civil-military relations in India and Pakistan, and an absence or lack of strategic culture in both countries, responsible.

In Pakistan, issues like Afghanistan, Indo-Pak relations, Kashmir and nuclear capability are areas of special concern to the military. The political leadership- when there is a civilian government - is either not briefed adequately or finds it difficult to assert on such matters. This is historical, almost traditional, and is expected to continue.

The opposite is true of India, where the military functions not only under the political control - as it should - but also under an assertive and suspicious bureaucracy. As a result, interaction and teamwork between military and political authorities on politico-military issues is less than adequate. The Government often decides politico-military issues without adequate military inputs and discussions. A lack of strategic culture in India is well known. George Tanham wrote about it in his research paper. However, it must also be mentioned here that the political leadership has now started taking greater interest in national security matters, particularly after the Kargil War.

Lesson No 5

Assumption and misperceptions, a fairly consistent feature, mostly in Pakistan, have been a major cause of Indo-Pak conflicts. Greater transparency and Confidence and Security Building Measures are necessary to reduce tension and chances of a war.

In all Indo-Pak wars, there is continuity not only of objectives but also of wrong assumptions and misperceptions. Before Kargil, Pakistan had assumed that the Indian military, due to prolonged and over involvement in anti terrorist and anti insurgency operations in Punjab, J&K and North East India, was tired and not in a fit shape to fight. Its weapons and equipment were obsolete since no modernisation had taken place for more than a decade; and that there was an acute shortage of officers especially at the junior leadership levels. All this was true but only to an extent.

As mentioned earlier, my statement in late 1998 that 'space existed between the proxy war and Indo-Pak nuclear umbrella, wherein a limited conventional war was a distinct possibility', generated a strong reaction in Pakistan. A part of the vernacular media in Pakistan mis-presented the statement as if it was a military threat/challenge to Pakistan. In February 1999, Lieutenant General Javed Nasir, former head of the ISI, then Chief Intelligence Advisor to Prime Minister Nawaz Sharif, a well-known Islamic hawk, wrote a highly publicised article "Calling the Indian Army Chief's Bluff". The crux of that article was that the Indian Army was incapable of undertaking any conventional operation. This was not only a gross underestimation of a possible adversary but also a poor assessment and misperception.

Some other assumptions and misperceptions which led to the Pakistani offensive operation in Kargil were:

- Nuclear umbrella allows "offensive action" without risk.
- International community would intervene or stop the war at an early stage.
- The coalition government in India, weak and indecisive, will either over-react or under-react.
- India is militarily weak and unprepared.
- Indian frustration will lead to escalation, putting the onus of escalation on India.
- Military operation under the garb of "Mujahideen" would focus attention on Kashmir and Pakistan would be able to claim this as a victory.

There are several such assumptions and misperceptions about the military, including nuclear capabilities, on both sides of the border even now. One of the problems is near opaqueness of matters military in both countries, which leads to considerable speculation and misreporting in the media. In a highly tense situation, misperceptions of the adversary often lead to a war. The answer lies in greater transparency and confidence and security building measures (CSBMs) at political, and more importantly at the military level. Over the years, several CSBMs have been agreed to between India and Pakistan. However, many of them have got eroded or diluted ever since Pak sponsored militancy was initiated in Punjab and J&K. Although the war in Kargil was another major setback to the CSBMs, hot lines between Prime Ministers and Director Generals of Military Operations were often used, which helped to prevent escalation of the Kargil War.

There is yet another politico-military assumption in Pakistan, that China, its strategic ally, would intervene in an Indo-Pak war. This was so in 1965, 1971, and no doubt in 1999. Kargil and Siachen Glacier lie very close to the Sino-Indian Line of Actual Control in Ladakh. The Pak COAS, its Foreign Minister Sartaj Aziz and Prime Minister Nawaz Sharif, all visited China during the Kargil War. But this assumption does not take into account the changed global and regional geo-strategic environment. The Chinese reaction during the Kargil War at the political level and on the ground was pragmatic and responsible. If anything, China leaned closer to India during the war. Chinese are and would be interested in the sale of weapons to their traditional strategic partner Pakistan, even in the continuation of limited tension between India and Pakistan, but it is highly unlikely today that they would consider physical intervention on the Indo-Tibet border to bail out Pakistan.

Lesson No 6

(a) Kargil War has re-established political sanctity of the Line of Control in J&K with the international community; (b) Militarily, over the years, the defence of Actual Ground Position Line (AGPL) in Siachen Sector, Line of Control (LoC) in the rest of J&K, and International Boundary have got linked. Any attempt to disturb status quo and re-draw the LoC or AGPL forcibly, is more likely to lead to conflict all along the Indo-Pak border.

After the first Indo-Pak War in 1947-48, in which Pakistani irregulars backed by Pak Army units attacked J&K, the two countries signed the Karachi Agreement on 27 July 1949 under the aegis of the United Nations Commission for India and Pakistan. The Karachi Agreement delineated and demarcated a Ceasefire Line (CFL) in J&K, which was signed by Indian and Pakistani military commanders as well as by UN Representatives.

In 1965, when Pakistan launched Operation Gibraltar followed by Operation Grand Slam in J&K, India retaliated by crossing the International Boundary (IB) in Punjab and elsewhere. Thereafter, fighting took place all along the CFL and the IB. Following the Tashkent Declaration, the two sides agreed to exchange the territories captured by each other across the CFL and IB and restored status quo ante.

The focus in the 1971 Indo-Pak War was on East Pakistan, now Bangladesh, although the war was also fought along the CFL and the IB on India's western border with Pakistan. After the war, under the Simla Agreement, both sides kept the gains they had made across the CFL. The resultant line was redesignated as the Line of Control (LoC), which was delineated and demarcated by military commanders of both countries and an agreement signed to this effect in December 1972. This was a significant transition from a 'military line' separating two armies through an UN arranged ceasefire in 1949 to a 'political divide', which could evolve into a boundary. The delineation of the LoC was done on two sets of maps, each containing 27 map sheets, formed into 19 mosaics, each sheet signed by military commanders. The LoC traverses 740 kms from the IB in the South up to NJ 9842, from which, in accordance with the unchanged definition of the 1949 Karachi Agreement, it runs 'North to the glaciers'. After militarisation of Siachen Glacier' area in 1984, this part of the line, North of NJ 9842, came to be known as the Actual Ground Position Line (AGPL). Post Simla Agreement, there have been a few occasions when both sides made efforts to improve their tactical positions along the LoC. But there were no major incursions till the Kargil War.

During the Kargil War, the Indian political aim given to the military was to get the intrusion vacated but not to cross the LoC. The international community endorsed the Indian position. The United States also insisted on restoration of the sanctity of the LoC. The joint statement signed by President Clinton and the Pakistani Prime Minister Nawaz Sharif on 4 July 1999, states the following about the LoC:

- "They (the signatories) also agreed that it was vital for peace in South Asia that *the LoC in Kashmir be respected by both parties, in accordance with their 1972 Simla Agreement*".
- "It was agreed between the President and the Prime Minister that concrete steps will be taken for the *restoration of the Line of Control in accordance with Simla Agreement*".
- "The President said he would take personal interest in encouraging expeditious resumption and intensification of those bilateral efforts once the sanctity of the Line of Control has been fully restored".

If the Kargil War had not ended as it did, the possibility of Pakistani and/or Indian forces crossing the IB could not be ruled out. In fact India had adopted a deterrent posture along the rest of LoC and the IB. Pakistan too had deployed its forces accordingly. It is obvious that over the years, the sanctity of the AGPL in Siachen, the LoC, and the IB have got linked militarily. Any attempt by either party to redraw the LoC or the AGPL through force can lead to retaliation and escalation of conflict elsewhere. The 'restrain' term of reference given to the Indian Armed Forces during the Kargil War came under severe public criticism in India and might not be acceptable next time. The lesson and conclusion we may draw here is that the post Kargil durability of the Line of Control has increased. This durability, or sanctity, provides a longer-term base for a future dialogue between India and Pakistan.

Lesson No 7

Post-Kargil, agreements like the Simla Agreement and Lahore Declaration will not inspire adequate confidence.

The Pakistani Kargil initiative was a major violation of the Simla Agreement, signed by the Prime Ministers of the two countries in 1971, which had maintained a reasonable amount of stability between the two countries for long. This war repudiated two important articles of the Simla Agreement: namely that (a) the two countries will settle their dispute through bilateral negotiation and (b) the LoC will be respected by both sides and not altered. Also, the war coming so soon after the Lahore Declaration created a deep sense of betrayal and of being let down in India. It took two years and considerable pressure from the international community for Indo-Pak political level dialogue to be resumed.

No agreement with Pakistan after the Kargil War shall inspire the same confidence in India. Despite the 'U' turn taken by Pakistan in its policies on Afghanistan and terrorism under US pressure, the Indian public does not trust or feel confident that President Musharraf's military regime, which initiated the Kargil War and subsequently took over the Pakistan Government in a military coup, will remain faithful to any Understanding/Agreement with India for long.

Lesson No 8

Secular India, which has a larger Muslim population than the entire population of Pakistan, would find it difficult to live in peace with a less than moderate Islamic Pakistan.

Behind Pakistan's attempts to achieve politico-military objectives in the Kargil War, the development of a Jihadi culture in Pakistan since the beginning of the Afghan War, the right wing reaction in India, and the thoughtless political rhetoric on both sides of the border, was a strong motivation. Pakistan was formed on a religious basis; the idea that Islam defines nationhood. Indians accept the establishment of Islamic Pakistan as a sovereign state but they reject the two nation communal ideology because it contradicts and challenges the Indian core values - democracy, secularism, federalism and social justice, as given in the Directive Principles of the Indian Constitution - fundamentally.

With the advent of the Afghan War and development of the Jihadi culture, the social environment on the sub-continent started changing. Increasing Islamisation of Pakistan, with moderate elements remaining mute spectators all through the Bhutto-Zia-Nawaz period, shifted the ideology from Islam being the foundation of its nationhood to being the basis of the state. This has sharpened the ideological conflict with India and also created some internal contradictions within Pakistan. In fact it has rejuvenated communal forces in both countries. While this is constitutionally checked in India, there has been little attempt to do so in Pakistan. The Army, the ISI, which is only an extension of the Pak Army, and some political parties in Pakistan, have continued to encourage this ideology till recently.

My observation is that secular India, which has more Muslim population than the entire population of Pakistan, and a less than moderate Islamic Pakistan, are unlikely to be able to live in peace.

After the events of 11 September 2001 and launching of Operation Enduring Freedom, it is obvious that the US is committed to stay in Pakistan and support the Pak President in his efforts to fight terrorism domestically and reform Pak Madrassas which have been churning out Mujahideen and

Taliban. This development has far reaching implications for India, the sub-continent, and the region. If this move works out successfully, we may see the emergence of a moderate Pakistan and a more conducive security atmosphere for tackling Indo-Pak disputes.

Lesson No 9

India's defence modernisation in the coming decade on account of Kargil may cause the arms race between India and Pakistan to continue. However, this would have a serious adverse impact on Pak economy and socio economics.

India spent nearly Rs 30 crore (US$ 6.9 million) per day during the Kargil War. Pakistan's expenditure would have been fairly close to that.

An important strategic lesson for India from the Kargil imbroglio is that Simla and Lahore types of agreements notwithstanding, the country cannot afford to be complacent and cannot let down its guard on matters concerning national security. The progressive decline in the Indian defence budget since early 1990s when the process of economic liberalisation began, had affected its armed forces' ability to modernise and to prepare for the type of war they were called upon to fight, or were expected to fight. Indians, after Kargil, have started taking greater interest in national security matters and would not be prepared to compromise on its requirements. This led to a 28 per cent increase in the defence budget soon after the War, and about 10 per cent increase in the year 2001.

The Pak economy on the other hand has been under tremendous pressure after Kargil. It was forced to cap its defence budget. In fact, the defence budget was reduced by Rs 2 billion last year and the Soviet Union type of economic phenomenon has been staring it in its face. (An analyst in the US National Defence University, Washington has already drawn the conclusion that acceleration of India's growth rate and relative stagnation of Pakistan economy will increase India's economic, military and diplomatic profile.)

The reduction of Pak defence budget, however, is unlikely to have any significant impact on the Indian defence budget. India is likely to maintain its defence expenditure between 2.5 to 2.75 per cent of its GDP in the foreseeable future to meet modernisation demands of its armed forces.

Lesson No 10

- There is no military solution to J&K problem.
- Annexation of J&K is more a military agenda than a political agenda in Pakistan.
- No major breakthrough can be expected on Kashmir dispute in the coming decade unless the military in Pakistan and a strong political centre in India are prepared to change their stance.

This was the fourth war over J&K, not counting the ongoing skirmishes in Siachen Glacier area and Pak sponsored proxy war in large parts of the State. That makes it obvious that the J&K problem cannot be resolved militarily by Pakistan or India.

There is no doubt that J&K is an important and a complex dispute identified by most Pakistanis. However, it is worth noting the hard-line consistency of military-bureaucratic elite over the issue, and slight lack of it in Pak political leadership. It allows the military elite to maintain its politico military status in Pakistan. FM Ayub Khan initiated the war in 1965 when he was the military ruler in Pakistan. As Prime Minister, Benazir Bhutto raised the pitch of this through shrill speeches and unrealistic promises. The same leader, politically more experienced but out of power now, sounds more conciliatory and accommodating on this issue. For Nawaz Sharif, Kashmir was not an electoral issue when he was returned to power in 1997. During elections, he focused more on domestic issues and seldom made any provocative statements on Indo-Pak relations. In the wake of new pressures due to a socio-economic crisis, the Kashmir dispute, though very much alive, was placed on a back burner. This was reflected in his talks with two Prime Ministers of India, IK Gujral and AB Vajpayee, and in the gradual decline of militancy in J&K. As in the past, Pak military-bureaucratic elite saw it as a threat to its importance, supremacy and status in the national power structure. By launching the war in Kargil, it was able to assert its authority and also revive national and international interest in the J&K dispute.

The Indian legal position on J&K is established through the Instrument of Accession signed by the ruler of J&K in October 1947 and subsequent resolutions in the State Assembly and the Indian Parliament. The problem is more difficult for India where the democratically elected government has to create a political consensus in the country. A ruling party in India would be committing 'harakiri' if it backs down from the Parliamentary resolution, without creating such a consensus. A coalition government will find it extremely difficult.

My observation is that the J&K dispute, which has been the cause of three wars and also the ongoing proxy war, is more a Pak military agenda for its own vested interest than a political agenda. Over the years, it has become the core issue for the Pak military, which must keep it alive, and at the centre of domestic politics and external policy.

India and Pakistan have hardly any option or room for manoeuvre to resolve the J&K problem. This dispute along with other fundamental ideological differences cannot get attenuated in the coming decade.

AFTER KARGIL PROGNOSIS

The biggest casualty of the Kargil War, apart from 1,200 lives lost on both sides of the LoC, was trust and confidence in Indo-Pak relations. The two nations took two years to travel the 'high road' from the Kargil War to the Agra Summit. Prime Minister Vajpayee's initiative to hold a summit with the Pak military ruler, considered in India as the architect of the Kargil War, was bold and courageous. Pak President General Musharraf himself acknowledged it.

The approach to the Agra Summit was cautious and bumpy when both sides began stating their case through the media. The summit started on a cordial note with the Government of India unilaterally announcing several 'people to people' confidence-building measures. But it ended on a jarring note, unable to agree to an acceptable joint statement.

General (President) Musharraf, with his suave, clever articulation and repeated assertion of his stand on Jammu & Kashmir to the media, won the Public Relations exercise handsomely but made no long-term gains: a tactical victory but a strategic loss.... like the Kargil War. It is not possible to conduct summit level negotiations through media, much less on the Indian sub-continent. The over enthusiastic electronic media coverage raised hopes of the people high and then brought them down as quickly. However, what also emerged clearly through this media hype was the fatigue and desire of educated people in India and Pakistan to resolve differences.

There was too much of 'form' and little 'substance' in President Musharraf's visit to India. If you ever need a lesson that adequate preparations are essential before a summit, here is one. The military President of Pakistan might be the sole arbiter in his nation, but the Indian Prime Minister is not. The political decision-making process in both countries is very different.

The messages that came across from Agra were that:

- According to Pakistan, relations cannot normalise unless India agrees to discuss Kashmir within the framework of Pakistani objectives.
- As per India, it is prepared to discuss Jammu & Kashmir, along with other Indo-Pak issues but there can be no surrender of Jammu & Kashmir or its territorial alienation from India. Also, Pakistan must give up sponsoring violence and terrorism in Jammu & Kashmir.

The only gains made during the summit were (a) that the two leaders got to know each other and their constituencies, and (b) they agreed to meet again and continue the dialogue. These gains were not small under the prevailing circumstances.

There is another important question beyond the next Summit: that of political, economic and social dynamics in Pakistan. Pakistan today stands torn between democratisation, the demands of military rulers, and of the, till recently, rising strength and influence of its religious leaders. There were about 150 Deeni madrassas (religious seminaries) in 1947. Their number today is more than 5,000. This number is related to the number of people living below the poverty line in Pakistan (130 million), which has increased fourfold in the last 20 years. Will General Pervez Musharraf, with US assistance, succeed in reforming these institutions, eliminating religious fundamentalism, and thus reducing Mullah power in Pakistan?

Pakistan's economy is in a bad state with a total debt amounting to about $ 65 billion. Will it be able to turn the corner now that US and other donor nations and institutions have resumed financial assistance to Pakistan?

Important geo-political developments have taken place on the sub-continent after 11 September 2001 and America's war on terrorism. Afghanistan is no longer the backyard or 'strategic depth' for Pakistan. The new Afghan government due to its own strategic and economic requirements, and under US and UN influence, is likely to follow independent but not unfriendly policies towards Pakistan. We can expect a 'forget and forgive' Pak-Afghan relationship if Pakistan does not support Taliban again or interfere in Afghanistan's internal affairs.

The US, whose influence in the region has increased considerably after the beginning of the war against terrorism, is likely to maintain a close relationship with Pakistan. It will ensure that the Jihadi infrastructure in Pakistan is gradually dismantled through 'carrot and stick' means. It is unlikely to abandon Afghanistan or Pakistan as it did from the former after the Soviet withdrawal in 1989. The Bush Administration has also declared that unlike in the past, it will not involve itself in a zero sum game and its policies and relationship with India and Pakistan will be independent of each other.

The terrorists' attack on the Indian Parliament on 13 December 2001 and subsequent deployment of armed forces of both sides on the border has once again increased tension between India and Pakistan. Another war has been averted in the nick of time through US diplomacy. The US has also put some Pak terrorist organisations - Harkat-ul-Mujahideen, Lashkar-e-Toiba and Jaish-e-Mohammed on the State Department's list of Foreign Terrorist Organisations. This will enable its authorities to deny visas and carry out deportations of suspected members of these organisations. However, if the US is unable to dissuade Pakistan from following its current terrorism/proxy war policies against India, we may expect Pakistan to act bold and continue with its hard-line stance in resolving Indo-Pakistan disputes.

What kind of elected government in Pakistan will there be after President Musharraf's promised election in October 2002? Will it lead to political stability or instability? The general impression is that in both contingencies, the Pak military would remain a dominant factor. What is also obvious is that a "failed" Pakistan would be disastrous for India and the region. This would lead to mass migration, mostly into India, which the Indian Government would not be able to handle.

As already stated, the Kargil War was the fourth to be initiated by Pakistan over J&K, not counting the ongoing skirmishes in Siachen Glacier and the twelve year old Pak sponsored proxy war. That, along with more difficult strategic and economic conditions prevailing on the sub-continent now, should make it obvious to both India and Pakistan that the J&K problem cannot be resolved militarily. Even when political attempts are made to resolve the issue in a hurry, it could lead to greater violence on both sides of the LoC.

Indo-Pak talks, which began after two years of the Kargil War, have once again got stalled after 13 December 2001. The hawks on both sides have taken over. The Jihadi terrorism in J&K has increased and so has the tension and insecurity on both sides of the border and the LoC. Such a situation between two geographic neighbours cannot go on forever but one can foresee that the talks, whenever resumed next time, will move at a snail's pace. Failure to move forward would have an adverse impact on both countries. It is also obvious that there is no alternative to a slow, gradual incremental peace process through political, economic and military CBMs. Peace cannot be created by dramatic gestures or a few meetings between the top leaders, but through gradually increased confidence building measures. India and Pakistan have a long way to go before they can create a win-win situation on any of their problems. The best hope is that both countries can agree to create a situation of trust and confidence: to live and let live.

Even if India and Pakistan do not fight a war in the future, only a miracle would avoid an 'armed peace' between them in the next decade.

7

Diplomatic Damage from Latest India-Pakistan Border Clashes

On 6 August 2013, five Indian soldiers were shot dead in an ambush in Indian-controlled Kashmir, near the India-Pakistan Line of Control (LoC). While it is unclear who was responsible for the attack, blame has been attributed to either militants backed by the Pakistan Army, or the Pakistani Special Forces themselves. Although Pakistan has denied any involvement and its Prime Minister, Nawaz Sharif, has sent his condolences over the killings, tensions have markedly increased. Intermittent exchanges of small arms fire across the LoC have occurred throughout the week, wounding several soldiers and civilians. The most recent incident occurred on 11 August, with both sides using machine guns.

Comment

While the incident on 6 August and the following border skirmishes are unlikely to escalate into more serious military actions, they are likely to damage the efforts of the Indian and Pakistani governments to improve relations between their countries. Both governments are showing restraint and a willingness to co-operate at the moment, but political pressure over a similar incident in January 2013, forced the Indian Prime Minister, Manmohan Singh, to suspend the official dialogue with Pakistan.

Talks between Indian and Pakistani bureaucrats over their territorial disputes were scheduled to restart this month, but that is now doubtful; many in India's opposition are stridently opposed to them taking place. The main Indian opposition party recently demanded that Singh's government cancel a planned meeting with Sharif in New York next month and even scale down relations with Pakistan by recalling the Indian High Commissioner to Islamabad.

With elections in India due next May, Singh's government is particularly susceptible to agitation from the Indian opposition and the notoriously jingoistic media, which could force it to take a harder stance against Pakistan. Although the current administration favours dialogue to reach a consensus with Pakistan, the public mood in India will make this politically difficult. Singh's government is frequently painted as being weak on border protection, owing to the incursions by Chinese and Pakistani forces at various times through the past year. Since the Indian Government is already contending with domestic anger over the rising cost of living, it is likely that it will heed calls to take some action to shore up its support, rather than just wait out the media storm before quietly restarting talks. While India's reaction is unlikely to be as extreme as the opposition and sections of the media are calling for, the government will almost certainly suspend the talks and make a diplomatic protest.

Perhaps a greater concern not just for relations in the sub-continent but for the region and beyond, is that this event highlights the Pakistani government's lack of control over at least some elements of its military forces and the militants aligned with Pakistan. The government of Prime Minister Sharif has been seeking to re-engage in dialogue with India for some time now, making it highly unlikely that it would have authorised such an attack. Consequently, although the efforts by Sharif to ease tensions and rebuild trust are widely seen as sincere, questions will again begin to rise about his government's ability to deliver on its peace agreements.

When India, or indeed any country, enters into security-based talks with Pakistan, the issue of how Pakistan can control its rogue elements and prevent them from tarnishing any deal, will need to be factored into the discussions. Given that Pakistan's democracy is newly established, it is unlikely to be able to give any reliable guarantees in this area. That alone may provide the Indian Government with a reasonable excuse for suspending the talks with Pakistan, now that it is politically expedient for them to do so.

INDO-PAKISTAN BORDER

India shares 3323 km long and complicated boundary with Pakistan. The India-Pakistan boundary is categorised under three different heads. The first is the international boundary also known as the 'Radcliff line'. It is 2308 km long and stretches from Gujarat to parts of Jammu district in Jammu and Kashmir. The second is the line of control (LoC), or the Cease Fire Line, which came into existence after the 1948 and 1971 wars between India and Pakistan.

This line is 776 km long, and runs along the districts of Jammu (some parts), Rajouri, Poonch, Baramula, Kupwara, Kargil and some portions of Leh. And the third is the actual ground position line (AGPL), which is 110 km long and extends from NJ 9842 to Indira Col in the North. The LoC and the AGPL has been a scene of constant tensions with border skirmishes and firing between the armies and border guarding forces of both countries. The LoC has been vulnerable to constant infiltration by foreign terrorists, Kashmiri separatists and Pakistani army regulars for long.

Like the Bangladesh boundary, the India-Pakistan boundary also does not follow any geographical barrier. It runs through diverse terrain like deserts, marshes, plains, snow clad mountains, and winds its way through villages, houses and agricultural lands making it extremely porous. Porosity of this border has facilitated various illegal activities such as smuggling, drugs and arms trafficking, and infiltration. Heroin and fake Indian currency are the two predominant items of smuggling along this border. Other items include saffron, textile, mercury, which are smuggled from Pakistan. The villagers adjacent to the border are alleged to be involved in smuggling in a big way. Money laundering is also quite rampant along the border. A large scale hawala network is flourishing in Punjab, especially in Ludhiana. In addition, the border population has also been subjected to hostile propaganda by Pakistan designed to mislead and sway their loyalties. The Sir Creek area, due to its peculiar terrain, makes the movement of border guarding forces very difficult and thus, provides scope for illegal fishing in the creeks.

DRAWING THE INDO-PAKISTANI BOUNDARY

The 1947 partition of South Asia has had lasting repercussions not only for the region, but also for the larger international community. Border tensions between India and Pakistan have taken on a new magnitude since both countries carried out nuclear tests in May 1998. Surprisingly, historians have paid little attention to the creation of the Indo-Pakistani boundary, a key element of the 1947 division. This article analyzes the problematic procedure and format of the body responsible for delineating that boundary through the province of Punjab, the Radcliffe Boundary Commission. It is part of a larger project that will examine links between the boundary-making process and the repercussions of partition, particularly mass violence.

The commission takes its name from its chairman, Sir Cyril Radcliffe. In the end, his boundary-making effort was a failure in terms of boundary-making, but a striking success in terms of providing political cover to all sides.

The British seized the opportunity to withdraw from their onerous Indian responsibilities as quickly as possible; the Indian National Congress, the avowedly secular but primarily Hindu party headed by Jawaharlal Nehru and Sardar Patel, took control of India, as it had desired for so long. The Muslim League, which claimed to represent South Asia's Muslims and was led by Muhammad Ali Jinnah, won Pakistan, the sovereign Muslim state for which it had campaigned.

Although the British had, in 1946, considered leaving India piecemeal, transferring power to individual provences as they withdrew, they concluded that such an approach was impractical. without defining the entity or entities that would come into power, they concluded that such an approach was impractical.

It would not be possible to hand over power without making it clear what international entity would take on that power; in order to define a new international entity, a new boundary was necessary. From a certain perspective, however, a rigorously and properly delineated boundary was not necessary to accomplish these political ends—any boundary line would do.

Due to this fact and to a myriad of political pressures, the Radcliffe Commission failed to draw a geopolitically sound line delineated and demarcated in accordance with accepted international procedure. The Punjab's population distribution was such that there was no line that could neatly divide Hindus, Muslims, and Sikhs. Radcliffe's line was far from perfect, but it is important to note that alternative borders would not necessarily have provided a significant improvement. There is, in contrast, a great deal to be said about flaws in the boundary-making *procedure*—and why those flaws existed.

Significance

This territorial division is significant on multiple levels. As an episode in imperial history, it marked the beginning of a global trend towards decolonization. For South Asian history, it meant independence for India and Pakistan. Unfortunately, it also inaugurated Indo-Pakistani tension. Conflict between Hindus and Muslims had existed on the subcontinent, to a greater or lesser degree, for many centuries, but the partition brought that conflict to the international level—and exacerbated it. The results include three wars, in 1948, 1965, and 1971, as well as the Kargil conflict of 1999. The problem of Indo-Pakistani tension took on greater urgency when both India and Pakistan tested their nuclear weapons in May 1998, and current events in South Asia demonstrate the need for continued attention to and greater understanding of this vital region. How did this division intensify the very conflict it was intended to resolve? Part of the answer lies in the drawing of the boundary. My primary goal is to clarify and analyze the boundary-making process, but having identified specific flaws in this division, I hope to lay them out in terms that might be useful for decision-makers considering partition as a tool to resolve conflict in other regions of the world.

Methodology

Because this project focuses on a controversial episode, which reasonable historians describe differently according to their own national or political biases, my first research priority was balancing these varied perspectives. Accordingly, I gathered archival material and conducted interviews in England, Pakistan, and India. In all three countries, I focused on government documents, examining material relating to the work of the Radcliffe Commission and to the repercussions of the Radcliffe Line. I also examined private papers, mostly of British officials serving the raj, but also, where accessible, the papers of Indian and Pakistani leaders. Regrettably, Radcliffe destroyed all his papers before he left India—in keeping, his biographer claims, with a lifelong habit of discarding material he no longer needed. As a result, it may be impossible ever to clarify Radcliffe's thinking completely. I have attempted to compensate through archival research and through interviews with Radcliffe's stepson and executor, with his private secretary on the Boundary Commission, and with the last surviving Pakistani official associated with the Punjab Boundary Commission.

This research explores the balance between structural influences and the role of individuals. My story centers on a small number of individuals: Radcliffe, the man who had responsibility for the boundary line; Mountbatten, the last viceroy of India; Nehru and Patel, leaders of the Indian National Congress; and Jinnah, head of the Muslim League. But my argument also has a great deal to do with the sweeping drives of British imperialism, Indian and Pakistani nationalism, and decolonization.

My conclusions about the forces that shaped the Indo-Pakistani boundary would seem to support a structural approach, but the lessons of this particular division could be read another way. If at any point enough individuals had decided to take another path—for example, if Radcliffe had withdrawn his services once he reached India and was informed of the August 15 deadline—the outcome could have been dramatically different.

Alternatively, if the key individuals had different backgrounds—for example, if all the Indian leaders had not been lawyers, but rather businessmen or engineers—the outcome could again have been very different. The story of the Radcliffe Commission concerns individuals attempting to do what they saw as best, and as a result both bowing to and struggling against the pressures of larger structural forces.

Historical Context

The 1947 partition was shaped not only by decades of Indian nationalist pressure on the British Government and by the rise of civil unrest in the subcontinent after World War Two, but also by Britain's precarious economic position in the aftermath of the war. After nearly two centuries as an economic asset, British India had become a liability at a time when Britain could least afford it. In addition, American pressure to decolonize the subcontinent influenced both international and British domestic opinion against the *raj*. British India became a political and symbolic liability as well as an economic problem.

These factors, combined with domestic political considerations for the newly elected Labour Party, meant that ridding itself of its responsibilities in India suddenly became a priority to His Majesty's Government (HMG).

However, Indian independence had not always been such an urgent goal for the British Government. The first half of the twentieth century saw a series of small steps towards self-government in South Asia.

Traditional imperialist historiography holds that these ventures marked carefully incremented progress, part of the process of training Indians to govern themselves. Other interpretations, including but not confined to South Asian nationalist schools, argue that these steps were actually sops intended to keep nationalists satisfied enough to prevent a more serious threat to British rule.

This view holds that HMG had no intention of letting go its "jewel in the crown"—until it had no choice. Many historians, imperialist and nationalist alike, trace the roots of partition to the Morley-Minto reforms of 1909. These changes increased Indian participation in their own governance, anticipating an eventual move to self-rule.

By creating separate electorates for different religious groups, however, these reforms also "embed[ded] deeply in Indian life the idea that its society consisted of groups set apart from each other.... The result was the flowering of a new communal rhetoric, and ultimately, of the Pakistan movement." Politicians found religious rhetoric useful for rallying support, with dangerous results. The elections of 1937 and 1945-46, in which both Congress and the Muslim League rhetoric played on communal themes, provided further evidence of a lack of political cooperation at the highest levels.

With the onset of the Second World War, the Government of India found itself in a difficult position. HMG declared war on India's behalf, without even a pretense of consulting Indian leaders. Indian politicians and public opinion were outraged. The prospect of civil unrest loomed. In 1942, with the Allies in urgent need of a reliable Indian base, Churchill dispatched Sir Stafford Cripps to India at the head of a Cabinet delegation charged with exploring the possibility of self-government after the war. Cripps offered an implicit promise that if India fought in World War II it would be granted freedom; Congress rejected this offer with Gandhi's memorable phrase that it was a "post-dated cheque on a bank that was failing." In the aftermath of Cripps's failed mission, Gandhi launched the "Quit India" movement, which the British repressed violently. Most Indians subsided into more or less supportive attitudes.

With the end of the war, Indian leaders and people alike expected to be repaid, with independence, for their wartime backing. In Britain, the Conservatives were voted out and the Labour Party took power, under Clement Attlee. Meanwhile, the India Office was losing patience with its viceroy, Lord Wavell. Relations between the India Office and Wavell had been steadily worsening throughout 1946.

Wavell, a career military man whose stolid exterior concealed a bent for writing poetry, had been viceroy of India since 1943. Left with the difficult job of guiding India through treacherous post-war waters, he sent increasingly blunt warnings to London that their Indian policies were misguided and inadequate to the challenges ahead.

Lord Pethick-Lawrence, Britain's Secretary of State for India, resented these warnings and paid less attention to them as time went on. In particular, Wavell's outline of potential partition boundaries, the first serious discussion of the issue, received little attention.

However, Wavell's "Breakdown Plan," calling for a withdrawal of all British presence in South Asia, alarmed HMG. Attlee sent another cabinet mission to India in hopes of negotiating a less drastic outcome. The resulting proposal, known as the "ABC Plan," called for a loose federation to consist of three groups of provinces, each of which had the option to "opt out" of the federation. This proposal met a curious reception. It was first accepted, then rejected, by Congress; the Muslim League initially announced that it would cooperate, but in the aftermath of the Congress decision it renounced constitutional methods and declared "Direct Action" Day on August 16, 1946. "Direct Action Day" became the "Great Calcutta Killing," and the next thirteen months saw rioting and violence across North India.

By the beginning of 1947, Pethick-Lawrence and Attlee had lost all confidence in Wavell, regarding him as "frankly defeatist." In February 1947, they asked him to resign, appointing Lord Louis Mountbatten, a career naval officer and cousin to the king, in his place. Although Mountbatten was given a June 1948 deadline by which to disentangle Britain from India, he concluded shortly after his arrival in India that a rapprochement between the various parties was impossible. Within a few months he decided to move the decolonization deadline up, to August 15, 1947.

INDIA-PAKISTAN: THE NEW VICTIMS OF AN OLD BORDER DISPUTE

India and Pakistan's decades-old territorial dispute is often portrayed as a dormant conflict, but for Zaigham Abbas it is anything but. His father Mumtaz Hussain was killed last August when India's Border Security Force (BSF) shelled the village of Bajra Garhi along the Sialkot Working Boundary in Pakistan.

"We were leaving the mosque after [morning] prayers when the Indians started shelling. The next thing I know, my father was hit in the ribs," Abbas said. "By the time the shelling stopped, he was lifeless," Hussain's widow Shama Batool added. "I don't think much could have been done to save him."

In the street, the neighbouring homes still bear the scars of battle, with pockmarked walls and smashed glass.

STUCK IN THE MIDDLE

Abbas is one of around 80,000 Pakistanis who live in the 45 Pakistani villages regularly affected by fighting along the zigzagging 1,800-mile border with India.

Of that, a 124-mile stretch in Kashmir remains disputed between the countries – demarcated by a "line of control". Further south, the divide in the Sialkot-Jammu region operates on the basis of a "working boundary", meaning the Pakistani government considers the land on the other side occupied.

Three full-scale wars were fought over the border, the first in 1947 and the most recent in 1999. Tensions have heightened after the coming to power of Hindu nationalist Narendra Modi in India in May 2014. In August he called off peace talks, while in October fighting intensified, with Modi taking a more aggressive tone. On the Pakistani side, too, calls for moderation have increasingly been sidelined.

Violence continues to wreck lives – on December 31, a rare attempt at a flag meeting spiraled out of control, with two Pakistani rangers killed after clashes which both sides accused the other of starting. "The firing continued for five hours before the bodies could be retrieved," said Major Ijaz, a media officer of the Pakistan Rangers. He insisted that the Indians began the violence but Indian media denied the claim.

In January, at least four civilians were killed on each side of the border, while dozens of others were injured. Thousands in both countries have fled their homes. When IRIN gained rare access to the Pakistani border region in late January, there was intermittent shelling, with civilians describing how they live in fear of the next attack.

Sumaira Raza, a resident of the village of Jooyian, said that she has had to flee on multiple occasions. "Every few days, we leave and lodge with our relatives in neighboring villages. Others who do not have this option simply spend their nights in open fields. This winter, it was so cold that many families in neighbouring villages allowed women and children who are not their relatives to sleep in their homes."

Other residents describe having to leave elderly or disabled family members behind as they fled. There are no specialised medical facilities in the areas and basic health units are unable to treat the severely injured. Though there is no set pattern as to when the fighting begins, villagers say it usually starts after sunset. "The shelling is getting more intense with each passing day," Farid, a farmer from the region, added. Others say they live in fear of Indian drones, which they say often hover over the area shortly before an attack. "When the village has fewer people, the shelling doesn't happen even if the drone comes but when the village is full and a drone comes by, we know shelling will happen," one teenager said.

Other villagers reported similar tales, but Ijaz would not confirm or deny such claims. Late last year India committed to buying 49 more drones to patrol the border.

IDPs of the night

The effects of the conflict on the population can be drastic. Shama Bibi said she went into early labour during clashes and struggles with post-natal depression, which she blames on the violence. "There was firing every day and at times we had to run for cover. Then came the September [2014] floods. The shelling stopped but our mudhouse collapsed. I walked for miles with my family in that condition. When my son was born, I didn't look at him," she said.

Even when peace reigns, risks abound. Both the Pakistani Rangers and the BSF have laid thousands of landmines across the border region, with many dating back to 2002. Shama Bibi says she went into early labour during clashes between India and Pakistan During floods in September 2014, some landmines are believed to have been swept across the border into Pakistan.

One of Ehsan's sons was partially blinded and another two crippled in a landmine explosion a decade ago. "The government has abandoned us. No one came to offer us even medical help," he said. Residents claim the Pakistan government has made no arrangements to move the villagers to other areas and there are no compensation schemes for those relocating. Sometimes local politicians arrange some support for those killed or injured, but it is arbitrary and limited. As such many are faced with a choice between leaving their land and livelihood for good and the safety of their loved ones. "I can either keep my family safe in another place or send my children to school," said farmer Ghulam Din who makes barely Rs8,000 ($78) a month. He moved his family from the border village Umeraanwali to a slum near Sialkot city where they are no longer in education. "I barely have money to feed them," he bemoaned.

Ironically the land he left behind could be some of the most valuable in Pakistan if the situation were different. Sialkot is among the most fertile parts of the country– yet the violence means there are few buyers for those seeking to flee.

INDO-PAK CEASE FIRE TENSIONS

In August 1947, India and Pakistan became independent. India's border with Pakistan was delineated in 1947 when the British Raj left India. Under the scheme of partition enshrined under the Indian Independence Act 1947, Kashmir was free to accede to India or Pakistan.

Hari Singh, who had ascended the throne of Kashmir in 1925, was the reigning monarch in 1947 at the conclusion of British rule. The Maharaja signed a standstill agreement with Pakistan, to ensure continuity of trade, travel, communication, and similar services between the two. Such an agreement was pending with India. Following huge riots in Jammu, in October 1947, Pashtuns from Pakistan's North-West Frontier Province recruited by the Poonch rebels, invaded Kashmir. The guerilla campaign was to frighten Hari Singh into submission and accede to Pakistan

The Hindu ruler Hari Singh allied himself with India when confronted with large numbers of infiltrators from Pakistan and appealed to the Government of India for assistance. The then Governor-General Lord Mountbatten agreed on the condition that the ruler accede to India. Once the Maharaja signed the Instrument of Accession, Indian soldiers entered Kashmir and drove the Pakistani-sponsored irregulars from all but a small section of the state.

India accepted the Instrument of accession of Kashmir, regarding it provisional. The Pakistani government immediately contested the accession, suggesting that the Maharaja acted under duress and that he had no right to sign an agreement with India when the standstill agreement with Pakistan was still in force.

India sought a resolution of the Kashmir Conflict at the United Nations. In January 1948, the Security Council adopted resolution 39 (1948), establishing the United Nations Commission for India and Pakistan (UNCIP) to investigate and mediate the dispute. In April 1948, by its resolution 47 (1948), the Council decided to enlarge the membership of UNCIP and to recommend various measures including the use of observers to stop the fighting.

In July 1949, India and Pakistan signed the Karachi Agreement establishing a ceasefire line to be supervised by the military observers. These observers, under the command of the Military Adviser, formed the nucleus of the United Nations Military Observer Group in India and Pakistan (UNMOGIP). The UN mission insisted that the opinion of Kashmiris must be ascertained. The then Indian Prime Minister is reported to have himself urged U.N. to poll Kashmir and on the basis of results Kashmir's accession will be decided . However, India insisted that no referendum could occur until all of the state had been cleared of irregulars

On 30 March 1951, following the termination of UNCIP, the Security Council, by its resolution 91 (1951) decided that UNMOGIP should continue to supervise the ceasefire in Kashmir. UNMOGIP's functions were to observe and report, investigate complaints of ceasefire violations and submit its finding to each party and to the Secretary-General.

There are several controversial cartographic frontiers in Jammu and Kashmir—the international border between Jammu and Kashmir and Pakistan that is known as the working border in Pakistan; the ceasefire line (CFL) of 1949 that was re-designated as the line of control (LoC) in 1972; the extension of the LoC beyond the last cited grid reference (NJ 9842) in the icy heights of the Siachen, a sector which is known as the actual ground position line (AGPL); and finally the segment east of AGPL, bordering on or controlled by China which is known as the line of actual control or LAC4.

In early 1965, relations between India and Pakistan were strained again because of their conflicting claims over the Rann of Kutch at the southern end of the international boundary and, in August, military hostilities between India and Pakistan erupted on a large scale along the ceasefire line in Kashmir. In his report15 of 3 September 1965, the Secretary-General stressed that the ceasefire agreement of 27 July 1949 had collapsed and that a return to mutual observance of it by India and Pakistan would afford the most favourable climate in which to seek a resolution of political differences.

On 4 September 1965, the Security Council, by resolution 209 (1965), called for a ceasefire and asked the two Governments to cooperate fully with UNMOGIP in its task of supervising the observance of the ceasefire. On 20

September 1965, the Council adopted resolution 211 (1965), by which it demanded that a ceasefire take effect at 0700 hours GMT on 22 September 1965 and called for a subsequent withdrawal of all armed personnel to the positions held before 5 August. The Council also requested the Secretary-General to provide the necessary assistance to ensure supervision of the ceasefire and the withdrawal of all armed personnel.

Since the hostilities extended beyond the Kashmir ceasefire line, the Secretary-General decided to set up an administrative adjunct of UNMOGIP, the United Nations India-Pakistan Observation Mission (UNIPOM), as a temporary measure for the sole purpose of supervising the ceasefire along the India-Pakistan border outside the State of Jammu and Kashmir.

As ceasefire violations continued to occur and there were no prospects for the withdrawal of troops, the Security Council met again in November and adopted resolution 215 (1965) of 5 November. By this decision, the Council called upon the Governments of India and Pakistan to instruct their armed personnel to cooperate with the United Nations and cease all military activity.

On 10 January 1966, the Prime Minister of India and the President of Pakistan, who had met in Tashkent at the invitation of the Chairman of the Council of Ministers of the Soviet Union, announced their agreement, Tashkent Declaration, that the withdrawal of all armed personnel of both sides to the positions they had held prior to 5 August 1965 should be completed by 25 February 1966 and that both sides should observe the terms of the ceasefire on the ceasefire line.

Violence along the LoC does not occur in a vacuum. Rather, it reflects the general state of relations between India and Pakistan. Increased violence along the LoC is noteworthy for several reasons. It could portend triggering events leading to a severe crisis, as was the case prior to and during the 2001–2002 "Twin Peaks" crisis. That crisis, sparked by the December 2001 attack on the Indian Parliament by the Pakistan-based extremist groups Lashkar-e-Taiba and Jaish-e-Muhammad, saw more than 2,600 incidents of firing along the LoC. Increased firing along the LoC also makes improved bilateral ties and crisis resolution harder. There is no comprehensive database of ceasefire violations along the LoC. A report states that in the year 2010, 44 ceasefire violations occurred and in the year 2011 -51, 2012- 93 , 2013 -195.

Pakistan had unilaterally announced a ceasefire on the LoC and International Border on November 26, 2003 which was immediately reciprocated by India. Close to 13 years after the ceasefire on the Line of Control (LoC) between India and Pakistan came into force, the number of ceasefire violations has gone up in the last couple of months. Out of the 151 incidents of ceasefire violations on the LoC this year, 110 of them have happened since September 2016 South of Pir Panjal, in Poonch, Mendhar, Naushera and Akhnoor sectors. Uri, Tangdhar, Keren, Machhil and Gurez sectors – areas north of Pir Panjal – have witnessed 21 ceasefire violations in the past two months. 4,675 Indian soldiers have lost their lives along the LoC in ceasefire violations by Pakistan since 2001. "These ceasefire violations are recorded because they are serious violations, where the exchange of fire is for at least 15-20 minutes. Use of direct and indirect weapons or prolonged firing of small arms is registered as a violation. We don't count a single burst of small arms as a ceasefire violation," explained a senior military official posted in Kashmir.

My research confirms commonly-held views that violence along the LoC has been increasing at a notable rate since late 2012, but does not confirm views of a correlation between diplomatic progress and increases in ceasefire violations. The increase in violence along the LoC since late 2012 is a clear and concerning marker of the deterioration of India–Pakistan relations on a broader scale. Whether or not ceasefire violations can be attributed to signaling related to high-level meetings, they carry the risk of escalating into a larger crisis or standoff if accompanied by a triggering event.

The cease fire violations are Pakistan Army's attempt to indicate its complete control over issues related to military and foreign policy. More importantly, many view the Pakistani Army as being the spoiler, not only destabilising democracy in its own country but also initiating obstacles for Indo-Pakistan peace.

The relationship between two countries would normally be judged by accepted principles of International Law. However, the relationship between India and Pakistan extends beyond legal relationship and has to been seen with historical, religious and cultural perspectives and their corresponding ramifications.

ANALYSIS OF TERRORISM IN KASHMIR AND THE INDIA-PAKISTAN DISPUTE

All these reasons have caused numerous wars and untold death and destruction for both India and Pakistan. However, the biggest fallout of the above factors has been rampant terrorism and the related proxy war between Pakistan and India since 1988. Terrorism has ravaged the valley and its people. This terrorism is not aimed at directly gaining any strategic advantage or territory from India. Rather, it is aimed at terrorizing and exterminating innocent and moderate Kashmiris to convert Kashmir into a radical Islamist region· Such a region would automatically be at odds with a secular, passive and Hindu dominated country like India. The region would therefore, naturally secede from India and possibly join Pakistan. This proxy war which employs the technique of terrorism rather than direct military action has completely changed the face of the Kashmir problem. It has converted the territorial dispute into a multifaceted social, economic, political, military and religious problem that must be resolved before Kashmir can ever experience peace and security.

This war is far more sophisticated and organized than the genocide in Congo and conflict in the Gaza strip. During the late eighties and early nineties, the Pakistani government and army, through the I.S.I. (Inter Services Intelligence), helped set up an entire terrorist network in Kashmir. Reports suggest that the I.S.I. had setup a war council consisting of approximately seventy hardcore terrorists· The I.S.I. has worked in conjunction with this terrorist network to achieve two major objectives. The first objective is the removal of all non-Muslims from the Kashmir valley, and the severing of all connections to the central government. By doing so, it hopes to change the demographics of Kashmir to make it more natural for Kashmir to become a part of Pakistan. In essence, they want to convert Kashmir from being a part of secular India into an Islamic nation. The second objective is to neutralize a large part of the Indian military forces by keeping them occupied and making them less potent in the event of a confrontation with Pakistan.

Many techniques have been employed to achieve these two objectives. The most important of these techniques is the establishment of a network of religious schools in the valley. These religious schools reject secularism and the secular, scientific syllabus prescribed by the government. Instead, these schools implant religious bigotry, communal hatred and radical religious fundamentalism in thousands of impressionable young minds throughout the valley· A network of hundreds of such schools has been established by the terrorist organizations throughout the valley· They have also destroyed many regular schools in the valley to force children to go to the religious schools or remain uneducated. They have also established a network of mosques throughout the valley· These mosques are instrumental in spreading religious fundamentalism. Together, these mosques and schools act as centres through which fundamentalism and violence have spread throughout Kashmir. These structures also act as important places for terrorist organizations to recruit people. These recruits, after being thoroughly indoctrinated and trained in terrorist training camps, add to the religious hatred brewing in the valley. Simultaneously, terrorists are also destroying Hindu temples and systematically exterminating Hindus to erase any link between Muslims and Hindus in the valley· This has further increased the communal tension in the valley.

Behind the scenes, the I.S.I. and the Pakistani army are supervising, controlling and supporting these terrorist organizations. They have armed the terrorists with the latest weapons and provide cover fire to help them infiltrate the L.O.C. into India. The I.S.I. coordinates between different terrorist organizations to effectively spread violence and create communal tension throughout the valley. The terrorists, with help from Pakistan, have created training camps in Kashmir, Pakistan and Afghanistan to indoctrinate and further train recruits. It was estimated that there were as many as 5,000 terrorists in various camps located in Pakistani Punjab and the North West Frontier Province.

The local government and administration are also deeply involved in the proxy war in the valley. In the early 1980's the local administration began to be penetrated by fundamentalists, some from terrorist organizations. Simultaneously, moderates in senior posts in the local government were systematically exterminated.

As a result, organizations like the Jamaat were able to organize black outs and major protests to bring the entire state to a standstill. Religious fundamentalists in high government positions also used government resources to provide logistical and monetary support to terrorists.

These fundamentalists discriminate against non Muslims in Kashmir, even denying them emergency medical aid or simple amenities like electricity and water.

It is interesting to note that on multiple occasions, security forces have uncovered evidence linking these terrorists with Pakistan and the Pakistani Army. In 1999, Security Forces recovered pay books and I.D. cards establishing the militants and 'freedom fighters' as regular soldiers in the Pakistani Army, specifically, the Northern Light Infantry.

It has become clear that Pakistan, through organizations like the I.S.I. covertly supported terrorism in Kashmir. This fact is further supported by the Centre for Contemporary Conflict in the U.S. which published an analysis of the Kargil conflict in 1999. The extent of Pakistan's involvement in the current situation in Kashmir is also evident in the sudden fall of Kashmiri groups that support an independent Kashmir like the JKLF (Jammu and Kashmir Liberation Front). The JKLF comprised largely of radical Kashmiris and unlike today's terrorist groups in the valley had few foreigners. However, as it became clear that the group did not support secession of the state to Pakistan, the group was suddenly marginalized and replaced by groups which supported secession to Pakistan. Clearly, the situation in Kashmir has become a Pakistan supported proxy war from an indigenous struggle for self-determination.

CONCERNS GROW IN PAKISTAN AND INDIA OVER BORDER VIOLENCE

For much of the past decade, the residents of this village near Pakistan's border with India have lived in relative peace, tending their water buffalo and goats, despite a history of tensions between the countries.

But this fall, mortar shells from India killed a 40-year-old rickshaw driver and several animals, residents say.

"I have sent my family to relatives and keep my door locked," said Mohammad Iqbal, 55. "When I am sure peace is restored, I will bring them back."

Recent attacks involving Indian and Pakistani troops have been the worst border violence since a 2003 cease-fire. Now, with snow falling on the mountainous border, fighting has subsided and displaced residents are trickling home.

But analysts fear the calm will be relatively short-lived. While few expect another war, the flare-ups illustrate the simmering tensions that may only increase as the two countries jostle for influence in Afghanistan while U.S. troops withdraw.

"This is the new normal," said Stephen P. Cohen, a senior fellow and South Asia analyst at the Brookings Institution. "This is going to be just like the Middle East, but only with two countries with nuclear weapons."

The fighting this fall, which included artillery and mortar fire, claimed civilian and military lives on both sides of the border. Ominously, it took place not only in Kashmir, which has been a source of tension for decades, but also farther south on the outskirts of Sialkot, an industrial area known for producingquality soccer balls.

Since predominantly Muslim Pakistan was separated from mostly Hindu India in 1947, the countries have fought two wars over Kashmir, which is divided between them but has a majority Muslim population.

Each side has blamed the other for the recent fighting.

Pakistanis speculate that the Indian government is becoming more aggressive toward its neighbor, in part to gain support ahead of national elections. Meanwhile, Indians accuse Pakistan of failing to rein in Islamist militants seeking an independent Kashmir. Some of the militant groups are widely suspected of having ties to the Pakistani military and intelligence services. The conflict started in January, when Pakistan accused Indian forces of killing a Pakistani soldier on the disputed border in Kashmir, known as the Line of Control. India then claimed Pakistani soldiers or militants crossed the border and killed three of its soldiers.

In August, the feud took a dangerous turn when five Indian soldiers were slain in Kashmir. Pakistan denied responsibility but shelling between the two sides escalated.

Last month, Pakistan's military accused India of firing 4,000 mortar shells and 59,000 machine-gun rounds during a two-day period that coincided with Pakistani Prime Minister Nawaz Sharif's meeting with President Obama in Washington. One of those shells killed the rickshaw driver in Tahir Joian.

"We were forced to retaliate," said Brig. Mateem Ahmed Khan, a senior commander for Pakistan's border force near Sialkot. He accused India of stoking the tension to undermine Sharif's visit to Washington. "It was a rain of fire coming down on our villages and posts," he said.

With Pakistan restricting Western reporters' access to the border, it is difficult to verify the claims of its military. In Tahir Joian, chunks of concrete were missing from walls and a hole was visible in a thatched roof, but there did not appear to be widespread damage.

Efforts to avoid crisis

When a reporter visited a Pakistani ranger outpost recently, soldiers were looking out over a tranquil border, listening to music from an Indian Border Security Force bunker about a quarter-mile away.

The sound of music across the border underscores a crucial point: Unlike previous conflicts in the 1990s and early 2000s, which led to fears of another major war, India and Pakistan are working to keeping their skirmishes from turning into an international crisis.

The directors of military operations for both countries hold weekly conference calls to try to keep hostilities in check. Khan recently met his Indian counterpart at the border to discuss matters such as how Indian forces can clear brush around their outposts without fear of being targeted.

Sharif, who campaigned on improved relations with India before taking office in June, is pressing for security and trade negotiations with Indian Prime Minister Manmohan Singh.

Though the two met in late September, Singh has appeared hesitant to engage in substantive talks, expressing concern that Pakistan is not doing enough to control Islamist militant groups including Lashkar-e-Taiba, responsible for the 2008 Mumbai terrorist attacks.

But many Pakistani analysts doubt that this country's military is to blame for the tension, since it is focused on battling domestic militants. A bloody insurgency by the Pakistani Taliban has claimed more than 45,000 lives.

"Pakistan is preoccupied with domestic issues at the moment, so the military would have no interest in heating up the Line of Control, none whatsoever," said Maleeha Lodhi, a former Pakistani ambassador to Washington. "In fact, it has an interest in assuring all is peaceful on the eastern front so it can focus on the western front" with Afghanistan, an area where many militants are based. Lodhi said Singh may be adopting a tougher approach to Pakistan because of Indian elections in the spring. Singh is stepping aside, but his Congress Party faces a stiff challenge from the BJP party, led by Narendra Modi, an ardent Hindu nationalist who wants to take a harder line with Pakistan.

The Afghanistan factor

Even after the elections, analysts fear, the India-Pakistan border could turn volatile as the two countries struggle for influence in Afghanistan. In recent months, Afghan President Hamid Karzai has been reaching out to India for military aid, a potential alliance that unnerves Pakistani leaders, who fear their country could become further isolated in the region. To Pakistanis, their nation's regional importance was highlighted this summer when U.S. officials turned to the country for help in trying to arrange peace talks between the Taliban and Karzai's government. The talks ultimately didn't happen. In Pakistan, some officials believe India escalated tension at the border to draw attention away from Pakistan's diplomatic efforts.

Today's WorldView

What's most important from where the world meets Washington, "India was anxious it was getting left out and that Pakistan was not taking it seriously," said Riaz Khokhar, Pakistan's foreign secretary from 2002 to 2005. Sushant Sareen, a researcher at the Institute for Defense Studies and Analyses in New Delhi, called Khokhar's comments "utter rubbish." The real cause of the skirmishing on the border, he said, was Pakistan's unwillingness to stop Islamist militant groups from crossing the border. In recent weeks, before snows in the Himalayan mountains made passage difficult, as many as 100 Pakistani insurgents sneaked into Indian territory, according to Indian intelligence and security officials. They say the insurgents plan to carry out attacks before the elections and stoke separatist fervor in Indian-controlled Kashmir. "Before, there was this looming American presence in the region that kept things from happening," Sareen said. "But now, with that focus shifting from the area, it's going back to business as usual."

PRODUCING AN ANALYTIC FRAMEWORK FOR IDENTITY: BEYOND WENDT'S SYSTEMIC THEORY

Identities, writes Rogers Smith, 'are among the most normatively significant and behaviorally consequential aspects of politics,' and analyses that incorporate them present a powerful challenge to behaviouralist and rational-choice approaches. Constructivists have demonstrated, as discussed earlier, that Smith's observation extends to the realm of international relations. Accordingly, identity has been a central concept in constructivist arguments, particularly for Wendt and other influential 'middle-ground' constructivists. Indeed, the integrity of the former's theory hinges on the strength of his conceptualisation of identity. But Wendt's highly-influential conceptualisation suffers from important—even severe—flaws. Thus, this chapter will engage with and critique Wendt's 'middle-range' framework and attempt to formulate a more convincing conceptualisation of identity—as well as its relationship with conflict—based on the insights of alternative accounts. I will also aim to show that rationalist/materialist explanations of identity formation and conflict are insufficient. Before proceeding, it is valuable first to elucidate what is meant by 'identity.' Identity essentially refers to our self-conception *in relation* to others.

Identities are not individualistic or personal, but are formed in a social context where individual and collective identities are co-constituted—leading us to identify with "our" social group—and 'defined [by our] interaction and relationship to others.' In the same way, national/state identities are also 'partly formed in relationship to other nations and states.' Accepting this, Wendt applies symbolic interactionist theory to the systems-level of inter-state relations and argues that states' social identities—and in turn their interests—are formed and sustained (or constituted) through *social interaction* with other states; an ongoing process which creates structures of shared knowledge (which are maintained by practices), leading to relatively stable identities as the social system into which states are embedded becomes a 'social fact.'

If social identities and structures of shared knowledge are competitive and zero-sum, conflict may ensue. However, while difficult to modify, identities 'are not carved in stone' and can change through 'social learning'; replacing, for example, Hobbesian cultures of anarchy and conflict with Kantian security communities. For Wendt, the 'daily life of international politics is an on-going process of states taking identities in relation to Others, casting them into corresponding counter-identities, and playing out the result.'

In contrast to Waltz's excessively materialistic 'proto-theory' of identity formation, Wendt endogenises states' social identities and regards them as socially constructed. Thus, 'anarchy is what states make of it.'Because he focuses on the level of the international system, Wendt also anthropomorphises states and distinguishes between their 'corporate' and 'social' identities—the latter referring to the sets of meanings about oneself a state derives from the social structures of international society through inter-state interaction, and the former denoting 'the intrinsic, self-organizing qualities that constitute actor individuality.' For states, this means domestic-level elements such as the constituent individuals, physical resources, and the shared beliefs and institutions which confer individuals with a collective function. Crucially, Wendt regards corporate identities as 'exogenously given' and 'ontologically prior to the state system'; in short, as 'fixed and pre-social entities'. Consequently, and because of his assumption of a unitary state, Wendt also brackets everything domestic.

Wendt's argument of social identities emerging through systemic interaction and his bracketing and exogenising of 'corporate' identities presents serious problems for his framework. As Sujata Pasic argues, by attempting to avoid an 'oversocialized approach,' Wendt, in effect, strips identity of its social-cultural content. 'Social' identity formation in Wendt's constructivism is curiously missing a notion of society and is presented as 'simply a by-product of repeated state interactions.' Similar to realists/rationalists, then, Wendt's conceptualisation of identity formation fails to engage 'the actual social levels of state sociality.'

Indeed, it is difficult to differentiate between identity and behaviour in Wendt's account; his framework demands us to deduce actors' self-conceptions/understandings merely from their behaviour. There is thus a compelling argument that Wendt's conceptualisation of identity does not entail 'identity' at all, but is simply an account of behaviour. The 'centrality of physical gestures' to Wendt's framework makes it 'impossible to analyse identity [formation and] transformation as a *discursive* process.' As does his treatment of 'corporate' identities. By bracketing the domestic, Wendt omits a considerable amount of the normative content that underlies identity formation and change. Maja Zehfuss demonstrates this by showing how post-Cold War contestations over German identity were not limited to the level of inter-state relations, but were equally present in domestic discourse and exerted a deep influence on German identity construction. Moreover, by joining rationalists in regarding states and their corporate identities as 'exogenously given,' fixed and pre-social, Wendt obscures the complexity of identity formation/change and the extent to which corporate identities are not 'bounded' categories or spatio-temproally fixed, but are often contested and even unstable; with a profound effect not only on states' 'social' identities, but also in some cases—and this is extremely relevant to explanations of nationalist conflict—their very existence.

Cederman and Daase and Pasic thus correctly stress the need to move beyond 'static [and statist] conceptualisations of identity' and endogenise and problematise *corporate* identities; that is, actors' 'very existence and extension in space and time,' including their membership, boundaries, and domestic institutions. Runa Das argues this analytical approach is particularly important in the context of India-Pakistan relations. Contra Wendt, this requires an appreciation of state sociality beyond systemic interaction between fixed, unitary states. Importantly, this analytical shift can be achieved within a framework of constructivism without sliding into postmodern relativism.

In developing such a framework, I draw on sociology, social theory and social psychology by incorporating the insights of four main analytical perspectives—Abdelal et al.'s conceptualisation of collective identity; Cederman and Daase's application of Simmel's sociational theory; Peter Gries's adaptation of social identity theory, and the concept of 'ontological security.'

While some may criticise such analytical eclecticism, Katzenstein and Okawara offer a strong defense of this approach by arguing that it is intellectually more important to make sense of empirical anomalies than it is to privilege parsimony. I formulate the core assumptions of the model around Abdelal et al.'s framing of collective identity as 'a social category that varies along two dimensions—content and contestation.' The aim of the framework is to conceptualise the social construction of identities and its influence on actors, and to demonstrate the impact of *contestation* on the content of identities and on conflict in international relations.

Content

Content describes the *meaning* of a collective identity, and may entail four types; *constitutive norms*, which define the boundaries and formal and informal rules of group membership; *social purposes*, or the goals that a group attaches to its identity; *relational comparisons*, through which a group defines itself in reference to 'Others,' and *cognitive models*, which refers to the 'understandings of political and material conditions and interests' that are shaped by a group's identity. Three core assumptions can be inferred from this reading of the content of identities, which I place under two categories: *identity formation* and *influence over actors*.

Identity Formation. The first core assumption centres on the argument that identities are socially constructed, and emphasises the 'social origins of identity.' Collective identities are not primordial, essentialist or natural—as, for example, Huntington's 'clash of civilizations' paradigm or Posen's neo-realist reading of ethnic conflict would suggest—but are 'constructed and reconstructed through historical action.' Nationalism, for instance, is one key discursive process which constructs national identities around mythical, 'imagined communities.'

Arguments for unity and the boundaries of community (including nation-states') are also embedded into these mythical constructions through the use of language, socially meaningful cultural symbols and imagery or 'frames,' and narratives of national identity (storylines about a nation's origins and history).These might be employed strategically by purposeful agents ('political entrepreneurs'), but such action is not merely instrumental; it can be principled and takes place within a normative structure that enables or legitimises it. The endogenising of corporate identities central to Simmel's sociational theory—which privileges neither actor nor structure and emphasises the dynamic interaction of both—helps capture this and overcomes the structural-bias of constructivists like Wendt, who have been criticised for paying insufficient attention to human agents. Social psychology perspectives—notably social identity theory—also suggest that we might respond to the mythological social-cultural cues of collective identities and assimilate into groups because of the desire to gain—and maintain—collective self-esteem. The second core assumption, related to the content type *relational comparisons,* is that there is always an internal-external dynamic to identity formation. Collective identities do not simply emerge from internal group processes.

Rather, identities are incomplete without an 'understanding of oneself in relation to others.' Several scholars have shown, for example, that European identity construction has always needed—including contemporarily—a constituting 'Eastern' 'Other'. Similarly, central to social identity theory is the notion of the 'looking-glass self,' where groups gain knowledge about their own collective identities through comparisons with others, leading to identity formation through in-group/out-group differentiation. In the realm of international relations, Others are also vital to a state's identity. Carl Schmitt argues that a state's authority over its self-definition depends on framing Other(s) as 'public enemies.' But contra Wendt, states' 'social' identities are also partly the product of the domestic socio-cultural practices that constitute their national identities. Barnett captures the internal-external dynamics of identity formation succinctly with his definition of identity as 'a relational construct that emerges out of international and domestic discourse and interactions.'

Influence over actors. The third core assumption is that identities shape and influence actors' actions, interests and understandings of material and economic conditions. Here the content types *constitutive norms,social purposes,* and *cognitive models* are particularly relevant. With respect to the former, depending on the degree of internalisation of constitutive practices, norms may influence actors by biasing choice through a 'logic of appropriateness,' where behaviour that is inappropriate for an actor's identity is consciously dismissed. *Social purposes* highlights the *purposive* content of collective identities and emphasises the role of identity in leading actors to infuse their practices with group purposes and to interpret the world through frameworks partly defined by these purposes. An identity's purposive content—based on the notion that *who we are influences what we do*—thus assists in defining group interests, goals, and preferences, while also producing obligations for the group to pursue practices that increase the likelihood of achieving its set of goals. Purposive goals might range from specific territorial claims to an abstract moral purpose, which Reus-Smit argues deeply influences international state practices and institutions. Finally, the *cognitive content* of an identity entails a group's model of social reality, or its epistemology and ontology. This can be conceived of as a *worldview* which enables a group to 'make sense of social, political, and economic conditions.' Vitally, this cognitive perspective suggests that identities 'are not things in the world but ways of seeing the world,' which help us orient our actions and conceptualise ourselves (and Others), and our interests and predicaments or threats; as well as our 'subjective perception and understanding of [our] communal past' or history. Actors are not compelled into certain forms of behaviour by material forces or the objective instrumental logic of rational-choice. Rather, as Risse et al. argue, it is 'collective identities [that] define and shape how actors view their perceived instrumental and material interests and which preferences are regarded as legitimate and appropriate for enacting given identities.'

Contestation (and conflict)

Identities are not 'natural,' fixed or stable entities. As Yosef Lapid points out, taking constructivism seriously requires us to treat identities as socially constructed, rather than primordial; as optional, rather than deterministic; as fragmenting/diversifying, rather than integrating/homogenising; and as multidimensional and dynamic, rather than undimensional and static. In short, we must 'problematize [the] dominant ontology and epistemology of stability and continuity that [has] hitherto informed depictions of… collective identity.' Thus, the second key dimension of identity is *contestation*. Abdelal et al. challenge the reifying of collective identities and argue that the content of identities 'is the outcome of a process of social contestation within the group.' However, I diverge slightly from this perspective because of its one-dimensional focus on *internal*contestation, which obscures the importance of external challenges to the content of an identity from 'out-groups.' Instead, I frame contestation around Thomas Berger's argument that cultures and identities 'are not static entities hovering above society,' but are reproduced through often imperfect primary/secondary socialisation mechanisms, while being 'under constant pressure from *both* external developments and internal contradictions.' Crucially, utilising social identity theory and sociational theory,

I centre the remaining core assumptions of the model on the argument that contestation dynamics are essential to understanding patterns of conflict in international relations, particularly 'enduring rivalries' such as India and Pakistan's.

Social Identity Theory (SIT). SIT emerged as a theoretical approach to intergroup relations in social psychology. Through robust experimental work using 'minimal-group' situations, SIT convincingly demonstrated that people seek a positive self-identity through identifying with a group, and favourably comparing this 'in-group' to 'out-groups.' These comparisons induce potential competition through in-group favouritism and out-group discrimination. Jonathan Mercer applied the insights of SIT to the level of the international system and argued that they provide theoretical and empirical support to neo-realist assumptions about state egoism, inter-state competition and conflict, self-help systems and the pursuit of relative gains—with the desire for a positive self-identity, rather than the anarchic international structure or material economic or security incentives, generating and driving inter-group and inter-state competition. Conflict, argues Mercer, is 'an inescapable feature of intergroup and interstate relations.' There are glaring errors in Mercer's application of SIT, however. Mercer conflates 'in-group love,' which SIT emphasises as emerging from in-group favouritism, and 'out-group hate/dislike,' which does not necessarily follow from favouritism towards in-groups. Inter-group competition, conflict, and aggression should thus be considered distinct from in-group bias. Many other applications of SIT to IR suffer from similar problems. Peter Gries challenges Mercer on the same grounds and offers a highly valuable framework for applying SIT to the identity-conflict debate in IR. Rather than viewing inter-state/inter-group competition or conflict as inevitable, Gries follows social psychologist Marilyn Brewer's argument that 'any relationship between ingroup identification and outgroup hostility is progressive and contingent rather than necessary and inevitable.'

Thus, Gries identifies conditions under which identification with nations may lead to international competition and conflict. To achieve this, he describes a four-stage process, with conflict as the final stage: (1) ingroup identification, (2) ingroup positivity, (3) intergroup competition, (4) intergroup conflict. According to SIT, once people identify with their 'ingroup,' they also attach positive attributes to it and favour it over outgroups. This creates a desire for *positive social identity*, and in order to obtain this and maintain ingroup positivity, groups engage in*intergroup social comparisons*, a process through which they seek external confirmation and recognition by outgroups of their social identity and the positive views they attach to it.

It is these *social comparisons processes* that lie at the heart of explaining when ingroup identification and ingroup positivity (stages one and two) may lead to intergroup competition and conflict (stages three and four). When ingroup positivity is not affirmed by significant Others, or when outgroups are perceived to impugn or *contest* the ingroup's identity, the latter's collective self-esteem is threatened, and anger and competition might follow. Here, argues Allen Whiting, nations may shift from espousing non-competitive 'affirmative nationalism' to competitive 'assertive nationalism,' and even 'aggressive nationalism':

Affirmative nationalism centres exclusively on 'us' as a positive in-group referent with pride in attributes and achievements. Assertive nationalism adds 'them' as a negative out-group referent that challenges the in-group's interests and possibly its identity. Aggressive nationalism identifies a specific foreign enemy as serious threat that requires action to defend vital interests.

Contestation of one's identity from an 'outgroup' through social comparisons is thus a vital prerequisite to competition and conflict. However, Gries identifies three conditions which need to be satisfied for competition to ensue. First, the comparisons must be made with a *salient other*: an external group that is a relevant and 'desirable object of comparison.' With regards to Pakistan, for example, while India is a salient other, Ecuador is not. Second, the comparisons must entail something that is *consequential* to the groups' self-conceptions: something each group *cherishes as part of itself*. For Pakistan and India, this may be the ideological foundations of their national identities; for example Pakistan's 'Muslim' identity and India's 'secular' self-conception. Third, the comparisons must be framed in *zero-sum terms*. Here, the notion of 'status' is particularly important. Thus, under zero-sum comparisons, Pakistan's status as a 'Muslim' nation might require hurting India's status as a 'secular' or 'Hindu' nation, and vice versa. One group's 'gains' in this regard will be the other group's 'losses.' All three of these conditions need to be met; if comparisons are inconsequential or not framed in zero-sum terms with a salient other, competition will not ensue. Moreover, even if these conditions are met, competition can be inhibited through 'social mobility'—denoting 'exiting' from a threatened social identity—or 'social creativity,' which entails reframing threatening comparisons 'to allow for positive distinctiveness.' Therefore, contra Mercer, competition is not an inevitable feature of ingroup favouritism.

Ontological Security and Sociational Theory. But how do we get from intergroup competition to intergroup conflict? Gries does not explore this in detail, but suggests the role of affect—particularly anger—might be crucial. Instead, I join Huysmans, Steele and Mitzen in emphasising the group/state's need for 'ontological security,' which is already implicit in the SIT framework. According to this perspective, states seek more than just the physical security that realists privilege. More importantly, they constantly require 'ontological security,' or security and stability in their self-understandings, which Anthony Giddens describes as essential to obtaining a sense of agency and self-identity.

States 'need to feel secure in who they are.' Deep uncertainty and anxiety—which in my model stems from threatening *contestations* (internal and external) to a group's identity—'renders the actor's identity insecure' (thus threatening collective self-esteem). To alleviate this ontological insecurity, states seek a stable cognitive environment. They thus pursue cognitive certainty by establishing *routinized relations* with significant others (such as those that threaten their ontological security), which in turn leads actors to 'get attached to these social relationships.'

Crucially, ontological security-seeking can conflict with physical security. If materially-harmful or 'self-defeating' conflicts can provide ontological security, states may become 'attached' to conflictual relationships because 'on-going, certain conflict' is preferable to deeply uncertain self-identities. This creates a sort of implicit 'dysfunctional [intergroup] collective identity' centred on physical insecurity and competition; a mutual, intersubjective social structure where each state nonetheless considers itself to be acting alone and contesting the 'Other.' In other words, a collective identity without a 'we' feeling. Here the traditional 'security dilemma' is turned on its head; the certainty conflict provides, rather than uncertainty, can cause and sustain conflict.

The need for ontological security offers a powerful structural explanation of 'intractable conflicts'/'enduring rivalries' (such as the India-Pakistan conflict) which seem pathological or irrational from a realist perspective—a perspective whose focus on 'material rationality' fails to explain the social construction of identities and the role identity plays in producing 'irrational' or 'self-defeating' conflicts. But the ontological security-conflict relationship also has a crucial *internal* component at the level of states' 'corporate' identities, which systemic theories omit by reifying nation-states. Threats to self-identity might emanate not only from external others, but also 'internal others'—a category Steele and Huysmans term *internal strangers*—who disturb the 'predictability and continuity' of a state's/nation's self-identity over time; thus endangering the 'realization of ontological security.' It is here that sociational theory is especially illuminating, for it also problematises 'corporate' identities—the boundaries of groups/nations/states.

Rather than reifying the boundaries of nation-states, sociational theory regards spatial mappings as socially constructed. For Simmel, 'the boundary is not a spatial fact with social implications, but rather a sociological fact that forms spatially.' This highlights a crucial link between ontological (in)security and ontological *survival*, which Mitzen and others do not explore.

For as Pasic writes, 'states, even with stores of military might at their disposal, only survive if the historical arguments for unity within them continue to convince an audience.' Ontological survival in this context is especially pressing when the ingroup and outgroup hold incompatible spatial representations and the situation might involve potential boundary transformations—as is the case with 'irredentist' conflicts. Consequently, deep ontological uncertainty—stemming not only from external contestations but also 'internal strangers' who threaten 'national unity' and identity cohesion—may intensify levels of ingroup discrimination and bias as groups/states urgently seek to establish firm and coherent boundaries.

This might be achieved through *internal violence*—which attempts to secure self-identities through efforts to homogenise populations and utilise violence as a 'vehicle for social integration' to 'defuse the danger that a "foreigner inside"' presents to the group's self-identity. More importantly, conflict with an outgroup might also be employed. Here, sociational theory highlights the importance of conflict—as an interaction process with an external Other—in creating the group consciousness necessary for secure identities.

Applying the Framework: Identity and the Enduring India-Pakistan Conflict

In order to sufficiently analyse and contextualise the India-Pakistan rivalry, it is essential to firstly appreciate the nature of the conflict. As T.V. Paul et al. demonstrate, the relationship between the two states does not constitute an ordinary conflict, but an *enduring rivalry*, denoting 'a strategic competition between the same pair of states over an extended period of time.' While the majority of inter-state conflicts are concluded relatively quickly, a small percentage become *enduring*, 'locking' the competing states into a robust conflictual relationship.

These 'enduring' or 'intractable' conflicts are defined by an 'outstanding set of unresolved issues,' 'strategic interdependence,' 'psychological manifestations of enmity,' and 'repeated militarized conflict.' The aforementioned features evidently characterise the India-Pakistan relationship, which has experienced four wars (three of them over the disputed territory of Kashmir), continual crises and hostility, 'proxy wars', and has even been on the verge of nuclear conflict (in 1990 and 2001-2).

Interestingly, realist and rational-choice approaches have tremendous difficulty in explaining enduring rivalries. For realists, who place material*power* at the heart of explanations of conflict, enduring rivalries should only take place between states whose material capabilities are relatively similar (major powers, for example). In asymmetric conflicts—such as India and Pakistan's—where one state possesses a substantial power advantage (in our case India), enduring rivalries should not develop because of the stronger side's ability to militarily defeat and impose its will on the weaker state.

But contrary to realist assumptions, the asymmetric India-Pakistan conflict has endured for over sixty years, despite Pakistan's repeated failures to militarily defeat or challenge India. Such conflicts appear similarly enigmatic to rational-choice theorists, with some even suggesting that repeated military conflicts are not 'enduring rivalries' with strong historical interconnections, but 'random events' occurring by chance. However, not only has this argument been challenged empirically, but it also seems 'ludicrous' to suggest that India and Pakistan's various conflicts have taken place 'randomly,' with no interconnections. Some realists/rationalists accept the substantive presence of these seemingly 'irrational' conflicts, but tend to implicitly regard them as aberrations or deviations from the 'rational' systems-level realist logic, and explain them with reference to 'second-image' causes such as bureaucratic self-interest.

However, this chapter will move beyond realism's materialism and methodological individualism and seek to analyse the enduring India-Pakistan rivalry utilising the identity framework developed—exploring the social construction of both states' identities and the influence of these intersubjective social structures on their interests, preferences, and understandings of the material world, and, vitally, on their conflictual relationship.

It will be concluded that the India-Pakistan relationship constitutes a 'dysfunctional [intergroup] collective identity,' characterised by deep ontological uncertainty—stemming from both 'domestic' and 'systemic' turbulence in the form of *threatening contestations to each state's 'social' but also 'corporate' identities*—and an on-going, zero-sum social comparisons process, with conflict providing an avenue for the realisation of ontological security and the maintenance of collective (in-group) self-esteem. To strengthen my argument and test its plausibility, alternative explanations of the conflict will then be critically analysed, before concluding the paper by situating its contribution within the wider debate on the India-Pakistan conflict and suggesting that constructivism offers researchers the opportunity to introduce IR theory as a serious tool in the study of the conflict without being constrained by excessively materialistic or parsimonious, systemic—and wholly inadequate—theories such as neo-realism.

Indian and Pakistani Identity Formation

In analysing the role of identity in India-Pakistan relations, it is crucial to recognise the socially constructed, as opposed to primordial or instrumental, quality of identity formation. Many adopt a primordialist interpretation and attribute the enduring rivalry to the irreconcilable worldviews of, and entrenched hostilities between, monolithic 'Muslim' Pakistan and 'Hindu' India—essentially explaining the conflict as an offshoot of Hindu-Muslim communalism. While superficially appealing, this argument fails to account for the centuries of relative coexistence and inter-social, cultural and religious connections and exchanges between generally pluralistic Hindu and Muslim communities prior to the twentieth century.

More fundamentally, it ignores the *socially constructed,* rather than natural, quality of both states' national and state identities; something this section aims to address, beginning with India. Much of 'modern' India's self-conception was originally formulated around Indian nationalist discourse and spearheaded by the highly-dominant Congress party before and following independence.

In particular, Jawaharlal Nehru was pivotal in helping to articulate the central features of Indian identity—not in a liberal-individualist sense, but as a purposeful agent embedded in a social structure consisting of the intersubjective ideas of the wider Indian nationalist movement. The first core element of India's self-conception was *Sarva Dharma Samabhava* (secularism), which was key in distinguishing India from the 'communal' and 'reactionary' Pakistani 'other,' highlighting the in-group/out-group differentiation element of identity formation. Indeed, Nehru himself defined India's self-image as 'a secular nation' by differentiating it with ' two-nation theory which Pakistan is sponsoring.'

The 'exceptionalism' of Indian democracy in South Asia as well India's espousal of non-alignment and its claim to moral leadership in the developing world were the other core 'differentiating markers' from the Pakistani 'other' in India's self-image. In addition, India was deemed a *modern* 'major power'; a successor to the British with a powerful regional and global mission that reflected its 'national greatness.' Narratives and frames were utilised to reify this self-conception; history was interpreted anew and multiculturalism presented as a natural feature of Indian civilisation, while 'pacific' ancient cultural and social traditions coupled with stories exalting the glories of India's past civilisations helped legitimise its 'benign' global role in the international system. Moreover, 'India' was transformed from a vast land of disparate provinces and princely states—described as a 'porridge of irregular and improbable jigsaw puzzle shapes' —into an 'imagined community' whose territorial borders were naturalised and embedded into the national consciousness through 'the popular sacralisation of territory,' embodied in the metaphor of *Bharat Mata*('Mother India').

While India's self-image has been based on secularism, Pakistan's identity was constructed on the mythical narrative of the 'two-nation' theory, popularly articulated by the Muslim League, which posited that the Muslims and Hindus of India represented two monolithic, incompatible civilisations who were based, as Jinnah declared, 'on conflicting ideas and conceptions.' Crucially, Pakistan's national (and state) identity as the homeland of India's Muslims and its self-image as an advanced, *modern* Islamic state was (and continues to be) constructed against the perceived threat of Hindu (the 'other') domination and majoritarianism. Thus, the notion of *parity* between 'Muslim' Pakistan and 'Hindu' India has been central to Pakistan's self-conception. As former Prime Minister Zulifkar Bhutto wrote:

One of the dominant urges for Pakistan has been to dispel the notion of seniority or superiority of Hindu India over Muslim India by creating a Muslim State equal and sovereign to the other State.

Moreover, being different from the Indian 'other' has been essential in providing 'a rationale for the two-nation theory and for Pakistan's battle for a separate identity.' Narratives have thus emphasised Pakistan's Islamic-Arabic roots and '[rejected] everything that was Indian' about Pakistan. Some have suggested the narratives and cultural symbols associated with the 'two-nation' theory were merely instruments in the power struggle between elites (and thus without normative content). However, while the 'two-nation' theory was certainly employed strategically by political entrepreneurs, such activity took place within a normative structure influenced by a mass, broad-based movement, and arose from a genuine fear of 'Hindu domination,' as elements of the Congress-led 'nationalist-secular' movement increasingly incorporated 'Hindu' symbols and policies. Similarly to India, Pakistan was socially constructed as an 'imagined community,' based on the narrative of the two-nation theory. This was achieved not merely through territorial state/nation-building, but more importantly through 'representational practices,' that 'in various ways attempted to inscribe something called India [and Pakistan] with a content, history, meaning, and trajectory.'

The identities of the two states, however, have not been stable and unchanging. Beginning in the 1980s, India's secularism began to decline and its conception of 'self' and 'other' was increasingly informed by the discourse of Hindu nationalism framed by the *Hindutva* movement, which attacked the 'pseudo-secularism' of the Congress for purportedly empowering religious minorities, particularly Muslims (the 'other'), at the expense of Hindus, and sought to 're-imagine' India as a virile and masculine Hindu *rashtra* (state). Narratives were employed to reconstruct Hindus as a homogenous in-group, with India's identity being re-articulated on the principle of *akhand bharat*, or 'one nation, one people, and one culture.' Critically, Hindu nationalism was invigorated by the 'Muslim question' and Pakistan; the Hindu *rashtra* was constructed in contradistinction to the Muslim and Pakistani 'other.'

Hindutva was further empowered by the formation of BJP governments, notably in 1998. Nevertheless, Hindu nationalist parties were compelled to moderate their agendas to remain in power because of the constraining effects of India's liberal-democratic structures. Thus, rather than forging a Hindu *rashtra*, India's self-conception has been defined by the tensions, compromises and even convergences between secular and Hindu nationalist narratives.

Pakistan also underwent 're-imagining' in the 1980s, as processes of *Islamisation*, particularly under Zia-ul Haq, sought to redefine Pakistan's identity on the basis of orthodox Islam. *Madrassas* and *Jihad* symbolised the new discourse, and fresh narratives about the nation's birth were employed to reconstruct Jinnah and the anti-colonial freedom struggle as Islamists that aimed to establish an Islamic state. Moreover, protecting Pakistan's Islamic identity and defending its 'ideological frontiers' became crucial for achieving national unity and stability in Pakistan's self-conception. As Zia-ul Haq declared, the 'preservation of [Pakistan's ideology] and the Islamic character of the country ... as important as the security of the country's geographical boundaries.' Islamisation has also been considered vital to the core aim of distinguishing Pakistan from the Indian 'other,' which is reflected in the fear that 'if Pakistan does not become and remain aggressively Islamic, it will become India again.'

Role of identity in shaping actors and foreign policies

The conceptions of identity discussed above have played a pivotal role in shaping both states' actions and understandings of their material and instrumental geopolitical and strategic interests—or their *social purposes*and *cognitive models*—as well as their foreign policies. As Gupta argues, 'cultural and ideological factors [have been] enmeshed with strategic calculations' of both states, which is reflected in their respective*strategic cultures*, which Ken Booth defines as perceptual frameworks entailing the 'traditions, values, attitudes [and] patterns of behaviour' of nations—or in Alistair Johnston's words their 'integrated set of symbols' —that shape states' security discourses and interactions (which are not merely determined by the 'rational' pursuit of instrumental interests). Within this context, one of the 'key elements of Pakistan's strategic culture,' notes Peter Lavoy, has been opposition to Indian hegemony.

This is characterised by what many describe as Pakistan's primary foreign policy goal; to achieve *parity*—politically, diplomatically and even militarily—

with India, and to eventually balkanise 'akhand bharat' (united India) in order to make it more manageable and less threatening. This *purposive goal* is not merely a prudent geopolitical strategy arising from threats to state survival by a hegemonic neighbour in an anarchic world, but has been intimately shaped by Pakistan's long-standing self-conception as a strong 'Muslim' state that is equal to 'Hindu' India and must challenge 'Hindu' majoritarianism and domination. For its part, India's own security and strategic discourses have centred on—even 'obsessed' over—the Pakistani 'other.' While realist analysts have derided the 'irrationality' of this preoccupation with a far smaller power, the strategy has been motivated by India's self-image as a secular nation that needs to challenge and demonstrate the artificiality of Pakistan's two-nation theory. The disputed territory of Kashmir attests to the centrality of identity to both states' geostrategic understandings, for the meaning and significance attached to it has been defined by their respective self-conceptions rather than narrow material incentives. For Pakistan, Kashmir is crucial to its 'Muslim' (and pan-Islamic) identity and the two-nation theory, while for India, as former Prime Minister Vajpayee commented in 2002, 'Kashmir is not a piece of land; it is a test case of secularism.' Identity has also played a fundamental role in the most significant security issue—the nuclearisation of the subcontinent. As Das and others have demonstrated, India and Pakistan's nuclear trajectories have been—to a considerable degree—shaped by their self-images. Thus, by pursuing a nuclear capability, India sought to act out its identity as a *modern* post-colonial state (and indeed a major power) established on the *modernist*principles of secularism, democracy, and scientific and technological progress. Similarly, Pakistan's nuclear programme sought to confirm its 'scientific and technological greatness' and self-image as 'the most advanced Muslim country,' while also being 'a symbol of defiance' to the Indian 'other,' and furthering its goal of *parity* with 'Hindu' India. Indeed, Pakistan originally contextualised its nuclear policy around its 'Islamic' identity, with Bhutto coining the term 'the Islamic bomb' and reasoning that:

The Christian, Jewish, and Hindu civilizations have [a full nuclear capability]... Only the Islamic civilization was without it ... but this was about to change.

The 1998 nuclear tests further demonstrated how conceptions of 'self' and 'other' have shaped both states' security discourses. For India, the tests reflected the increasing salience of *Hindutva* as a source of Indian identity, as the Hindu-Right BJP government overturned India's longstanding policy of nuclear ambiguity to showcase the nation's 'nuclear teeth,' dubbing the tests 'Operation Shakti' as Hindu nationalist discourse situated it in the context of 'the cult of manliness and virility' that defined the Hindu *rashtra*—in contradistinction to the Muslim and Pakistan 'other.' Realist analysts explained the tests as instances of instrumental power politics vis-a-vis Pakistan, and especially China, but this fails to appreciate that the tests were actually strategically counter-productive and *not* constructed against 'the China threat.'

Rather, the tests most importantly represented what Talbot terms the 'Hindutva bomb'—aimed primarily at the Pakistani/Muslim 'other.' Pakistan's subsequent 'tit-for-tat' explosions were also framed within the context of its Islamic identity as an advanced Muslim state reacting to the domineering threat of the Hindu 'other.' Thus, the tests were constructed as the 'Islamic bomb' responding to the 'Hindu bomb,' which also reflected the increasing importance of an orthodox Islamic identity to Pakistan's strategic culture and its foreign policy and security discourses. In India, *Hindutva* was further energised by the post-September 11th security context, as the 'cult of manliness and virility' informed India's new, more aggressive, policy of 'coercive diplomacy' vis-a-vis Pakistan. The Pakistani/Muslim 'other' was now constructed as a despotic *Jihadi* state and 'the epicentre of world terrorism'; as well as a threat to Indian civilisation.

As the preceding discussion has shown, India and Pakistan's identities have shaped their respective understandings of the material world, informed their interests and influenced their foreign policy and security discourses.

8

Kashmir's Siachen Glacier Outpost in India-Pakistan Conflict

India and Pakistan have talked about removing troops from the world's highest battlefield in the disputed Kashmir region, but military outposts of the two nuclear powers remain in the frozen Himalayan terrain. More troops have died from hostile weather conditions in the Siachen glacier area than from military action since sporadic fighting began there nearly three decades ago. A ceasefire came into effect in 2003.

Avalanches have taken their toll in the region, where the altitude rises to 6,700 metres, temperatures plunge to –70 C and frostbite can set in within seconds. "It's totally insane to be fighting a war at these altitudes," Rifaat Hussain, who teaches political science at Islamabad's National Defence College, told Time magazine in 2005.

An avalanche at the entrance to the Siachen glacier on April 7, 2012, buried more than 100 Pakistani soldiers. Another 24 Pakistani troops were killed in 2010. Up to 20,000 troops deployed Conflict in the area began in 1984 when India occupied the heights of the 78-kilometre-long glacier, fearing Pakistan wanted to claim the territory. Pakistan also deployed its troops.

Reuters has reported that since then, up to 20,000 Indian and Pakistani forces combined have faced off against each other in the mountains above the glacier, which has melted to half its earlier size. The conflict between India and Pakistan over Kashmir and other areas of disagreement goes back more than 50 years. While Mahatma Gandhi and his followers were spreading non-violent resistance against British rule, another movement was making headway in India. Muslims were demanding greater say in government. Hindus were the majority and therefore held most of the political power.

In August 1947, a solution came for both causes. India won independence from British rule, and a new state, a Muslim state, was created. This new state was given the name Pakistan, which means "land of the pure."

A history of war

The old country was split, with various regions holding votes to decide whether they wanted to be a part of India or of Pakistan. The results came in and the new borders drawn up. But the transition had more than a few problems. For one, the announcement of the new borders caused the greatest migration in human history as millions of Muslims left India for Pakistan while millions of Hindus left Pakistan for India.

Secondly, the new nation of Pakistan consisted of two separate chunks of land, which sat at opposite sides of India, a problem that would later lead to the creation, following a bloody war, of yet another new country, Bangladesh. Then there was Kashmir. With the deadline for the vote passed, Kashmir had failed to choose whether it wanted to be part of India or Pakistan, leaving the issue unresolved. It didn't take long for Pakistan and India to begin fighting over it.

Only two months after independence was won, tribesmen from Pakistan's North West Frontier province invaded Kashmir. At the time, the population of Kashmir was about 80 per cent Muslim. The invasion caused Hari Singh, the Maharajah of Kashmir, to sign an accord joining Kashmir with India. Indian troops were sent in to defend what was now Indian territory.

'LINE OF CONTROL'

The war ended on Jan. 1, 1949 with the United Nations creating a ceasefire line, known as the "line of control." Azad Kashmir, a region in northwest Kashmir, was given to Pakistan.

In 1965, war broke out again in Kashmir and continued until both governments signed a ceasefire agreement negotiated by the British.

Kashmir has remained a contentious issue. Since 1989, more than a dozen Islamic militant groups have been fighting for Kashmir's independence from India or its merger with neighbouring Pakistan.

More than 68,000 people, mostly civilians, have been killed in the conflict. India and Pakistan resumed peace talks that were interrupted by the Mumbai attacks in 2008. The United States has offered a $10 million US bounty for the founder of the Pakistani militant group blamed for the attacks that killed 166 people. Hafiz Saeed founded Lashkar-e-Taiba in the 1980s, allegedly with Pakistani support to pressure India over Kashmir.

KASHMIR CONFLICT EBBS AS NEW WAVE OF MILITANT EMERGES

One of a new wave of young, educated separatist militants active in the Indian-administered parts of Kashmir, Wani has much support in his village of Tral, a cluster of traditional homes and mosques amid green fields and woods in a fold of the dry hills in the south of "the valley", as the most famous, richest and strategically important part of the disputed Himalayan former princedom is known.

"Everyone in the village supports Burhan," said a friend, requesting anonymity for fear of detention by security forces as a militant sympathiser.

Kashmir, which was split between Pakistan and India after the countries gained their independence from the UK in 1947, still makes headline news. Seven towns in the Indian portion are under an indefinite curfew following sporadic clashes between local Hindus and Muslims that have killed three people, officials said.

Last week, India accused Pakistan of sending commandos to kill five of its soldiers stationed on the line of control, the de facto border dividing the two parts of Kashmir. But overall levels of violence are lower now in Kashmir than at any time since an insurgency that pitted groups of young Muslim Kashmiris enrolled in Islamist groups, and later extremists from Pakistan too, against Indian security forces first flared more than two decades ago. In total, more than 50,000 militants, soldiers, police and civilians are thought to have died in the fighting in India's only Muslim-majority state. Human rights abuses have been perpetrated by all sides.

At its height in 2001, 4,500 deaths were recorded, according to the Institute for Conflict Management, a Delhi-based thinktank. Last year, only 117 people were killed. And though there have been spectacular attacks against military targets and scores were injured in rioting in July after four protesters were shot dead by security forces, officials in Srinagar, Kashmir's summer capital, say there are now no more than 200 militants operating in the valley, whereas at the peak of the insurgency there were up to 20 times as many.

The unrest that has often paralysed cities and the economy in recent years has almost died away. Tourists now throng the houseboats on Dal lake or make pilgrimages to Hindu holy sites.

"I have never been worried while here. The image of Kashmir elsewhere in India is totally wrong," said Meha Sao, from the southern state of Maharashtra, on holiday in Srinagar.

Nor, despite the sentiments expressed by the friend of Wani the militant, is support for violence as widespread as it once was. "You do find some local support in pockets but these pockets have shrunk dramatically, which is why it is so difficult for the militants," said Omar Abdullah, the chief minister.

A militant hardcore still exists, particularly in southern areas such as Tral. And even if less numerous, the new militants appear highly motivated. Wani is believed to have been involved in at least one of the recent attacks on security forces.

Tral village is tense. After three militants and a policeman were killed in a recent clash nearby, leaders of Hizb-ul-Mujahideen, the group Wani is believed to have joined, warned locals to stay away from security personnel, whom they planned to target.

Observers say the new recruits to militancy are different from volunteers over the past 20 years. They are younger and better educated. Wani is one of the youngest. His father, Muzaffar Ahmed Wani, 50, said his son had left home overnight two years ago to join the militants, aged just 15. "He said nothing to anyone. He just said he was going out and didn't come back," he said.

Though pious and brought up in a family that is supportive of the extremists, Wani had shown no sign of wanting to take up arms until he was detained and beaten by security forces, his father, the head of a local college, said.

"He was thinking of revenge only for 15 days after being released. So he got in contact with the militants. Or maybe they heard about him and got in touch. Then he went. It was only 10 days before his exams. But I am proud of him," his father said.

It is almost certain that Wani will be killed. Few active militants surrender. Most prefer to die when cornered by security forces. "We are ready for him to die," his father said. "We are facing oppression every day. I look around and I see only ashes. There is only less violence because there is a lack of faith. Anyone with true faith joins the militants."

'We are not scared of death, we are just scared of detention'

Three hours' drive to the north, in the tough town of Sopore, the family of Muzamil Amin Dar have already faced what Wani has accepted is inevitable.

Dar, 26, was killed last October. Accounts of how and why he had joined the extremists differ. His family says Dar, a college graduate who had landed a highly paid job as a hospital medical technician with a monthly salary of £200 seven months before going underground, was not interested in radicalism.

This changed, they say, after his detention by security forces when guns were found in a well in the Dars' garden. Police say he was a member of the

Pakistan-based Lashkar-e-Taiba group, one of the most violent organisations operating in the valley, for five years, was the mastermind of a Delhi bomb plot and was wanted for several local militant attacks including the killing of a policeman.

Over recent years Dar had become increasingly devout. He had stopped his father, an electrical repair man, from watching television and convinced another brother to leave a bank job which, Dar said, involved usury.

"Once I was watching a cricket match and he unplugged the television and shouted at me not to waste my time on trivial things," Dar's father, Mohammed Amin, said.

After his son disappeared, there was no news. Then last October, the family heard firing only a mile from their home. A huge military operation was under way. Two militants armed with assault rifles and grenades were holed up in a house, they heard. Then they learned one was Dar.

Security forces asked Dar Sr to negotiate with his son but he refused, fearing they would kill him as he came out to surrender. After nearly 12 hours of shooting, his son, badly wounded, called him and told his father to "live life according to Islam".

He died the next morning when explosions brought down the house he and the other militant had hidden in. "We miss him a lot," his father said. A policeman and a paramilitary were wounded in the firefight. Such encounters were once regular occurrences. Now they are rare. A senior Indian official in northern Kashmir said the extremist groups had been forced to change tactics in recent years because they lacked weapons.

"They have moved from insurgency to terrorism. But if they had thousands of guns they would have thousands of fighters," he said.

This, most analysts believe, is underestimating the degree to which decades of conflict have undermined support for militancy locally.

Some suggest that security officials in the disputed province exaggerate the threat from extremism to justify wide-ranging powers of arrest and detention – and a broad measure of immunity from prosecution for human rights abuses – granted early on in the conflict.

One factor is declining official support for the extremists in Indian Kashmir from Pakistan over the past decade.

Another is the growing disparity between the economies of the two neighbours, which have fought three wars over the state. Indian growth has undermined the argument for accession to Pakistan in Kashmir – though much rhetorical support for independence remains – and sapped enthusiasm for any return to a hugely disruptive violent struggle.

However, Abdullah, the chief minister, said economic development was only a partial solution. "You will always be plagued by the reality that there is a political issue that formed the basis for this trouble and it will have to be resolved, today, tomorrow, the day after, at some point," he said.

During a short bout of rioting in Sopore, a hotbed of insurgent violence in northern Kashmir, last month, young men spoke of their anger.

"We are not scared of death, we are just scared of detention, for our families," said Shakeel Ahmed, a 24-year-old pharmaceutical representative, before returning to throw stones at the police. "The level of militancy is low now, it is true, but it will rise, God willing."

THE RISE OF KASHMIRI SECESSIONISM IN INDIA

While the post-1947 political history of Kashmir was at times turbulent and a separate ethno-national consciousness among the Kashmiri Muslims remained consistently strong, it was only in the late 1980s that widespread frustration among the Kashmiri Muslims against some of their own leaders and the policies pursued by New Delhi erupted into a full-blown secessionist movement against India.

The rise of secessionism in Kashmir is attributable to certain fundamental changes that took place in the state in the 1980s. As a result of demographic changes and the spread of modernisation and communications, a younger, more educated and more politically conscious generation emerged in Kashmir in the 1980s. Economic development and employment opportunities did not expand commensurately, however, leading to a rise in unemployment among the educated poor. Moreover, starting from the early 1980s, the Congress government at the centre indulged in vote fraud and subversion of the electoral process in Kashmir in order to further the interests of the Congress Party in the state. This first led to the dismissal of the legitimately elected National Conference government of Farooq Abdullah, the son of Sheikh Abdullah, in the state in 1984. Subsequently, the Congress Party led by Rajiv Gandhi and Farooq Abdullah's National Conference entered into an electoral alliance and blatantly rigged the state elections of 1987. This blatant electoral abuse encouraged by the Congress and Farooq's 'betrayal' led to widespread resentment among the Kashmiri Muslims against the Indian government and the National Conference.

In the early 1990s, the secessionist movement in Kashmir split into two main branches. In the first branch were those who advocated the creation of an 'independent' state of Kashmir to be achieved by the secession of Kashmir from India and the POK from Pakistan followed by the merger of these areas.

The main secessionist organization espousing this view is the Jammu and Kashmir Liberation Front (JKLF) which wants a sovereign, secular and democratic Kashmir that would include all Kashmiris irrespective of their religious affiliation. The JKLF position is unacceptable to the Hindu and Buddhist minorities in Kashmir since both these communities fear that in an independent Kashmir, the Muslims would dominate due to their substantial numerical majority.

The Hindus of Jammu and the Buddhists of Ladakh have, therefore, called upon the Indian government to protect their status in Kashmir. These communities have made it clear that if Kashmir secedes from India, then only the Valley should secede since it is predominantly Muslim. But this view is unacceptable to the JKLF which claims to represent the whole of Kashmir.

The second current of Kashmiri secessionism was represented by the Muslim fundamentalist groups and religious elites in the Valley who wanted to make Kashmir either a part of Pakistan or, at the very least, an independent Islamic state with close ties with Pakistan. The principal insurgent groups that advocate this kind of religious nationalism and pro-Pakistan sentiments are the Harqat ul-Ansar and the Hibz ul- Mujahideen.

Pro-Pakistani sentiments are also demonstrated by the All-Party Hurriyat Conference, an umbrella organisation of various political parties in Kashmir. These fundamentalist organisations regard Kashmir as a region which legitimately should be under the control of Muslims. Hence, they look upon the Hindu and Buddhist minorities as 'outsiders' and resort to violence against them.

In the initial years of the secessionist movement, nearly all Hindu families were driven out by the insurgents from the Valley. Politically motivated violence against Hindus in the Jammu region (mainly with the aim to alter the demographic balance of the Jammu province) was also carried out. Further, Buddhists in Ladakh were targeted for violence and intimidation leading to a Buddhist counter-mobilisation.

In this climate of spiraling political violence and 'ethnic cleansing', the pro-India leaders among the Kashmiri Muslims became sidelined or were eliminated by the insurgents for being 'soft' on India. Violence also broke out within the ranks of the insurgents over ideology and strategy. The insurgents did not even spare the members of their own community from intimidation and violence in order to maintain a strong hold over them. The Onset of the Indo-Pakistan 'Proxy War' Over Kashmir With the outbreak of insurgency in Kashmir, a 'proxy war' erupted between India and Pakistan which is still ongoing. This proxy war is being fought on three different planes.

International Diplomacy

Since 1989, India and Pakistan have carried out an international diplomatic tug-of-war over Kashmir. Since the outbreak of the insurgency, Pakistan has tried to 'internationalise' the Kashmir dispute by highlighting in international forums the human rights abuses carried out by the Indian military in Kashmir and asking for international mediation in the dispute and the holding of UN-sponsored plebiscite to ascertain the wishes of the Kashmiri people regarding the state's future political status.

The strategy worked initially. Under intense Pakistani lobbying, the Organisation of Islamic Countries (OIC) voted for sanctions against India for human rights violations in Kashmir in May 1993. In Britain, the Labour Party raised the Kashmir issue in the Parliament and called on the British government to put pressure on India to honour the Kashmiris' right to self-determination under UN supervision. In the United States, the Clinton Administration also criticised India for human rights violations in Kashmir leading to strains in India-US ties.

However, as the conflict dragged on, Pakistan's diplomatic initiatives failed to bring about international pressure on India to hold a plebiscite in Kashmir for a number of reasons. First, reacting to the international outcry over human rights abuses, the Indian military reformed its operating methods in Kashmir.

Emboldened by this development, the Indian government started encouraging foreign dignitaries to visit Kashmir to see firsthand the destruction and massacres caused by the Kashmiri insurgents and foreign 'volunteers' who were armed and trained by Pakistan. Indian diplomats also presented this 'evidence' in international forums and foreign capitals.

The Indian government further argued that the 'real problem' in Kashmir is one of 'cross-border terrorism' directed at India by Pakistan, and called upon the western states to brand Pakistan as a sponsor of terrorism in Kashmir. India also categorically ruled out any international mediation in Kashmir by moving a unanimous resolution in a joint sitting of the two houses of Parliament which stated that Kashmir is an inalienable part of the Republic of India.

Secondly, the US placed more stress on curbing the conventional and nuclear weapons proliferation in the subcontinent and undertaking confidence building measures (CBMs) between India and Pakistan than pressing for a plebiscite in Kashmir. The end of the Afghan war and the collapse of the Soviet Union also downgraded Pakistan's importance to US national security interests. Further, the rise of Islamic fundamentalist forces in West Asia and Pakistan's strong links with fundamentalist groups in Afghanistan and Kashmir did not go down well with the Clinton administration. Additionally, the US concern over Pakistan's clandestine nuclear weapons programme resulted in the suspension of US military aid under the Pressler Amendment.

Thirdly, in spite of the presence of several 'irritants', Indo-US relations witnessed an upswing in the 1990s, attributable mainly to the convergence of politico-economic and security interests between the two states and the reduction in India's apprehensions about a possible US hegemonic role in world politics after the Gulf War.

Indicating the growing cooperation between the US and India, a number of high-ranking American officials visited India in the 1990s to discuss trade and security issues. The two countries held several joint military exercises. India's market-oriented economic reforms have also found favour in Washington. The evolving friendship between India and the US further eroded Pakistan's appeal to the West on behalf of the Kashmiri secessionists.

Fourthly, Pakistan's diplomatic effort to garner support from the Islamic world for its position on Kashmir also received setbacks. To be sure, the Islamic countries voiced their concern about the plight of the Kashmiri Muslims and the highhanded measures undertaken by the Indian army~ yet they stopped short of endorsing Kashmir's independence or accession to Pakistan due to India's patient diplomacy in the Islamic world.

India established a working relationship with the Rabbani Government in Afghanistan and secured a promise of Afghan neutrality on the Kashmir dispute. Prime Minister Rao visited Uzbekistan and Kazakhstan in May 1993 where he secured support for India's position that the Kashmir dispute must be settled bilaterally within the framework of the Shimla Agreement. India was also able to procure the backing of Iran for its position on Kashmir. Under pressure from Iran (and China), Pakistan had to withdraw a resolution it had tabled in the International Conference of the Human Rights Commission at Geneva in March 1994 denouncing India for violating human rights in Kashmir.

Finally, Pakistan's position on Kashmir evoked considerable opposition from China. Beijing is particularly concerned about the 'demonstration effects' of Kashmir's independence on the Xinjiang autonomous region. In 1993, Chinese troops had to quell an armed uprising in Xinjiang and the continued army presence may well engender further resentment and separatist sentiments among the region's 10 million Muslims.

Signs of orthodox Sunni practice are steadily increasing in Xinjiang, and developments in Kashmir and Central Asia are being watched closely, feeding hopes for a successful independence movement. Secessionists in Xinjiang could also influence other separatists among China's Tibetan and Mongol populations and threaten China's hold on the Tarim Basin, an oil producing area essential for the PRC's economy. Acting on these fears, China indicated to Pakistan that while it would like to see a negotiated solution to the Kashmir dispute, it would not accept any form of independence for Kashmir. Thus, in spite of the international concern about the plight of the Kashmiris, Pakistan's diplomatic efforts to win international support for a UN-sponsored plebiscite in Kashmir proved to be unsuccessful. This was a major setback for Pakistan's Kashmir policy.

Insurgency and Counter-Insurgency

The outbreak of secessionist sentiments in Kashmir in 1989 provided Pakistan with a golden opportunity to loosen India's hold over the region by providing military and financial help to the various insurgent groups that sprang up. In implementing this policy, Pakistan benefited immensely from the Afghan war. During the height of the Afghan war, the United States trained and equipped the Afghan mujahideen (freedom fighters) and 'volunteers' from neighbouring Muslim countries for guerrilla operations against the occupying Soviet forces and government troops. These operations were run by the Pakistani military's Inter Services Intelligence (ISI) directorate under the supervision of the US Central Intelligence Agency (CIA) officials from bases in the border regions of the North-West Frontier Province in Pakistan. As a result, the ISI developed an expertise in unconventional warfare and established close ties with the Afghan *mujahideen.*

Once the 'proxy war' between the US and USSR ended in Afghanistan in 1989, the ISI turned its attention towards Kashmir. Initially, the ISI provided covert military support and training to the pro-independent JKLF. Most of the ISI-run training centers for Kashmiri insurgents were located in Azad Kashmir and along the Pakistan-Afghanistan border. Further, large quantities of sophisticated weapons, including Stinger antiaircraft missiles and automatic rifles, which the US had brought into Pakistan to be used by the Afghan *mujahideen,* were diverted to the Kashmiri insurgents.

By 1992-93, with the emergence of strong pro-Pakistan secessionist groups such as the Hizb-ul-Mujahideen and Harqat ul-Ansar, the ISI stopped supporting and funding the JKLF. The Pakistan government also cracked down on JKLF's leaders and sympathisers in Azad Kashmir. Along with the training and support that it provided to the Kashmiri insurgents, the ISI also encouraged veteran guerrillas of the Afghan war, who were left aimless after the Soviets withdrew from Afghanistan, to infiltrate into Kashmir to carry out a *jihad* (Holy War) against India.

New Delhi responded to the insurgency by dismissing the local government and declaring president's rule (direct rule by the central government) in Kashmir. India also responded to the insurgents through a massive show of force. As the secessionist movement grew in strength in the early 1990s, India's military presence in Kashmir escalated simultaneously. Numerous reports of the Indian army's highhanded and repressive behaviour towards the Kashmiri Muslims started to filter out and the army operation in Kashmir drew heavy fire from human rights groups and activists in India and abroad. It also led to the widespread alienation of the Kashmiri Muslims from the Indian state. As the stalemate in Kashmir continued in the 1990s, India's approach towards taming the insurgency centred on doing several things. The main requirement was to win back the confidence of the Kashmiri civilians by clamping down hard on the insurgents who were regularly infiltrating the LoC from the POK.

One way the Indian military attempted to do this was to raise, train and arm small anti-insurgency forces composed of former Kashmiri insurgents who were captured by the Indian security forces and were 'persuaded' to give up the secessionist struggle. Another policy which was strictly implemented was to exercise tighter control over the behaviour of the regular security forces in order to reduce the instances of human rights abuses by the security personnel. It was felt that when the security environment of Kashmir improves, regular military personnel could be gradually withdrawn leaving charge to the paramilitary forces.

The Indian government was also keen to re-start the political process in Kashmir as and when the security environment improved. For this purpose, the government kept open the lines of communication with several Kashmiri Muslim groups, including the All Party Hurriyat Conference and the Jammu and Kashmir Democratic Liberation Front (JKDLF). Improving the security environment and the re-starting of the political process in Kashmir were the stepping stones for holding state elections, which was viewed by New Delhi as the only way to erase secessionist sentiments from the minds of the Kashmiri Muslims.

Throughout 1995 and early 1996 the Indian government prepared the ground for elections in Kashmir. In May 1996, elections for the Indian national parliament were held and the people of Kashmir voted for the first time after 1989. In spite of the call for poll boycott by the insurgent groups, voter turnout in Kashmir during the national parliamentary election was around 35-45%, although many voters claimed that they were forced to vote by the Indian troops stationed in Kashmir.

The national election of May 1996 was followed by state elections in Kashmir in September 1996. This election was widely publicised by India as a "rejection of the insurgency" by the Kashmiri people. Voter turnout was around 53%, not much less than the 56.7% for India as a whole in the general election in May. With many pro-independence and pro-Pakistan groups boycotting this poll, the National Conference led by Farooq Abdullah won easily and formed the government.

In the aftermath of the 1996 state elections, there was quiet optimism in New Delhi that a new beginning has been made in Kashmir. While there was no denying that the reconstruction of Kashmir was an enormous task, the return of Farooq Abdullah to Kashmiri politics after a gap of seven years was seen by many experts as an opportunity for moderate Kashmiris, who were sidelined during the armed insurgency, to re-enter Kashmiri politics.

Critics further felt that Farooq Abdullah's re-entry into Kashmir politics offered India a chance to win back the loyalty of the Kashmiris~ however, it would all depend upon how quickly the National Conference government could bring 'genuine' democracy to Kashmir and jump-start Kashmir's devastated economy. Political freedom and economic opportunity were thus seen as the key to solving the insurgency in Kashmir.

Low-Intensity Border Skirmish

Since the late 1980s, as tensions between India and Pakistan flared up, the two sides appeared to be on the brink of war on at least three different occasions~ incredibly, they moved back from the brink all three times. The lack of war, however, did not imply that the LoC was quiet. On the contrary, throughout the 1990s, Pakistani troops stationed along the LoC and on the Siachen Glacier, the world's highest battlefield, have periodically resorted to firing and shelling of Indian 'forward positions' and border villages. It is generally believed in India that these unprovoked firings serve two purposes for the Pakistani military: one, to infiltrate armed insurgents into Kashmir under cover of gunfire from across the LoC and, secondly, to scuttle any initiatives for the resumption of bilateral dialogue between the two states. On almost every occasion, the Indians returned the fire.

There are compelling financial, political and strategic reasons for the existence of simmering 'low-intensity' tension across the LoC and the Siachen, rather than open warfare. First, a conventional war (let alone a nuclear one) between India and Pakistan today will be economically and financially ruinous for both states given the astronomical rise in the cost of warfare and the state of their respective domestic economies.

A short conventional war between India and Pakistan would cost some US$2.5 billion, twelve times more than the cost of the last India-Pakistan war in 1971. Some Pakistani estimates put Pakistan's cost of fighting a conventional war with India today at US$350 million per day. Similar studies done for India place the figure at US$400 million per day. Given the state of the Indian and Pakistani economies today, such exorbitant expenses would be difficult to meet.

Secondly, the 'political cost' that India and Pakistan would have to pay domestically as well as internationally for initiating a war today would be astronomical given that both states possess nuclear weapons.

Finally, Pakistan's conventional military capabilities, in spite of the substantial modernisation it has undergone in the last decade, still remains weak compared to India. Its armed forces have also been badly hit by the stoppage in American military aid since 1990. On the other hand, the modernisation of the Indian armed forces and the maintenance of a steady supply of ammunition, equipment and spares for its Soviet- made inventory have been badly hit by the demise of the Soviet Union. The prolonged use of the military in domestic political problems and foreign misadventures has also generated battle fatigue and affected morale within the armed forces. As a result, neither side today would be capable of inflicting an overwhelming defeat on the other side in a conventional war.

This is precisely the sort of scenario in which, if a conventional war is waged, both India and Pakistan might be inclined to carry out a nuclear 'first strike' against the other to break the military (and political) deadlock once and for all. To prevent even an inadvertent escalation of a conventional war to a nuclear showdown with catastrophic consequences, both sides need to ensure that a conventional war between them does not erupt in the first place and that the "logic of deterrence" works.

THE KASHMIRI REVOLUTION INTENSIFIES - INDO-PAK CONFLICT

In the midst of the Kashmir Muslim insurgency, tensions between India and Pakistan became so intense that in May 1990, the Pakistani military headed by General Mirza Aslam Beg was willing to use nuclear weapons to "take out New Delhi." It was President Bush's National Security Advisor Robert Gates and Assistant Secretary for Middle Eastern and South Asian Affairs who reportedly helped arrest a deadly encounter between them by visiting India and Pakistan. The two countries, however, increased their exchange of cross-border firing along the LOC. Prime Minister Benazio Bhutto, who was dismissed in the summer of 1990 by Pakistan's President Ghulam Iushaq Khan at the prompting of the military, took a hostile stance toward India to appease the Khan (which she admitted in June 1999) after she was reelected in October 1993. She called India an "imperialistic power and aggressor" in Kashmir. Despite these hostile relations, India and Pakistan held several rounds of talks at foreign secretary levels between 1990 and January 1994, but without any results as they took irreconcilable positions on Kashmir. For example, Pakistan insisted that India stop its counter-insurgency operations, while India insisted that that the talks should focus on Pakistan's cross border aid to the Muslim militants. Following Bhutto second dismissal by President Farooq Leghari, at the orders of the military, Nawaz Sharif took office as Prime Minister in February 1997. Indo-Pak relations temporarily thawed. In March of that year, for example, a dialogue at foreign secretary level was resumed. In April, Pakistani Foreign Minister Gohar Ayub Khan met India's Prime Minister, I.K. Gujral, at the Non-Aligned Movement (NAM) meeting in New Delhi, and in May, the two Prime Ministers met at the South Asian Association of Regional Cooperation (SAARC) summit held at Male, the foreign secretary level but also to form eight joint "working groups" that would look at, for the first time since 1972, the Kashmir issue. Subsequently, by September, foreign secretaries held three meetings despite of artillery exchanges at a number of points along the LOC. In September, the Prime Ministers met again in New York when they attended the UN General Assembly session. This situation, however, changed after the March 1998 parliamentary elections when the BJP-dominated United Front won the election and formed a coalition government that took a hard stand against Pakistan. The Home Minister, L. K. Advani, of the new government threatened to go after the terrorists even into the Pakistan-occupied Kashmir. Indo-Pakistani tensions increased following the nuclear testing in May 1998. This also caused concerns in the international community that the Kashmir conflict would become a catalyst for war that would include the use of nuclear weapons by both countries.

Both countries were severely condemned by the international community and the U.S., Japan, and some European countries imposed sanctions. Following mutual testing, the tempers of both countries were so high that on July 29, when Vajpayee and Sharif met at the tenth summit of the SAARC held in Columbo, Sri Lanka, the encounter failed to break new ground.

Sharif insisted that no progress was possible between the two countries unless the "core issue" of Kashmir was resolved. He characterized the meeting as "zero" and warned that India's "intransigence" was pushing the region to the brink of war. India's foreign secretary, K. Raghunath, responded by terming Pakistan's obsessive focus on the single issue of Kashmir as "neurotic" and that serious dialogue should not be used to "pursue a limited agenda or promote a propagandist exercise."

Intense hostility along the LOC at that same time left contrast, when they met on September 23, for the second time at the UN General Assembly session, in New York, there was a dramatic change in the tenor of their encounter. It was friendly and they agreed to try to resolve the Kashmir issue "peacefully" and to focus on trade and people to people contact.

For example, India agreed to buy sugar and powder from Pakistan. After a decade of absence, Pakistan's cricket team visited India in November 1998.

In February 1999, Pakistan allowed India to run buses from New Delhi to Lahore and following an invitation by Sharif, Vajpayee visited Lahore. His visit is commonly known as bus diplomacy and at the end of their summit they issued the Lahore Declaration that was backed up by a clearly spelled out Memorandum of Understanding (MOU).

In the MOU the leaders agreed to engage in consultations on security matters, to include nuclear doctrines, to initiate confidence-building measures in both nuclear and conventional areas, and to establish appropriate communications mechanisms to help diminish the possibility of nuclear war by accident or misinterpretation.

They also agreed to continue their respective moratoriums on further nuclear tests unless their "supreme national interest" was in jeopardy. This declaration, however, was not well received by some elements of the Pakistani military branch including General Musharraf. The Pakistani military provoked a mini war called the Kargil war within the India-occupied Kashmir, during May to July 1999 that undermined the Indo-Pak relations.

THE INSURGENCY AND POLITICAL SYSTEM

Contrary to the popular view that the insurgents picked up their guns in response to an undemocratic political system, in no way was the movement fighting for greater democratic rights. In fact, as already shown, they had already picked up their guns prior to the election. Their cause was religiously and ideologically fuelled. In many ways, the ruling National Conference party had encouraged this atmosphere through a range of propaganda campaigns. Even as far back as the 1984 election, Farooq Abdullah and the National Conference deliberately tried to create revulsion against India for their own political ends. These Propaganda ads tried to demonstrate that India's iron fist was bleeding Kashmir. There is little evidence of Indian repression in this period, and it seems likely that the National Conference was trying to use this as a way to hide the poor and corrupt performance of the State Government. Indeed, perhaps if India had done more to intervene in State affairs, it could have abated the insurgency that followed.

The Role Of Pakistan

Having failed to take Kashmir by force, and unable to win the hearts of the Kashmiris by offering them a democracy when they themselves had a military dictatorship, Pakistan had to woo the Kashmiris by its ideology of communalism.

Before the insurgency in Kashmir began, there was an insurgency movement in neighboring Punjab, which had also been split between India and Pakistan in 1947. That died out by the late 1980s, when the Sikhs that had taken up arms against India had realized they were being used by their Pakistani sponsors and gave up arms. And so Pakistan's attention turned to Kashmir. One major reason Pakistan needed to sponsor insurgency in India was to gain intelligence on India, and its army. After suffering three consecutive defeats, each time after attacking India unprovoked and by surprise, Pakistan was fearful India would be tempted to launch a pre-emptive strike against Pakistan to destroy its army to ensure Pakistan never again attempted to invade India.

The Pakistani view is that they are providing moral support to the Kashmiri People in their fight for freedom against the brutal Indian Army who commit excessive humans rights abuses on the oppressed Muslims living in India, a non-Muslim country. The Indian perspective is that they are dealing with a proxy war by Pakistan who have never accepted the Kashmiri's democratic reaffirmation of their accession to India. The Kashmiris themselves are split between supporting Pakistan, India and independence. But while the Pakistanis and Indians live in relative peace, it is the Kashmiri who suffers the most while the issue remains unresolved.

The slogans: "Pakistan se kya rishta? La ilaha ilallah" (What is the relation with Pakistan? There is no God but God.) followed by "Azaadi ka matlab kya? La ilaha ilallah" (What is the meaning of freedom? There is no God but God.) indicate that Pakistan for Kashmiris meant Islam, and freedom for Kashmiris meant Pakistan. Those who coined and floated these slogans went on to form the Jammu Kashmir Liberation Force (JKLF). The JKLF wanted to liberate Kashmir. In fact its founder, Hashim Qureshi, later fled to Western Europe for asylum after the Pakistanis hijacked his organization and used its members to fight India as part of a religious struggle rather than for the independence he had desired.

In 1990 a report showed that almost a thousand of the elite Kashmiri Muslims were on the payroll of the ISI. In 1993, with pro-independence insurgents separating from the pro-Pakistan factions, Pakistani border troops shot and killed some thirty Kashmiri youth on their way to POK for training.

Slowly but surely the ties between Pakistan and the Kashmiri youth were being severed.

Republic Day

In addition to the Afghan War, local Kashmiris also watched on TV as mass movements against authoritarianism arose in East Europe and Central Asia. The most significant of these was in Romania, where on Christmas Day 1989, dictator Nicolae Ceausescu was executed. Less than a month later was to be Kashmir's turn.

Perhaps the most significant event was the insurgents successful kidnapping of India's Home Minister. In December 1989, there was a change in the Federal Government in India, with Rajiv Gandhi losing to VP Singh's Government. Singh's deputy, the Home Minister, was Mufti Mohammed Sayeed, the current Chief Minister of Jammu & Kashmir. Just weeks after being sworn in, his daughter was kidnapped near Srinagar by insurgents who demanded the release of their colleagues from prison. Mufti, holding the third highest office in India behind the President and Prime Minister, broke India's policy of non-negotiation with terrorists and released the captured insurgents and his daughter was released. The whole episode has subsequently been referred to by insurgents as a key moment when they were able to show their Kashmiri people that India could be brought to its knees.

These incidents gave the Kashmiris fighting for independence a great deal of confidence, unlike the early years when dreams of independence were always viewed as a practical impossibility. Many Kashmiris felt that independence was imminent after the fall of the communist era, and some locals remarked that they thought the reality of independence was only a matter of weeks away.

Kashmiri Independence Day

January 20, 1990 was to be Kashmiri Independence Day. This date was chosen a few weeks prior as the day the masses would take to the streets and take power from India, effectively their army, for the Kashmiri people (and they would subsequently become a Republic and/or join Pakistan). Most Kashmiris were convinced that this would occur, and in fact the largest exodus of Kashmiri Pandits occurred on January 19.

Despite the fact that the masses were limited to Srinagar, and not regions of the State such as Ladakh and Jammu did not mean it was not a very real threat. There were reportedly between January 1 and January 19, 1990, 319 violent acts - 21 armed attacks, 114 bomb blasts, 112 arsons, and 72 incidents of mob violence. In fact the Indian Government was so desperate they sent Jagmohan, the former Governor of the State, on the night of 18th January to make a last ditch effort to save the Kashmir Valley. He was able to organize a last minute blockade that stopped people from leaving their local neighborhoods so they could not reach the main streets and mobilize into a large crowd. The momentum of the masses was soon lost, and such a mass protest was never attempted again.

Exodus of Pandits

One reason why Kashmiris were uncomfortable in joining Pakistan was its large non-Muslim minority, who would have no place in Islamic Pakistan. Hence by resorting to the systematic killings of Hindus, as well as spreading fear amongst them through newspaper ads and pamphlets ordering them to leave or face death, Pakistan was able to overcome this major obstacle.

With most of the Hindus gone by January 1990, and the secular minded Muslims powerless to help them return, Pakistan was able to strengthen its claim on Kashmir. There was religious indoctrination, by misusing mosques and other available platforms, in a bid to frighten the secular Muslims.

Kashmiri Pandits

The crimes against humanity perpetrated against the Kashmiri Pandits were tragic. While genocide occurred on a small scale, it is more likely that the objective was to drive them away rather than wipe them out. The dozens of killings and rapes were always followed by warnings for Pandits to get out, which suggest that the attacks were more as a statement rather than intent for mass genocide.

But what was most surprising to Pandits was how there were large demonstrations in several Kashmiri cities by common Kashmiris with the slogan: "Asi gachi Pakistan, batni rosin batta gatssin." In Kashmiri this means: We will become a part of Pakistan, Pandit women can stay with us but Pandit men must leave." They could understand why the extremists wanted them to leave, but were shocked when the masses joined in.

The Momentum Dies

The list of innocent persons who fell prey to the bullets of terrorists is again illustrative of the Islamization drive. The victims included prominent educationists and subscribers to secular ideals.

Not only Pandits, but Muslims such as Professor Mushir-ul-Haq, Vice Chancellor, Kashmir University, and Maulana Mohammad Syed Masoodi, a renowned Muslim scholar were among such victims at the hands of the terrorists. Libraries of Universities were destroyed for having unislamic books, and freedom of speech was suspended. It was clear the movement was not against India, but all things unislamic in their eyes.

While comparisons to Nazi Germany are fraught with danger, it does seem the population were caught in a mass hysteria that they now admit was a mistake. I have heard many anecdotal stories from others who have met with Kashmiri Muslims in Kashmir who have shown much resentment in not doing anything to stop the fundamentalists. It is difficult to determine if they genuinely wanted an Islamic State of Kashmir, or if they merely followed the trend as if it were a fad.

THE KASHMIR WAR AFTER KARGIL

The real war is the one in J&K: in this larger conflict, Kargil is just something of a footnote. But Kargil's impact on security in the rest of J&K might be mildly described as a calamity. 58 battalions of the Army engaged in counter-terrorist operations have been withdrawn for border deployment in the war's wake. 36 of these have been withdrawn from Kashmir and 22 from the Jammu Province. Just 14 Central Reserve Police Force (CRPF) and 6 BSF battalions have been moved in to take their place. A further six have been sent in for the Amarnath Yatra, and these may stay on until the 1999 Lok Sabha elections. With the prospect of a permanent manning of the LoC, no one has any cogent idea of just how the shortfall will be met in the long-run. During the 1998 Lok Sabha elections, moreover, 354 additional companies, each of approximately 125 men, had been deployed in J&K. This time round, at least 500 companies will have to be brought in to even meet the 1998 security levels. At least two significant elements of the war in J&K have already become evident. First, since last summer, the mountain heights of the State, areas of little political significance, have seen large concentrations of Pakistani and Afghan terrorists, as well as an assortment of other "freelance seekers of martyrdom". Received military wisdom has it that these groups lack the motivation or resources to fight a losing battle in the Kashmir Valley. But a more plausible possibility also exists. By building-up numbers on the heights dominating Doda, Banihal, the Rajouri-Poonch belt and Kupwara, terrorist groups will dominate the principal lines of access to the Kashmir Valley. Read in the context of recoveries of increasingly heavy weapons in recent months, ranging from mortar and anti-aircraft guns to a Grail anti-tank missile launcher, some argue that current deployment patterns suggest terrorist groups are preparing to support Pakistan troops in a conventional engagement.

The second key element of terrorist activity in months to come is certain to be the engineering of a deterioration in communal relations, pushing Muslims out of Hindu-dominated areas south of the Chenab river, and Hindus from the predominantly Muslim areas to its north. Such migrations will give a *de facto* demographic legitimacy to Pakistan's objective of securing some variant of the Owen Dixon plan. These processes have been in place at least since 1997, although they gathered momentum after the Pokhran II tests and Advani's promise of a "pro-active" policy in J&K. In a broader sense, revanchist groups in Pakistan believe the communal war they are engaged in is merely part of a larger struggle against supposedly-Hindu India. These faultlines, ironically but unsuprisingly, are precisely those that shape the *mentalité* of the Hindu Right.

Even as much of J&K finds itself without security cover, there is substantial evidence that cross-border infiltration of terrorists has been unusually high in summer 1999. Field intelligence officials in Kupwara and Baramulla estimate that at least six hundred terrorists have moved in since March, often occupying positions at heights above 4,000 metres. Anantnag, too, has seen sharp rise in the numbers of Pakistan and Afghan terrorists active in the district, with over two hundred reported to be based in the district. While most groups of terrorists have been avoiding frontal engagement with state forces, there is little doubt that the period since the Kargil conflict broke out has seen a marked escalation in violence in the State.

A secondary thrust of terrorist activity 1999 summer unveiled itself with the murder of Deputy Inspector General S.K. Chakravarty, Joint Director G-Branch Mahendra Raj, and Sub Inspector K. Bhaskar during a raid on the BSF's Sector Headquarters at Bandipore on July 13. Evidently, the increased targeting of security force personnel represents, at once, a shift in strategy as well as a radical enhancement in weapons capabilities and the proficiency of the foreign militants who have come to dominate the movement in J&K. This has been a progressive trend of the past three years, as the steadily worsening ratio of security force personnel to militants killed demonstrates. This ratio has declined from 1:5.79 in 1997, through 1:4.54 in 1988, to 1:3.20 in 1999. Worse, with the thinning out of security forces in the wake of Kargil and the escalation in Pak-backed militant activity, this ratio fell to 1:2 in June 1999 year, as compared to a ratio of 1:5 in June 1998. If the massacres and violent attacks this summer mark a vertical escalation in the conflict in J&K, there are also signs of a generalised horizontal escalation in the Leh region.

Last month's arrest of a twenty-five member terrorist cell from the Turtok area of Leh, led by local resident Ali Bhutto, has made it clear that conflict can be expected in this until-now quiet region. Bhutto's arrest, outside Leh, has been treated with little concern. But terrorism had similar low-key origins elsewhere as well. In Poonch, the first sign of an offensive was the arrest of Ayub Shabnam in May 1990. Shabnam, who went on to spend five years in jail, was believed to be responsible for the training and distribution of weapons to several local operatives. But he, like Bhutto, had little knowledge of Pakistan's broader objectives. Few took the incident seriously, until Poonch went up in flames after 1993.

Bhutto was picked up along with his cell, which included two police constables, in a series of raids that began on June 7. The group had hidden 25 Kalashnikov assault rifles, one heavy machine gun, one general purpose machine gun, a sniper rifle, a rocket propelled grenade launcher and several kilogrammes of explosive material, brought in by Bhutto's Skardu-based brother, Ibrahim Sangsang. Sangsang, interrogators of the Turtok cell discovered, had made several trips accross the LoC in 1998, handing over weapons to relatives and associates in five villages. All the five villages, Turtok, Pachathang, Thakshi, Thang and Chalungpa were captured by India in the war of 1971. Bhutto's father had been instrumental in asking villagers, against Pakistan Army advice, to stay in India on the grounds that it was wrong to leave the land of their birth. Interestingly, dozens of villagers in nearby Bogdang village were issued rifles by the Pakistan Army in 1971 to wage a guerilla war against advancing Indian troops. Few complied, and the rifles were instead put to use poaching mountain goats.

Ibrahim Sangang's story illustrates the rich relationship between broad ideological factors and purely local issues in the emergence of terror. Sangsang had, by local accounts, been intimate with local officials and the military authorities, even having been sponsored to visit New Delhi for a Republic Day parade in 1987. But by 1994, Sangsang found himself embroiled in a series of legal disputes. Most emerged from a criminal assault on a police officer, the outcome of a violent dispute over the use of a diesel generator set that powered several villages. Under pressure from the criminal justice system, Sangpapa fled accross the LoC, where the ISI appears to have offered him a better deal as against several years in jail. But several larger factors appear to have been at play in the five villages. The *Noor Baksh* sect that historically dominated the region, an eclectic*Sufi*-inspired faith drawing both from *Sunni* and *Shia* custom, has been under sustained seige from ultra-conservative *Ahl-e-Hadis* prosletysers. The *Ahl-e-Hadis* have been closely associated with terrorist groups in J&K, notably the *Lashkar-e-Toiba* and the *Tehreek-ul-Mujaheddin*.

The near-unchallenged growth of revanchist religious groups both in Pakistan and in J&K is certain to prepare the real ideological agenda of events to come. In J&K, as the RAC Report illustrates, the National Conference has begun to tear away from its historic character as a secular, modernising force, and recast itself as a Muslim communal formation. The tendency has been most marked in Jammu where, as I have pointed out earlier, leaders of the far-Right *Jamaat-e-Islami* have shared platforms with the National Conference. These trends will be reinforced from across the border as, most disturbingly, the future of Pakistan's establishment elite has never been more unsure than in recent years.

Back home, economic hardship and the inability of a corrupt government to bring relief has made Pakistan's Islamic fundamentalists more popular with ordinary folk and – crucially – with the military, which for decades has helped the Westernized elite to curb Islamic fervour. As Jamaat [e-Islami] leader Qazi Hussain Ahmad pointed out at a well-attended convention in Islamabad in October, the income gap between junior and senior officers has been widening as the economic crisis worsens.

In the first of his seminal articles on the Kargil War, Aijaz Ahmad had written, "The Pakistan we are dealing with was born not once but twice". He outlined the crisis of identity that emerged from the creation of Bangladesh, and the reinvention of Pakistan not as the home of sub-continental Muslims, but of a mythically pure Islam, subsidised by West Asian wealth. Nothing worked as magically in restoring the self-confidence of the Pakistani state and its privileged classes as the infusion of petrodollars. But this new sort of money brought with it a new and curiously effective commodity as well: petro-Islam. A hybrid thing, born of centuries of ferocious conservatism so characteristic of the desert, but also of the unprecedented levels of wealth that was newly gained but was the product neither of a settled history nor of accumulated labour but of chance, that the black gold flowed here rather than elsewhere. It was a curious kind of Islam, equally ferocious in its piety and in its consumerism.

To those who have noted the organic links between the emergence of a new middle class through the 1980s, and the rise of the Hindu Right through India, Ahmad's description of petro-Islam will be disturbingly familiar. In both India and Pakistan, the forces of reaction are far from spent, driven, as both now are by nuclear power. The end of the war on the Kargil heights, it is almost certain, is profoundly unlikely to mark the begining of peace.

NATIONAL SECURITY LESSONS

The Kargil War of 1999 was a rich teaching experience for India in the national security arena in many respects. For one thing, it represented the country's first exposure to the "CNN factor," in that televised images of the fighting showcased in Indian living rooms each evening helped the government and armed forces to mobilize domestic support for Operation Vijay while, at the same time, demoralizing the literate Pakistani rank and file. Making the most of that tool, the Vajpayee government interacted skilfully with the nation's media in building domestic and international appreciation of the fact that India had been attacked without provocation by Pakistan and accordingly was in the right in its chosen response. The Vajpayee government interacted skilfully with the nation's media in building domestic and international appreciation of the fact that India had been attacked without provocation by Pakistan and accordingly was in the right in its chosen response.

As the counteroffensive unfolded, Indian media coverage of combat events was detailed and extensive, with numerous television channels showing a constant flow of scenes from the war zone in a manner reminiscent of CNN's coverage of the 1991 Persian Gulf War. Some analysts in New Delhi suggested afterward that this media coverage helped to serve as a force multiplier for Indian combat operations, since it was more credible by far than Pakistan's version of ongoing events. It definitely served as a morale booster for the Indian populace. Shortly after the campaign ended, the Indian government convened a Kargil Review Committee, chaired by the eminent international security scholar and strategist K. Subrahmanyam, which was charged with determining how Pakistan's forces had succeeded in crossing into Indian-controlled territory and establishing a foothold there without having been detected in due time by military intelligence. It concluded on the important media-coverage count that the showdown against the Pakistani intruders was "India's first television war" and, as such, was an experience that "knit the country together as never before." A major shortcoming highlighted by the war experience was a significant deficiency with respect to the provision of timely indications and warning of impending crises.

As for the country's vigilance over its perennially volatile border with Pakistan, a major shortcoming highlighted by the war experience was a significant deficiency with respect to the provision of timely indications and warning of impending crises. Although the Indian Army had a brigade of troops fielded in the Kargil sector to monitor activities there and the IAF possessed Canberras, Jaguars, and MiG-25Rs capable of overseeing the area by means of medium-and high-altitude aerial photography, local civilians noticed the intruders before the Indian Air Force did. In an early comment on the air contribution to the campaign, a serving IAF air commodore frankly admitted that Pakistan's intrusion into the high reaches of the Kargil sector made for "a surprise bordering on shock." A clear lesson emanating from this experience, he noted, was the "urgent requirement to improve our surveillance and reconnaissance capability. We cannot afford to be surprised again." Similarly, the Indian Army chief at the time, General Malik, later recalled that India's surprise at the incursion "reflected a major deficiency in [the country's] system of collecting, reporting, and assessing intelligence." Clearly, the IAF needed a better nationwide, real-time intelligence, surveillance, and reconnaissance capability.

As for the good-news part of the story, this intelligence, surveillance, and reconnaissance deficiency has since been substantially improved upon by India's placement of indigenous reconnaissance satellites on orbit. In October 2001, the Indian government launched its first Technology Experiment Satellite, which substantially improved the quality of its overhead intelligence product as a result of the satellite's one-meter resolution. India's spaceborne synthetic aperture radar capability provides all-weather, around-the-clock coverage, and the Indian Army also now maintains a constant vigil in the area with its inventory of Israeli-made Searcher and Heron unmanned aerial vehicles. In addition, today there are five times the number of troops permanently garrisoned in the Kargil sector than at the time of the Pakistani incursion in 1999, consisting of four brigades totaling nearly 20,000 troops.

Today there are five times the number of troops permanently garrisoned in the Kargil sector than at the time of the Pakistani incursion in 1999.

A major interservice shortcoming highlighted by the first two weeks that followed the initial detection of the incursion was the near-total lack of transparency and open communication between the Indian Army and the IAF with respect to the gathering crisis. Without question, the onset of the Kargil confrontation revealed a lack of effective air-ground integration in India's joint arena at the most senior leadership level. On this point, one IAF airman later lamented the "complete loss of synergy between air and land forces" at the start of the operation that had been occasioned by "the late induction into the fray of airpower and, hence, the denial of the optimum employment of its attributes of offensive action," notwithstanding the fact that "we were fighting a clearly defined enemy within our own territory." Another IAF airman, noting how the army at the outset had "looked to fight a classical high-altitude battle on its own," asked rhetorically whether it was, at least during the campaign's first two weeks, a case of "my war, can you help" rather than "our war, let's do it together."

This inclination at the outset to go it alone, it might be noted, was not just an idiosyncratic Indian Army trait. The since-retired director of operations of the PAF during the Kargil crisis, Air Commodore Kaiser Tufail, similarly noted the PAF leadership's "surprise" at having been told of what the Pakistan Army leaders had authorized, adding that "we all were ... piqued at being left out of the army's planning [and] were given to believe that this was a 'limited tactical action' in which the PAF would not be required."

Bibliography

Ajey Lele: *Strategic Technologies for the Military : Breaking New Frontiers*, Sage, Delhi, 2009.

Ajoy, Ghosh : *China-Pak Conflict : Threat to South Asian Security*, Reference Press, Delhi, 2003.

Akbar, M. K. : *Kargil Cross Border Terrorism*. South Asia Books, 1999.

Alastair Lamb, *Kashmir: A Disputed Legacy 1846–1990*, Hertingfordbury, Herts: Roxford Books, 1991.

Anadish Kumar: *World Guide to the Partition of INDIA*. Amazon Digital Services, 2010.

Anderson, J.: *Transnational Democracy: Political Spaces and Border Crossings*, Routledge: London and New York, 2002.

Anil, K.C.: *Military and Democracy in South Asia : Challenges, Politics and Power*, Sumit Enterprises, Delhi, 2009.

Arend, A.: *International Law and the Use of Force*, London, Routledge, 1993.

Azad, Maulana Abul Kalam: *India Wins Freedom*, New Delhi, Orient Longman, 1959.

Bamzai, P. N. K.: A *History of Kashmir*, Delhi: Metropolitan, 1962.

Barber B.R.: *Strong Democracy. Participatory Politics for a New Age*. Berkeley, University of California Press, 1984.

Barua, Pradeep: *Gentlemen of the Raj: The Indian Army Officer Corps, 1817–1949*, 2003.

Benjamin, Joseph : *China-Pak Relations : Prospect and Retrospect*, Reference Press, Delhi, 2004.

Bhalla, Alok: *Stories about the Partition of India*, New Delhi: HarperCollins, 1994.

Bhaskara Rao: *Military Conversion : Impact on Science and Technology*, Discovery, Delhi, 2003.

Bhat, T.P. : *India and China : Trade Complementarities and Competitiveness*, Bookwell, Delhi, 2008.

Bhatia, Shyam: *India's Nuclear Bomb*, Ghaziabad: Vikas Publishing House, 1979.

Bort, E.: *Boundaries and Identities: The Eastern Frontier of the Asia,* Edinburgh: International Social Sciences Institute, University of Edinburgh, 1996.

Chaudhary, M.: *Partition and the Curse of Rehabilitation.* Calcutta: Bengal Rehabilitation Organization, 1964.

Chitkara, M.G. : *Indo-Pak Relations Challenges Before New Millennium,* APH, Delhi, 2001.

Coakley, J.: *The Territorial Management of Ethnic Conflict,* London: Frank Cass, 2003.

Cochran, Thomas B. *Nuclear Weapons Databook.* Cambridge, MA: Ballinger Publishing Company, 1987.

Deepak, B R : *India and China : 1904-2004 : A Century of Peace and Conflict,* Manak, Delhi, 2005.

Digumarti Bhaskara Rao: *Military Conversion : Impact on Science and Technology,* Discovery, Delhi, 2003.

Digumarti Bhaskara Rao: *Military Conversion : Impact on Science and Technology,* Discovery, Delhi, 2003.

Dixit, J.N. : *India and Regional Developments : Through the Prism of Indo-Pak Relations,* Gyan, Delhi, 2004.

Dominique Lapierre: *Freedom at Midnight.* London: Collins, 1975.

Donnan, H. and Wilson, T. M.: *Borders: Frontiers of Identity, Nation and State,* Oxford: Berg, 1999.

Duncan, Francis. *Rickover and the Nuclear Navy: The Discipline of Technology.* Annapolis: Naval Institute Press, 1990.

Evelyn Goh, *Meeting the China Challenge: The U.S. in Southeast Asian Regional Security Strategies,* DC: East-West Center, 2005.

Gao, Mobo: *The Battle for China's Past: Mao and the Cultural Revolution,* London, Pluto Press, 2008.

George Perkovich: *India's Nuclear Bomb: The Impact on Global Proliferation,* University of California Press: Berkeley, 1991.

Ghosh, Ajoy : *Indo-Pak Conflict : Threat to South Asian Security,* Reference Press, Delhi, 2003.

Gupta, Alka R. : *Indo-Pak Security Discourse : South Asian Context,* Radha Pub, Delhi, 2010.

Gupta, S.: *Disrupted Borders: An Intervention in Definitions of Boundaries,* London: River Oram Press, 1993.

Heathcote, T. A.: *The Indian Army – The Garrison of British Imperial India, 1822–1922.* David & Charles. Newton Abbot, Devon. 1974.

Herken, Gregg. *The Winning Weapon: The Atomic Bomb in the Cold War, 1945-1950.* Princeton: Princeton University Press, 1988.

Hoffman, Bruce, *Inside Terrorism,* New York: Columbia University Press, 1998.

Holsti, K.: *The State, War, and the State of War,* Cambridge, Cambridge Univ. Press, 1996.

Imtiaz, A.: *State and Foreign Policy: India's Role in South Asia,* New Delhi, Vikas, 1993.

Javed, A.: *Secular and Nationalist Jinnah,* JNU Press, Delhi. 1999.

Jha, Prem Shankar : *India and China : The Battle Between Soft and Hard Power,* Penguin Books India, Delhi, 2010.

John L. Esposito: *Islam: The Straight Path,* Oxford University Press, 1998.

Juvale, R.P. : *Military Strategy and Diplomacy,* Cyber Tech Publications, Delhi, 2010.

Kanjilal, Kalidas, *The Perishing Humanity,* Sahitya Loke, Calcutta, 1976

Kapur, Ashok: *Pakistan's Nuclear Development,* New York: Croom Helm, 1987.

Kunju, N. : *Indo-Pak : Nuclear Cold War,* Reliance, Delhi, 2002.

Lamb, Alastair: *Kashmir: a disputed legacy, 1846-1990,* Oxford University Press, 1991.

Lifton, Robert Jay and Mitchell, Greg. *Hiroshima in America: A Half Century of Denial.* New York: Avon Books, 1995.

Matinuddin, General Kamal, *Tragedy of Errors: East Pakistan Crisis, 1968–1971,* Wajidalis, Lahore, Pakistan, 1994.

McPhee, John. *The Curve of Binding Energy.* New York: The Noonday Press, 1992.

Navnita Behera, *State, identity and violence : Jammu, Kashmir and Ladakh,* New Delhi: Manohar, 2000.

Nevile, P.: *Lahore: A Sentimental Journey.* New Delhi: Penguin, 1993.

Pash, Boris T. *The Alsos Mission.* New York: Award House, 1969.

Posen, B.R.: *The Sources of Indian Military Doctrine,* Ithaca, 1984, Cornell Univ. Press.

Prasad, Lal Bahadur : *Indian Political System and Law,* New Delhi, Shree, 2005.

Quereshi, Major General Hakeem Arshad, *The 1971 Indo-Pak War, A Soldiers Narrative,* Oxford University Press, 2002.

Qureshi, A. Iqbal : *Islam and the Theory of Interest,* Kitab Bhavan, New Delhi, 1994.

Raghavan, G.N.S. : *New Era in the Kashmir Polity, A Study of Omar Dynasty,* 1996.

Rhodes, Richard, *The Making of the Atomic Bomb,* New York: Simon and Schuster, 1988.

Rosen, P.: *Societies and Military Power: India and its Armies,* Ithaca, Cornell University Press, 1996.

Salik, Siddiq, *Witness to Surrender,* Oxford University Press, Karachi, Pakistan, 1977.

Santhanam, K., Sudhir, Saxena and Manish, *Jihadis in Jammu and Kashmir: A Portrait Gallery,* Institute for Defence Studies and Analyses/Sage, 2003.

Sherwin, Martin J. A World Destroyed: *The Atomic Bomb and the Grand Alliance.* New York: Vintage Books, 1977.

Singh, Amarinder : *A Ridge Too Far: War in the Kargil Heights 1999*. Motibagh Palace, Patiala. 2001.

Singh, Jasjit: *Kargil 1999: Pakistan's Fourth War for Kashmir*. South Asia Books. 1999.

Spear, Thomas: *The Oxford History of Modern India.* Delhi: Oxford University Press, 1978.

Spector, Leonard S., *Going Nuclear*, Cambridge, MA: Ballinger Publishing Company, 1987.

Sumantra Bose, *The Challenge in Kashmir : democracy, self-determination and a just peace,* New Delhi: Sage, 1997.

Sumner, Ian, & Chappell, Mike: *The Indian Army 1914–1947*. Osprey Publishing. Oxford. 2001.

Sutton, J., *Technology and Defence Market Structure*, MIT Press, Delhi, 1998.

Totten, Samuel et al., eds., *Century of Genocide: Eyewitness Accounts and Critical Views*, Garland Reference Library, 1997

Victoria Schofield, *Kashmir in Conflict* I.B. Tauris, London, 2005.

Winkler, Allan M. *Life Under A Cloud: American Anxiety About the Atom*. New York: Oxford University Press, 1993.

Index

❑❑❑